DECISIONS DISCORD & DIPLOMACY
FROM CAIRO TO KABUL

**ADMIRAL WILLIAM J. FALLON,
U.S. NAVY (RETIRED)**

DECISIONS DISCORD & DIPLOMACY
FROM CAIRO TO KABUL

COPYRIGHT © 2025 BY WILLIAM J. FALLON

All rights reserved. No part of this publication may be reproduced or transmitted in any form or by any means, electronic or mechanical, including photocopying, recording, or any information storage and retrieval system now known or to be invented, without permission from the author.

ISBN 978-1-962729-10-9 (PAPERBACK)

PUBLISHED IN THE UNITED STATES OF AMERICA BY FORTIS, AN ADDUCENT NONFICTION IMPRINT

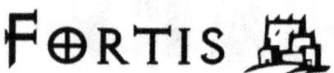

ADDUCENT, INC.
JACKSONVILLE, FLORIDA
ADDUCENTCREATIVE.COM

CONTENTS

FOREWORD i
PREFACE iv
CHAPTER 1 1
   Surprise, Contemplation, And History 1
CHAPTER 2 22
   Early Exposure To The Middle East 22
CHAPTER 3 46
   Major Command Responsibility In War 46
CHAPTER 4 56
   Gulf War 1991 56
CHAPTER 5 60
   Operation Provide Comfort 60
CHAPTER 6 66
   Iraq Redux? 66
CHAPTER 7 74
   Iraq Again: Drama In Jordan 74
CHAPTER 8 81
   War In Bosnia 1995 81
CHAPTER 9 88
   Increasing Responsibility 88
CHAPTER 10 92
   September 11, 2001 92
CHAPTER 11 101
   Al Qaeda And The War On Terrorism 101
CHAPTER 12 110
   Osama bin Laden 110
CHAPTER 13 122

Washington, Politics, and Iraq as the Epicenter 122

CHAPTER 14 .... **136**
Moving Toward War In Iraq: 2003 136

CHAPTER 15 .... **150**
The 2003 Invasion Of Iraq: Why It Happened 150

CHAPTER 16 .... **154**
Learning The Ropes: Preparing For USCENTCOM 154

CHAPTER 17 .... **165**
Senate Armed Services Committee Confirmation 165

CHAPTER 18 .... **173**
Commander USCENTCOM 2007-08 173

CHAPTER 19 .... **177**
Important Voices And Interests 177

CHAPTER 20 .... **189**
Behind The Power Curve In Iraq 189

CHAPTER 21 .... **202**
The Conundrum: Afghanistan And Pakistan 202

CHAPTER 22 .... **217**
In The Crosshairs 217

CHAPTER 23 .... **236**
Planning Ahead 236

CHAPTER 24 .... **240**
A New Front In The Iraq War 240

CHAPTER 25 .... **245**
The Surge Was Successful, But Then What? 245

CHAPTER 26 .... **258**
Long-Term U.S. Security Posture In Iraq 258

CHAPTER 27 .... **272**
Something New Every Day 272

CHAPTER 28 .... **292**
Afghanistan: The Best Of Intentions 292

CHAPTER 29 .... **305**
  New Issues, New Decisions 305
CHAPTER 30 .... **313**
  Engaging With The Media: Accuracy A Challenge 313
EPILOGUE... **324**
BIBILIOGRAPHY **345**
GLOSSARY **347**
ENDNOTES.. **360**
INDEX **402**
ABOUT WILLIAM J. FALLON **430**
ABOUT JOHN F. LEHMAN JR. **431**

TO THE MEN AND WOMEN OF THE ARMED FORCES OF THE UNITED STATES OF AMERICA.

FOREWORD

The United States' long historical involvement in the Middle East has deep roots, going back to the first Barbary War in 1801. Its modern history began with President Franklin D. Roosevelt's meeting with King Abdulaziz, the founder of Saudi Arabia, on the deck of the cruiser *USS QUINCY* in the Great Bitter Lake of the Suez Canal in February 1945. Another Navy warship, the destroyer *USS MURPHY,* facilitated the Saudi monarch's movement to the meeting as well. From these nautical beginnings, the U.S. relationships with Middle Eastern states evolved through the Cold War confrontations with the Soviet Navy, the Arab-Israeli wars, and ultimately, to the 1980s, with U.S. naval forces often serving as the primary interlocutors for U.S. interests. Real U.S. combat involvement in the region began in the 1980s, coinciding with my service as Secretary of the Navy, and again, naval forces were in the vanguard of those operations.

The 1980s marked the beginning of nearly 40 years of continuous U.S. direct military involvement in the region. A few U.S. military or naval officers engaged in those operations over the entirety of their careers, which makes Admiral William "Fox" Fallon's new book *Decisions, Discord, and Diplomacy, From Cairo to Kabul* essential reading for those seeking to understand the long-term effects of that engagement. Fallon actively served in U.S. naval aviation combat units from the time of the Iran Hostage rescue mission of 1979 through the 1991 Gulf War. He was one of the first of the most elite aviators to command an air wing as the "Super CAG," commanding Carrier Air Wing Eight from *USS THEODORE ROOSEVELT* during 1991 strikes on Iraq and later, having been promoted to Rear Admiral, led the *ROOSEVELT* Carrier Strike Group during operations in the former Yugoslavia in 1995 and 1996.

His shore-based assignments are no less informative. He spent time on the ground in Saudi Arabia as a liaison officer serving in the OPERATION PROVIDE COMFORT Joint Task Force. He also worked with the Kurds in the wake of DESERT STORM. He was the Navy Vice Chief of Naval Operations during the 9/11 attacks on New York and the Pentagon. He later commanded the Atlantic Fleet and Fleet Forces during OPERATION IRAQI FREEDOM. Service as Pacific Commander (PACOM) followed, and his career concluded as Commander of Central Command (CENTCOM) from 2007 to 2008. Few officers have commanded at so many levels in the Middle East as Fox Fallon had before assuming the role of CENTCOM, and he has a story to tell on that service that unfolds in his book.

That story begins with the decision to invade and conduct regime change in Iraq, a choice Fallon says had been decided long before evidence was in place to support that move and in the absence of any concept of what would happen after the Saddam Hussein regime was toppled. He details his arguments with the Bush Administration on how to address the CENTCOM region of responsibility, as opposed to just focusing on the problem within Iraq.

Fallon had broad discretion to function as the Pacific (PACOM) Commander, but he rapidly found himself under scrutiny in CENTCOM, with the Bush Administration intensely focused on his command choices and decisions. In true naval officer fashion, Fallon set out to view the region in a strategic sense but ran afoul of a presidential administration and the Army command in Baghdad, which wanted to run an Iraq campaign at a very discrete theater level. As Fallon relates, local Army staff response to a fact-finding mission, the Admiral dispatched to Iraq:

> "Believe me, he (Fallon) knows nothing about this AOR," and "Tell your boss get out of MNF-I business." Further, "we need to concentrate now on today's fight, get the 'now' done, then in mid-January or so we can evaluate where we are. We don't see any real reductions (force levels) until the end of 2008 at the earliest."

Fallon found similar problems in Afghanistan, with too many disparate strategies at work in Kabul that were often at cross purposes to one another. Combating the international opium trade, creating literate Afghan soldiers, and trying to fight the Taliban all at once frequently did not work and never satisfied government leadership in Washington. He had to focus on the wider region, which often involved Byzantine processes, from Islamabad to Cairo.

Fallon looked for a broader solution to the Iraq and Afghanistan wars than just the troop surge in Iraq and being at cross purposes with the Bush Administration's support for a continuation of the surge, he had no choice but to resign.

Fox Fallon's account of his service in the Middle East, from squadron commander in the 1980s to Central Command leader 30 years later, in many ways well describes the United States' detached and unfocused policies of the post-Cold War era. Fallon discusses the Cold War Navy Maritime Strategy as a highly successful means of focusing globally, not just locally, on a strategic opponent. However, this global focus was lost with the end of the Cold War. Likewise, the United States' national strategy, writ large, lost focus geopolitically with the demise of the Soviet Union and engaged in many short-term tactical fights in Iraq, Afghanistan, and the wider Middle East without regard for the possible, adverse strategic outcomes from the decision to seek short-term military success.

As was the case with the Vietnam War, the nation continued to pour blood and treasure into a fight with the tactical hope that victory lay just past the next troop surge. Despite the false promise of the Goldwater-Nichols legislation that regionally deployed commanders could lead their own campaigns, Fox Fallon and others found that, like Vietnam, civilian presidential advisors were constantly issuing additional 'stick and rudder' orders that muddled the strategic situation and made ultimate success less possible with each new round of intervention.

The need, as Fallon says, to fight rear-guard actions in Washington, D.C., consumed more time and effort than fighting two wars in the theater, even with a staff one-third larger than his PACOM staff. It calls to mind something that the civilian head of counterinsurgency in Vietnam, Bob Komer, said of the Vietnam War: "The U.S. grossly misjudged what it could actually accomplish with the huge effort it eventually made, and thus became more and more wound up in a war it couldn't 'win,' the way it fought it."

Admiral Fox Fallon offers an intriguing insider's perspective into operations at the height of the Iraq and Afghan wars, and his views implicitly foresaw the catastrophic, chaotic, and shameful American withdrawal from Afghanistan in 2021. A tactical focus on the immediate fight may not always address broader strategic challenges.

His insightful narrative not only recounts the internal tensions and difficult choices of high-level military command but also is a stark reminder that strategic clarity is essential when committing lives and resources to prolonged conflict. As readers explore the experiences and hard-earned wisdom Fallon shares in the pages ahead, they will better understand the complexities of war, diplomacy, and the crucial need to balance immediate battlefield decisions with a coherent long-term vision. Lessons that resonate profoundly in today's uncertain geopolitical landscape.

—John Lehman, 65th Secretary of the Navy

PREFACE

The motive behind this book is simple: I have a story to tell. It is about my experiences, particularly during a complex and busy year in command of all U.S. military forces in the volatile region stretching from East Africa through the Middle East to Central Asia. I made many decisions. I inherited the consequences of many others. The outcomes of these decisions continue to shape events in our world today. Others have written their views of history; this is mine.

From 2000 to 2008, circumstances placed me and others with whom I interacted in positions to make crucial decisions that played a part in national and international events. Today, I am motivated to share my personal and often unique experiences, offering background, context, and insight into these historical episodes to help make our world a better place. Events are not always as they seem. The complexity of decisions and the influence of actors and conditions, often unseen and unappreciated, determine the course of history. A comprehensive understanding of history benefits from diverse, sometimes differing, perspectives and explanations of occurrences. This book is my experience.

I served on active duty in the United States Navy for 41 years. The last eight years of my service were at four-star rank in four different positions with national and international involvement: in Washington, in the Atlantic, in the Pacific, and in the Middle East. As a senior military officer in positions of increasing responsibility, I witnessed and participated in actions of historical significance around the globe. My background is unique. Given the command positions I held and my extensive interactions with senior U.S. and foreign leaders and policymakers, it is incumbent upon me to record these firsthand experiences and their relationship to the outcomes. My vantage point was close to, yet distinct from, that of other witnesses to the events I will describe to the best of my ability, drawing on notes and memory within the context of the existing historical record.

In early 2001, I was the Vice Chief of the United States Navy in the Pentagon, the second most senior position in the Navy. I was on the scene during the transition from Bill Clinton to George W. Bush and the arrival of Secretary of Defense Rumsfeld and Deputy Secretary

Preface

Wolfowitz, participating in most of the discussions and decisions in the first years of that administration. Some months later, I was in the Pentagon when one of the 9/11 terrorist suicide aircraft struck, killing 42 of our Navy people among the thousands to die that day. The consideration of and planning for the resulting retaliatory attack on Al Qaeda and the Taliban in Afghanistan, the War on Terror, and the subsequent invasion of Iraq were all events in which I was intimately involved.

Next, I took command of the U.S. Atlantic Fleet and Fleet Forces Command, responsible for the readiness and deployment of all operational Navy forces. In 2005, I assumed command of U.S. Pacific Command, headquartered in Honolulu, directing U.S. military activities throughout the Asia-Pacific region, with a focus on China, India, and North Korea, as well as interactions with our allies in the area.

My final active-duty military assignment was as Commander of U.S. Central Command, responsible for the Middle East, Horn of Africa, and Central Asia from 2007 to 2008, during the critical period of the "Surge" in Iraq and the ongoing war in Afghanistan. That period at U.S. Central Command is the focus of this book; however, many previous events in which I participated influenced or precipitated activities that I will recount.

The responsibilities inherent in a U.S. Geographic Combatant Commander position are significant. I led U.S. Pacific Command, the largest geographically, spanning more than half the Earth's surface and accounting for 60% of the world's population. Subsequently, I commanded U.S. Central Command, then arguably the most demanding, with two major wars raging at the time. As Commander of these regions, I served as the interface between the highest-level political decisions and their implementation, reporting directly to the President through the Secretary of Defense. These are critically important appointments with an essential role in the formulation and execution of national security policy. Complementing this was close and frequent interaction with the leaders of other countries, a vital component of international relations and foreign policy.

Early chapters of the book include events and episodes in which I was involved that may seem peripheral or irrelevant but were important in shaping my later thinking in more senior positions. Likewise, two short historical narratives regarding the modern history of Iraq and the life of Osama bin Laden are incorporated, as that knowledge and understanding should have led to better decisions.

Desired takeaways from reading this book include an appreciation of how bureaucratic and decision-making processes work in the political-military realm of Washington and other national capitals and the key role of the Combatant Commander at the interface of policy and operations. Also, to expose readers to the importance of what I describe as "the tyranny of agendas" and the good and bad influences these often-competing special interests have on decision-making. Impactful, too, is the reality that random, seemingly unconnected events have on outcomes. Finally, readers will see a consistent lack of strategic thinking and planning, a focus on short-term reactive responses, and the troubling recurrence of poor decision-making due to lack of knowledge, inattention, or hubris. These challenges continued through subsequent and current administrations in Washington, with consequences still in play. Throughout, I recount the importance of knowledge and its application to strategic thinking, essential to the future well-being of our nation.

This book is about people and human interaction, day-to-day activities that sometimes profoundly influence our past, present, and future lives. I have recounted anecdotes and experiences to put a human face on the story rather than just an abstract recitation of detail.

A recurring theme is the impact and influence a single individual has or may have on the course of events. As is often the case in life, an action or decision by one person can make all the difference between good and bad outcomes, success or failure. A life lesson for me has been the importance of doing and questioning what I hear, read, and even see. Appearances are often deceiving. My experiences have reinforced an optimistic faith in the genuine better nature of people and the need for initiative and action in every domain of life to affect actual outcomes. I admire action that gets results and makes this world a better place, never activity for its own sake.

This book has been in work for over a decade, albeit inconsistently, due to my dawdling and distractions. I drew upon an extensive series of personal notebooks dating back several decades and logs and records meticulously maintained by my diligent staff over the years.

Preface

Additionally, books, periodicals, and articles have offered views on many of the events described in this book. I have endeavored to credit the authors appropriately, whether agreeing or disagreeing with my experiences.

Several people have earned my profound appreciation for their encouragement, assistance, inspiration, and insistence that I complete the task. Particular thanks to Ray O'Brien, Tom Bowditch, Leann Barber, Kitty Moe, Dave Frost, Colin Powell, Christi Fallon, Susan Fallon, Robert Draper, and Dennis Lowery. Thanks also to Alisha Frederick Reyes, Yousef Allan, and Harry Gerwien for their photographs.

A GOOD DECISION IS BASED ON KNOWLEDGE
AND NOT ON NUMBERS.
—PLATO

UNITED STATES CENTRAL COMMAND AREA OF RESPONSIBILITY 2007

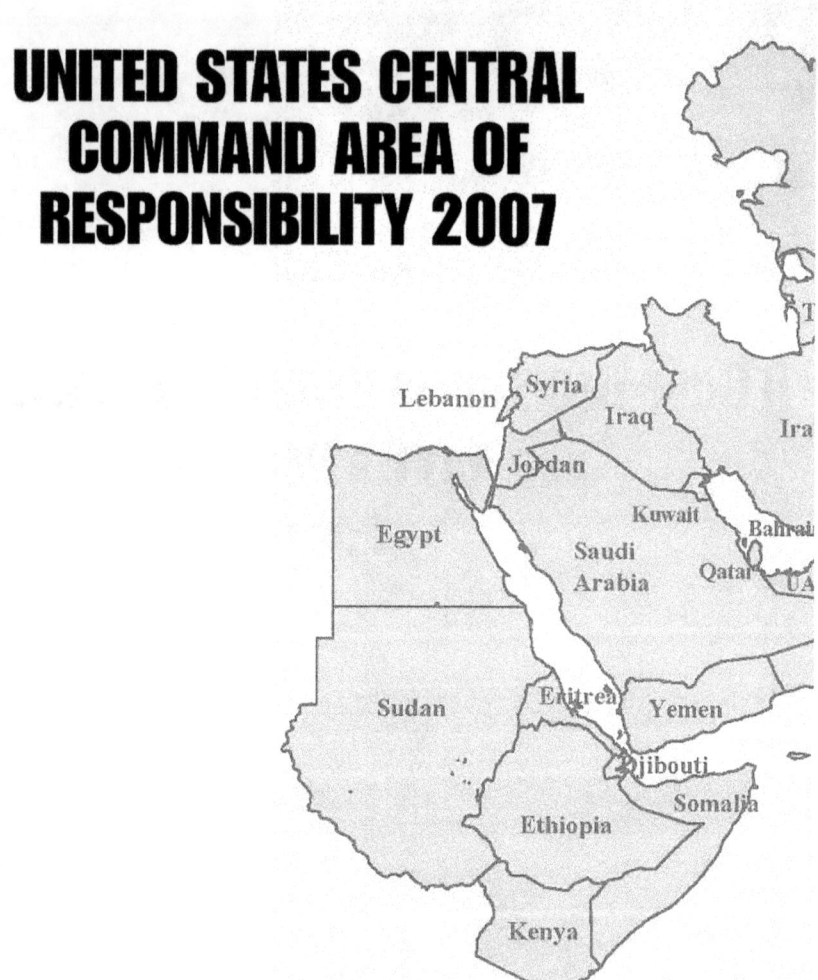

CHAPTER 1
SURPRISE, CONTEMPLATION, AND HISTORY

THE SUMMONS

> "...Deep into that darkness peering, long I stood there wondering, fearing, doubting, dreaming." [1]

I remembered the words from Edgar Allan Poe's iconic poem, *The Raven,* as I sat in darkness, staring out of the airplane window enroute from Honolulu to Washington in early January 2007. I had been in charge of U.S. Pacific Command for almost two years, busy with issues throughout the vast region, especially with China and North Korea. But the United States had been at war in both Afghanistan and, particularly, Iraq for almost four years. These lengthy conflicts drew resources and diverted attention away from the Asia-Pacific, which I viewed as the most critical long-term area of focus for our country. American casualties in Iraq were mounting, and the military situation on the ground was stagnant and seemingly stalemated. Also, the political atmosphere in Washington was toxic as patience was wearing thin, and the bipartisan divide was opening. Change was coming one way or another.

A few days earlier, just after Christmas, I received a phone call from General Pete Pace, the Chairman of the Joint Chiefs of Staff. He asked if I could return to Washington to meet with the new Secretary of Defense, Bob Gates, who had only been in office for a few weeks. I did not know Secretary Gates, and in fact, we had only spoken for a minute when we bumped into one another in the hall at the Pentagon, and I had introduced myself about 10 days prior.

But Pete Pace and I had known each other professionally and socially for many years. His request to return struck me as odd, given that I had just been back in Washington and was in the middle of the Christmas holidays. I asked Pete, "What is this about?" He replied, "The Secretary said he would like to chat and get to know you." I said, "OK, sure; how soon do you think I ought to come back?" "How about tomorrow?" was the reply. When I asked again what was happening, Pete offered a vague response and asked me to call him the next day with an estimated arrival time.

When Pete indicated that the Secretary wanted me there as soon as possible, I immediately recalled a phone call I had received several days earlier from a longtime acquaintance in the Washington media. She asked me if I had heard the rumor. I asked, "What's that?" She said, "That you're going to CENTCOM." CENTCOM is shorthand for U.S. Central Command, responsible for all military operations in the Middle East, Central Asia, and the Horn of Africa, one of six U.S. military Geographic Combatant Commands. I replied, "I don't know anything about that... and where did you pick it up?" She said, "Oh, this rumor has been running around town the last couple of days." My suspicions raced.

In truth, I was not surprised, but I doubted that I would be asked to go to CENTCOM, primarily because I was a naval officer. It would also be very unusual to move from one large combatant command like the U.S. Pacific Command to another, particularly where we were engaged in two ground wars.

But now, as I flew through the night over the dark Pacific, peering intently toward an invisible ocean, I recalled several background factors that might be at play. First, the now-retired former Vice Chief of Staff of the Army, General Jack Keane, and I had many recent conversations lamenting the situation in Iraq. We were dismayed by the lack of progress in pacifying the country and the steadily rising casualty figures among our troops. Jack and I had known one another for years and served as Vice Chiefs of our respective services in the Pentagon. We agreed that the current strategy in Iraq was going nowhere and needed to be changed. During one of several conversations, he suggested that I ought to be running CENTCOM. I told him that he would be a much better choice, and they ought to bring him back out of retirement, as had been done with the current Chief of Staff of the Army, General Pete Schoomaker. We agreed to disagree, but Jack pointedly said that he could not do it for family reasons.

I knew that Jack was politically well-connected with the George W. Bush White House, particularly with Vice President Cheney's staff, and that he had been working with Fred Kagan and others at the American

SURPRISE, CONTEMPLATION, AND HISTORY

Enterprise Institute during the autumn of 2006 in an attempt to draft a new strategy for U.S. forces in Iraq.

In addition to grousing with Jack Keane, I had consistently expressed my frustration and need for change in meetings with the Joint Chiefs and combatant commanders that Secretary Rumsfeld would hold every few months in Washington. I could have been minding my own business in my own command. However, in addition to the overall impact on the Armed Forces, many thousands of troops usually assigned to me at Pacific Command were currently deployed in Iraq, absorbing heavy casualties along with the other troops. So, this was my business.

At one point during the autumn of 2006, I told Pete Pace that I would like to see the President to express my view about the need for change in operations in Iraq. Pete did not think that was a good idea and told me so straightaway, but he also said the team back in Washington was working hard on new options.

President Bush was under intense political pressure from the Democrats in Congress to withdraw U.S. troops and end the war. Partisanship was rife, the media had soured on the war, and correspondingly, public opinion was mounting to end the conflict.

Several weeks earlier, in November 2006, I had just returned from a trip to Afghanistan and Iraq, visiting with forces typically assigned to my command in the Pacific but who were deployed to the combat zones. The visit confirmed my suspicion that things were not going well. I was dismayed by the lack of positive momentum on the battlefield; for example, most of our troops were spending their time inside the fortified walls of so-called FOBs (forward operating bases).

In one area of western Iraq near the town of Haditha, the Marines working there seemed undermanned and under constant threat of fire from the enemy. Marines occupied the town, but the surrounding desert areas were in the hands of insurgents who came and went at will, placing the Marines on the defensive and under attack whenever they moved. I could sense fear in their eyes.

On my way out of the country, I stopped in Baghdad to meet with General George Casey, then the Commander of MNF-I (Multinational Forces-Iraq), and discussed my observations. Particularly, the need for additional troops in western Anbar province. George responded positively and orchestrated troop movements between the Army and Marines to improve the situation.

The overall impression from my visit to the combat zones was that we had people working extremely hard in dangerous conditions, but that, however well-intentioned the direction and plans, strategically, the situation continued to deteriorate, and we were basically treading water.

HOW DID WE GET HERE?

My future was uncertain, but I recalled my knowledge and prior experience in the region. A reading of history shows scant U.S. engagement in the Middle East until after World War II, when the U.S. Navy accepted a British invitation to share their facilities at the port of Manama, Bahrain. During the next three decades, a small Navy force, typically one ship, was the region's only permanent U.S. military presence.[2]

This began to change with the enunciation of the so-called "Carter Doctrine" in 1980, in response to the Soviet invasion of Afghanistan and concern about security of oil supplies originating in the Persian Gulf. This new policy declared that the U.S. would use military force, if required, to defend national interests in the Persian Gulf. Still, the U.S. footprint was minimal until the buildup following the Iraqi invasion of Kuwait in 1990 and the subsequent DESERT STORM combat operation in 1991.

My first personal, detailed education about the geopolitical and military issues of the region took place in 1977–78 when I was a student at the U.S. Naval War College. The staff there had the foresight to focus our attention on the Gulf area at a time when most of us knew next to nothing about the region. And so, we learned about the geography, the history, the politics, and some of the complexities of relationships among the peoples in the area. I had an opportunity to put this academic learning into practice several years later when, in 1980, I spent most of the year in the north Arabian Sea on board the aircraft carrier *USS DWIGHT D. EISENHOWER,* deployed in response to the Iranian seizure of U.S. hostages at our embassy in Tehran.

That deployment was long and frustrating. The ship set what was then a modern U.S. Navy record, steaming continuously at sea for five months, most of the time during weather conditions known as the southwest monsoon. I have had a longtime fascination with the weather, at one point contemplating a career in meteorology, but flying from the aircraft carrier during that period was quite challenging and exposed us to the ferocity of the elements. It was extremely hot and muggy, the wind blowing almost continuously at 25 to 30 or more knots, the seas very rough with the ship landing area in constant motion, and the visibility usually less than a mile, day and night, week after week.

But the most wearisome aspect was that we did little other than steam and fly in circles in the north Arabian Sea and Gulf of Oman for months. It was my unwelcome introduction to what is known as "presence" operations. The ship was somewhere in the Middle East in an ill-defined attempt to deter entities from something untoward. The Soviets? The Iranians? Someone else? Or just to be nearby in case the decision was taken to attempt another hostage rescue? We did not know, and it seemed we were accomplishing little. Although not under fire, we were essentially treading water again, a recurring situation in my experience. Our professional consolation was that we were on station, doing our jobs, and in a high state of readiness to execute any mission we might be called upon to complete.

In hindsight, we could have learned lessons from that 1980 experience, and several of them were pertinent to our situation in 2007.

The strategic backdrop to the increasing U.S. military presence in the region was complex but essential to remember. In 1980, key factors included:

- The Cold War had intensified, highlighted by both the U.S. and Soviet Union vying for regional allies and seeking to undermine and discredit the other side.
- The Soviet Union invaded Afghanistan in 1979, resulting in the aforementioned Carter Doctrine and the U.S. beginning military material support to the mujahideen against the USSR.
- In 1979, the Iranian revolution displaced our longtime Persian ally, the Shah, and a key tenet of the new theocratic regime in Tehran featured extreme hostility toward America, declared to be the "Great Satan."

DECISIONS, DISCORD & DIPLOMACY

- During our time on the north Arabian Sea station in 1980, Iraq invaded Iran, beginning an almost decade-long conflict that featured horrendous casualties on both sides, widespread use of chemical weapons by Iraq against military and civilian targets, extensive financial and military support from around the world, principally to Iraq. Subsequently, the U.S., while siding with Iraq, also provided some material support to Iran, evolving into the so-called "Iran-Contra" scandal.
- Great Britain, unable to sustain the cost of empire, had almost completed its colonial withdrawal from "East of Suez," precipitating a partial power vacuum, especially around the Arabian Peninsula, where the British had ties to most of the kingdoms and sultanates.

Another event during that 1980 deployment was unsettling to me then and remained in my memory as a cautionary lesson. We left Norfolk, Virginia, in early April 1980 on board *USS EISENHOWER*, knowing only that our destination was the Indian Ocean, to which we proceeded directly at high speed without pause. Just before departure and without explanation, our air wing received a surprising addition: two large RH-53D Sea Stallion helicopters. Speculation abounded, but most of us surmised that the helicopters had something to do with a potential hostage rescue attempt. Rumor had it that more of these helicopters were embarked in *USS NIMITZ*, already on station in the northern Indian Ocean.

In those pre-computer days, aside from handwritten letters from home, access to news from the outside world was limited to irregular teletype reports, which the ship's public affairs people would receive and then distribute once or twice a day on mimeographed sheets of paper. Being a news junkie and thinking ahead about the uncertain nature of our deployment to a distant part of the world, I packed a new, state-of-the-art shortwave radio receiver in my belongings, only to discover that signal reception in my small quarters three levels below the weather deck was nonexistent due to many layers of reinforced steel decking separating me and the outside hull of the ship.

Engaging in a bit of unauthorized ship alteration, I ran a shielded antenna wire up through the decks into a catwalk alongside the flight deck. I surreptitiously affixed a small antenna onto the bulkhead outside one of our squadron maintenance shops. It provided reasonably good high-frequency (HF) reception at certain times of the night (mostly).

After weeks of high-speed steaming with little news, I was in the habit of trying to tune in to the BBC midnight world news. As we were rounding the Horn of Africa near the Cape of Good Hope, I was pleased to recognize the chime of Big Ben, then stunned to hear the newsreader report the failure of OPERATION EAGLE CLAW, an attempt to rescue the American hostages in Tehran. To my knowledge, this was the first time anyone on the ship knew of the operation.

Assuming that our embarked helicopters were reinforcements for those already on *USS NIMITZ*, I could not understand why the mission execution would not have been delayed an additional week or so to get our helicopters into position. My misgiving was borne out by the subsequent Holloway Commission investigation into the mission failure, which noted that "...Additional helicopters would have reduced risk... were operationally feasible...and could have been made available..."[3] I wondered who in the chain of command knew that additional helicopters were en route, very close to the scene of action, and why that option was not suggested to the President.

This is one of several events during my career that caused me to think hard about complex mission execution and the importance of ensuring that appropriate information is available to those responsible for making key decisions.

Fast-forwarding to 2007, the Cold War had ended, but Russia and China had reemerged as contenders for relevance and influence in the Middle East.

U.S. military involvement in Afghanistan and later military presence on the Arabian Peninsula fueled an Islamic extremist backlash, directly resulting in the 9/11 attacks on the U.S. and continued pushback against America in parts of the Islamic world.

Iranian–U.S. relations remain hostile, with indirect military opposition to U.S. operations in both Iraq and Afghanistan being provided through proxy forces.

DECISIONS, DISCORD & DIPLOMACY

The 1990 Iraqi invasion of Kuwait, the U.S.-led military response to that incursion, and the long-term frustration with Saddam Hussein's malfeasance led to the 2003 Gulf War and the current mess in Iraq.

Great Britain has mainly gone from the region, replaced with U.S. military and commercial interests in most of their former colonial empire, including Iraq and Afghanistan. We are there purportedly for stability and security, undoubtedly noble aspirations. But honestly, residents view us as the new outsiders, and we are resented for our military footprint in many of these places, as were the British. After a brief hiatus, the Russians are again meddling, seeking influence and renewal of their recently lost prestige. And the Chinese, with a keen interest in Middle East energy sources and potential economic partnerships, are increasingly seen in the region. The Iranian Revolutionary regime is still in place. It seems to have benefited from additional regional influence since our incursion into Iraq.

Saddam, the despot, is gone, but the country of Iraq has descended into turmoil and increasingly deadly sectarian conflict between competing militias and terrorists bent on eliminating their opponents and forcing the withdrawal of U.S. forces.

My assessment is that although once loath to commit military forces, we have, over time, usually in response to perceived crises, ramped up our security presence to the current large footprint, sustaining it at great expense. The strategic benefit of this is major influence, albeit heavily tilted toward military power and the unhampered flow of energy resources to trading partners out of the region.

But what are the strategic costs? In addition to our national resource outlay, the intense focus on the Middle East has diminished our attention on other regions, particularly the Asia-Pacific. What could we have learned from the past, particularly from the situation in 1980? In hindsight, the first answer would be to exercise extreme caution about inserting ourselves into complex regional and domestic issues far from home.

The Middle East has a long history of instability and conflict. Foremost, the Shia-Sunni religious strife has been ongoing for centuries. Exemplified in the current day by predominantly Shia Iran versus the mostly Sunni Gulf States, continuing the age-old religious conflict with proxies in Iraq. Civil wars have been raging in Yemen since the collapse of the Ottoman Empire, and Somalia is a poster child for a failed state.

Yes, we have democracy and standards of human decency and behavior that we would like to emulate, and we also have immense resources. But judicious use of power in pursuit of long-term objectives is a lesson often verbalized and seldom heeded. I recognize that advice is not easily followed, particularly when a good argument can be made that events threaten national security, as was the case for pursuing Al Qaeda in Afghanistan. Unfortunately, an equally compelling argument could not be made for our invasion of Iraq.

Since the end of the Cold War, the U.S. has been too quick to use the military in response to global challenges. We seem to have forgotten about the other instruments of statecraft. As the sole remaining superpower, we saw military muscle as the solution to most issues. And here we are, stuck in a stalemate in Iraq with thousands of casualties and profound strategic implications for the outcome. Looking out the window and seeing dawn breaking, I realized that I had been musing for several hours and decided to try to close my eyes and get a little rest during the remainder of the flight.

WASHINGTON D.C.

Arriving at Andrews Air Force Base in mid-afternoon, I changed into my dress uniform and proceeded to the Pentagon to meet General Pace at his office. We had a pleasant chat, but I received no further insight from Pete regarding what the Secretary had in mind. Pete said that Secretary Gates was expecting me upstairs in his office.

When we were alone and after only a few minutes exchanging pleasantries, the Secretary came to the point. He said, "We are considering nominating you to be the Commander in CENTCOM. What do you think about that?" I did not indicate that I had any forewarning about this, but I asked him, "Why me?"

He seemed a little surprised, but I continued, "Mr. Secretary, you know I am considered an 'old guy,' I've been around the institution for quite a while, a four-star Admiral for more than six years already, and I'm Navy. I believe that all CENTCOM commanders have been ground officers, Soldiers, or Marines. The fact that I am not does not bother me. But I'm sure it will cause some heads to turn."

He said, "Yes, we know this, but also that you are very experienced." I took that to mean that I was not timid and accustomed to making decisions. He then asked me if I knew Army Lieutenant General Petraeus. I said, "No, we've never met." He then told me that the decision had already been made in the White House to nominate General Petraeus as the ground commander in Iraq. That surprised me, but I immediately saw the pieces falling into place. I knew that Jack Keane was high on Dave Petraeus and that they had a remarkably close personal relationship. In fact, Jack had helped to save Dave's life some years earlier when the latter was accidentally wounded during a training mishap in Kentucky. I was certain that Jack had been pushing the White House to have Dave take over as the commander in Iraq.

This selection had not been announced publicly and struck me as unusual. Typically, nominations for three and four-star officers were sent up from the services through the Joint Staff to the Secretary of Defense, who would then forward them to the White House. At the time, Dave was a three-star Lieutenant General, and the Commander in Iraq was a four-star General. Also, as Secretary Gates had only been in the job for several weeks, I doubted that he knew Dave any better than he knew me. It became clear this was being orchestrated across the river at the White House.

Secretary Gates said, "You know General Petraeus has a reputation of being pretty strong-willed, but so do you," or words to that effect.

Hmmm, I could already foresee a problem if Petraeus had a direct line to the White House, potentially end-running the chain of command. I told the Secretary that if I were to be appointed CENTCOM Commander, I would have no desire to be a standby or babysitter; rather, I would have to be the Commander. The command structure could be problematic if the White House has already handpicked the force commander in Iraq, who should be subordinate to the CENTCOM Commander.

He said, "Yes, I understand. You would be the Commander." We then spent about 30 minutes discussing the situation in Iraq and the region. I was impressed with his knowledge of detail, particularly his big-picture

SURPRISE, CONTEMPLATION, AND HISTORY

strategic grasp of the situation. He then asked, "Well, what do you think?" I said, "I'd like a little time to consider it."

I had only been the Commander in the Asia-Pacific for a little less than two years, and we had many initiatives underway- quite a lot was going on out there. I also needed to consider the ramifications of going into CENTCOM with my most important subordinate commander (Petraeus), who had already been selected. Gates asked how much time I needed, and I replied that I could let him know the next day if that would be okay. He said fine, so I left and briefed Pete Pace about the meeting.

My son was deployed with his Navy squadron then, but my three daughters all lived in the Washington area. I called each of them, and we arranged to meet that evening at a small restaurant in Arlington that we frequented when I was in town.

Meanwhile, I contacted a couple of my senior mentors who were wise in the ways of Washington: retired General Colin Powell, former Chairman of the Joint Chiefs, and former Secretary of State and retired Marine General Jack Sheehan. These well-connected and savvy friends advised me in the strongest terms not to accept this new position. Their rationale was similar: that it would be a no-win situation given the existing military stalemate in Iraq and the poisoned political atmosphere in Washington.

I was grateful for their wisdom, but they offered that this would be a difficult choice for me, given how strongly I felt that the military situation needed to be straightened out and that I had some ideas to change the current trajectory. And, of course, there was a keen sense of duty, plus the fact that thousands of military personnel normally assigned to Pacific Command, including my son, were fighting in the combat zones. They understood and reiterated their opinions but would offer any assistance if I accepted the position.

When my family gathered at the restaurant that evening, my daughters were curious to learn why I was back in Washington. When I explained what was being proposed, they collectively offered their thumbs-down opinion, and one of them pulled out her cell phone and called my wife, who was back in Honolulu. My daughter outlined what I had just told them and opined that, although they opposed it, "You know, Dad will probably do it anyway." My wife was skeptical about the proposal but said she would support my decision. After dinner, I told the girls I had some work to do but would let them know what I decided.

Returning to my room and thinking about it for a while, I called Jack Sheehan again to share what was going on in my mind. He suggested some sleep and that we get together in the morning at a local Arlington diner, Bob and Edith's, where we would occasionally have breakfast. At 6:00 AM, we rendezvoused in the parking lot, walked into the diner, and were both surprised to see, sitting at a table in the corner, three then-serving government officials, each known to us.

Our acquaintances were even more surprised to see us than we were them. One said aloud what they were all thinking: "What are you doing here?" We mumbled something and pushed past them to another table. In a stage whisper, someone else said, "There must be something going on," and engaged in animated conversation while glancing at Jack and me several times.

During our short breakfast, I told Jack that I was inclined to take the new assignment but was wary of the potential difficulties that might arise in the chain of command, given the decision already made to nominate General Petraeus as the ground commander. Jack asked if I had raised this issue with Secretary Gates. When I said that I had, he suggested that I might draft a memo about what we had discussed just to have a record of the conversation. Although I wondered how this would be received, I agreed with him that it might be a particularly good thing to do for a record rather than just trying to recall a conversation.

I went to the Pentagon and called my former administrative assistant, Peggy Handy, who was still working for the Navy staff. I asked her if she could type a letter for me. She kindly agreed, and we went to her office, where I dictated a short memo recounting the previous day's conversation with Secretary Gates. I signed it and brought it with me to discuss with Pete Pace before I went to see the Secretary. I told Pete that I would accept the nomination, but he was quite surprised when I showed him the memo and asked if I really intended to share it with the Secretary.

SURPRISE, CONTEMPLATION, AND HISTORY

4 January 2007

MEMORANDUM FOR THE SECRETARY OF DEFENSE

    Per our conversation of last evening, it is an honor to be considered for this appointment and I am inspired by your confidence in my abilities.

    I would like to summarize and gain your concurrence in my understanding of the task at hand and the operating parameters.

    That my mission as Geographic Combatant Commander would be to lead the military effort to establishing conditions of stability and security in Iraq and throughout the region. That I would work in concert with the other U.S. agencies and international partners to achieve the policy objectives of the U.S. Government. That a revised U.S. strategy which refocuses and unifies diplomatic, political and military efforts in Iraq to achieve security and stability, enabling Iraqis assumption of these responsibilities is imminent.

    That I assume responsibility and accountability for the military implementation of this strategy and your policy guidance for Iraq and the theatre. That I would have the operational flexibility to assume a more aggressive approach on the ground if required to achieve the desired policy objectives. That the soon to be appointed new U.S. ground commander in Iraq would report directly to me in the execution of his tasks. That it is your desire that I be available to assume these responsibilities as soon as practicable.

    If this accurately reflects your intentions and vision in this assignment, it would be my honor, if confirmed, to undertake these responsibilities.

Very respectfully,

William J. Fallon
Admiral, U.S. Navy

Copy to:
DEPSECDEF
CJCS

Later, when I arrived at Secretary Gates' office, his staff told me he was going out but would see me immediately. I told the Secretary I would be pleased to accept the appointment, but I wanted to share the memo with him and see if he agreed with what was in writing. He read it, looked at me, and said, "Yes." I said, "In that case, I'm your man. I'll do whatever it takes to succeed in the new assignment."

REFLECTIONS

The next several weeks were a whirlwind of activity as I had ongoing full-time responsibilities as Pacific Commander, but I knew I had to start preparing for the upcoming duties at CENTCOM. Although rumors and leaks about my change of position were soon everywhere, the official announcement was not made until some days later, after President Bush gave a televised briefing about the changes he was instituting, including the troop "surge" in a speech entitled "The New Way Forward in Iraq."[4]

Before returning to Washington to receive background briefings and prepare for my confirmation hearing, I needed time to think about how we had gotten to our position and what lessons could be pulled from the past as a foundation for the new work ahead. I took about a week off and went to my vacation cabin in Montana to unwind and start getting up to speed on the Middle East.

DESERT STORM and the first Gulf War started in January 1991. I reflected on my participation in that conflict and the subsequent activities in Iraq, in the region, in Washington, and on my most recent visit to Iraq, a little over a month prior.

The overall security situation in early 2007 was grim. The conflict on the ground in Iraq was stalemated, Congress was bitterly divided, mostly down political party lines between supporters and opponents of the war, and the media was, by and large, against the war, as was a growing segment of the American people. I sensed a critical juncture very soon and was about to assume a key role in deciding the outcome of the conflict in Iraq. I knew that virtually everything I said would be scrutinized and used either in support of or against the opinions and inclinations of listeners.

It was also apparent to me that for the Bush Administration, Iraq, teetering on the brink of disaster, was its number one issue, and that the course of the war would define the future and legacy of the President. I expected my upcoming confirmation hearing to be a good illustration of the passions and widely divergent interests and expectations of Congress.

Before taking over in CENTCOM, I needed to know the facts, particularly about Iraq, so that actions contemplated would have the benefit of a detailed appreciation and understanding of the situation. And not just of activities currently underway, but also the decisions taken to get us into the conflict, and why. Just as important are the lessons that could be learned from history about what had gone on in Iraq and the region in the past. In summary, everything, the good and the bad.

SURPRISE, CONTEMPLATION, AND HISTORY

As for recent history, I was starting off on reasonably solid footing because of my involvement in most of the military activities regarding Iraq that had gone on for the past decade and a half. I went off by myself and focused on a bit of history.

IRAQ

The current state of Iraq is situated on land occupied by human beings before recorded history. Known for centuries as Mesopotamia, a part of the ancient Fertile Crescent, the land and its people have been nourished and sustained by the great Tigris and Euphrates River valleys for eons. As the site of several of the great civilizations of Western history, the land has seen many empires, kingdoms, dynasties, invaders, and religions coming and going. Turmoil and conflict, particularly in recent centuries, have been the norm for the region, as the local inhabitants and the world's great powers contested control of the land, people, resources, or geographic position.

During the past century, two key factors have influenced the course of events in what is now known as the Republic of Iraq.

First, the discovery of oil and its use and dependence as an energy source by modern societies worldwide, and second, the collapse of the more than 600-year-old Ottoman Empire as an outcome of the First World War. Regarding the latter, the victorious Western colonial powers, France and Great Britain, both coveting the Middle East, secretly discussed dividing the bulk of the crumbling Ottoman Empire into spheres of their own interest, even before the war's outcome was decided.

Further to this point, I remember attending a luncheon discussion at the Pentagon with the highly regarded historian and expert on Islam, the late Bernard Lewis, in November 2001, shortly after 9/11, at which he talked about potential motivations for the attacks. After reminding us of a common historical mistake, a tendency to judge others by ourselves, he opined that there is an intense focus on history in the Middle East and that "...for the Arabs, several events loom large in a perception of declining power and influence over the last several centuries, and the biggest of all was the collapse of the Ottoman Empire."[5] This sense of grievance persisted and was later cited by Osama bin Laden as partial justification for his actions.[6]

Decisions, Discord & Diplomacy

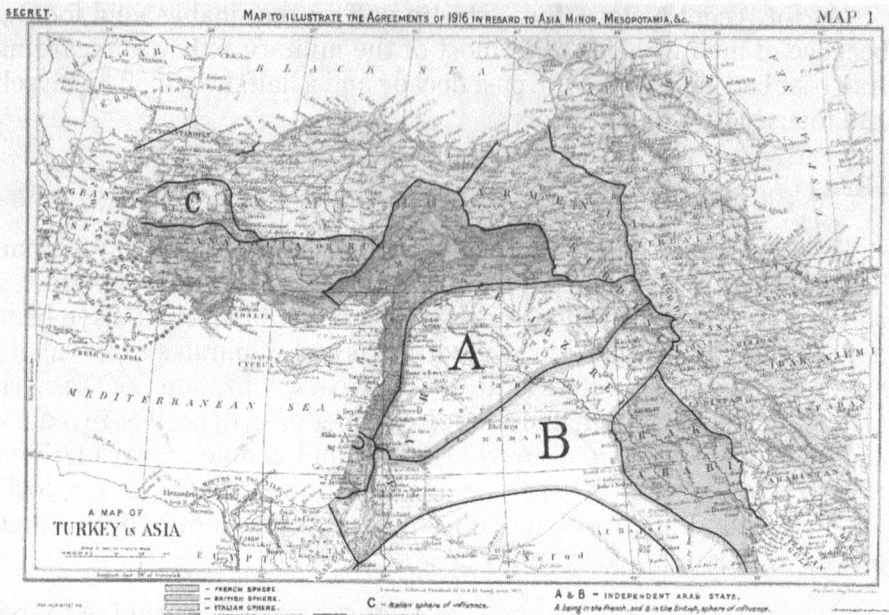

Original Map depicting the Sykes-Picot agreements carving up the former Ottoman Empire into French (A) and British (B) sectors, along with Italian (C), Russian, and a small International) sphere.

The infamous Sykes-Picot Accord of 1916 partitioned, without consultation with the Arab inhabitants, much of the Middle East between the two colonial powers. Before this secret agreement, the outside powers had been fomenting unrest and insurrection by the desert tribes against the Ottomans. In fact, while Sykes and Picot were deliberating, other British representatives negotiated with selected Arab leaders to recognize their independence after the war.

These actions and the subsequent betrayal of their aspirations by the colonial powers dismayed the Arabs, sowed seeds of revolution among the people of the region, and had a direct influence on events that correlated to the eventual seizure of power in Iraq by Saddam Hussein. Great Britain, which already had a significant economic, military, and diplomatic presence in what became Iraq, was highly desirous of controlling events to secure its oil supplies, originating in the newly discovered oilfields there and in Iran, and to safeguard supply lines to India and the Empire "East of Suez."[7] Owing to the obvious mistrust and perception of betrayal by the British, trouble began almost immediately.

SURPRISE, CONTEMPLATION, AND HISTORY

Meanwhile, the British military, which had been pressuring the Ottomans from the south, continued a slow grind up the Tigris and Euphrates River valleys from the Persian Gulf, an invasion they began in 1914 on the al-Faw Peninsula. With nearly 200,000 troops committed, this so-called Mesopotamian campaign would take until 1918 to reach Baghdad after defeats and victories. It also featured insurrections against the British by their erstwhile Arab allies, a foretaste of the challenge ahead. The British continued their advance northward, eventually seizing the city of Mosul in November 1918, after the armistice that ended World War I was in effect, solidifying their hold on Mesopotamia.[8]

Following the Treaty of Versailles in 1919, the idea of the League of Nations to create "Mandates" was put forth to govern territories formerly occupied by the Ottomans, with the idea that the territories would eventually achieve self-governance. The British were awarded the mandate for Mesopotamia (as well as Palestine) and united the Ottoman-era provinces of Baghdad, Basra, and later Mosul into the new nation-state of Iraq. But many in the local populations suspected that they were merely getting fresh masters in place of the old. The new colonial rulers quickly faced resistance from several secretly formed Arab groups intent on mobilizing the population to seek self-determination. This pattern of behavior continues, as demonstrated by opposition to the current American presence in Iraq.

The Iraqi Revolt of 1920, a large pro-independence insurrection, began in Baghdad, included both Sunni and Shia participants, and soon spread throughout most of the country before being crushed by a strong and bloody British military response, featuring extensive use of the Royal Air Force (RAF) to bombard the opposition.[9] The RAF was the principal tool of British response then for the same reasons that U.S. airpower is a primary instrument today. It advantageously uses a technology edge and minimizes manpower on the ground.

The British installed the Hashemite Faisal ibn Hussein, with the support of his ally and friend from the Arab revolt against the Ottomans, T.E. Lawrence "of Arabia" fame, as king, although they continued to rule the country more or less effectively through administrators, including the skilled and influential Gertrude Bell and the RAF. Lawrence and Bell spoke fluent Arabic and were Oxford-educated, bright, well-traveled, and knowledgeable about the Middle East. Interestingly, both were

British intelligence agents assigned to the Arab Bureau in Cairo during World War I, whose opinions about the region and its people were well regarded. Both are also good examples of the outsized influence that savvy individuals can have on history.[10]

Significantly, the installation of a minority Sunni as king in a new nation-state with a large Kurdish and majority Shia population, as well as the establishment of an indigenous Iraqi army, led almost exclusively by Sunni officers who had served under the Ottomans, would enhance Sunni influence and power, and foster Shia and Kurdish discontent. This minority Sunni dominance persisted and was a root cause of growing internal friction and violent conflict as time passed. In the current experience, the U.S. reversed this initiative and installed Shia leadership in Baghdad. To date, this has also been a fraught experiment. The British mandate was supposed to last for 25 years, but in the face of political, economic, and military pressure, they departed in a decade.

As a result of the uprising, British military control in Iraq was passed to a civilian High Commissioner and his administrators, who faced continual challenges and disputes from the monarchy and other groups. The costs involved in maintaining control and appearances by the British continued to grow. During the 1920s, after lengthy negotiations, local and statewide governing structures were established, and an agreement was reached for Britain to support Iraqi membership in the League of Nations. The mandate ended, and the Kingdom of Iraq was accepted as a member of the League as an independent state in 1932, although close economic and military ties with Britain continued for many years.[11]

During the same timeframe, the area of southern Mesopotamia, now known as Kuwait, was experiencing similar issues, which planted seeds of eventual conflict involving Saddam Hussein's Iraq and Kuwait in 1990. The dissolution of the Ottoman Empire and the growing aspirations of Ibn Saud on the Arabian Peninsula led to competing territorial claims by both Iraq and Saudi Arabia for the lands controlled by Great Britain that eventually became the state of Kuwait. Both Arab states voiced claims on the land rejected by the British. Still, they were kept alive in the same historical context Bernard Lewis cited during our 2001 discussion.[12]

SURPRISE, CONTEMPLATION, AND HISTORY

Meanwhile, in Iraq, despite well-intentioned efforts by King Faisal to form a more inclusive state governance before he died in 1933, dissension and disputes became a hallmark of Iraqi politics.

Faisal was succeeded by his young and inexperienced son Ghazi. His untimely death several years later resulted in the ascendancy of the even younger and less experienced Faisal II. Both monarchs were ill-equipped and ineffective in dealing with the many more powerful and increasingly violent political operatives. The Army, which intermittently intervened in government until the rise of the Ba'ath party, overthrew the monarchy in a 1958 coup d'état, assassinated the king, and established the "Iraqi Republic," a one-party state under a military junta.

Despite continued factionalism, a decade of moderately successful governance saw some progress in unifying the various ethnic, tribal, religious, and political interests until overthrown by yet another coup engineered by Ba'athists with the support of the Army in 1968.[13]

The Ba'ath Party, which translates as "renaissance," originated in Syria in the aftermath of World War II, espousing the ideology of Ba'athism, a combination of Arab nationalism, secular, socialist alternative to the imperial colonial rulers and the monarchs they installed. Although the founders envisioned a Ba'athist entity that unified all the Arab lands and peoples into a single Arab state, the Ba'ath Party took root in only two countries, Iraq and Syria. An early member of the revolutionary Arab Socialist Ba'ath Party in Iraq was Saddam Hussein, who, from age 20 onwards, was a key figure in the party's rise.

The momentous 1968 coup, supplanting the regime that had ousted and assassinated Feisal II 10 years earlier, was engineered by the Ba'ath party and military leaders. Saddam was deputy to the coup leader, Ahmed Hassan al-Bakr, and assumed powerful positions in the party and government of Iraq during the next decade. Although al-Bakr was *de jure* president, Saddam amassed increasing power. He became the country's de facto leader, eventually forcing al-Bakr to resign in 1979, and formally assumed the presidency.[14]

The almost quarter-century rule of Iraq by Saddam Hussein was ruthless, rife with corruption, bloodshed, and perfidious persecution of anyone suspected of fomenting political challenge or unrest. The avowed socialist state increasingly provided most employment, ensuring a population beholden to the regime and solidifying its position with favors and payoffs to reward loyalty. Rampant cronyism, with Saddam installing relatives and tribal affiliates, often lacking required experience or qualifications for positions, who only professed fealty to Saddam, led to the gradual bankrupting of the economy, accelerated by the generally downward trend in oil prices after the boom of the 1970s.

Although occupying some key positions in the governing power structure, the Shia and Kurdish populations were assumed untrustworthy. They were often the subjects of brutal persecution and heinous, inhumane torture. Iraq was a fiercely secular state, although Saddam kept up Islamic religious appearances and dispensed favors and tokens of benevolence to curry favor with clerics not already killed or forced into exile. The personality cult of Saddam was carefully nurtured into an image of benevolence and affection for his people, with ruthless enforcement by the ever-present Mukhabarat secret police and intelligence service.

Internationally, Saddam benefited from playing off the Cold War powers, and he amassed an impressive arsenal of military hardware, including weapons of mass destruction, specifically a wide range of militarized deadly chemicals. Sensing opportunity and perceiving military weakness in the wake of the 1979 revolution in neighboring Iran, Saddam moved to seize the oil-rich Iranian province of Khuzestan just across the Shatt al-Arab from Iraq, justifying his invasion by citing long-term grievances and unresolved (to his satisfaction) border disputes. What he thought would be an easy military victory for his large army instead turned into an almost decade-long bloodletting stand-off with hundreds of thousands of casualties on both sides.

The long conflict drew military support for Iraq from Western powers in addition to the USSR, all wary of the potential long-term regional damage by an active and hostile revolutionary regime in Tehran. In addition to accelerating the economic decline in Iraq, the war was challenging for Saddam because of close religious ties between mainly Shia Iran and the large majority Shia population in southern Iraq. The conflict included attacks on oil tanker shipping in and out of the Persian Gulf by both sides, with military actions also causing damage to U.S. warships. Specifically, an unintended missile attack on the *USS STARK*—a frigate—by Iraq and another U.S. vessel, which struck an

Iranian mine. These attacks caused considerable damage and U.S. casualties.

An enduring and horrendous feature of the conflict was the Iraqi use of chemical weapons against Iranian military forces and the civilian population on numerous occasions. The regime also conducted chemical attacks against the Kurdish population in Iraq, the infamous Al-Anfal campaign, punishment for insurgent activities, and perceived cooperation with Iran. Saddam's blatant use of chemical weapons of mass annihilation during the war became a focal point for international attention. It would play a pivotal role in subsequent events.[15]

Saddam's regime was also interested in nuclear and biological weapons and constructed, with significant help from Western countries, research facilities during the 1970s. France supplied Iraq with the equipment and technical assistance to build a nuclear reactor called Osiraq, which was nearing completion at the Tuwaitha nuclear research center near Baghdad. Fearing that the facility could be used to produce fissionable material for nuclear weapons, the site was bombed first by the Iranians and then destroyed by an Israeli air attack in 1981. It is still debatable whether that facility could have produced weapons-grade material, but in any event, it resulted in the Iraqi nuclear and biological programs being hidden from public scrutiny and pursued in secret.[16]

The stalemated Iran-Iraq war was finally terminated by a U.N.-brokered cease-fire in 1988, with an estimated loss of over half a million casualties and the original borders essentially unchanged. The protracted war devastated the economies of both countries and left Iraq, in particular, with staggering debt, most of which was owed to its Sunni Gulf neighbors.

Eager to improve the country's economy, Saddam greedily eyed its tiny oil-rich neighbor, Kuwait, and began a campaign in the manner of his "justification" for the Iran War in which he alleged border violations and a historical claim to Kuwait as a province of Iraq, reviving arguments from the 1920s and 30s when Great Britain effectively ruled the entire area. Having rebuilt his military, he decided to attack again and ordered the invasion of Kuwait in August 1990.

CHAPTER 2

EARLY EXPOSURE TO THE MIDDLE EAST

In this chapter, I recount events and experiences from earlier years that were formative in my understanding of the region and development as a leader. In many respects, they connect historically to later decisions in the Middle East. My participation in these episodes allowed me to observe and contemplate actions taken, responses, and consequences that proved invaluable in later years in similar circumstances. Additionally, some anecdotes provide information about historical decisions that were previously unknown or little understood by the participants.

THE LEVANT-LEBANON 1983

Iraq and Afghanistan were not the only places in turmoil during the 1980s. Spillover effects from the Iran-Iraq War and related events resulted in a series of crises in the Levant, particularly in Lebanon. I was familiar with that country since a 1966 Navy visit to the capital, Beirut, finding it vibrant, beautiful, and the crossroads for Middle Eastern economic and cultural affairs, in addition to its key geographic location. The previously cited collapse of the Ottoman Empire had a profound impact on this area as well. In accordance with the Sykes-Picot arrangement, Lebanon and adjacent Syria were included in the French Mandate and under domination by Paris until World War II. The transition from colonial rule to emerging statehood throughout the region was rife with conflict. Lebanon was initially the exception as it peacefully established a confessional government with power apportioned among the country's major religious sects. This changed in the mid-1970s when civil war erupted, continuing through the 1980s.

I found myself deploying, in the rank of Commander, to the region on Navy ships several times during the late 1970s and into the 1980s, most notably as Executive Officer (second in command) and then commanding officer of a carrier-based A-6 attack squadron, VA-65, in *USS EISENHOWER* (IKE), and later as Deputy Air Wing Commander in *USS NIMITZ*.

Early Exposure To The Middle East

The background for our presence in and offshore Lebanon in those days dates back to the end of the British mandate for Palestine, the emergence of the state of Israel, and the displacement of hundreds of thousands of Palestinian Arabs, mostly into Jordan, during the 1940s through the early 70s. Guerrilla fighting between Jordanian-based Palestinian militants and the Israelis escalated. Israeli counterattacks into Jordan were an affront and provocation to the Jordanians, but most importantly, the growing Palestinian presence in Jordan was openly challenging the government of King Hussein. Following months of cease-fires and broken deals, the king decided he had had enough and directed his army to crush the militants, beginning in late summer and fall of 1970, remembered by the Palestinians as "Black September" and giving rise to the terrorist organization of that name. The head of the Palestinian Liberation Organization (PLO) and nominal leader of the militants, Yasser Arafat, and his fighters were forced out of Jordan and fled into southern Lebanon.

The PLO and its allies established a de facto "state within a state," quickly joined the factional fighting that was destabilizing politically fragile and militarily weak Lebanon, and reinitiated attacks on Israel using new bases in south Lebanon. Escalating violence during the 1970s resulted in an Israeli incursion into south Lebanon in 1978 to push the PLO back from the border.

During part of this time, I was in Israel and could travel freely around the country, meeting people from all walks of life. I was struck by the vibrancy of the society, but also by the unease that people felt in response to repeated terrorist attacks. To this point, I visited the site of the PLO terrorist massacre of 38 Israeli civilians in an attack on a civilian bus on the coastal highway between Tel Aviv and Haifa, which prompted the Israeli response. Another observation was the apparent difference in economic circumstances between the Jewish and Arab-Israeli citizens and the onerous security measures in the West Bank, which would later fuel the infamous violence of the "intifadas." I also toured the Israeli-Lebanese border to learn about the terrain and issues.

Continued PLO-instigated violence against Israel resulted in a full-scale Israeli invasion of Lebanon in June 1982, aimed primarily at the PLO but encountering significant resistance from various Palestinian militias and the Syrian Armed Forces. The Syrian army was initially welcomed by the Lebanese government as a stabilizing factor, but then switched sides to support the PLO and its allies and occupied a large part of the country with its army. Both Israel and Syria refrained from all-out war, but the fighting included main force ground, air, and naval units.

Inflicting significant losses on Syrian and Palestinian forces, the Israelis drove north to surround Beirut. A U.S.-brokered cease-fire enabling the withdrawal of the PLO from Lebanon also included the insertion of a U.S., French, British, and Italian multinational force (MNF) to facilitate the PLO pullout and safeguard civilians. The MNF was quickly withdrawn following the PLO evacuation but was soon reinserted for "peacekeeping" purposes in response to the assassination of Lebanese President-elect Gemayel in September 1982, several massacres of civilians, and renewed fighting between the various forces around Beirut.

The second iteration of the MNF was initially successful in supporting the government of Lebanon, separating the combatants, and helping to stabilize the situation. Still, it increasingly came to be seen no longer as a neutral force but biased in favor of the Lebanese government and army (LAF) by militias opposed to the government. The MNF, and particularly the U.S. contingent of Marines based at the Beirut International Airport (BIA), began to come under attack by militia groups, which shelled and fired rockets at their positions. Yet another unhelpful addition to the witches' brew of combatants was the Iranians, who began to actively support the Shia militias with weapons and training, eventually using Hezbollah as its principal proxy in Lebanon.

The watershed event that first dramatically signaled things had changed was the suicide terrorist truck bombing of the U.S. Embassy in west Beirut in April 1983, which killed 63 people. I arrived shortly thereafter and spent most of the next six months just off the coast of Lebanon on the aircraft carrier *USS EISENHOWER* as part of a large flotilla of U.S. and allied warships supporting the MNF.

U.S. Secretary of State George Schultz was then engaged in diplomatic efforts with Lebanon and Israel to terminate hostilities and effect an Israeli withdrawal as violence against the MNF escalated during the summer of 1983.

The mission of our offshore naval forces at that time was not well defined. We provided a military "presence" to demonstrate U.S. interest and indirect support of the MNF. Recalling that this was the height of

Early Exposure To The Middle East

the Cold War, a large fleet of Soviet warships was also in the Mediterranean, and our aircraft carrier was "shadowed" 24 hours a day by a Soviet intelligence collecting ship, which we knew was passing real-time tactical information to Moscow and to their Syrian allies in Damascus. Over the next several years, events in and around Lebanon allowed me to view the conflicted regional political and military interests firsthand and acquire professional experience at every level, from tactical to strategic.

We knew that the insertion of U.S. Marines ashore as part of the MNF was a hotly debated topic in the Reagan Administration. We hosted numerous visitors from Washington who wanted in-person observation, including the National Security Advisor, Bud McFarlane.[17]

All U.S. aircraft initially remained offshore except for helicopters on supply missions to the Marines and some photo-reconnaissance flights. Frustration mounted among the offshore forces as Marines began to take casualties, and we were not authorized to respond. The task force commander, Rear Admiral Jerry Tuttle, was particularly aggressive and repeatedly pushed the chain of command above him for permission to retaliate. Admiral Tuttle was well known as a tough, assertive, and tactically astute boss who always demanded that we perform to higher levels of execution.

The situation ashore deteriorated rapidly when the Israelis decided to pull back their forces from the outskirts of Beirut to positions south of the Litani River in south Lebanon. U.S. negotiators had been urging a withdrawal to occur in conjunction with a Syrian disengagement from Lebanon. Agreement on the latter was never concluded, but the Israelis decided to pull back unilaterally, and the action was taken without prior notification. The result was a security vacuum into which the competing militias raced to occupy key terrain and re-engage in hostilities. It was difficult to keep track of all the factions and their shifting alliances. At one point, our intelligence briefers identified more than 30 separate groups involved in conflict.

The French began to fly reconnaissance missions along the coast from their aircraft carrier, *FS Foch*, which was rotating off Lebanon with aircraft carrier *FS Clemenceau*. One of the planes was hit by a surface-to-air missile fired by an unknown combatant, which exploded in the tailpipe area of the aircraft, severely damaging it. The startled pilot,

Lieutenant Clary, whose hair allegedly turned white from the incident, was able to miraculously land back on his ship.[18]

With then Commander (later Admiral and subsequently Ambassador to China) Joe Prueher, CO of VA-65 in the north Arabian Sea, summer 1980 on USS Dwight D. Eisenhower

About this time, Admiral Tuttle summoned me. He directed our CAG (Commander Carrier Air Group-all the planes on the carrier), Commander Joe Prueher, later Admiral and Ambassador to China, and me to visit *Foch* to see what the French were thinking and areas where we might cooperate. Joe and I were longtime friends and had flown together for several years. I also knew some French pilots and spoke a bit of their language. We had no difficulty accepting this task, knowing that French cuisine, supplemented by the occasional glass of wine, was far superior to our typical shipboard culinary fare.

Warmly received and reintroduced to some old friends, we gained valuable insight from our colleagues, who were much more familiar with Lebanon. We also jointly planned a potential strike against a particularly interesting target. In the process, I enviously discovered that the French

EARLY EXPOSURE TO THE MIDDLE EAST

had a valuable and rare navigation planning tool, a terrain map of Lebanon about 2.5' x 3.5' in size, called a "bumpy chart."

The topography of Lebanon is particularly challenging; steep mountains climb abruptly at the coast to an altitude of about 10,000 feet, then drop away precipitously to a wide valley, the Beqaa, before rising again along the Syrian border. When I asked my French confreres where they obtained the chart, they exclaimed, "La Librairie à Beyrouth!" and offered to get another one for me, promptly sending a junior officer to downtown Beirut by helicopter. That precious chart, which I gratefully accepted from my comrades, was passed down from air wing to air wing on Navy aircraft carriers in the eastern Mediterranean for several years, eventually ending in my hands in 1987. Most graphics and print had been worn off, but the "bumps" remained. Admiral Tuttle was pleased with the results of our visit and reciprocated with the French Admiral.

The situation ashore continued to deteriorate.

The U.S. provided some logistical support and ammunition to the Lebanese Armed Forces (LAF), reinforcing the view that we were not neutral in the conflict. One of the more unusual requests received was to assist the Lebanese Air Force, which had only a few aged, 1950-era Hawker Hunter jet fighters that were airworthy. The Air Force wanted to help the Lebanese army in the fight against the militias, but had no weapons to employ from the aircraft. Responding in typical Navy "can-do" fashion, we shipped several pallets of 500-pound bombs by heavy helicopter to a rudimentary aircraft staging area on the coastal highway north of Beirut toward Byblos.

Our squadron ordnance officer, Lieutenant Preston Swift, and a small team of ordnance technicians flew to the site by helicopter. They ingeniously rigged a mechanism for attaching the weapons (one bomb per plane) to the aircraft and a mechanical method for the pilot to release the bombs on target. Upon their return to the ship, our sailors regaled us for days with entertaining stories about the LAF pilots, in leather helmets and white scarves, taking off and landing on the highway amidst incoming rocket attacks that rained down on the aircraft and our men, all of whom thankfully returned unscathed.[19]

Although we were not permitted to fly overland or engage in hostilities, we trained with the Marine forward air controllers (FAC), who were situated on the roof of what became known as the Marine Barracks at BIA. The Marines often asked us over the radio to help suppress incoming fire aimed at them. But the Rules of Engagement then did not allow us to return fire. Although we chafed at these restrictions, the satisfaction we might have gained by responding with live ordnance would not have altered the overall situation.

We routinely had aircraft on close air support (CAS) alert status on the ship, ready to respond, if necessary, when the rules would permit.

One morning in September, I had the "Alert 15" (aircraft ready to launch within 15 minutes) 0400-0800 watch, teamed with pilot Lieutenant Commander Ron Alexander. Our A-6 Intruder attack aircraft was positioned on the number one catapult, ordnance loaded and ready to go, along with another A-6 and two A-7 Corsair II attack aircraft. I was the senior man and the mission commander.

We had briefed in the pre-dawn hours and were all strapped into our cockpits, ready to start engines when notified. Sometime after the sun came up, probably about 0700, the Air Boss (the senior officer in the ship's "tower") called down to us and said it appeared nothing was happening that morning and if we wanted to climb out of the cockpit to stretch our legs and go, a couple of us at a time, and get some breakfast (with flight gear on), it would be fine. No sooner had Ron and I gone down to the next level below the flight deck and picked up trays in the chow line... the shrill whistle of the boatswain's pipe screamed. He excitedly announced over the ship-wide public address system, "Now launch the alert CAS!" Dropping the trays and pulling on our helmets, we sprinted back to the airplane, jumped in, started the engines, closed the canopy, and were fired off the catapult about five minutes later.

As the other three aircraft in our flight launched and pulled alongside to rendezvous, we headed to the beach. I called up the Marines on the radio for further direction. We were immediately and unexpectedly given a hot mission to attack tanks and troops threatening the Marines and LAF from nearby high terrain. As we were already receiving anti-aircraft fire and uneasy about our ability to distinguish friend from foe in this cluttered and dynamic environment, I directed the other three aircraft to remain just offshore while I went in to investigate. Using a unique feature in the A-6 radar, the Marine FAC could pinpoint the area of concern. When I turned on an infrared aiming device, I could clearly see a couple of tanks surrounded by troops on the move. Accelerating the aircraft to attack speed and altitude, we received the coded clearance to attack, armed the weapons, and rolled into our dive-bombing run. Almost immediately, the FAC signaled us to "Abort, abort...pull out, pull out." We were able to 'safe' the weapons and pull up and away, avoiding anti-aircraft fire, and headed back out to the coast.

Later, the reason for the abort was explained. U.S. Navy cruisers and destroyers, and the recently reactivated battleship *USS NEW JERSEY,* were patrolling just off the coast to provide fire support for the Marines, and some were given the same target tasking we had received. As the big ship guns began to fire, the FAC realized we did not need to test the potential collision between incoming shells and our aircraft and called us off just in time. This was the first and only over-the-shore aerial attack mission of that deployment.

Several days before this event, a significant turning point had occurred in the Lebanese Civil War saga when U.S. warships off the coast began firing large-caliber guns against the various Shia militias in direct support of the LAF ashore. Most of us eagerly applauded this decision as we wanted to assist the MNF, particularly the Marines and the LAF. Unfortunately, the tactical success of these missions was soon overshadowed by a new reality: the U.S. was clearly seen to be teamed with the LAF against the Muslim militias and their Syrian allies. We were deeply enmeshed in the turmoil without clear-cut objectives or a strategy.

Our ship, *USS EISENHOWER,* had been on station continuously for about three months and was given a welcome reprieve with a scheduled port visit to Naples, Italy. As we headed west, Admiral Tuttle again summoned me. He expressed his reluctance to leave the Marines at BIA without air cover. He wanted a plan to be able to respond on short notice to any request for help. He put his finger on a chart at the Strait of Messina, about a thousand miles from Beirut. He said he wanted us ready to fly back to Beirut from any place at sea between those two locations.

I was put in charge of this mission. We drew up a plan with several A-6 and A-7 attack aircraft, appropriate ordnance loads, and a scheme to refuel in-flight using other air wing aircraft to ensure we could make it there and back. When the planning was completed and briefed to the

Admiral, he turned to me and said, "OK, Fox (my naval aviation nickname), tomorrow morning, you're going to take that flight to Beirut to prove you can really do it. Any questions?"

With a bit of anxiety, the next morning, I got to verify the planning that we had done as the flight was launched from the flight deck with full live ordnance combat loads and headed back to Beirut, about 750 miles. Nearing the coast, I broke radio silence and called our friend, the Marine FAC, on the barracks roof and told him I had a large flight with a heavy ordnance load. He said, "I have just the place I'd like you to put those bombs to silence some guys that have been shooting at us." We both knew that the Rules of Engagement would not permit that, so I proposed an alternative, asking if it would be OK if we did a live-fire-power demonstration just off the beach, hoping that it might be seen by the combatants up in the hills. With his concurrence, we rolled the aircraft in, flying at low altitude, with each pilot, one after the other, dropping our strings of bombs into the water not far off the Beirut Corniche. It must have been quite a show, certainly well received by the Marines, whom we could hear cheering over the radio. We soon discovered that our demonstration proved inadequate in deterring what came next.

Two days later, on Sunday morning, October 23, I received a telephone call at my hotel room in Naples directing me to return to the ship immediately, as there had been a terrorist bombing at BIA. Two hundred and forty-one U.S. service personnel were killed, including the Marine FAC team.

The aircraft carrier quickly returned to the coast of Lebanon amid speculation around the world as to who was responsible for the truck bombings of both the U.S. Marine and French barracks (which killed an additional 58 French service personnel) that Sunday morning.

Several days later, I was sitting in our squadron ready room doing paperwork when one of the pilots who had just landed came in reporting he had just seen something strange on the flight deck, "...a Navy Commander in dress blue uniform got off the COD (Carrier Onboard Delivery, a small passenger aircraft used to ferry people, mail, and high-priority parts from shore to the aircraft carrier) with a briefcase chained to his wrist!" A short time later, the squawk box (intercom between key offices on the carrier) bellowed, "... The Admiral wants to see XO Fallon in the war room ASAP..."

Early Exposure To The Middle East

When I arrived in the war room, the Flag Staff planning and operations center, I saw Admiral Tuttle, the CO of IKE, Captain Ed Clexton, CAG Joe Prueher, and the mysterious visitor with a briefcase still affixed to his wrist. The Admiral motioned us to go to his cabin-office next door. Once inside, the Commander undid the lock from his wrist and opened the briefcase. The Admiral explained that the guest was a courier from Washington conveying highly classified briefing materials, who had been dispatched by Vice Admiral James "Ace" Lyons (later Admiral and Commander-in-Chief of the Pacific Fleet), the policy planning chief on the Navy staff. From intelligence information available in Washington, the planners had identified a target that they concluded was connected to the Beirut barracks bombings.

I recognized the site immediately, as one the French Navy pilots highlighted when we visited the *Foch*. We learned that it was called the Sheikh Abdullah Barracks, near Baalbek in the eastern Bekaa, formerly occupied by the LAF, and now being used as a training site by Shia militia connected to Iran, along with Iran's Islamic Revolutionary Guard Corps (IRGC) and Quds Force operatives then in Lebanon.

Admiral Tuttle appointed CAG Prueher as the strike lead, me to fly with him, and immediately plan a strike to destroy it with the following guidance, "Fox, I want you to turn that place into a 40-acre plowed field!" Admiral Tuttle often referred to his youthful years growing up on a potato farm in Indiana.

It was a challenging task, and we quickly started planning. The barracks was a compound with numerous buildings of assorted sizes and shapes outlining a big parade field and would require a large amount of heavy ordnance from as many aircraft as we could muster. We decided on a unique configuration of 12 1000-pound bombs plus a centerline 2000-pound external fuel tank per A-6. It was the maximum aircraft carrier launch weight permitted for the aircraft.

The task was also challenging for the deck crews as each weapon had to be manually lifted into the bomb racks. After several days of intensive planning by a handpicked team, we briefed the Admiral. We gained his approval for a night attack to our tactical advantage. He said that he thought Washington was ready to authorize this retaliatory strike imminently and to get prepared.

DECISIONS, DISCORD & DIPLOMACY

Within a few days, the ship buzzed with anticipation. Everybody knew something was up, although only a handful of us had the details. The Admiral then met with all the key people on the ship and, without revealing the target, broke the news that we would conduct a large strike operation. He said confirmation from higher authority was pending, but we were to prepare to go that night. The entire ship-airwing team began to work through the thousands of actions necessary to conduct this operation.

After dark, the aircraft carrier and other U.S. ships began an elaborately detailed deception plan to "shake" our Soviet tattletale so they could not see the aircraft weapons loading and other preparations. The launch was set to enable a target time in the wee hours of the morning. After midnight, with the ship racing to close the distance to the coast, the aircrews went to the flight deck. We all did a walk-around preflight of our heavily loaded aircraft, climbed into the cockpit, and Joe started the engines.

With adrenaline pumping, we followed the signals of the aircraft flight deck spotting crew. We taxied into position behind the number one catapult as the lead aircraft in the flight, with the other aircraft similarly moving toward and lining up behind the other three catapults. Following instruction from the tower, our catapult director signaled to spread the folded wings, lower the flaps, and move forward to the catapult launch shuttle, which would fling the aircraft into the air. At that moment, within seconds of launch, the director signaled us to stop. All aircrews were directed to park their aircraft, shut down engines, and return to the ready rooms. The Admiral never clarified exactly what happened, whether higher authority gave or rescinded the strike authorization, or, more likely, that it was all a "final exam" engineered by Tuttle to ensure we were ready.

Not many days later, on November 17, Admiral Tuttle received a call from the French Admiral, who said, "Allons" (Let's go) with the joint French–U.S. strike. He was ecstatic and passed the word to immediately begin all necessary preparations. But then, to my chagrin, he called for me to come down to the war room and stay with him instead of going on the strike with Joe, saying, "You know all the details of the strike, plus you interacted with the French, and I need somebody who will understand all of this and can keep track of it for me." He then pointed

Early Exposure To The Middle East

to a chair and a cupful of newly sharpened pencils with directions to "start taking notes."

But when he called to advise his boss, the Commander of the U.S. Sixth Fleet, he was told in no uncertain terms that the U.S. would not participate in the strike. After fruitlessly arguing to countermand that direction, Admiral Tuttle hung up the secure radio circuit and angrily snarled, "OK, cancel the strike aircraft, but I still want to launch the fighters and jammers (electronic support) to help the French."

The French flew the strike against the barracks at Baalbek alone, using Super Etendard attack aircraft and F-8 Crusader fighter jets, while we provided support from a distance and "a wall" of F-14 Tomcat fighters high overhead to ensure the Syrian Air Force did not interfere. The damage was minimal.[20]

Shortly thereafter, IKE was relieved by two newly arrived carriers, *USS INDEPENDENCE* and *USS JOHN F. KENNEDY*. Still, Admiral Tuttle and his staff remained as the Commander of Task Force 60 with the new ships. A couple of weeks later, as we were enroute back to the U.S., we learned about an airstrike conducted by planes from *INDEPENDENCE* and *KENNEDY*.

Surprisingly to us, it was not against the barracks but in retaliation for anti-aircraft fire directed by the Syrians against one of the U.S. reconnaissance flights on the day prior. The strike was militarily ineffective and an embarrassment to the U.S., with the loss of two aircraft shot down, one pilot killed in action, and another taken captive by the Syrians. The ramifications of this debacle were too numerous to recount, but the bottom line is that the strike did not resolve anything involving Lebanon and left most of the issues festering.

This recitation of events in the Levant that transpired in 1983 indicates the rapidity with which things happen in the national security realm, the complexity of issues, and the necessity for continuous, informed decision-making by leaders.

Involvement by the U.S. military was for the best of intentions, peace, and stability in the country. Still, as has been demonstrated countless times throughout history, events take their own course once the shooting starts. Contemplated decisions require prudent analysis of alternative circumstances and understanding where they fit into the long-term national strategy. The major actors in this situation each had their own, and in most cases, differing agendas and motivations for their actions. Some were complementary to ours, but many were not. The U.S. had powerful military capabilities at hand, but actions were limited by the understandable overriding desire to not get involved in a major conflict. Yet policymakers wanted to demonstrate U.S. leadership and not appear weak in the face of challenge. The Marine Barracks at BIA was a tempting target in quite different circumstances than when the troops first arrived. Many warning signs were either not understood or not acted upon.

And in hindsight, the "setup" for the disastrous retaliatory airstrike of 3 December doomed it to failure. Short notice, hurried planning, bad choice of difficult targets (mobile anti-aircraft guns and missiles), wrong time of day for execution (flying into the rising sun with targets in deep, shaded valleys), pressure from the tactical level to "do something" in retaliation, impromptu weapon selection (generally whatever was already loaded or handy), the list could go on and on! But by far the most critical and, to date, inadequately explained factor was the chain-of-command decision-making, all the way back to Washington. Why those targets? Why that time of day? And who in the chain of command understood enough detail to make prudent decisions?

Several years later, in an address to the staff at the Naval Strike Warfare Center at the Naval Air Station Fallon, Nevada, which was initiated by Secretary Lehman as a direct result of the December 3 fiasco, Admiral Tuttle admitted, "The reason you are in this room is because I screwed up!" Accepting part of the blame, he said he should never have allowed the mission to proceed.[21] His admirable acknowledgment of responsibility still does not explain the whole story of this event.

LEVANT—LEBANON 1984-85

In the autumn of 1984, I deployed again to the region in *EISENHOWER*, this time as commanding officer (CO) of VA-65 with many of my same superb squadron mates but a new leadership team above us in the chain of command. My bosses were the Air Group Commander (CAG) Commander (later Rear Admiral) Bob Ellis, ship CO Captain (later Admiral and Pacific Commander) Dick Macke, and the Battle Group Commander Rear Admiral Jim Flatley. Receiving the turnover from the outgoing carrier and proceeding to the eastern

Early Exposure To The Middle East

Mediterranean, we were not surprised to inherit the Sheikh Abdullah Barracks as the number one contingency target for planning and potential execution. Happily, the "bumpy chart" came with the turnover package.

 By the time of our arrival, the MNF had been withdrawn from Lebanon, but the civil war was still raging. Terrorist attacks were common, and just before our arrival, another major truck bombing decimated the new U.S. Embassy annex near Beirut. The attack, which killed 23 people, mostly Lebanese but including two U.S. service personnel, used the same MO as the previous suicide truck bombings in Beirut and was quickly attributed to the Shia Hezbollah proxies of Iran.

Renewed emphasis was placed on planning for that target in the Bekaa. I was designated the Navy strike lead and chief planner. As our work the previous year indicated, the number of structures at the barracks required many weapons to provide the desired degree of damage. Also, as a result of the prior U.S. and French air strikes in the Syrian-controlled areas of Lebanon, the air defenses had been increased.

Given the single U.S. aircraft carrier in the region, the decision was taken to increase the number of strike aircraft assigned to the mission on IKE. Six additional A-6 aircraft from a sister squadron on another carrier were transferred to IKE, increasing the aircraft assigned to VA-65 from 16 to 22, along with additional aircrews and maintenance personnel. The level of complexity in the plan was significantly increased by tasking to be able to conduct the strike from anywhere in the Mediterranean, which would require support from large USAF KC-135 or KC-10 tanker aircraft.

Admiral Flatley was satisfied with the plan but relayed that higher authority wanted it reviewed and discussed with me in person. The two of us flew off the ship to Naples to meet with the Sixth Fleet Commander and Admiral William (Bill) Small, the Commander of U.S. Naval Forces in Europe, who had commanded my squadron, VA-65, in Vietnam, and quickly grasped the detail. After a phone conversation with USCINCEUR (Commander-in-Chief U.S. Forces Europe), Admiral Small made a small jet transport aircraft available and told us to immediately fly to the higher headquarters near Stuttgart, Germany, to brief General Rogers, the Commander USEUCOM (shorthand for U.S. European Command, one of the six U.S. military Geographic Combatant

Commands, responsible for all military operations in Europe, Africa, and the Levant). Arriving during a snowstorm in the middle of the night, we slept for a few hours. Then we met with USAF General Richard Lawson, the Deputy Commander. Emphasizing the importance of the mission and that he would listen to my briefing in a few minutes in the conference room, he offered the following advice, "Commander, don't try to B.S. the CINC (Commander-in-Chief)."

We entered a conference room with a large horseshoe-shaped table crowded with senior officers and a row of chairs behind. Sitting at the center of the table, U.S. Army General Bernard Rogers motioned for Admiral Flatley to take a seat and welcomed us. I had never seen so many stars (on uniforms) in one place in my life. Every one of the generals and admirals in the room peered intently at me as I delivered my plan with the help of a few transparencies on the screen behind me.

After replying to many questions, several particularly pertinent ones by General Rogers himself, he asked me to leave the room. Unbeknownst to me, until then, I was followed by a team of U.S. Air Force officers briefing their attack plan for the same target using United Kingdom-based F-111 fighter-bombers. Sometime later, I was recalled to the room. General Rogers announced that he had selected my plan to be executed if and when determined by the National Command Authority. He said he had high confidence as briefed, but expected that circumstances might cause me to want to change the plan sometime in the future. He was okay with that, so I just returned and told him what needed to be done. He became quite animated and said, "Do not take guidance or direction from anyone in Washington. If anybody tries to meddle with your plan, you let me know, understand?"

"Yes, sir," I replied, wondering, "how did he know?" Because, in fact, I was under pressure from the Navy back in Washington to take on that mission for the Navy and try to execute it under any circumstances. By way of background, this was an extremely complicated operation, and agreeing to do it at short notice, from long range, at night, with rendezvous and multiple refueling from Air Force tankers, put it right at the edge of my comfort level with little margin for error. In my view, the closer we were to the target at launch, the better. I understood that higher-level commanders wanted flexibility to move the aircraft carrier around, but I spent the next several months resisting outside pressure to change my stance.

Early Exposure To The Middle East

In this regard, Admiral Flatley supported the plan and our flight crews. His staunch support in standing up against some poor ideas from Washington probably cost him more senior positions in the Navy. The squadron, air wing, and ship were "on the hook" for that mission for the remaining six months of the deployment. To maintain the highest readiness, we repeatedly practiced every aspect of the strike, including nine nighttime mid-air rendezvous missions with the USAF refueling tankers, several at full scale with all 16 strike aircraft.

It seemed that challenges from the bureaucracy and resistance to requests for outside assistance were the norm during that deployment. For example, to ease the difficulty in aircrew identification of the target, I requested long-range oblique photography from USAF SR-71 "Blackbird" reconnaissance aircraft that had been available in the past. But, I was told this was not obtainable and that I should use overhead satellite imagery, which was claimed to be of "much better resolution." But senior intelligence people missed the point; it was the low-angle, oblique, "pilot's eye view" that we needed. In addition to not grasping our need, I was also aware that some senior people in the Air Force were trying to retire the SR-71 and did not welcome a "demand signal" from the fleet.

As an aside, later on, I had similar difficulty as a four-star commander when some in the Air Force wanted to retire the U-2 reconnaissance aircraft, which at the time provided unique intelligence. In 1984, I finally took matters into my own hands to increase the likelihood of success of the mission and to assist our aircrews in the mission execution.

The A-6 aircraft was designed as an all-weather attack vehicle and depended on accurate radar scope interpretation to find most targets at night. An advantage in this regard was radar scope photography (RSP). If available, it offered, in effect, a "sneak peek" at what the target would look like on radar.

Another unique attribute of the A-6 was the ability to precisely deliver weapons at night when the target was neither visible nor directly distinguishable on radar. In this case, a technique known as radar offset bombing was used. If one could find and readily identify a strong radar return in the vicinity, it would be possible for the aircraft computer to accurately measure the bearing and distance to the otherwise invisible target. The barracks were difficult-to-find targets, and we needed to identify something nearby that we could recognize and use as an aiming point.

I discovered that Baalbek was the site of an ancient Roman temple with a massive structure that would offer a good radar return. But we needed pictures of it and surrounding structures to be sure it could be distinguished. I initiated the request through intelligence channels to the CIA, asking if they could get someone on the ground to take photos for us. The request was turned down. I was told putting someone there was "too dangerous" then. Recalling that Tom Stewart, a former active-duty Navy friend, had previously been assigned to UNIFIL, the UN Peacekeeping Mission in Lebanon, I asked him if he had ever been to Baalbek. His reply was, "Yes, I visited the site of the ruins of the famous Roman temple there." Inquiring if he had taken any photos, he replied in the affirmative. I asked him if he could expeditiously send me copies of whatever he had, and then I added, "Don't ask!" He "got it," and I had the pictures in my hands within a week. They were exactly what we were looking for, enabling us to compute an offset aiming point.[22]

The remaining piece of the puzzle was to acquire RSP so that the bombardier-navigators would know exactly what to look for to increase the likelihood of mission success. With all other options exhausted, I acted, had a recording device affixed to one of the aircraft, and advised Ron Alexander, my regular pilot, that we would have a special mission that night. After completing our assigned training event, I told Ron that we needed to "disappear" for a while. Descending to wave-top level and below the radar horizon of the Soviets, Syrians, and our own ships, we turned off our lights and all other radiating electronic equipment, headed for the coast north of Beirut, and began the steep climb necessary to top the 10,000-foot mountain peaks. Accelerating to maximum speed and skimming over the top of the peaks, we pointed toward Baalbek, about 30 miles distant, and turned on the radar.

Locating the city, I put the radar cursors on what I thought were the ruins and visually tried to confirm it on the FLIR (forward-looking infrared) sensor, but we were still too distant, so I turned on the RSP recording device. Obtaining the necessary photos, we turned around and got back out to sea as quickly as possible, rejoining the aircraft, getting ready to recover on the carrier. Swearing Ron to secrecy, we had the pictures developed and distributed to the flight crews assigned to the

Early Exposure To The Middle East

mission. Several days later, CAG Bob Ellis mentioned that he had heard that RSP of the target area had suddenly appeared. I said, "Yes, I saw that, and it will really be helpful…"

On one occasion, IKE was anchored at Palma de Mallorca in the far western Mediterranean for a port visit when we were ordered to get underway immediately and return to the Levant at top speed, prepared to execute the mission. The squadron's motto during that deployment was "It could go at any time." But the actual execution order never came, and we later passed the planning over to our relieving sister squadrons as IKE returned to the U.S.

Lessons learned and takeaways from that deployment were many.

At a personal level, it was gratifying to see our sailors work so hard toward mission accomplishment despite challenges, changes of direction, and frustration. They never let the nation or me down during seven months and countless hours of physically and mentally exhausting work. The standards were high, and they met or exceeded expectations with no public recognition except our thanks and, later, a couple of ribbons on their chests from the Navy. I do not doubt that had the execution order been given, our people would have excelled. Why? Because we had the right tools and, more importantly, well-trained people who believed they were making a difference, and leadership that supported us.

Having been put through the paces earlier in my career by bosses with exacting standards, I also relearned the necessity of training hard with acute attention to detail. 'Practice makes perfect' is a saying with much merit. Although I doubted we would be perfect, we would be as close to it as possible, and the best way to make that happen was practice, with an honest and fastidious assessment of the results. Numerous issues competed for my time and attention. Still, I tried to keep the big picture in focus, certain that some assumptions would be incorrect, things would go awry, and had contingencies and alternative courses of action thought out in advance.

Differing agendas were constantly in play, whether service priorities, intelligence community preferences, scheduling issues, inattention to detail by higher authority, and, of course, the reality of time and place in history, to wit, the height of the Cold War and the conflicted regional conflicts. Indecision by the national political leadership about how to deal with events in the Middle East and actions related to national priorities and strategy was a problem then, as they are now. As I saw it, my task was to lead our people to the highest possible readiness for many contingencies and to provide my best advice to higher authority based on experience and observation.

BACK TO LEBANON AGAIN 1986-87

With then Captain (later Rear Admiral) "Bad Fred" Lewis, Commander CVW-8 in the Mediterranean Sea, spring 1987 on USS Nimitz.

In late 1985, I was assigned as the Deputy Commander of Carrier Air Wing Eight in a new leadership scheme, which I will describe later. Following a fast-paced couple of months learning to fly in some different aircraft, I reported to my new boss, Captain (later Admiral) "Bad Fred" Lewis, CAG-8. We spent several months training in the U.S. Then we reported aboard our new home away from home, *USS NIMITZ*, for deployment to the north Atlantic and the Norwegian Sea. During that time, at the apex of the Cold War, I gained firsthand experience with the Navy's Cold War Maritime Strategy against the USSR. The brainchild of Navy Secretary John Lehman and a group of bright, forward-leaning, and big-picture-thinking strategists, the master plan fit in well with the

Early Exposure To The Middle East

national security strategy of the Reagan Administration and was a significant factor in bringing the Cold War to conclusion. We understood and practiced the operational execution fundamental to the strategy's success. Regrettably, this big-picture thinking soon dissipated.

In late 1986, we deployed from Norfolk again in *NIMITZ* with Captain (later Rear Admiral) Gene Connor as carrier CO and Rear Admiral (later Admiral and Pacific Fleet Commander) Barney Kelly as our embarked Flag Officer. Steaming first to the Mediterranean, then back into the Atlantic, south around Cape Horn at the tip of South America, and into the Pacific, ending up in San Diego.

Shortly after arriving in the Mediterranean, the ships of the U.S. Sixth Fleet embarked commanders, and all supporting Navy commanders, were directed to convene at an unprecedented event near Augusta Bay, Sicily, for a meeting with the new Sixth Fleet Commander, Vice Admiral Ken Moranville. All fleet ships, including the aircraft carriers *KENNEDY* and *NIMITZ*, were anchored in the bay. Other commanders flew into Sicily for the meeting, which was held in an atmosphere of high security due to the ongoing terrorist threats in Europe at the time. The conference agenda explained the Maritime Strategy, its application to the southern flank of NATO in the Mediterranean, and the Commander's expectations regarding our strategy execution. This was another example of the well-coordinated, worldwide implementation of strategic thinking that helped to conclude the Cold War favorably.

Not long after I was last there on *EISENHOWER*, my return to the Mediterranean included being handed the target planning folder for the Sheikh Abdulla Barracks (and "bumpy chart") again. But on this deployment, another more immediate priority, in addition to the Cold War, was the challenge of Muammar Qaddafi's Libya. U.S. forces had conducted airstrikes on Benghazi and Tripoli just a few months earlier in response to Libyan provocations, and Libyan aircraft were once again threatening U.S. forces in the Gulf of Sidra. Initially, our top task was to develop contingency plans for additional potential strikes in Libya.

Vice Admiral Moranville visited *NIMITZ* soon after we arrived in the area. He was aggressive and forceful, challenging our aircrews to be ready at a moment's notice for combat against Qaddafi's Air Force. Inquiring whether we were also prepared for the Lebanon target barracks, he assumed that Bad Fred would lead it. Captain Lewis said, "No, Fox will be the strike leader." The Admiral was dubious and said, "OK, Fox, I want you to lead a rehearsal with live ordnance tomorrow, and I will fly and observe the mission and see how you do."

The next day, we flew the mission over water in a mirror image of the actual strike. When we returned to the ship, I was summoned to the war room where Admiral Moranville gave me a 'thumbs up' and said, "You've got it."

Not long after that, Fred Lewis received a message from Captain (later Admiral and Chief of Naval Operations) Jay Johnson, Admiral Moranville's operations officer and right-hand man for aviation matters. The Admiral was planning to be in Nice, France, for business and wanted Bad Fred and me to fly in and meet with them the next day. Complying as directed, we flew into a French military airfield. We were surreptitiously escorted to a small hotel in cold and rainy Nice. Jay Johnson arranged a vehicle to bring us to the meeting at a different hotel. At this time, extreme caution was being exercised due to the ongoing terrorist activity of kidnappings and assassinations against U.S. officials.

When we got to the new hotel about midafternoon, the sight of Admiral Moranville caused me to chuckle. He was seated in a darkened corner of the hotel restaurant, which was otherwise deserted, with his back to the wall, drinking a cup of coffee. He was in civilian attire, as we all were, except for a dark, bulky Navy raincoat over his other clothes. He got up to greet us, and I noticed the pockets seemed heavily weighed down. The reason became readily apparent as he pulled a large revolver from one pocket and several clips of ammunition from the other: his own personal last-ditch defense against the terrorists.

The Admiral indicated that we would have to go to Stuttgart again to discuss the Barracks target with the European Commanders, but first, he launched into an animated discussion about the tactics I planned to use. Jay Johnson quickly suggested that we go to another, less public location. The Admiral agreed, saying, "Fine, let's go up to my room. And Jay, get a bottle of whiskey and some glasses." We sat around the table in his room for the next couple of hours and debated the plan. As did we all, the Admiral had extensive combat experience in Vietnam, but recent technological changes necessitated new tactics. After a thorough discussion, the Admiral said we needed to fly up to Stuttgart in the morning and update the "big boss," General Rogers, and the new deputy, USAF General Thomas Richards.

First thing the next morning, the four of us were on a small military jet, flying to Stuttgart, and again landed in a snowstorm. General Rogers was called away to another task, but as he was familiar with the plan and me, he had us brief the new Deputy Commander, General Richards. Following a delay due to the storm, the aircraft finally returned to Nice, and Fred and I flew back to *NIMITZ*.

Some takeaways from this episode included the senior leadership's diligence for that mission and the value of probing questions into execution in light of the botched raid in December 1983.

The Barracks strike was never conducted, much to the chagrin of Admiral "Ace" Lyons, author of the original proposal, who lamented to me on every occasion of our subsequent meetings for the remainder of his life. But I have long since concluded that whatever tactical success might have ensued, it would have done little to alter events in Lebanon or the world. Other matters took precedence in 1987, particularly the approaching culmination of the Cold War and the focus on Europe, the ongoing Iran-Iraq War, the attacks on U.S. ships there, and the aftereffects of the Iran-Contra scandal in Washington. Much effort was expended in the planning and revising of never-executed operations. Still, I learned a great deal by observing the actions of my superiors and the impact of coincidental events on decision-making.

A BREAK FROM THE MIDDLE EAST

Shortly after returning from the deployment on *NIMITZ*, having been selected to the rank of Captain, I received orders to report to the staff of Commander Naval Air Force Atlantic in Norfolk as the Air Wing Training Officer. My new boss, Vice Admiral Dick Dunleavy, a charismatic and much-admired Bostonian, allowed me lots of running room. It was my great fortune to enjoy the company of a crackerjack team of superb professionals in our office, many of whom went on to the most senior positions in the Navy.

The job encompassed much more than the title might imply and proved invaluable. It enhanced my professional knowledge, behind-the-scenes, big-picture understanding of the Navy and its operations, and unprecedented leadership insight. In addition to the obvious title of the job, I led the team that conducted the pre-deployment readiness assessment of all carrier air wings as part of what was known as an operational readiness evaluation (ORE), effectively the 'graduation exercise' for each of the aircraft carrier/air wing teams to certify them ready for deployment.

I was responsible for the budget and funding for all naval aviation ships, squadrons, and units on the East Coast of the U.S. I also had other duties regarding the integration of new aviation technology into the fleet, coordination of activities with our Pacific Fleet counterparts, and advice to the Commander as he desired. Another interesting aspect of the job was being the head of a board that reviewed the cases of individual aviators to determine their fitness for continued service as a pilot or naval flight officer. This task demanded intense focus on the personal, technical, and organizational aspects of their careers and a decision about their futures with often profound implications for them and the Navy. For example, if we made a judgment to continue a pilot in service and he or she was later the cause of a fatal aircraft mishap, the resulting loss could include that individual and other people, as well as the aircraft.

The job was an advanced responsibility, accountability, and professional standards course. Observation of behaviors and leadership by key individuals under pressure was vital to my own development and opinions about the performance of others when faced with stressful circumstances. Another critical takeaway was the absolute necessity for honest appraisal and assessment of self and others.

I next took command of Medium Attack Wing One at NAS Oceana in Virginia Beach. The wing included all the Navy East Coast A-6 Intruder medium attack squadrons plus the fleet replacement squadron (FRS), which was charged with training new and returning flight crews and maintenance personnel for duty with the fleet. The command was known in the Navy as a functional wing, overseeing all squadron readiness, training, and preparation for deployment with the operational carrier air wings.

Concisely, my staff and I needed to know everything about the people, airplanes, equipment, and mission to successfully prepare them

Early Exposure To The Middle East

for deployment with the fleet. We conducted inspections and made hard judgments regarding assessment of people and equipment. We were viewed as the "experts" in every aspect of the A6 community and held accountable for the same. We supported the squadrons after they deployed in distant parts of the world, working hand in glove with the CAGs. We were a ready resource for the squadron commanding officers. In this job, I came to understand how all the aspects of the term 'readiness' come together and how to accurately measure it. The necessity for making trade-offs in situations with limited resources and the consequences of not getting them right were powerful lessons then and for the future.

CHAPTER 3

MAJOR COMMAND RESPONSIBILITY IN WAR

The first Gulf War of 1991 had aspects that were pertinent to the U.S. decision to invade Iraq in 2003. I was a participant as a major operational commander during the 1991 liberation of Kuwait, and I will offer insight into some lessons about command decisions and the processes involved.

GULF WAR 1991

I had taken command of Carrier Air Wing Eight (CVW-8) early in 1990, training to deploy on the aircraft carrier *USS THEODORE ROOSEVELT*. We were scheduled for an exercise in the north Atlantic in the autumn and then to proceed to the Mediterranean in 1991. The "TR," as we called her, was nuclear-powered and the Navy's newest operational aircraft carrier.

The air wing was unique in the Navy. At the time, the Navy was experimenting with several different wing configurations. It was known as the "TR Air Wing." Largest in the Navy at the time, the wing was composed of ten squadrons: two F-14A Tomcat, two F/A-18A Hornet, and two A-6E Intruder, plus one each EA-6B Prowler, S-3A Viking, E-2C Hawkeye, and SH-60 Seahawk helicopter squadrons.

As soon as we learned that Iraq had invaded Kuwait, I had a strong hunch that our schedule would change and we would be headed to war. This necessitated an immediate modification to our training plans and an intense focus on the impending combat operations. In addition to myself, the CAG (Carrier Air Group Commander in Navy parlance), there was only one pilot in the entire wing who had any prior combat experience, and this meant that we were going to have a very steep learning curve to prepare our aircrews for what they were likely to face.

There would not be an official decision to deploy TR and CVW-8 to the Gulf area until late in the year, but I instilled the idea in the minds of our people that we were going to go to war in Iraq to ensure that we had the right focus on essential survival skills and operational proficiency for aerial combat. The intelligence reports that we began to receive about Iraq were quite ominous, noting the recent combat experience of the Iran-Iraq War and the huge resupply of modern military equipment from Russia, France, and other arms suppliers.

On paper, the air defenses in Iraq looked quite formidable and particularly difficult for our planning because it was a mix of Russian, Chinese, French, German, and other new systems. Still, we were unsure how well these systems might be integrated. Our air wing did have a terrific opportunity to train out in the desert at Naval Air Station Fallon, Nevada, where we practiced tactics against some very capable simulation systems and skilled "aggressor" aircrews who flew against us using the best available intelligence about the tactics the Iraqis would employ. There was some confidence because, during the Iran-Iraq War, the Iranians flew some of the same type aircraft the U.S. forces possessed, particularly F-14s and F-4s, and seemed to do well against the Iraqis.

It did not take long before it became evident that the U.S. was quite serious about raising a coalition of forces to retake Kuwait. Again, we were not sure that our ship and air wing would be part of the effort, but my instinct was that, as we were the largest, newest, and most capable ship and air wing team, we would get the call to battle.

My immediate boss was Rear Admiral, later Vice Admiral David "Frosty" Frost, Commander of Carrier Group Eight, composed of TR, CVW-8, and several cruisers, destroyers, and other ships. I felt fortunate to be working for Frosty, a very experienced fighter pilot, former commanding officer of "Top Gun," the Navy Fighter Weapons School, and an aircraft carrier. Dave's Carrier Group staff was also excellent, with lots of experience and several officers who were well-known to me.

The CO (commanding officer) of TR, the "home" for our airwing and the Carrier Group staff, was Captain, later Admiral, Charles Stevenson "Steve" Abbot, a former attack aviator, Rhodes scholar, and nuclear engineer. By interesting coincidence, I had the pleasure of becoming acquainted with Steve's colorful and warmly entertaining father, retired Rear Admiral Lloyd "Doc" Abbot, many years earlier and long before Steve and I met. "Doc" was a World War II veteran aviator and former carrier CO who was still piloting planes in his eighties.

As Frosty, Steve, and I would all be working closely together on TR, it was important and our good fortune that we got on well and brought diverse and experienced backgrounds to our tasks. We each presumed that we would be involved in the coming conflict, and this expectation brought focus and intensity to our planning and preparation.

One evening, an interesting professional topic came up after a training exercise in Florida as Frosty and I relaxed at a restaurant over dinner and a bottle of wine. By way of background, I should explain that the traditional sequence for positions of increased responsibility for those of us in carrier aviation was, for the fortunate few lucky enough to be chosen for air wing command, to then shift over to ships, with the ultimate prize being selected as "skipper" of an aircraft carrier.

That tradition was abruptly changed a few years earlier by the former Secretary of the Navy, John Lehman, in the wake of that poorly executed 1983 retaliatory airstrike during the Lebanese Civil War, in which the two U.S. Navy aircraft were shot down. Lehman desired more experienced air wing commanders with in-depth intelligence preparation and focus on big-picture employment strategy to engender better decision-making. He set in place a trial reorganization, quickly dubbed the "Super CAG" program.

In the new structure, the "Super CAG" would have the rank of Captain and report directly to the Admiral in charge of the Battle Group, vice reporting to the carrier CO as had been the prior practice. The new structure would have a deputy, functioning like the traditional CAG but reporting to the "Super CAG." As noted, I was selected as the deputy for the first trial with "Bad Fred" Lewis on NIMITZ in 1986-87. The idea was quite controversial at the time, with most of the "old salts" predicting a return to the more traditional structure in short order. However, this was not to be, and the program soon became standard throughout the Navy.[23]

In any event, Frosty, who had come up under the traditional system of sequential ship command, asked me how I felt about it and whether I would not be happier having carrier command, traditionally the plum in naval aviation. Replying that in the early days, I felt whipsawed between trying to make it work and being advised by our elders that the system would revert. Despite some prior misgivings, I said I felt content in the current situation. We then discussed the agreed-upon likelihood of an upcoming war, and Frosty asked me what I thought about leading my airwing in combat from the cockpit. I said, "Of course, I want to fly in the lead." He told me that he did not think that was a good idea because of the significantly increased intelligence information to which I had been exposed, and that in the new CAG program, the concept was that I would be taking a more strategic approach to exercising the operations. He asked, "What if you get shot down?" and said he was unhappy with the idea of my flying with that risk. I pushed him hard, but he smiled and said, "We'll see." Some months later, in his cabin on TR on the night before our first mission in the war, which I was leading, he said with a grin, "So what do you think now? Would you rather be doing this or up on the bridge commanding the ship?" I laughed and said, "You know the answer to that," he said, "Yeah, I do," with a big smile.

Another issue in our preparation for the war concerned intelligence information and sharing that information among the services. In mid-December, the decision having been made that we were deploying to the war, along with five other aircraft carriers and their accompanying ships, I went to Frosty and confided in him my concern that we were not being given all the information that was desired and available. The specific need was for current order-of-battle data and analysis, namely the Iraqi air defenses' type, numbers, and disposition. I had asked my Navy colleagues in the other air wings, but they had no more information. Frosty suggested that we take a quick trip up to Washington from Norfolk, as he had a friend in Joint Staff J-3, current operations division, whom he thought would have the info. As we sat in his Pentagon office and I questioned him about what we needed, I was dumbfounded when he told us there really was nothing else; that we had it all. When we walked out, I told Frosty, "I flat out don't believe him. I do not understand why he won't give us what I'm certain is more available information." We both had calls to make on other people in the building, so we split up and agreed to meet a little later.

I called an old friend I knew was well-connected in the intelligence world. He asked, "Do you know Colonel John Warden of the Air Force?" I said, "I do not," but I recalled that he was the Pentagon's head of the Air Force "Checkmate" planning cell.[24] I received a call to go to a specific room in the basement of the Pentagon, which I did. Knocking on the door and announcing myself, I was led to Col. Warden's office, where I received a pleasant greeting. John asked what he could do for me, and I explained that I was an Air Wing Commander about to deploy for the war and needed the most up-to-date order-of-battle information. He said, "Let me show you around, and you can have anything you find that might be of use to you."

As I walked through his planning spaces, I was astounded. What I saw was exactly what we were looking for. I asked John if I could have some classified charts and other background materials. He said, "Sure, whatever you need." I was figuratively blown away as I had never experienced this open willingness to share from a sister service. After passing the good news to Frosty, I called my staff intelligence officer, Tony Cothron, down in Norfolk, and directed him to get in his car and bring some other people with him because I had a treasure trove we needed back on the ship.

As an aside, Frosty and I mused about the real story, whether the Joint Staff Admiral did not know or whether there was some other reason behind the secrecy. In any event, we were far too busy to waste time looking backward. Reviewing our planned tactics resulted in immediate changes based on the information we gleaned. I did note that virtually everyone in the Navy was trying to help as we prepared to deploy, and they bent over backward, responding positively to every request.

Shortly before we were due to depart Norfolk for the Middle East, I came up with a doozy when I asked if we could make an exceptionally substantial change to the ship ordnance load-out. For background: weapons loads on ships getting ready to deploy, particularly the copious amounts allotted to the aircraft carriers, are usually determined and loaded well in advance. In our case, TR was alongside the pier in Norfolk, had completed pre-deployment training, the ordnance was aboard and stowed, and the ship was being loaded with food and the remaining last-minute items, as we were due to leave in about 10 days, just after Christmas 1990. I asked to change a large percentage of the bomb load-out from the more numerous 500-pound weapons to the heavier 1000 and 2000-pound bombs. My rationale was that, given the particularly formidable Iraqi air defenses we now understood from the information gleaned from the USAF in Washington, I wanted our attack aircraft to be more appropriately armed with fewer, heavier weapons, making them more effective and more survivable. This was an extraordinarily heavy task for the ship's crew and all the supporting folks in Norfolk. Still, they did it with incredible, mostly hard manual labor in the amazingly short few days we had left. It was an impressive performance that I have never forgotten. Once we got into combat, we saw it was the right decision.

TR departed Norfolk for OPERATION DESERT STORM on December 28, 1990, and crossed the Atlantic and Mediterranean at high speed with the whole air wing aboard, except for a few airplanes that had flown ahead to help protect the gathering force in the Persian Gulf. We marveled at the large coalition of willing, if not altogether able, forces that had been put together against Saddam's invasion of Kuwait.

In another example of unselfish assistance, a German naval task force departed its home ports over that Christmas holiday to rendezvous with our TR Task Group for one significant and much-appreciated reason. Although Germany did not deploy troops or ships to the war as part of the Coalition, their Navy was eager to help. We knew France had provided Iraq with modern and capable weapon systems. One of them, the anti-ship Exocet missile, was also a main armament on German warships. We were genuinely concerned about this weapon and its capabilities, but had no experience with it, particularly the electronic signature and how well we could distinguish and hopefully deceive it. Joining with the German destroyers in mid-Atlantic for only a couple of hours, they fired some of these missiles directly at our ships (with fingers crossed, at what was calculated to be just beyond maximum range), giving us an unprecedented and invaluable live-fire experience. We were indebted to our German allies for this altruistic contribution to the Coalition.

As the time drew closer to the imminent start of the war, Frosty and I were summoned to a meeting in Bahrain with the Commander of the U.S. Seventh Fleet and all U.S. Naval Forces involved in the war, Vice Admiral (later Admiral and Navy Vice Chief) Stan Arthur, who desired a face-to-face meeting with as many of the naval commanders as possible. Although the ship had just passed into the eastern Mediterranean, a long way from Bahrain, we climbed into one of our S-3 Viking long-range aircraft. We flew from TR down and across Egypt and Saudi Arabia to land at the Manama airfield in Bahrain. We arrived just before dusk to an amazing sight; aircraft of every size, shape, and description from countries worldwide that had joined the Coalition were parked on every square foot of the ramp space. As it turned out, the only available space for us was under the wing of a giant C-5 Galaxy transport aircraft.

DECISIONS, DISCORD & DIPLOMACY

The meeting with Admiral Arthur and the other commanders was valuable and unprecedented in recent times, as we got to meet face-to-face with our Navy and Marine Corps counterparts, exchange information and ideas, and prepare to support one another in the coming conflict, which we learned would commence a few days later, on January 17, 1991. A disheartening disclosure at that meeting came from the group tasked with clearing anti-ship mines in the Gulf. Their assessment was that the number of mines was substantially higher than we had previously calculated. Doing the job could take months rather than weeks, thus greatly complicating the planned operations.

Following the conference, some of us got together to talk about tactics. I wanted to ensure that my counterparts had the latest intelligence information we received in Washington (we had passed the key points to them) and had appropriately modified their tactics. I was chagrined to learn from one of my former squadron mates that a couple of the other wings planned to proceed with the more traditional attacks they had previously practiced. We discussed the challenges of attacking most of the heavily defended Iraqi targets in the old style.

My former colleagues agreed, but unfortunately, they could not convince their wing commanders. They suffered some immediate losses as a result. After dinner, a few of us found our way to a pub in downtown Manama frequented by businesspeople from the region. Most patrons were Arabs, and I joined in some fascinating conversation. The majority opinion was that there would not be a war. Of course, I had just come from the meeting at which the hour and night for the start of the war had been disclosed. I listened in amazement as some of these gentlemen offered their rationale for no war, predominantly that Saddam was too smart to get tangled up in another war, and/or the Saudis would buy him out to preclude a conflict. I could only exclaim, "Really?" One of the gentlemen there asked me if I had ever visited Baghdad. When I replied negatively, he said, "You would love it; great nightlife and the most sophisticated city in the Middle East." Would not he have been surprised to learn that I was, in fact, planning a visit some night very soon!

The war started on January 17 and lasted less than seven weeks until February 28. For Air Wing Eight, the combat operations were intense, and the overall performance of the air wing was superb. The flight crews did a magnificent job, and the support they received from the squadron maintenance personnel, crew of TR, and the Group 8 staff was exemplary. We cherish the memories of our three lost airmen: Lieutenant Commander Barry Cooke and Lieutenant Junior Grade Patrick Conner of Attack Squadron 36 and Lieutenant Robert Dwyer of my CVW-8 Airwing Staff, killed in action. The courage and tenacity of these men and their colleagues made the conflict come to a quick and victorious conclusion.

Fast-forwarding past many of the details and experiences of the Gulf War, we pick up the story in the final days of the conflict.

The ground assault by Coalition forces to expel the Iraqi military from Kuwait began on February 24. It was concluded about one hundred hours later. Events unfolded quite rapidly, and the air wing was deeply involved in supporting the operations from the air. To set the scene, the four Navy aircraft carriers in the Gulf had moved much farther north from our original launch positions near Bahrain at the start of the conflict. The Iraqi threat to our ships had been generally eliminated by numerous airstrikes around the northern Gulf. The new launch positions significantly shortened the flying time to the target areas in Kuwait and Iraq. They reduced the need for additional fuel from the U.S. Air Force and Coalition tankers.

A good part of the Persian Gulf was fouled and blackened by the crude oil that Saddam had ordered dumped into the sea. Our ships did their best to stay out of the highly polluting and corrosive drifting oil slick, an area of approximately 100×45 miles on the surface. The Iraqis had also blown up and set ablaze, beginning in late January, almost all the oil wells in Kuwait, and as a result, the air overhead of those drilling rigs and for hundreds of square miles downwind was blackened and dangerous when inhaled, severely restricting visibility for our aircrews.

When flying at night, the combination of burning oil wells, heavy smoke, and intense anti-aircraft fire reflected from the smoke and low clouds was dangerously eerie and reminded me of a scene from Dante's Inferno. To make matters more challenging, the weather turned bad with low clouds, intermittent rain showers, and blowing dust mixing in with the man-made mess.

Although most of the low-altitude close air support of the ground forces was being conducted by attack helicopters, Air Force special-purpose A-10 ground attack jets, and Marine Corps Harrier ground attack "jump jets," the air wing had significant assets dedicated to this air support when needed. The rapid movement of the attacking ground forces and the many Coalition aircraft in proximity was a cause for considerable concern about fratricide within our own forces. This combination of the rapid troop advance, often well ahead of the published timelines, and the inability to clearly see from the air through the weather and smoke made it anyone's guess where the FEBA (Forward Edge of the Battle Area) really was in those final hours of the conflict.

After listening to the aircrew debriefings and the confusion that seemed to be growing, I elected to fly out on a mission in an A-6 Intruder attack aircraft and see for myself what was going on. As predicted, the weather was awful, and we had to get down under the clouds to about five hundred feet just to see the ground. We did a reconnaissance run along a north-running road in eastern Kuwait and received a fair amount of ground fire from Iraqi troops, many of whom were moving north to escape the ground offensive. We discovered a vehicle refueling site with several tanker trucks, attacked it, and set it ablaze. My assessment was that it was dangerous to be flying that low in the conditions described. I shifted our missions to avoid the battle area except for those aircraft holding high overhead in case they were needed for close air support.

When I landed back on the ship, a new issue was creating quite a stir. During the previous night of February 26-27, a large column of Iraqi forces was reported fleeing north from Kuwait City on Highway 80. Coalition forces spearheaded by U.S. Marines had been rapidly advancing on Kuwait City from the south, and we assumed that these Iraqi forces were attempting to withdraw. Most of the forces that were deployed by Saddam in Kuwait at the time of the DESERT STORM operation were regular Iraqi army troops. The best-equipped and most proficient forces in the Iraqi army were five divisions of the Republican Guard, which were arrayed north of Kuwait City and into Iraq south of the Euphrates River Valley. These troops were well dug into defensive positions and put up formidable air defenses when we flew over them.

As the Marines and other Coalition forces pushed north into Kuwait City, the U.S. Army, with French and British divisions, were sweeping in from the west in the so-called "left hook" maneuver and, by the night of February 26 and continuing on the 27th, was combating Republican Guard divisions. It did not seem surprising to us that the Iraqi forces, being pressured from both the south and the west, would be trying to extricate themselves from Kuwait City before they were trapped there.

CHAPTER 4

GULF WAR 1991

Unfortunately, given the state-of-the-art communications at the time, we were not receiving real-time reports of ground action. In short, we did not know until much later that the column of Iraqi vehicles coming out of Kuwait City had been cut off about 50 miles north of the city by Coalition air attacks and was strung out and stalled for many miles. While I was airborne, distant from the ship, media reports hyping photos of extensive damage were circulating around the world, indicating that Coalition forces were pummeling that convoy, destroying most of the vehicles and inflicting heavy casualties on the Iraqis in a scene described as "shooting ducks in a pond." After the fact, it was determined that the number of Iraqi troops killed was actually several hundred. Still, much larger numbers were being reported in the media. Many had simply abandoned their vehicles and tried to escape into the desert or nearby swamps.

Also, after the fact, it was discovered that many of these vehicles were filled with booty: valuables, personal belongings, carpets, and furniture that had been looted from homes and businesses in Kuwait. But at the time, in the firestorm of reaction to photos of the damaged vehicles, the perception was that our forces were just indiscriminately killing people.[25] This was exacerbated by a Radio Baghdad claim attributed to Saddam and reported in the media that he had ordered a cease-fire and withdrawal from Kuwait. It took some time for Washington to sort things out and deny this assertion, reinforced by the experience with strong Iraqi resistance on my just-concluded flight. Nonetheless, there was noticeable sensitivity to the images being circulated by the media.

As there was little information on the ship other than the media reports, Admiral Frost asked me what we were doing out there. Steve Abbot opined that it seemed we were just perpetrating a massacre, and we ought to stop. I was a bit frustrated and replied that our airwing was not flying in that area of the battlefield, and from what I had just witnessed, it was clear that both sides were doing what they were ordered to do, aggressively pursuing the war.

Gulf War 1991

With so many conflicting stories and the literal fog of war on the battlefield, it was not surprising that many people, including me, were wondering who had the complete big picture. Remember, this was still the early digital computer days, and we only had two satellite telephone lines on the ship. I asked my intelligence team to do their best and sort through whatever information they could glean to get an accurate picture of what was happening in northeast Kuwait and southern Iraq. Still, my number one concern at that moment was to try to prevent a "friendly fire" incident involving our aircrews, given the confusion on the battlefield.

About this time, I received a rare phone call. On the other line was my longtime friend from Vietnam War days, Captain Lyle "Ho Chi" Bien, who was in Riyadh as our Navy liaison to the air component commander. He said, "Fox, they're going to call this thing to an end early tomorrow, so if you have any work that needs to be done or targets you think you need to hit, you'd better do it quickly." I asked if we could get any extra fuel from the big Air Force tankers because I had in mind sending our strike aircraft farther north into Iraq to try to knock out bridges to preclude the escape of the Republican Guard divisions. He replied negatively that we would just have to do our best with what we had.

I reported this to Frosty and asked to recall and rearm our jets for one last big strike against bridges north of Basra toward Amarah on the highway to Baghdad. He concurred, so as darkness fell, the flight deck crews labored strenuously to reload the aircraft with heavy ordnance. We launched as many aircraft as possible when things were organized shortly before midnight. Again, they were hampered by bad weather but had some success. After the aircraft landed back on the ship, we were informed that the cease-fire was going into effect in a few hours, and the conflict would be over.

I assumed that Coalition ground forces had continued east toward Basra and the Tigris River to seal off the escape route north for the Iraqi forces, thus the timing for the cease-fire declaration. But this was not the case.

Given the rapid advance of the ground forces and the overwhelming success that they were achieving, Washington authorities were deliberating with CENTCOM about when and where to stop the offensive. Scenes of destruction on the "Highway of Death" and the resulting media outcry, plus Saddam's false claims of a cease-fire and withdrawal, sharpened and accelerated the discussions and led to the cease-fire declaration on 28 February. Meanwhile, Iraqi forces, and particularly most of the Republican Guard divisions, rapidly withdrew unimpeded to the north into Iraq because those routes had not been sealed off by our ground forces. I believe that the battle's confusion with the rapidly advancing Coalition forces and the severe weather made it virtually impossible to tell exactly where all the forces were on the battlefield. The concern and pressure from Washington to stop attacking, based on the overall success of the advance, plus the ugly media reports, combined to bring things to a halt before the job was quite finished. The fact that those Republican Guard units could escape intact had repercussions for the future. In the immediate aftermath of the cease-fire, Saddam claimed a "victory," bragging that his army stopped the powerful Coalition from advancing farther into Iraq.

Several days following the cease-fire and after the weather cleared, we were able to send reconnaissance aircraft over the area of the previous battlefield. We saw that many Iraqi forces had simply disappeared, confirming their escape. Much discussion and second-guessing ensued in the world media about the decision to halt the offensive campaign at the Kuwait-Iraq border and not proceed to Baghdad. President George H.W. Bush, who made the decision to stop the offensive, said then, and again upon reflection some years later, that the objective of the war was to expel Iraqi forces from Kuwait and not to march to Baghdad.[26] He was pleased with the victory but unhappy with how the conflict ended. How much difference it would have made if the bulk of Saddam's army had been prevented from escaping and stripped of their equipment is still being debated. I agreed with the decision to not advance to Baghdad but believed it was a significant blunder to cease hostilities before ensuring that the Republican Guard divisions were neutralized. Those enemy troops were used to suppress the Shia and Kurdish rebellions. They remained the strong nucleus of Saddam's army, keeping him in power and discouraging further attempts to unseat him.

That confusion reigned, and decisions up the chain of command were based on sketchy or inaccurate information, is now clear. A telling indicator is that the decision about where to accept the surrender of the

GULF WAR 1991

Iraqi forces and to dictate the terms of the cease-fire reflected what was occurring on that last day and night of the conflict. Coalition Commanding General Norman Schwarzkopf considered three proposed locations and ultimately chose a small airfield by the town of Safwan to the west of Basra, Iraq, assuming it was in Coalition hands. In fact, it was not, and when the error was discovered, U.S. Army forces had to quickly advance ten more miles to seize and occupy the site.[27] A decision made at the surrender meeting between General Schwarzkopf and the Iraqis that promptly came back to haunt world leaders was to accede to a request from the Iraqis to allow them to fly armed helicopters if they avoided Coalition forces. Saddam soon used these vehicles to deadly effect in suppressing insurrections by the Shia in the south and the Kurds in the north of Iraq.

While the people of Kuwait rejoiced in their liberation and the Coalition celebrated its' victory, Saddam assessed his situation and found that despite the pounding his country had taken and lives lost in the conflict, for him, much remained the same. Against long odds, he remained in power, his borders were unchanged, the core of his army and security forces had escaped with most of their equipment, and he still enjoyed support from a majority of the "Arab Street." But internal unrest was on the upswing in Iraq. No doubt inspired by Saddam's defeat at the hands of the Coalition and President Bush's call for them to revolt and overthrow their despotic leader[28], the Kurds in the north and Shia dissidents in the south rose against him within weeks of the cease-fire agreement at Safwan.

In the south, Saddam moved quickly to resume several punishing initiatives begun after the Iran-Iraq War to clear out opposition from Shia dissidents. He had his forces renew the effort to drain the vast marshlands between the Tigris and Euphrates Rivers to eliminate places of refuge. He put the military and security forces to work attacking the towns and villages that he perceived to harbor his opponents, taking deadly advantage of the armed helicopters that he retained by the terms of the recently concluded cease-fire. As the non-government organization (NGO) Human Rights Watch described it, "When the March 1991 uprising confronted his regime with the most serious internal challenges it had ever faced, government forces responded with atrocities on a predictably massive scale... Shooting them en masse and using helicopters to attack unarmed civilians as they fled the cities."[29]

CHAPTER 5

OPERATION PROVIDE COMFORT

In the north, Saddam's forces set upon the rebelling Kurds with particular vengeance, sweeping northward through the mountain valleys of their homelands. The Kurdish people, mindful of long-standing violent persecution, including many instances of the use of lethal poison gases against them during the Iran-Iraq War, fearfully fled their towns and villages in a mass exodus over the mountains toward Turkey.

Meanwhile, the nations that had agreed to have their forces join in the remarkably broad-based and successful coalition to evict Saddam from Kuwait gratefully rejoiced in the small number of personnel casualties and eagerly pulled their forces back home. There was clearly little appetite for any further military action against Saddam by most of the Gulf War participants. U.S. forces were part of this large-scale withdrawal from the region, and most of the ships from the Navy fleet headed home soon after the cease-fire. However, in the case of TR and CVW-8, as we were the last of the six aircraft carriers and air wings to deploy before the war, we remained on station while the others left. In the Gulf for several weeks, we then proceeded to the Red Sea. We assumed station off the northwest coast of Saudi Arabia, covering the withdrawal of U.S. and allied forces.

Locally, as Saddam accelerated his pursuit of the opposition Shia, and mainly the Kurds, concern mounted in Washington and some other capitals about what to do in response to his renewed genocide.

CENTCOM issued warnings to Iraq about the use of military aircraft other than helicopters. Subsequently, USAF fighters based in Turkey shot down several Iraqi fighter-bomber aircraft that were flying against the Kurds. As international concern mounted, and in response to U.N. Security Resolution 688, the U.S. and some Coalition partners rapidly put together a new military-led effort in reaction to the humanitarian crisis that was escalating in northern Iraq.[30] Reports were received that hundreds of thousands of Kurdish men, women, and children were fleeing, many on foot, over the steep mountains in harsh weather. The new plan was dubbed OPERATION PROVIDE COMFORT (PC).

Operation Provide Comfort

In early April 1991, TR/CVW-8 was ordered through the Suez Canal and into the Mediterranean Sea. None of us was quite sure about the details of what was going on, nor what we could contribute, but we rapidly moved north and began coordinating with other U.S. and allied forces as the ship headed to the northeast corner of the Mediterranean between Syria and Turkey. Arriving at a point as close as we could get to Iraq, we received permission to do a reconnaissance flight to find out firsthand what was happening.

Launching from the carrier in a section (two aircraft) of F-14 Tomcat fighters equipped with reconnaissance pods, I flew east over Turkey, refueled from an Air Force tanker, and then crossed the Iraq border to see if we could get an accurate assessment. The terrain in this part of Iraq consists of long, narrow valleys generally running east and west, interspersed with rugged mountains. Armed and prepared to respond if attacked by Iraqi military personnel, we methodically flew up and down the valleys searching for refugees as well as Iraqi military forces.

We found deserted towns and villages, but no sign of any people. As we worked our way south onto the plains of northern Iraq to the east of Mosul, we detected electronic surveillance of our aircraft. We began to see some Iraqi ground forces. Returning north, we went down to low altitude, searching for refugees, eventually finding several groups of displaced people in large concentrations close to the Turkish border. Already, some of these folks obviously had been the recipients of humanitarian assistance as we spotted groups of similarly colored blue and olive tents. People on the ground initially fled from our aircraft, assuming we were Iraqi military looking for them. As we returned and flew low, rocking our wings, the refugees began to wave, realizing we were not Saddam's Air Force. We took photos and plotted the locations of these encampments before running low on fuel and returning to Turkish airspace and back to the aircraft carrier.

OPERATION DESERT STORM had been commanded by General Schwarzkopf, as Iraq was in the CENTCOM area of responsibility. During the conflict, some air operations had been conducted against Iraqi forces in the northern part of the country by Coalition, mostly USAF, aircraft based in Turkey. These forces were under the command of the European Theatre (USEUCOM) Commander, General John Galvin; as Turkey is in the USEUCOM area of responsibility, General Galvin coordinated these operations with CENTCOM. Given the long distances involved, the operations in the north were complementary to the rest of DESERT STORM forces, which attacked Iraq from the south.

The decision was made in Washington to put USEUCOM in charge of OPERATION PROVIDE COMFORT since the activity was in the far north of Iraq along the Turkish border. The headquarters was established at Incirlik Airbase near Adana in southeast Turkey. This NATO facility had been the principal launch site for most of the air operations from the north during DESERT STORM.

The assigned Commander of what became a Joint Task Force (JTF), eventually including a mix of U.S. forces from all services and ten Coalition partners, was U.S. Army Lieutenant General John Shalikashvili (future Chairman of the U.S. Joint Chiefs of Staff). His deputy in the JTF was USAF Maj. Gen. Jim Jamerson, who had led the northern air operations during DESERT STORM, and Chief of Staff, Marine Brigadier General Tony Zinni, future Commander of USCENTCOM. Each of these officers had regular assigned duties at U.S. European Command (USEUCOM) and were well known to General Galvin and each other, which made the transition easier. A major component of the ground forces was the newly arrived 24 MEU (Marine Expeditionary Unit), commanded by USMC Colonel Jim Jones, future Marine Corps Commandant and Commander USEUCOM.

The TR/CVW-8 ship/ airwing team was now assigned to JTF PROVIDE COMFORT. Our new boss on TR, Rear Admiral Robert "Rocky" Spane, who had relieved Frosty after the war, sent me to Incirlik, Turkey, to establish face-to-face relationships and to understand what we could do to help the effort. The entire command structure and assigned forces were a pickup team of disparate capabilities pulled together without notice. But I was immediately impressed with the assembleds no-nonsense approach and task-focused direction. Most of the units involved were well-prepared and experienced. The commanders rapidly analyzed the situation and, with a good understanding of the strategic objectives, made quick and sound decisions.

First priority was to alleviate the humanitarian crisis and, second, to provide security for the people fleeing from Saddam's forces and eventually enable them to go home. The task that I was given was to provide air cover for the JTF personnel on the ground and the refugees.

OPERATION PROVIDE COMFORT

Our mission was to protect and, if necessary, respond to any Iraqi attacks against JTF personnel or refugees, to deter Iraqi attacks by our mere presence, and to contribute what information we might gather from in-flight observation to inform the intelligence picture. We would share this responsibility with the USAF and some Coalition partners flying out of Incirlik airfield. As these were long-range missions from the aircraft carrier, flying over Turkey into Iraq, typically three- or four-hour duration, we would be refueled in mid-air by large Air Force tanker aircraft over Turkey, much as we had been doing during DESERT STORM, so our pilots were quite proficient at this task.

As was explained to me, and as I had seen from the air on the previous day, the situation on the ground was complex and confusing. The big picture was that the Kurdish Peshmerga militia had led an insurrection against Saddam soon after the cease-fire and proceeded to attack and dislodge the Iraqi army from several towns and cities in northern Iraq. The vastly larger Iraqi security forces counterattacked and quickly took back the occupied towns, pushing north toward the Turkish border. The Kurdish population, mindful and fearful of a rerun of the 1980s "Anfal" persecution and use of poison gas against them by Saddam, began to flee en masse toward the Turkish and Iranian borders with little more than the clothes on their backs.

The JTF people on the ground had the challenging task of going into Iraq, invading in a sense, with us as air cover from Turkey, coordinating with many national and NGO relief organizations in providing immediate assistance in the form of water, food, and shelter for the refugees, and confronting Iraqi security forces that had reoccupied some towns close to the Turkish border. Aided by U.N. Security Council Resolution 688 and support from most world governments, JTF PROVIDE COMFORT expelled, with only minor conflict, Iraqi security forces from the majority Kurdish areas in the north, eventually enabling the return to their homes of most of the people who had fled and survived the exodus over the mountains. It also established a "no-fly zone" north of the 36th parallel, precluding Iraqi military air operations over the new safe zone in addition to what was essentially a "no-go zone" for Iraqi security forces on the ground.[31]

This work was completed in less than four months. JTF PROVIDE COMFORT set an exemplary standard of collaborative accomplishment in a complex environment involving humanitarian needs and military security. Cooperation between the political, military, civil, operational, and tactical levels was effective and enabled mission accomplishment.[32] The operation extended the Coalition collaboration demonstrated during DESERT STORM and was highlighted by a good understanding of the situation on the ground and clear enunciation of political guidance from national leaders. As a result, the Kurdish area of northern Iraq avoided oppression by Saddam for the remainder of his regime. Regrettably, the exemplary execution of this operation and the reasons for its success were largely forgotten in the run-up to the 2003 war in Iraq.

This was a teaching moment. I learned much about Iraq, its people, and the operation and functioning of a joint service and multilateral JTF from PROVIDE COMFORT. In the 90 days or so that we were committed to the operation, I became familiar with northern Iraq's terrain and cultural features. The geography and the place names are embedded in my mind. I also got to witness the beauty of that area and gain an understanding of why the Kurdish people are so drawn to it. When we arrived, it still looked like winter; the rugged mountains were covered with snow, and the ground at lower altitudes was drab gray or brown.

Over the next several weeks, an amazing transformation occurred: as the snow melted, the valleys turned green with grass, and the land was carpeted with wildflowers. The seemingly barren earth in the rolling hills south of the tall mountains turned green as far as the eye could see. The new shoots of grain that fed much of the country rapidly matured in the short growing season when water was available from the melting snow. Farmers appeared everywhere, tending their crops in pastoral scenes at odds with the ever-present human conflicts in the region.

The Kurdish people who call that place home have longed for their own state for centuries. The problem is that these people live in multiple and distinct political states of Iraq, Iran, Turkey, and Syria; none of these countries will voluntarily surrender any territory to create a separate Kurdish state. And so, the Kurdish leadership and their Peshmerga militias are typically in conflict with one or all of the governments of the states in which they reside. There are long-standing rivalries between the two dominant clans of Kurds, the Barzani and Talabani, who often engage in fighting and killing one another. An interesting observation is that despite the nearly constant conflicts, the Kurds are skilled at forming short-term political alliances in each of these countries and participate in many aspects of political and military life. This behavior was on display during Saddam's rule and is still a fact of life in Iraq today, as Kurds occupy key government political and military positions.

One other fascinating discovery while over-flying northern Iraq was a long line of ridgetop mansions deep in the Kurdish heartland and in a particularly scenic area with fantastic views in all directions. On a scale of grandeur like others in and around Baghdad, these palaces were constructed for family members and favored associates of Saddam. Stunning architecture, swimming pools, and elaborate gardens were the norm. Not all the structures were completed, but all were abandoned and looted during my observation. In retrospect, I thought about the complex functioning of Iraqi society with the oppressive minority Sunni political leadership coexisting with the Kurdish population, with which it was usually at odds. We clearly had little understanding and appreciation for the complexities of human existence in Iraq.

During our brief time as part of OPERATION PROVIDE COMFORT, I met many superb military and diplomatic leaders with whom I would work again in subsequent commands. A legacy of the success of PROVIDE COMFORT was the adoption of the general template of organizational structure, command and control, and integration of civil and military aspects to facilitate mission accomplishment in the now-changed post-Cold War security environment. Key lessons learned from the operation were directed for implementation in the U.S. military by the then Chairman of the JCS, General Colin Powell, and his successor, General Shalikashvili. Again, unfortunately, many of these lessons were abandoned and forgotten in the run-up to the war in 2003.

CHAPTER 6
Iraq Redux?

A little over a year later, in July 1992, I was a senior Navy Captain in rank, settling into my Pentagon office in a new assignment as Deputy Director of Naval Aviation Plans and Requirements. In the interim, I attended the National War College in Washington with many of my fellow operational commanders from DESERT STORM.

The Pentagon assignment was my first official Washington job since starting active duty in the Navy 25 years earlier, although I had spent a lot of time in Washington and picked up valuable experience and insight in another assignment about a decade earlier. As I took the measure of the new responsibilities, I felt professionally comfortable, having spent most of the previous years in service with the naval aviation operating forces. But then, a couple of weeks later, I received an unexpected phone call from an acquaintance and former boss, Rear Admiral Dave "Snake" Morris, who inquired, "How's it going in the new job"?

Replying that I was just settling in and things were going well, he said, "Fox, you better get your sea bag ready because you're going to be taking a trip real soon." It would be an understatement to say that I was surprised. I asked, "Really... Where might I be going? And for how long?" He said, "Somewhere hot, right away, and I don't know for how long." When I probed for more detail, he said, "I'm just giving you a heads up, but you're going back to the desert, and you'd better find your passport and get your immunizations up to speed, quickly. Someone will give you the official word soon, but they picked you!" I replied, "Thanks, I think," my head spinning. I quickly dialed home, and my son Bill, a junior in high school and the only person at home at the time, answered. I asked him to go up to the attic and see if he could locate my cruise box, bring it downstairs, open it, and lay out some warm-weather clothes. He said, "Dad, what's up?" I replied, "I don't know for sure, but it looks like I'm going to be taking a trip very soon; more details to follow."

About an hour later, I was called to the office of the Washington D.C. head of naval aviation, Rear Admiral Riley Mixon, the senior of the carrier group commanders during DESERT STORM, with his flag on the carrier *USS JOHN F. KENNEDY*. Smiling, as was his usual manner, he asked if I was up for a trip. I feigned surprise, and he continued that he didn't know all the details, but there was an urgent need to put together a small planning staff with current knowledge of naval aviation strike matters, and I was selected to head it. The authorities wanted me down in Tampa to meet with CENTCOM staff officers right away, and I would then be headed to the Middle East, probably Saudi Arabia. Inquiring if I had a current passport (I did), he suggested I meet with Rear Admiral Dave Rogers, the new Naval Forces Central Command Commander in Tampa. Riley said his staff would arrange to get me a flight to Tampa the next day, and folks at CENTCOM would take it from there.

Lacking even written orders and without further information, I boarded a commercial flight to Tampa the following afternoon. I arrived at CENTCOM headquarters several hours later. For background, the command arrangements at CENTCOM were somewhat awkward regarding the Navy, as Admiral Rogers' office was in Tampa, but the naval forces in the region were operating out of Bahrain under the command of Rear Admiral "RAK" Taylor. The good news was that I knew both.

The hasty briefings at CENTCOM were sketchy. Their priority task was to get me to Riyadh, Kingdom of Saudi Arabia (KSA), as soon as possible, where they said I would learn the details. To that end, I was informed that an Air Force KC-135 aircraft would leave in a couple of hours to take me there, along with some communications equipment. I put on a flight suit and flight jacket, boarded the aircraft, and was shown to a jump seat behind the pilots, which would be my deluxe accommodation for the trip to the Middle East. To make things more "enjoyable," at that time, there was a problem with KC-135 aircraft windscreen cracks at high altitude, so the aircraft were restricted to relatively low altitudes until further notice. That meant a slower flight with refueling stops en route. Adapting quickly, I exchanged my seat for a plush perch atop a pallet of cargo behind the cockpit, where I could roll up in a spare blanket and get some much-needed shut-eye in the horizontal position.

Arriving in Riyadh about 24 hours later in the wee hours of the morning, the aircraft was directed to park on the far side of the airfield on an unlit patch of tarmac. We were quickly escorted off the plane, bypassing all the standard customs and immigration procedures. I was taken to a temporary billeting location on the Riyadh Air Force Base for some rest and instructed to meet my chaperone in the morning for escort to a briefing.

After a short snooze, shave, shower, and breakfast, I was taken to Riyadh's Royal Saudi Air Force (RSAF) headquarters. I had never been to the place but recalled it was where the air war had been conducted during DESERT STORM. Meeting with several Air Force Colonels typically assigned to 9th Air Force headquarters at Shaw Air Force Base in South Carolina and double-hatted as the Air Component Commander for CENTCOM, I finally received the big picture.

In light of Saddam's continued persecution of the Kurds and particularly the Shia in southern Iraq, Washington was considering restarting (or finishing) the war (DESERT STORM Act II). They wanted planning to commence immediately for that possibility. The people on hand who had just arrived a few days before me were essentially the same crew that had planned and executed the DESERT STORM air war under Air Force Generals Horner and Glosson a year and a half earlier. I was to be the senior Navy representative for the planning. At that time, the staff was a total of one: me. It was immediately apparent that this was not some token effort but a serious undertaking likely to result in military action. The aircraft I traveled on brought essential command, control, and communications equipment with more to follow, plus many additional personnel. As I was the second most senior person on hand, and to meet the desire to have a decision-maker available 24 hours a day, I became the officer in charge for a 12-hour shift; the night shift, naturally! The work effort so far had been at senior staff level, principally digging out the plans for DESERT STORM and updating them. The Saudis were aware at some senior levels, but there was no public disclosure.

As I absorbed the intent and objectives of my new assignment, I also realized that I was a party of one, without written orders and an orphan on a staff of folks who were quite used to working together and had a keen sense of what they wanted to do. I asked about accommodations and discovered that a few more senior officers were billeted in the nearby U.S. Military Training Mission (USMTM) compound. The more junior folks were living outside the city at Eskan Village. The latter facility was built some years earlier by the Saudis to attract Bedouin tribesmen into the more urban environment.

Iraq Redux?

That plan did not work, and the facilities were made available and used during the war by the U.S. military, who were working in Riyadh. Many were at the RSAF HQ that we now reoccupied. I was told there was no room at the USMTM compound and that I would need to find a hotel room, which the staff would fund. Thanks to a helpful staff member and assistance from the U.S. embassy, I was able to arrange accommodation, which included a room and meals, in the nearby Le Meridien Hotel. I also called back to U.S. Naval Forces Central Command (USNAVCENT) in Tampa for written orders and some additional Navy people with key skill sets, which I enumerated. Thus, fixed administratively, I set my body clock for the night shift and started to dig into the planning that had been done to date. Except for being out of the normal workday loop for key decisions, I welcomed the night shift as daytime August temperatures in Riyadh were about 120°F.

However, it did not take long before I made an unsettling discovery. My Air Force planning colleagues were setting up an operational structure that fundamentally minimized the Navy's contribution. In fact, it looked like a rerun of DESERT STORM in which Navy aircraft were relegated to the sides of the battlefield, while the Air Force attack and fighter zones had all the prime airspace into the heartland of Iraq. This arrangement caused much heartburn in the Navy during DESERT STORM, particularly for our fighter aircrews, who found little action on the flanks while the USAF engaged most Iraqi aircraft. When I challenged this repeating construct, I was told that Navy aircraft did not have the appropriate sensors to positively identify friend from foe. I replied that most air-to-air engagements required positive VID (Visual identification) and that our Navy aircraft, particularly the new F-14 and F/A-18s, had excellent beyond-VID sensors.

My vociferous objections were dismissed. This blatant marginalization was not only wrong but also failed to take advantage of the significant capabilities the Navy would bring to this operation. While I seethed, I found out that Admiral Rogers was on his way to Riyadh and would be here in a couple of days. I also reflected on how different this non-inclusive mindset was from Colonel Warden's "shirt off his back" attitude before DESERT STORM.

Lieutenant General Michael "Mike" Nelson, USAF, had recently relieved General Horner as the Commander of Ninth Air Force/CENTAF and arrived in Riyadh to take charge of our nascent operation. I considered going to him immediately with the problem, but decided to wait for Dave Rogers, a combat-experienced naval aviator, to gain his assessment. When the Admiral arrived, I told him we had a significant planning issue. I explained the impact this exact same setup had on the Navy the previous year. Dave was taken aback and asked if I had raised this issue with General Nelson. I replied, "No, sir, as you are the senior naval officer in CENTCOM, I thought it better to use our Navy chain of command and advise you first, but I am quite prepared to speak with General Nelson."

Dave thanked me and said he wanted to speak with General Nelson to alert him to the issue. I was asked to report to General Nelson's office within an hour. I went in, we met alone, and he asked me to explain the problem, which I did in detail and expressed my chagrin that this was evidently what had occurred before DESERT STORM, driven by the same Colonel in charge. After many questions and a good discussion, he thanked me for bringing this to his attention.

Within a couple of days, the Colonel at issue was gone. A new senior planning officer, Colonel Chuck Wald, USAF, arrived. The plans were appropriately revised, and we had no further problems. General Wald later became the four-star Deputy Commander at EUCOM, and we have collaborated many times since.

General Nelson proved to be a superb boss, keeping us and the ever-growing staff focused on the tasks. Over the next few weeks, it became apparent that there was strong resistance in Washington and elsewhere to a full-scale resumption of war with Iraq, and other options were requested. The action that received the most attention was establishing a no-fly zone like that in northern Iraq in connection with OPERATION PROVIDE COMFORT.

Requests for Coalition support resulted in Saudi, British, and French air forces joining what became Joint Task Force Southwest Asia (JTF-SWA). Strong political support among the participants favored inaugurating the no-fly zone. I had reservations about this course of action, principally because, unlike northern Iraq, Saddam had many ground forces prosecuting the Shia and robust anti-aircraft defenses in the area under consideration for the southern no-fly zone. I assumed it would take significantly more assets to make it effective. But given the strong outcry over Saddam's oppression of the Shia marsh Arabs in

Iraq Redux?

particular, the "no-fly zone" option was selected and went into effect on August 27, 1992, from the 32nd parallel south over southern Iraq and became known as OPERATION SOUTHERN WATCH. The no-fly zone was later extended north to the 33rd parallel over Iraq. This operation became a decade-long cat-and-mouse game between Coalition aircraft and Saddam's forces, a resource-intensive drain on USAF and USN air assets. It included several episodes of intense short-term air attacks in response to Iraqi violations of UNSCR 688 or hostile acts against Coalition aircraft.

My stay in Riyadh lasted a little over three months before I was relieved by then Captain Tim "Timbo" Keating, USN, who also took over from me some years later at USPACOM. The luxurious accommodations in the Meridien Hotel evaporated soon after my arrival, and I was moved into a small apartment in the USMTM compound. But as this was pre-9/11, I had access to an automobile and unrestricted travel about town. Although there was not much time for leisure activities, I did get to take in the local sites and culture, sample the food, and visit the souks. This interaction with the Saudi populace at both the average citizen and senior official levels provided some interesting insight that would be useful later in my time in the Middle East.

On one occasion, I accompanied General Nelson to a meeting with Prince Salman, who was then the defense minister of Saudi Arabia. The prince made it clear that they wanted Americans out of the KSA as soon as possible. Although they supported SOUTHERN WATCH, they did not want foreign military personnel on their soil any longer than was necessary. To illustrate the point, he waved a finger at us (there were several U.S. officers at the meeting) and said, "You must all leave," and then, pointing to me, continued, "But you (Navy) should stay, nearby, not on the land."

Saudi citizens were generally quite friendly, but I found life in the streets repressive by Western standards. Women were forbidden from driving, female access to restaurants and even little falafel or custard shops were restricted to side entrances or pick-up windows. An "abaya" that did not extend all the way to the ankles would typically result in harsh words or a whack on the legs from the ever-present Mutawa, which were the religious police. Court-sentenced stoning or limb amputations as criminal punishment still took place every Friday in public at the central square.

DECISIONS, DISCORD & DIPLOMACY

My Saudi bodyguard at the RSAF bunker was watchful and solicitous, often treating me to hot tea and delicious dates during the long night watches. We chatted frequently. At one point, he also shared with me his unhappiness in his relationship with one of his three wives, whom he said was "just trouble." I told him I regretted not having any advice as I was unfamiliar with such complex domestic matters.

When the time came for me to leave KSA, I had an interesting experience at the airport. As I had entered the country in the dead of night without any documentation, I queried our embassy about procuring an exit visa to use on the way out. They "helpfully" sent over a piece of paper with some official-looking KSA palm tree stamps and lots of Arabic script, which I did not understand, and guidance to hand over to the authorities with my passport when clearing immigration.

I arrived at the Riyadh International Airport at about two in the morning for my Austrian Airlines flight to Vienna. The terminal was deserted except for one lengthy line of Pakistani ex-pat workers attempting to leave aboard a B-747 back to their country. The treatment they were receiving at the hands of the Saudi immigration processing personnel was disgusting. In addition to verbal harassment, passports were seized and thrown on the floor for no apparent reason, workers were jostled and pushed, and all were treated with disdain and disrespect. Of course, these were the people doing all the jobs the Saudis did not care to do.

As I queued up, wondering what kind of reception I would meet, I was waved to another checkpoint, where I handed my passport and "visa" to the official. He flipped through the passport and asked where my entry stamp was. I explained that I did not have one because I arrived on a military aircraft on official business, but that the official-looking piece of paper should explain this. That response did not work, so he brought me to a group of his comrades who asked the same question. Unsatisfied with my explanation, they discussed among themselves what to do. I noted the continuing mistreatment of the Pakistani men nearby but assumed the officials recognized that I was an American military officer and doubted they would treat me as they were doing to the other men.

I correctly surmised that the discussion among themselves was whether to call and awaken their superior officer, which eventually they

Iraq Redux?

did. He arrived impeccably groomed and dressed about 30 minutes later, invited me to be seated at his desk, and asked, "What is the problem, sir?" When I explained again and added that I had been here in the military, helping to protect the country during DESERT STORM, he smiled broadly, introduced himself as a KSA army major in a tank battalion during the conflict, and signaled to his men to bring over some tea. We chatted amiably for about ten minutes while the Austrian Airlines station manager paced nervously nearby, pointing to his watch and the obvious imminent departure of my scheduled flight. The major said, "Sir, any time you need to leave, please feel free to do so." Collecting my passport, I bid him adieu and hurried to the aircraft.

In retrospect, DESERT STORM was a successful example of political finesse in building a large international coalition as well as an operational and tactical success, resulting in the rapid defeat of Saddam's army and expulsion of his Iraqi invaders with minimum loss of life to Coalition forces. Yet within the next year and a half, we became engaged in two more military efforts involving Iraq; one in the north that averted a humanitarian catastrophe and stabilized the region at minimal short and long-term cost, and one in the south that resulted in a decade-long continuation of low-level military conflict, did not resolve the persecution of the Shia and left a legacy of escalating resource expenditures. We also established a large and continuing U.S. military presence in the Middle East that was not desired nor appreciated by most in the region and would be a significant cause of the terrorist activity that resulted in the 9/11 attacks on the U.S. mainland in 2001.

We still faced two hostile regimes in the Middle East, one in Tehran and the other in Baghdad, which kept drawing attention and resources when the end of the Cold War with the USSR offered many opportunities to focus on different parts of the world.

CHAPTER 7

IRAQ AGAIN: DRAMA IN JORDAN

In the spring of 1995, I received a new set of orders on short notice. At the time, I was a one-star Rear Admiral serving on the staff of the NATO Supreme Allied Commander, Atlantic, as the Assistant Chief of Staff for Policy. I had spent the previous year and a half immersed in new post-Cold War policy issues. Spending a lot of time at NATO headquarters in Brussels, I saw firsthand the alliance grappling with its relevance and appropriate structures for the future. Meanwhile, long-term President Josip Broz Tito had died, and Yugoslavia had imploded into ethnic and religious civil war, posing the first serious political and military challenge for the NATO alliance since the collapse of the USSR. A familiar story was playing out with a humanitarian crisis, military conflict, and widespread insecurity as the former state of Yugoslavia fractured into historic, separate ethnic and religious entities that had been united for the previous 30-plus years under Tito's iron rule. In response to the crisis, NATO mobilized air and naval forces to the Adriatic Sea and nearby Italian air bases. It enforced a no-fly zone as the political leaders debated precisely what else to do.

My orders were to report to the Mediterranean and take command of Carrier Group Eight, in a familiar setting, on TR with CVW-8 embarked, relieving Steve Abbot, then in command of Group 8. After a brief training period in the U.S., I made the rounds of senior leaders in the NATO chain of command in Europe. I reported on board TR, relieving Steve of command. In addition to being the Group Commander, I was designated as the Commander of Task Force 60 (CTF-60), responsible for the operating naval forces in the U.S. Sixth Fleet. My bosses at the next three levels in the chain of command above me were also double-hatted as NATO commanders who would facilitate matters if NATO decided on further action in the former Yugoslavia.

In addition to the aircraft carrier and air wing, the operational forces assigned to me included about a dozen cruisers, destroyers, frigates, submarines, and a large replenishment ship. U.S. forces also included an Amphibious Ready Group with a Marine Corps Special Air Ground Task Force (MAGTF) with about 2000 embarked Marines under the very able command of the late Colonel, later Lieutenant General Marty

IRAQ AGAIN: DRAMA IN JORDAN

Berndt, which had already conducted a dramatic rescue of USAF pilot Scott O'Grady who had been shot down over Bosnia earlier in the year. We were operating primarily in the Adriatic Sea near the coast of the former Yugoslavia. There was another maritime squadron of NATO destroyers, frigates, and several national task groups of various ships and forces. Expectations were high that the conflict would escalate into more complex combat, and we would be called upon to be a key part of it as the civil war and associated atrocities continued to escalate on the ground.

In early August, we received permission to let the carrier go into port for about a week in southern France, a lovely place to relax in midsummer. But it was not to be. A new Iraq-related crisis was beginning to unfold.

Visions of sunny beaches on the Côte d'Azur vanished as we received an urgent message to cancel the port visit to Cannes and steam east at top speed. As the ship proceeded to the eastern Mediterranean, about a two-day transit from our then location, we received an outline of what was happening. On August 8, 1995, several high-ranking Iraqi officials defected to Jordan in a motorcade from Baghdad. The senior persons were Major General Hussein Kamel al-Majid, Oil Minister and former head of the Military Industrialization Corporation (MIC)[33] in Iraq, which, among other tasks, oversaw the weapons, including weapons of mass destruction (WMD) programs.

Accompanying him was his brother, Saddam Kamel al-Majid, commander of Iraqi special forces. Both men were cousins of Saddam Hussein. More intriguing was that their wives, Raghad and Rana, who happened to be Saddam's daughters, and their children were with them.[34] Jordan's King Hussein had granted asylum to the entourage, as he had to many thousands of Iraqi refugees. However, he soon received threatening messages from Baghdad, followed by a visit from one of Saddam's sons, Uday, and another general from the al-Majid clan, demanding the immediate repatriation of the defectors or else! With this dilemma in his hands, the king called Washington, asking for help. TR/CVW-8 and our escorting cruiser, *USS ARKANSAS*, were the immediate response team, albeit without a plan. An issue that surfaced immediately was that our force was currently assigned to EUCOM and the U.S. Sixth Fleet (Italy-based).

DECISIONS, DISCORD & DIPLOMACY

In contrast, Jordan was in the CENTCOM area of responsibility, and the U.S. Fifth Fleet (Bahrain-based) was the naval commander. Although my staff labeled the next few days as "The Great Eastern Mediterranean Taffy Pull" (picture each of those four commanders yanking on my limbs), we established a good flow of communication between all parties and never had an issue with command and control. The focus of our thinking over the next two days was to devise a scheme to deter Saddam from moving into Jordan to reclaim his family members by force, which he threatened to do. It was clear that our only real option was to use our air assets, but how? To do this practically and effectively would require overflight access to Jordan through another country's airspace.

The significant distances would not allow much time for our aircraft to remain on station before returning to land and refuel aboard the aircraft carrier. We proposed a solution that was a novelty in this sensitive area of the world; if Jordan would allow it, we could stage a detachment of armed fighter and attack aircraft from the air wing at an airfield of their choosing in Jordan to provide an immediate response capability to deter Saddam from sending military forces into the country. King Hussein readily agreed and designated a desert air base between Amman and the Iraqi border for our use.

But the bigger challenge was to get permission to fly from the carrier to that airfield, the shortest distance being over Israel, with armed military aircraft, something that, in my experience, had never been granted. Fortunately, we had Martin Indyk, a skilled and well-connected U.S. ambassador in Tel Aviv. After explaining to him what we were trying to do and why, he was able to get Israeli permission for the multiple overflights of the armed strike/fighter aircraft and a small detachment of maintenance personnel to sustain them in the desert.

Things worked according to plan; the Jordanian Air Force was a gracious host, and our aircraft's presence and visible flights over Jordan did the trick. Over the next few days, a follow-on plan was put in motion to have a Fifth Fleet Amphibious Ready Group with assigned Marine MAGTF in *USS NEW ORLEANS* transit the Red Sea and put the Marines ashore at Aqaba for a hastily conceived exercise and land-based presence in Jordan.[35]

IRAQ AGAIN: DRAMA IN JORDAN

Several days later, I climbed into the back seat of an F-14 and flew into the air base in Jordan to congratulate our folks for a job well done and to thank the Jordanians for their hospitality. While there, I reprised an experience from my time in Saudi Arabia a few years earlier. Taking a short stroll alone to stretch my legs, I felt the desert's unique and uncanny total silence. One cannot hear anything, but there is another sense of heaviness, perhaps like an unseen but palpable blanket enveloping everything. An extraordinary experience and a timeout from very hectic days.

After about a week, we could recall the aircraft to the ship and leave the coast of Israel with the objective accomplished. But as part of Iraq's continuing and circuitous story, it would be useful to discuss what else happened in connection with this incident.

Saddam was furious at the defection of his cousins, sons-in-law, and daughters, although he sent word about six months later, alleging that all was forgiven and they should return home to Iraq. Amazingly, they did, and to no one's surprise, the al-Majid brothers were killed shortly thereafter.[36]

Hussein Kamal al-Majid was intimately familiar with Saddam's WMD programs and brought with him reference material that he later shared with Rolf Ekeus, then head of United Nations Special Commission (UNSCOM), the Special Commission, trying to verify the U.N.-directed dismantlement of Saddam's WMD programs.[37] Kamal also shared the information with CIA and MI6 debriefers.[38] It is interesting to note that before the defection of Hussein Kemal, UNSCOM inspectors were convinced that significant information about WMD programs was being withheld by the Iraqis. Ambassador Ekeus, who had flown to New York the day before the defection, was eager to interview Hussein Kemal when he learned that the latter was willing to share "weapons secrets."

Meanwhile, back in Baghdad, the Iraqis were highly agitated, no doubt, because they feared Kamal would reveal details about the WMD programs that were being covered up. Saddam had grand expectations for U.N. sanctions relief in exchange for coming clean on WMD, but if Kamal revealed evidence to the contrary, that expectation could be doomed.

Rolf Ekeus, still in New York, on the next day, received a phone call from General Amir Rashid, then head of the MIC, on behalf of Iraqi Foreign Minister Tariq Aziz, "...pleading that he come back to Baghdad as soon as possible." A few days later, on August 13, UNSCOM received a formal letter from Rashid blaming Kamel for ordering the cover-up of WMD information "...keep it secret under threat of death."[39] (See below). Baghdad was clearly squirming and seeking a way out of its perfidy. Ekeus then returned to Baghdad for several days of intense discussion with Tariq Aziz, Rashid, and other persons connected to Iraqi WMD programs. Some previously withheld information was made available to the UNSCOM inspectors, with Kamel fingered as the culprit of the deception. As Ekeus was preparing to leave his hotel to fly to Jordan on 20 August, he received a phone call from Rashid insisting that they go together to a poultry farm allegedly belonging to Kemal. Breaking a freshly installed lock on a chicken coop door, the inspectors discovered hundreds of thousands of pages of documents, microfilm, floppy disks, videotapes, and photographs relating to WMD programs.[40] Discovery of this trove of information confirmed prior Iraqi subterfuge and expanded knowledge about concealed WMD programs, but also detailed the destruction of significant parts of laboratories, equipment, and missiles and the termination of much of the Iraqi WMD programs.

Several days later, Ambassador Ekeus met with Hussein Kemal in Jordan and confirmed most of the information later extracted from the chicken coop "discovery" in Iraq, but with a completely contrary story regarding subterfuge, attributing it to Tariq Aziz and others in Baghdad. The revelations surrounding the defection to Jordan and the subsequent avalanche of newly available WMD-related material took some time to be digested by UNSCOM, debriefed to the U.N., and shared with interested capitals worldwide. The conclusion by UNSCOM was that the bulk of the Iraqi WMD programs had been discontinued, with the weapons and equipment destroyed. But suspicions lingered that the Iraqis were still hiding something, probably information and plans that could facilitate a restart of programs in the future.

The subsequent four years, until UNSCOM was dissolved and superseded in 1999 by UNMOVIC (U.N. Monitoring, Verification and Inspection Commission), featured complex and intense international political and military pressure involving Iraq. The proposition was that comprehensive, punitive U.N. sanctions would be lifted once Iraq was verified to have destroyed all WMD and ceased the related development programs. But Baghdad's equivocating statements, obfuscation, and deceit continued to fuel suspicion.

> DISTRIBUTION SLIP:
>
> RE ✓   AH __   JLR __   95-23865
> CD ✓   CV __   JB __
> JS ✓   HR __
> TT ✓   CW __
> JM ✓   IM __   Others: REPUBLIC OF IRAQ
> NS ✓   RS __
> MS __ RD ✓   E OF THE PRESIDENT OF THE REPUBLIC
> JL __ SB __
>   'ARY INDUSTRIALIZATION CORPORATION
>   NATIONAL MONITORING DIRECTORATE
>
> Sir,
>
> Following the flight of Hussein Kamel from Iraq, a number of those working at the Military Industrialization Corporation confessed to us that from 1991 to the time of his flight from Iraq Hussein Kamel had ordered them to conceal some important items of information relating to former activities and not to communicate them to Mr. Tariq Aziz or to Lieutenant-General Amir Rashid, who are entrusted with the direction of relations with the Special Commission and the International Atomic Energy Agency (IAEA). Hussein Kamel had intimated to them that this was an instruction that had emanated from higher authorities and had required them to keep it secret under threat of death.
>
> We have obtained some to these items of information and are continuing our endeavours in this direction, and we are prepared to communicate them to you. We request you to come in person to Baghdad as soon as possible so that you can be informed of them. I have sent a similar letter to Mr. Hans Blix, Director General of IAEA, and have requested him to send a delegation to Baghdad for the same purpose.
>
> (Signed) Amir Muhammad RASHID
> Lieutenant-General
> Engineer
> Director, Military Industrialization Corporation
>
> 13 August 1995
>
> His Excellency Mr. Rolf Ekéus
> Executive Chairman
> Office of the Special Commission
> New York

Summed up succinctly by Charles Duelfer, former UNSCOM Deputy Chairman, "As Saddam's truthful disclosures about WMD were going up, trust in his statements was going down."[41] Solidarity for continuing sanctions among the members of the U.N. Security Council dissolved, and attitudes about Saddam became ambivalent.

A well-intentioned U.N. initiative aimed at easing the impact of sanctions on ordinary Iraqi citizens, dubbed the "oil for food" program, was manipulated by the cunning Saddam to further enrich himself. This scandal further antagonized the U.S. and was viewed as more evidence of mistrust. The corruption surrounding this program further eroded support for sanctions and weakened UNMOVIC, the new U.N. WMD inspection initiative.

There is ample documentation now that what Kamel said was true and verified after the 2003 invasion of Iraq, when no WMD were found.[42] The gist of the issue is that the part of Kamel's testimony in which he admitted that the WMD program continued for some years after the Gulf War before being halted was used as evidence of Saddam's dishonesty and as "proof" of a continuing weapons program, while his statements to the effect that the programs were eventually terminated in the 1990s were omitted from the dialogue. This incident played a pivotal role in the buildup to the decision to invade Iraq in 2003.

CHAPTER 8

War In Bosnia 1995

OPERATION DELIBERATE FORCE

After wrapping up operations in Jordan and a short port visit to Haifa, Israel, we began a transit westward to return to the Adriatic Sea. On August 28, the central market in the city of Sarajevo was the target of a deadly mortar attack attributed to the Bosnian Serb militia. More than 40 civilians were massacred in this second attack on the same marketplace by the same parties during the ongoing civil war in the new state of Bosnia-Herzegovina, instigating worldwide outrage. This attack triggered the decision by the NATO governing body, the North Atlantic Council (NAC), to respond militarily in what was dubbed OPERATION DELIBERATE FORCE, a two-week bombing campaign by the NATO air forces against the Bosnian Serbs and their allies in the former Yugoslavia.[43]

The next day, I received a signal to return at top speed and be prepared to participate in the commencement of NATO retaliatory strikes the following night. During this operation, we would be working in the NATO chain of command. My immediate boss was the late Vice Admiral (later Admiral and my predecessor as Vice Chief of Naval Operations (VCNO)) Don Pilling, the U.S. Sixth Fleet Commander, who reported to the late Admiral Leighton "Snuffy" Smith, Commander of Allied Forces Southern Europe in his NATO role. We discussed the potential for offensive operations with both admirals when I arrived to take command of CTF-60. But at the time, the NATO high command was reluctant to commit to air attacks against the Serbs. Admiral Smith was a seasoned combat aviator in Vietnam, and given his experience and mine, Admiral Pilling, a surface warfare officer, told me he expected there would be a lot of direct dialogue between Admiral Smith and me. His confidence-building and helpful comment was: "You do not need to ask my permission. Just do what you think best and keep me informed."

The initial targets assigned to the air wing were not received until late August 30, offering limited time to plan and study before the expected target times that night. More challenging was that they were small, e.g., a mobile surface-to-air (SAM) missile launcher, and extremely difficult to find from the sky at night. Admiral Smith called me and said to launch the strike aircraft as soon as we cleared the Strait of Otranto at the mouth of the Adriatic Sea. TR was steaming at maximum speed, but we were racing the clock to get into position in time.

By sheer happenstance, I had another challenge on board *TR* that evening. A planned overnight media visit, not directly connected with the conflict in the former Yugoslavia, had just arrived on the ship, numbering more than two dozen international print, radio, and television crew members. Featured in the group were several well-known prime-time TV correspondents, including CNN's Brent Sadler and NBC's Linda Vester.

The initial strike launch was to be conducted in secrecy to avoid alerting the Serbian anti-aircraft forces. By nightfall, the ship was a beehive of activity as maintenance and ordnance crews raced to prepare the aircraft in the fierce wind on the flight deck. The media guests quickly surmised what was going on. They asked for a briefing to explain the activity, which I could not do until after the strikes were completed. Although this event was before the advent of cell phones, we did have one ship-to-shore radiotelephone circuit, which I had quickly secured until further notice.

About midnight, the ship began to launch the strike aircraft that would join other land-based NATO air forces for the initial attack. Fortunately, just before assuming command of CTF-60, I had visited the NATO Combined Air Operations Center (CAOC) in Vicenza, Italy, which had responsibility for all air operations over the former Yugoslavia, and met with the director, USAF Major General (later General and Commander of ACC) Hal Hornburg and his boss, Commander of Allied Air Forces Southern Europe, Lieutenant General (later General and USAF Chief) Mike Ryan. I also got to see several of the Allied air commanders whom I had previously known. The CAOC directed all the air operations during OPERATION DELIBERATE FORCE, and we maintained a good relationship.

As the aircraft returned safely from the first night of operations, I reviewed the results of their attacks. I found them to be far less successful than desired. But I appreciated aircrews' difficulty finding their aim points, among the most difficult assigned that night, while adhering to prudent altitude restrictions to avoid anti-aircraft fire. Nonetheless, I expected an earful from Admiral Smith, which came a few hours later. Weapons delivery accuracy improved dramatically after that first night, to the highest in my professional experience, and salvaged our credibility with Admiral Smith.

Of course, the media folks were champing at the bit to get information that they could report. I immediately recognized a significant dilemma; the media people on TR had front-row seats and could see what was happening before any media announcement from Brussels or Washington. What ensued was a two-week information release tug-of-war between NATO headquarters and TR. Admiral Smith initially obtained a commonsense release authority to brief the onboard reporters and allow them to telephone unclassified reports to their bosses. But soon thereafter, the PR folks in Brussels embargoed all information release without their approval.

Because TR/CVW-8 was the closest "airfield" to the combat zone, we often became "first responders" with the aircraft launching in full view of the media cameras on the ship. As the on-scene commander, I was asked frequently in those first few days to provide on-camera remarks and answer questions, resulting in being seen in news reports worldwide.

As might be expected, Navy headquarters back in Washington was overjoyed with the publicity, especially as our aircrews were doing an outstanding job. I received several telephone calls from Washington, encouraging me to make more appearances and asking if we could take additional media people on the ship. Soon, I received another call, this time from "Snuffy" Smith. His deafening voice in my earpiece advised me that Brussels was fed up seeing me as the spokesperson of NATO for the operation and to "Get your face off the TV! NOW!!" Debating this issue was fruitless, although I knew he understood the dilemma.

Meanwhile, despite the distractions, our aircrews were doing a terrific job, in coordination with our NATO allies, to degrade the Bosnian Serb defenses and ability to continue their savage attacks. U.S. Navy surface ships and submarines assigned to my force also launched Tomahawk land attack cruise missiles (TLAM). In fact, the success of this short air campaign was the lever that resulted in the Dayton Peace Accords, which stopped the conflict in Bosnia-Herzegovina.[44]

Another event during this period remains prominent in my memory. During one of the early combat missions, a French Air Force two-seat Mirage 2000 fighter-bomber was shot down, with the crew reported missing. In the tradition of U.S. Naval Aviation, we make every attempt to rescue or recover any downed pilots or aircrews. Recognizing that we were the closest available launch platform and had a unique asset on board the carrier at that time, a U.S. Navy SEAL platoon, several of the staff, and air wing leadership suggested that we attempt to recover the missing aircrew.

Initially, we had no actionable intelligence information. But shortly thereafter, one of the reconnaissance aircraft returned after recording a photo with what appeared to be the tactical callsign of the downed aircraft, EBRO 33, spelled out on the ground with rocks, a reasonable and expected communication attempt to get the attention of aircraft overhead. Additionally, thermal images of two human figures were detected nearby. I directed that a combat search and rescue mission (CSAR) plan be drawn up, knowing this would be challenging under any circumstances, deep in enemy-controlled territory, particularly given the mountainous terrain and numerous enemy combat forces. My confidence was bolstered because I had personally observed the SEALs training under the very able leadership of the platoon commander, Lieutenant Drew Deley. We also had several specially configured HH-60 helicopters that would be valuable for this operation.

After receiving the mission planning briefing from our people, I had misgivings about the quality of the briefing but decided to ring up Admiral Smith, tell him about the proposal, and ask for his permission to launch it, pending some refinements. Snuffy was highly supportive but said he wanted to see the briefing himself. First thing next morning, I jumped in a helicopter with the briefing officer. I flew over to his headquarters in Naples, about a 75-minute trip across Italy. My apprehension about the briefing was well-founded, as less than 10 minutes into it, Snuffy called it to a halt, threw everybody else out of the room, launched into a very justifiable tirade about my questionable judgment, and advised me not to come back unless I had a much better plan.

WAR IN BOSNIA 1995

Returning to the carrier, I called the CAG, Captain Gary "GarJack" Jack, and DCAG, Joe "Condo" Capalbo, competent leaders with whom I had previously worked. I asked them to put their best planning team together to produce a better plan, particularly a solid briefing. In my experience, the air wings typically were excellent at this, and even though the briefing officer would not be leading this rescue attempt, he would know how to put it together.

A few hours later, CAG said they were ready to brief me, and as I listened, I found it vastly superior to the morning effort. I called Admiral Smith and told him I would like another go. He allowed me to have the briefing over a classified video connection, confirming that he supported the initiative but wanted to ensure it was done correctly. With his blessing, I gave the order to attempt the mission that night.

Just before midnight in the early morning of 6 September, the carrier went to maximum speed to close the distance to the coast as the ship became alive with a bustle of activity. Of course, the media quickly noticed the heavily armed SEALs moving through the hangar deck to board the helicopters and the supporting package of fighter and attack aircraft taxiing toward the catapults. The weather was not good, but we had carefully reviewed the strict mission go/abort criteria with helicopter and SEAL team commanders and sent them on their way with the intention of returning to the ship before daylight.

Several hours later, the mission commander signaled an unsuccessful effort with the flight returning to the ship. After landing, the debriefing revealed the aircraft had run into impassable stormy weather in the mountains and enemy ground fire that damaged one of the helicopters. The helicopter squadron (HS-3) mission commander, Bob McGee, made a good decision in aborting the mission and returning to the ship. Fortunately, none of the men were injured. We did not reattempt the mission during several subsequent nights because of the continuing severe weather, and, more importantly, the attempt had clearly alerted the enemy to what we were about.[45]

With the media clamoring for information, I decided to take them into confidence. I briefed them on the outlines of the mission, what we were trying to do, and the reasons for our lack of success. I asked them for their agreement to embargo any information to their media outlets until such time as we could successfully complete the mission or that other circumstances made it unnecessary, given the danger to the missing flight crew and our own people. In exchange, I gave them enough details to satisfy their quest for information and access to a couple of the participants so they could get their first-person accounts. I also made myself available to them later when we could discuss it openly.

To their credit, the entire group kept their word, and none of this information leaked. Some days later, after we had left the theatre of operations, an announcement was made in Paris that the flight crew had, in fact, been captured after ejecting from the aircraft and were being held captive by the Serbs. Our team was flying into a trap. This information had never been passed to me previously. The bottom line is that we undertook that mission needlessly at significant risk to the participants, which I found unsettling. I did not know when the information about the capture of the aircrew was available to the political leadership in Paris after the aircraft had been shot down. Still, we certainly did not know, possibly due to the politics of the situation. I found out later that the USAF had also attempted a rescue mission from an air base in Italy that was unsuccessful for the same reasons as ours.[46] Once the information that the French aircrew were prisoners of war became known, the media with us on the carrier then told their stories. We supported them in every reasonable way.

These fast-paced couple of weeks in the Adriatic offered many teaching moments. At the top of the list was the outstanding performance of our people in dynamic, dangerous, and stressful situations. Repeatedly, our service personnel rose to the challenge of executing their assigned tasks, assuming that their military and political leaders were making good decisions in the orders they issued.

Exposure to the competing objectives of international political leaders was a foretaste of things to come. At this point in time, there were conflicts of interest between NATO and the EU, in addition to the ugly and complex civil war on the ground in the former Yugoslavia. In the specific CSAR event, which I directed to rescue the French pilots, I was fortunate to not have people killed or seriously injured in carrying out my orders. In hindsight, I made the decision to launch that risky mission, having violated one of the cardinal tactical rules previously learned through bitter experience in Vietnam. Establishing a voice communication link with the survivors to confirm their presence on the ground should have been a prerequisite for a mission of this type. Our French colleagues were courageous and professional, and the chain of command above me supported my decision, which should have been more prudent. Unfortunately, I would see this scenario again in the coming days in Iraq.

In a gratifying manner, the honorable behavior of the large and diverse group of media members on board TR helped shape my long-term attitude of openness and trust in dealing with members of this profession for many years.

I saw and felt again the long meddling arm of my own Navy in Washington, seeking to influence events to their advantage, albeit with the best of intentions, but without a nuanced understanding of the events in the Balkans.

CHAPTER 9

INCREASING RESPONSIBILITY

Soon after returning from that deployment in late 1995, I was reassigned as the Deputy Commander of the U.S. Atlantic Fleet, relieving Rear Admiral (later Admiral and Chief of the Navy) Vern Clark and working for Admiral "Bud" Flanagan. This staff assignment exposed me to a higher level of decision-making across the entire Navy. The fleet was in the middle of the post-Cold War downsizing. Two challenges were prominent. First was the necessary long-range vision and planning for the Navy of the future in a changed strategic environment. Second was a stream of essential business decisions in allocating resources to maintain the fleet and readiness of our people and assets in a reduced fiscal environment.

Less than a year later, I was nominated, then confirmed by the Senate, to the three-star position of Deputy Commander of U.S. Atlantic Command (USACOM), working for Marine Corps General Jack Sheehan, who was additionally double-hatted as NATO Supreme Commander Allied Forces Atlantic (SACLANT). The U.S. responsibilities of this command had recently been changed by General Powell to focus on a revised organization and training of all U.S. Joint Forces in keeping with the recently congressionally mandated reorganization known as the Goldwater-Nichols Act. The changes occurring on the command's U.S. and NATO sides during this period made the assignment dynamic and most interesting for me.

Two highlights of that tour stand out. First, on the NATO side, the collapse of the USSR and dissolution of the Warsaw Pact dramatically shifted the strategic balance of power, particularly in eastern Europe. It was certainly no surprise that most of the former Warsaw Pact countries and many states that had formally been part of the USSR wanted to join NATO. Seeking long-term protection under the NATO security umbrella against the possibility of a revanchist Russia, most countries received a welcoming reception from the U.S. and several key NATO allies.

However appealing and emotionally understandable this major expansion of NATO to the east was, in my view, strategically shortsighted and not in the better long-term pragmatic interest of the

Increasing Responsibility

United States, as well as complicating the unwieldy structure of an alliance that has grown to more than 30 member countries. Nevertheless, the Baltic states, formerly part of the USSR, were admitted. Ukraine was enticed to consider joining the alliance with most former Warsaw Pact countries. The NATO alliance continued to grow, now totaling 32 nations with the addition of Finland and Sweden.

Russia has historically had a deep paranoia about invasion from the West, certainly understandable given the realities of the 19th and 20th-century assaults by Napoleon and Hitler. Despite the country's vast size, the largest landmass in the world, it craves buffer states to attempt to insulate itself from future invasion.

The NATO Partnership for Peace (PFP) initiative of the 1990s was a great idea to expose the militaries of these eastern European countries to NATO structures and standards without antagonizing Russia. Regrettably, the political stampede to admit new NATO members prevailed, sowing the long-term seeds of future conflict with Russia. It seemed to me that we had an opportunity, particularly during the 1990s, to reach out to a severely traumatized and weakened Russia to try to help it recover in the way we treated Germany and Japan after World War II. Instead, we touted our "victory" over them in the Cold War. We missed that excellent opportunity to help ourselves and the rest of the world.

The rise of Vladimir Putin and the return to totalitarian rule in Russia was highlighted by the sense of grievance and anger demonstrated in Putin's remarks, coincident with the recent Russian invasion of Ukraine. No matter the possibilities back in the 1990s, the situation today, because of Putin's brazen and unjustified continuing assault on Ukraine, has dramatically changed the strategic landscape. Ukrainian membership in NATO is again being openly discussed by the member states. It seems much more reasonable today than 30 years ago. Putin's effort to discourage membership in NATO clearly backfired with the accession of Finland and Sweden, [47] as a direct result of his naked aggression. This episode is yet another example of recurring historical themes that demonstrate the need for knowledge and understanding of the past.

The second prominent initiative, on the U.S. Atlantic Command, renamed U.S. Joint Forces Command in 1999 (U.S. only side of the command), was a revised joint organization and training scheme involving all the U.S. Armed Forces to leverage the capabilities of each of the services in a practical but more efficient manner. This creative approach, championed by General Powell and his successor General Shalikashvili and implemented by Admiral Paul David Miller, followed by General Sheehan at USACOM, in the vision of OPERATION PROVIDE COMFORT, was a key change to service employment doctrine. Initially resisted and paid lip service by the services, it eventually took hold in the mid-1990s until it was severely diminished by the pressures of the war in Iraq, particularly on the Army and Marine Corps.

The most beneficial result of this new joint approach was an expansion of thinking to identify and employ unique capabilities of each of the services and, additionally, those of our allies and partners where applicable, in a combined manner, to optimize the attributes and skills of the participants best suited to the operation at hand. An enhancement of this was a major outreach to include civilian agencies, both government and non-government organizations (NGO), in the planning and execution of modern missions, the majority of which include many nonmilitary aspects such as humanitarian assistance, peacekeeping, and nation-building.

COMMANDER, U.S. SECOND FLEET AND NATO STRIKING FLEET

The next three years, from 1998 to 2000, were a highlight of my career as a three-star Admiral commanding a seagoing operational fleet with a dedicated flagship, *USS MOUNT WHITNEY,* specially configured for command and control. I was also double-hatted as the NATO Striking Fleet Commander, with a staff of allied officers and command of the combined NATO fleets when assigned. There was a third hat, as the standing U.S. Joint Task Force (JTF-150) Commander in the Atlantic in case of national contingencies, for which I reported back to General Sheehan.

I will fast-forward past many details of this command, save one. The most beneficial experience that helped to prepare me for greater operational responsibility was undergoing several weeks of intense training under General Sheehan and USACOM in my JTF Commander hat. The exercise objective was to train my staff and me to conceptualize

Increasing Responsibility

and execute a complex problem using joint forces, certain of which were assigned from each service. The first phase of the operation was in the form of a computer-assisted exercise that took place at a special facility for a week of nonstop, continuous operations with all hands present 24 hours a day. This format enabled a wide range of scenarios that could be explored by computer, severely testing the staff and my decision-making without employing actual service units or equipment, and the expense that entails.

The second phase of the operation was conducted while embarked in *USS MOUNT WHITNEY* for about 10 days of a live training exercise at sea and ashore over a vast area of the western Atlantic and Caribbean Sea. This phase employed people, ships, aircraft, and equipment in the actual operational environment, subject to weather, equipment malfunction, logistic sustainment, human error, and all the vagaries one would encounter in a real-world challenge. The training was focused on the three-star operational command level and was invaluable but has regrettably also disappeared due to the demands of the war in Iraq on people and equipment.

CHAPTER 10

SEPTEMBER 11, 2001

THE PENTAGON

The morning of September 11, 2001, dawned clear and refreshingly cool after weeks of summer heat in Washington, D.C. Driving into the parking lot outside my office in the Pentagon, I noticed the intense blue of the cloudless sky. Almost a year earlier, and now a 4-star Admiral, I had assumed responsibilities as the Vice Chief of Naval Operations (VCNO), effectively the Chief Operating Officer of the Navy, working for Admiral Vern Clark, the Chief of Naval Operations.

It had been a busy year, beginning on my second day in office when the *USS COLE* was attacked by terrorists in the port of Aden, Yemen, on October 12, 2000, resulting in the loss of 17 sailors killed and dozens more wounded.[48] Following the November 2000 national elections, a new Republican administration under President George W. Bush assumed office the following January. On February 9, 2001, U.S. Navy submarine *USS GREENEVILLE* collided with a Japanese fisheries training vessel near Hawaii. The *Ehime Maru* sank with the loss of nine lives, mostly young Japanese students. The incident caused a furor in Japan and was an embarrassment for the new U.S. Administration, which had merely a handful of new appointees at their desks. In the Department of Defense, only Secretary Rumsfeld had been confirmed. Two weeks later, I was dispatched to Tokyo as a presidential envoy to personally convey the condolences of the U.S. to the people of Japan at the loss of life in the collision. Greatly assisted by U.S. ambassador to Japan, the late Honorable Tom Foley, I met with Prime Minister Mori and the immediate families of most people lost in the collision, calming the uproar in Japanese public opinion and the media.[49]

During most of the year 2001, on an almost weekly basis, U.S. and Coalition aircraft enforcing the Iraq no-fly zones were engaged in weapons exchanges and attacks in response to Iraqi provocations, and suspicions about potential Iraqi WMD swirled. Saddam Hussein continued to be an expensive thorn in the foot of the U.S., and the new

SEPTEMBER 11, 2001

administration began to focus attention on ways to confront and remove him.

A meeting had been scheduled for 0830 that morning of 9/11 in the Office of the Chief of Naval Operations (CNO), to be attended by me, Admiral Vern Clark, and Captain Bob Erskine to discuss senior officer assignments. We were seated at a small conference table in the middle of his office, each on a different side of the table.

A television video display without audio was on the wall behind the CNO. Sometime after the meeting was underway, I noticed that Bob kept looking up at the television screen, which was very uncharacteristic of him; typically totally focused on the issue under discussion. I nudged him with my foot under the table to get his attention. Looking at the television screen, he said, "Something's wrong... it looks like there's been an airplane crash into a building."

We then turned around to look at the screen and saw the image of smoke pouring from a recognizable World Trade Center tower; we turned up the sound. The television reporter made a comment that indicated there had been a horrible accident and a plane had flown into the building. I recall saying aloud, "That was no accident because the weather is beautiful with crystal clear visibility this morning all up and down the East Coast."

Shortly thereafter, we observed the second tower being struck, and all realized that a real crisis was unfolding. I called down to our command center on the first floor of the building and spoke to our Navy operations officer, Vice Admiral Tim Keating, the same officer who had relieved me in Riyadh years earlier, and asked him if he could find out any more details about what was going on. "Timbo" reported that the aircraft involved had been hijacked and that there were reports that other aircraft were now in similar circumstances. I recall looking out the window at the perfectly cloudless sky and thinking that the flight path for the secondary runway into Reagan National Airport went right over the Pentagon.

A bit later, we asked Timbo to come to our office in person so we could talk with him and see if we could get any more information from Admiral Bob Natter, commanding our Atlantic Fleet at his headquarters down in Norfolk. Bob confirmed the hijackings and said that fighter aircraft had been scrambled from Langley Air Force Base and other places to find and intercept other aircraft believed to have been hijacked. Shortly thereafter, we felt a heavy impact and shockwave that reminded me of a large bomb explosion. We all knew instantly that the building had been hit. Tim Keating is fortunately alive because he had just left a discussion where the aircraft, American Airlines Flight 77, impacted our Navy Command Center on the first floor. The command center was destroyed, and many of our Navy personnel were killed, along with thousands of other lives lost in New York, Pennsylvania, and at the Pentagon. Other events of that day are still vividly etched into my memory, but we will save them for later.

Soon after the impact, and when it became evident that these were a series of terrorist attacks and there was at least one more hijacked aircraft headed toward Washington, the CNO and I decided to split up to make sure we would not both be wiped out in the next attack. Vern moved to the Washington Navy Yard, where there was a small command center. I gathered key staff and told them to meet me at the nearby former offices of our Bureau of Naval Personnel, less than half a mile away on a hilltop overlooking the Pentagon. Most of the Navy and Marine Corps offices in this large multi-wing building had been vacated several months earlier, although few people remained. In their inimitable style, the Marine Corps headquarters staff had only partially vacated their offices, which were still equipped with telephones. Although they had moved most of their equipment out of the building, it was temporarily stored down the road at Quantico, Virginia.

Within a couple of hours, the Marines had loaded critical communications equipment into their trucks and made a quick trip from Quantico, arriving outside the building where we agreed to set up a joint Navy-Marine Corps operations center until further notice. At that time and still to this day, I have never witnessed a closer working relationship between the Navy and Marine Corps than over the next several weeks. The immediate task for all of us was to determine casualties and the status of our personnel in the Pentagon that morning.

AFTERMATH

People at the scene that horrific day reacted in every imaginable manner, from hysterical screaming and cowering, frozen fear, to immediately helpful human responses such as attending to the injured, leading survivors to safety, and seeking to be useful in any and every way.

SEPTEMBER 11, 2001

Some of our folks demonstrated brilliant initiative, leadership, and selfless courage, while others shied away from responsibility and failed their shipmates in the hour of need.

Once it appeared there were no more airborne hijacked airliners, and as we tried to get organized, my top priority was to ensure continuity in command and control down through the operational fleets was maintained. The Navy Command Center in the Pentagon took a direct hit from the hijacked aircraft and was totally destroyed.[50] Admiral Bob Natter, the Commander of our Atlantic Fleet in Norfolk, was requested to take Navy responsibility and appropriate actions until we could reestablish functionality, and he did a superb job.

The next task was to finish determining who among our Navy staff was dead, missing, or alive. In this regard, I soon discovered that we did not have master lists of names, addresses, phone numbers, or next of kin for the entire staff. In the operational Navy, every ship, squadron, and unit maintains a "Recall Bill" with that information to effect a rapid muster or roll call in an emergency. We did not have such lists on that day. Most Pentagon workers were civilians, so they were unfamiliar with the concept. Some probably would have objected based on private personal information being made public. To make matters more challenging, many folks were understandably reluctant to re-enter the building after being evacuated, and some just went home without thinking about advising anyone in their offices of their status among the living. Some were incommunicado, in shock or fear.

Coming up with accurate numbers was complicated by the low probability of near-term recovery of identifiable remains of the deceased and the fact that the injured were taken to hospitals throughout the Washington metropolitan area. As their top priority task, I assigned the senior leaders from each staff element to produce an accurate list of the missing, by whatever means they could determine. As afternoon turned to evening, it became increasingly clear that we had suffered many casualties within the Navy Command Center, although a few were from other organizations in the building. But it would be several days before we were confident of exact numbers and names.

By late afternoon, thanks primarily to the Marine Corps staff, we were reasonably functional in our temporary headquarters, communicating within the Department of Defense and, to some extent, with the outside world. There were several incidents of high drama and anxiety. One was a decision on what to do about a civilian passenger aircraft inbound from the Atlantic that apparently was not in communication with air traffic control authorities. A discussion on a secure communication link with Vice President Cheney included an option to order the aircraft shot down, suspecting it was another terrorist attack. Fortunately, fire was held, and eventually, the plane was intercepted and got back in communication with the appropriate authorities.

As the day wore on, some incredible stories of personal bravery, ingenuity, and lifesaving in the Pentagon became known. In one instance, Captain (later Rear Admiral) Dave Thomas and Navy flight surgeon (M.D.) Lieutenant Commander Dave Tarantino were checking for survivors in a wrecked area of the command center when they heard a moan. Using their flashlights in heavy smoke with fires all around them and coming closer, they discovered injured civilian Navy contractor and retired Commander Jerry Henson trapped at his desk and under a heavy pile of debris. Using near super-human strength, Tarantino lay on his back and leg-pressed the debris a few inches while Thomas pulled the victim. It was enough for Henson to wriggle free. The three escaped through a small hole in a wall kept open by another rescuer, Navy SEAL Commander Craig Powell, before the ceiling collapsed and the place was completely engulfed in fire.[51] Jerry Henson and I had served together during the Vietnam War in sister squadrons flying the same type aircraft. We shared many mutual friends and common experiences. When I visited him in the hospital several days after the terror attacks, he gratefully relayed some of the details of his heroic rescue.

Later that evening of 9/11, I took a break and walked outside. One of the first things I saw was a converted camper food truck parked next to the building. It was staffed by several retired Navy chief petty officers who had driven up from Norfolk, about four hours away, when news of the attack that morning became known. On a very emotional day, I was moved by the initiative and generosity of these men, who just wanted to do something helpful and stayed with us for several days, providing water, coffee, soft drinks, and snacks on their own nickel to anybody who wanted refreshment. I recall numerous instances at that time of

SEPTEMBER 11, 2001

similarly generous Americans and many others around the world trying to help in ways large and small. People really came together.

Walking down the hill to the chain-link fence facing the Pentagon, I gazed at the still-burning building (and my former office) with flames lighting the night sky and smoke still pouring from several places, defying the best efforts of firefighters. I felt immense sadness and anger as I contemplated what had happened on this day: our country attacked at home for the first time since the War of 1812, and thousands of people killed. Who did it? Why? What could we have done to prevent it? What else was coming? I did not know the answers yet, but I knew we would be busy in the coming days.

Back in the office, accounting for missing members was evolving into two groups of names: those about whom we were still essentially clueless and those who were missing but presumed deceased based on information from colleagues, next of kin, and circumstantial evidence. Contemplating the list of names of the presumed dead brought familiar faces to mind.

Petty Officer Brian Moss, an Electronics Technician from Oklahoma and the Cherokee Nation, whom I had met and observed several times during the previous year, was as sharp-looking and impressive acting a sailor as any I had ever known. Recently assigned to the Navy staff at the Pentagon, he had previously been with the Navy Ceremonial Guard. This elite Washington unit represented the Navy in highly visible official functions in and around the nation's capital. Admired as a leader and role model for the younger Sailors of the Guard, Brian was married, the father of two young children, and a most welcome addition to the Navy headquarters staff.

Commander Patrick Dunn, a Naval Academy graduate from New Jersey, had served with me previously on the Second Fleet staff and on *USS THEODORE ROOSEVELT*. A red-haired Navy officer of Irish descent with a quick wit and a ready smile, he had recently shared that his wife Stephanie was pregnant with their first child.

Petty Officer Michael Noeth, a draftsman and illustrator from New York, was also a talented artist recently commissioned to copy portraits of Navy dignitaries lining the walls of the Pentagon. I recalled with a smile my first meeting with Petty Officer Noeth. It was a Saturday afternoon, and I had been working alone, catching up on some

DECISIONS, DISCORD & DIPLOMACY

paperwork. On the way home, as I closed the door to my office and looked down the hall, I saw a tall Sailor in dress uniform pointing out various display artifacts and paintings. His companion was a diminutive older woman, bright-eyed and smiling, who immediately put me in mind of a leprechaun. Although I did not know him, he recognized me and introduced me to his grandmother, Muriel Kuhn. Beaming at her grandson, she proudly relayed that she was from New York City and that Michael was a fine arts graduate of the Fashion Institute of New York. We chatted amiably for several minutes as Muriel happily filled me in about Michael's career in the Navy, his childhood growing up in New York with his artistically talented mother, Merrilly, and how pleased she was that her grandson was serving at the Pentagon. Thoroughly charmed by my elfin new acquaintance, I reflected on how fortunate the Navy was to have such diverse and talented people, strongly supported and encouraged by proud families.

But on that terrible evening of 9/11, one could only imagine the anxiety and fear in the minds and hearts of our families as they awaited news about the fate of their loved ones. Regrettably, over several days, it was determined that a total of 42 of our Navy staff shipmates serving in the Pentagon were killed. Additionally, I learned that a good friend, Wilson "Bud" Flagg, and his wife, Dee, were on the American Airlines Flight 77 aircraft that terrorists crashed into the Pentagon. Bud, a Navy fighter pilot who remained in the naval reserve, rising to the rank of Rear Admiral, was also an American Airlines pilot and was probably in the jump seat when the hijackers commandeered the aircraft.

Funerals and memorial services for the deceased help bring some closure for families. One particularly memorable and emotional experience was the celebration of life for Petty Officer Marsha Stallworth Ratchford in Alabama about a month later. I had earlier agreed to a speaking engagement there at the request of "Doc" Abbot, which had to be postponed after 9/11. Learning that the funeral was scheduled for Mobile, we adjusted the trip to attend both events. Ratchford was an Information Technology specialist who joined the Navy 15 years earlier after growing up in a large extended family. She was only 34, had three young children, was married to another Navy Petty Officer, and served in the Pentagon.

Due to the large crowd of mourners, the funeral service was changed from the family church to the largest historically Black church in Mobile.

SEPTEMBER 11, 2001

After paying respects and extending condolences to the family, we were invited to be seated in the front, from which we could closely observe the traditionally long and emotional service. A series of heartwarming tributes by family and friends, homilies by clergymen backed by spiritually uplifting music from an orchestra outfitted in Navy uniforms (the members admitted they were not in the service but thought the attire was fitting to the occasion), conveyed the image of a loving and close relationship. Marsha was highly regarded for her exemplary service to the nation and her example as a role model for her family. Steadfast and determined, she came from humble circumstances to excel in achievement, leadership, and stern but loving mentorship. The poignant and inspirational stories of her life and the indelible impression that her example left on others were unmistakably genuine and truly moving.

The most memorable part of the service was near the end when the senior clergyman, a bishop, delivered a final unforgettable homily. After highlighting Petty Officer Ratchford's strong faith in God, achievements, and good work during her life, the preacher warned the assemblage using the following analogy. He said, "The Lord is, in some respects, like a hippopotamus in that he can see EVERYTHING, not only what is being done in the open (in clear air), but what is done out of sight" (in this example, underwater). The unmistakable message was that someone, as well as the hippo, is always watching what we do. He continued, "People watched sister Marsha, saw the good that she did, and we should all act like her." This exceptional Sailor and human being was laid to rest in the historic Mobile National Cemetery.[52]

For other families, long-term care for the injured kept their attention. Among several cases that I followed closely was the recovery of Lieutenant Kevin Schaefer, who was severely burned at the Pentagon Navy Command Center.[53]

In the days immediately following the attack, I made the rounds of area hospitals to look in on our wounded. I had heard that Kevin was very gravely injured, and there was some doubt that he would survive. He had been taken to the Washington Hospital Center Burn Unit, as this was the facility with a reputation as the best in the area for treatment of burns.

DECISIONS, DISCORD & DIPLOMACY

As we entered the hospital, a couple of my young staff assistants were trying to help me expedite my way to the rooms of the injured. When we arrived at the burn center, the entrance was barred by a no-nonsense nurse who firmly informed us that no visitors were getting into the intensive care unit because of the seriousness of the condition of the injured, and "Please leave!" When I began to query her about the condition of our patients, she put up her hand and said, "Sorry, we can't release any information."

As I felt my jaw tighten, the door swung open and out stepped a man in a white medical coat with a calm demeanor and a reassuring smile. He introduced himself as Doctor Marion Jordan, the chief surgeon and head of the burn unit. He reported that Lieutenant Schaeffer was in critical condition with burns over almost half his body and suffering from jet fuel inhalation in his lungs, but that he was receiving the best care available. The doctor reported that he was personally treating Kevin and then twisted the lapel of his medical frock to reveal a Navy Medical Corps insignia pinned to the back of it. Dr. Jordan served for several years as a Navy surgeon before returning to civilian practice. I was relieved and chuckled when I saw it and heard the doctors' reassuring words, "Don't worry, Admiral, we're taking good care of the Lieutenant."

And that they did. All but one of the nine critically injured burn patients from that day survived, thanks to the expert care they received at that trauma center under Dr. Jordan's direction. Although Kevin and another of the Pentagon severely injured that I came to know, Army Lieutenant Colonel Brian Birdwell, spent several months at the hospital, sometimes hovering close to death with complications from their injuries, both eventually recovered and have gone on to live productive and exemplary lives. Kevin, Brian, and I were recently reunited, although sadly, for a Celebration of Life for Dr. Jordan, who tragically died in a motor vehicle mishap.[54] We each agreed that this beloved physician's leadership, experience, and skill saved their lives and others in those fateful days in 2001.

CHAPTER 11

AL QAEDA AND THE WAR ON TERRORISM

AFGHANISTAN

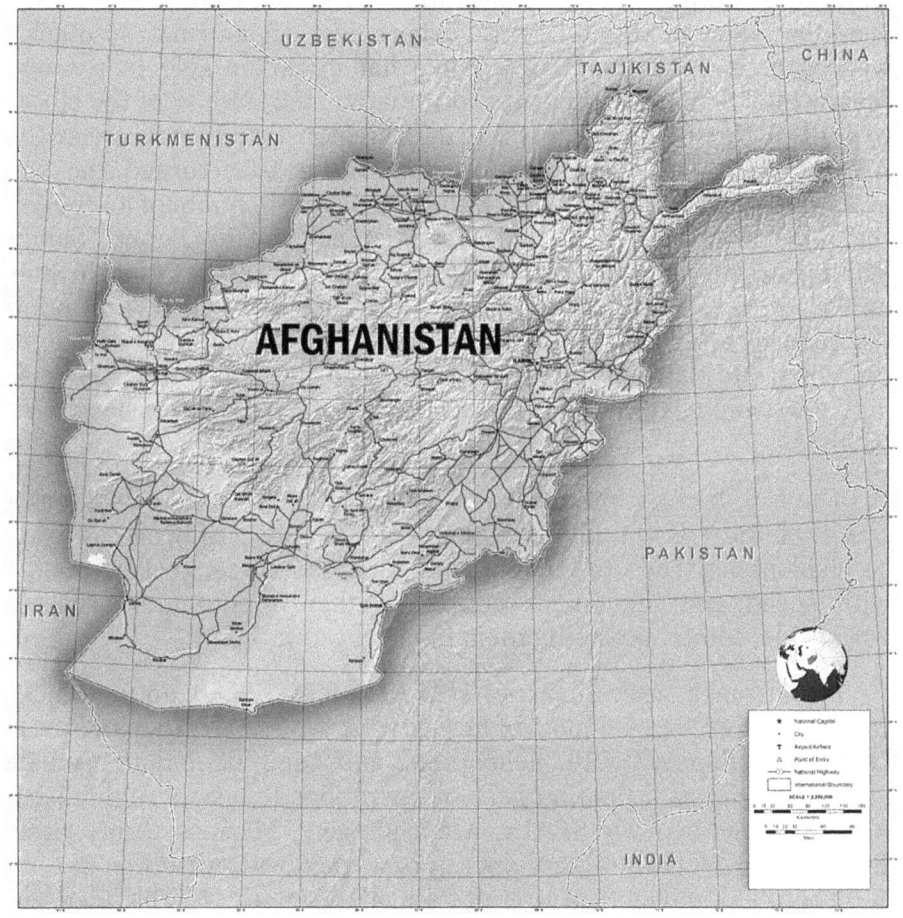

Map courtesy of U.S. CENTCOM

After the fact, intelligence information about the attacks began to come in very quickly. By the next day, Al Qaeda (literally "the base" in Arabic) and its leader, Osama bin Laden, were identified as the perpetrators. Attention during the next several days shifted rapidly to Afghanistan, where Al Qaeda was being sheltered and supported by the Taliban government. As the shock and disbelief of the attacks transitioned to anger and calls for retaliation, President George W. Bush sensed the mindset of the American people and passed the word within national security circles to prepare a military response within 30 days.

U.S. Military activity in Afghanistan was the responsibility of the CENTCOM Commander, but back in Washington, we knew that there were few assets or capabilities anywhere near Afghanistan, so quickly, we began to think about who and what might be able to respond. Meanwhile, demonstrating shrewd initiative, the skipper of the closest major U.S. Navy combat capability in the region, the aircraft carrier *USS ENTERPRISE*, after consultation with his bosses, turned the ship around and headed back to the Middle East within hours of learning of the attacks in New York and Washington. Captain James "Sandy" Winnefeld (later Admiral and Vice Chairman of the Joint Chiefs of Staff) and his crew, in the Indian Ocean, were near the end of a 6-month deployment and headed to a port visit in Cape Town, South Africa. He did not know many details then but correctly surmised that his vessel and crew would likely be called upon, and he turned the ship back to the north.[55]

The U.S. had no military bases near Afghanistan. As a landlocked country hundreds of miles from the ocean, simply getting access would be challenging. The operational commanders and services responded with speed and ingenuity, pulling together a potpourri of assets worldwide, sometimes using them in novel ways.

For instance, aircraft carrier *USS KITTY HAWK*, steaming quickly from Japan, exchanged most of her air wing for a large group of Special Operations Forces (SOF), helicopters, and equipment that used the aircraft carrier as a floating base of operations to access Afghanistan. Mixed groups of Navy SEALs, Army Rangers, Marines, Army Green Berets, and CIA paramilitary operators worked with Air Force B-1 and B-52 bombers and tactical aircraft from all the forces. New blended with old. For example, troops on horseback or camels sometimes used modern radios and Global Positioning System (GPS) devices to call in strikes from high-flying aircraft.

In short order, expeditionary bases were established on the ground to support troops, helicopters, and logistic aircraft in OPERATION

AL QAEDA AND THE WAR ON TERRORISM

ENDURING FREEDOM.[56] Most of the manpower was from the U.S., although several key U.S. allies (U.K., Canada, and Australia) joined with the Afghan Northern Alliance militias in attacking Al Qaeda and their Taliban supporters.

The initial prosecution of Al Qaeda and their supporting hosts, the Taliban in Afghanistan, was slow going despite the overwhelming technological advantage enjoyed by the U.S. and its allies. This was primarily due to rugged terrain over a large geographic area, a relatively small number of Coalition troops, and determined resistance by the Taliban and Al Qaeda.

The turning point in the operation came in early November when Coalition and anti-Taliban Northern Alliance forces linked up and routed the Taliban, capturing the key northern city of Mazar-i-Sharif. Kabul fell shortly thereafter, with Taliban and Al Qaeda remnant forces falling back to Kandahar in the south and the mountainous area in eastern Afghanistan known as Tora Bora, which became the site of the last organized resistance to the Coalition.

The Taliban leader, Mullah Omar, escaped, apparently across the border into Pakistan, where he went into hiding until he died in 2013. The principal target of the entire operation, Osama bin Laden, slipped away from Tora Bora into the mountains of NE Afghanistan and then to the tribal areas of Pakistan, where he remained in hiding until killed by U.S. Navy SEALs in 2011.[57]

Representatives of the various tribes and ethnic entities from Afghanistan met in Bonn, Germany, in December 2001 and selected Hamid Karzai as leader of a transitional government. Karzai was later elected as president and continued in power until 2014.[58]

The international community pledged support for the new government in Afghanistan, and the outlook for the country's future seemed quite bright in those closing days of 2001. We would not have imagined that the situation would descend back into decades of chaos.

But Osama bin Laden and his key henchmen had escaped, eluding the retribution that was intended in response to the 9/11 attacks. Their patrons, the Taliban, lost their immediate grip on power but merely blended into the countryside and across the border into Pakistan to fight another day.

The optimistic outlook for a stable and secure nation governed from Kabul turned out to be elusive and ultimately unattainable. Twenty years later, the U.S. and some of its Coalition partners were still mired in conflict in Afghanistan, supporting the elected but fractious government and battling a resurgent Taliban, remnants of Al Qaeda, and other tribals, aided and abetted by a duplicitous government in Pakistan. Twenty years of continuous conflict and an inability to sustain countrywide security sapped political will.

In 2021, the Biden Administration declared its intention to withdraw all U.S. military forces and, by August 31, 2021, completed a poorly executed and embarrassing drawdown that ended in a chaotic and costly-in-lives evacuation from Kabul airport.[59] In summary, the presence of the American military in Afghanistan ended in an ignominious fashion, with the country again ruled by the Taliban.

THE LONG WAR (A FOCUS ON COUNTERTERRORISM AND THE MIDDLE EAST)

The popularization of the term "Long War" has been attributed to U.S. Army General John Abizaid, my predecessor as CENTCOM Commander in 2004, to explain the complex and protracted conflict in which we were engaged. He identified "Salafist Jihadists" as the crux of the problem for the United States and non-Muslim entities.[60] Embracing violence and at odds with many in the Islamic as well as the Western world, these radicalized Sunni Muslims were viewed as committed to propagating a strict and puritanical form of Islam around the globe. The term took on a life of its own as it was expanded to include virtually all aspects of conflict involving Muslims worldwide. Soon after I took command at CENTCOM, I told the staff to stop using the term 'Long War' as the negative connotation of a seemingly endless war outweighed the desired benefit of encouraging steadfast perseverance.[61]

Meanwhile, by year-end 2001, attention in Washington was rapidly shifting from Afghanistan to an all-encompassing focus on what became known as the Global War on Terror (GWOT). Announced by President Bush in a speech less than a week after the 9/11 attacks, the GWOT, an acronym also known as the War on Terrorism, became the focal point for most U.S. government activities. It seized on a profound shift in attitudes among the American people, reflecting their anxiety and insecurity as a result of the attacks.

All manner of change in the name of security began to affect daily activities throughout the country. Barricades appeared around most public buildings; foot and vehicular traffic were rerouted; Pennsylvania Avenue in front of the White House was closed. Extensive security checks were initiated at airports and entrances to many buildings. A cabinet position of Director of Homeland Security with a large workforce was announced.

The new mindset was soon extended beyond domestic affairs as President Bush put the world on notice during an address to a joint session of Congress a fortnight after the terrorist attacks by stating, "…every nation in every region now has a decision to make. Either you are with us, or you are with the terrorists…"[62]

Most people and most national governments in the world expressed strong sympathy and solidarity with the citizens of the U.S. in the wake of the terrorist bombings. However, the unrelenting fixation on the GWOT by the Bush Administration and the expanding emphasis on entities alleged to be supporting or harboring terrorists, highlighted by the infamous "axis of evil" designation assigned to Iran, North Korea, and Iraq by the President in his State of the Union speech of January 29, 2002, caused people in other countries to question and gradually weaken support for the antiterrorism effort.[63]

But within the U.S. government, seemingly no effort or funding was spared in the ramp-up of counterterrorism activities. Soon after 9/11, congressional appropriations of "emergency" funds in the form of "supplementals" (monies allocated over and above previously agreed and legislated budget amounts) began in response to administration requests. These GWOT monies were substantial and underwrote the expanding counterterrorism effort for over a decade.

In 2009, the Obama Administration changed GWOT to OCO (Overseas Contingency Operations) Funds. Still, they continued to be used to support supplementary budget expenditures. The total amount of these funds through 2021 was over $2 trillion.[64]

In the months following 9/11, commentators in the media and citizens around the country speculated about when things would return to "normal." But as time went on, the old normal seemed elusive as anxiety and a lingering sense of disbelief pervaded the psyche of our citizens. It seemed that things would never be the same again. The shock to the American people from this brazen and unprecedented attack permeated every level of society, from individuals and families to the top of the government. The long recovery process remained, and caring for the injured, lingering images of the damaged and destroyed buildings, and nonstop media attention to all the above kept this issue front and center. Leaders vowed a cleanup, recovery, increased security, and a war on terrorists. The administration was fixated on homeland security and the Global War on Terrorism.

In response to Bush Administration requests in the immediate aftermath of 9/11, Congress passed two significant pieces of legislation. The first, Public Law 107 – 40, a short Joint Resolution of Congress commonly known as the Authorization for Use of Military Force (AUMF), granted the President authority "...to use all necessary and appropriate force against those nations, organizations, or persons he determines planned, authorized, committed, or aided the terrorist attacks that occurred on September 11, 2001, or harbored such organizations or persons..."[65] This broadly stated authority was used by President Bush to send troops into Afghanistan seeking Al Qaeda and the Taliban, who harbored them. It was also interpreted as authority by President Bush and his successors to target militants in other countries around the world. The law currently remains in effect. The Senate voted in March 2023 to repeal the two specific AUMF laws related to Iraq, but not P.L. 107-40. The subject is still under review in Congress.

The second major piece of legislation was Public Law 107 – 56, a lengthy document commonly known as the USA Patriot Act of 2001. It was enacted "to deter and punish terrorist acts in the United States and globally, to enhance law enforcement investigatory tools, and for other purposes" (primarily anti-money laundering and other financial issues). Seeking enhanced domestic security, it expanded certain surveillance powers of federal law enforcement and intelligence agencies and made numerous changes to existing statutes relating to the privacy of telephonic and electronic communications, immigration, money laundering, and the Foreign Intelligence Surveillance Court (FISC).

Significantly, it expanded federal officials' authority to intercept and track communications for law enforcement and intelligence-gathering purposes.⁶⁶ This statute has been reauthorized several times since it was enacted to include changes and adjustments to sunset clauses for specific provisions. Critics of this legislation have claimed that it infringes on individuals' rights and civil liberties. Whether or not these claims are justified is still being debated. But a significant consequence was a wave of anti-Muslim sentiment that swept the country, combined with immigration restrictions contained in the legislation to project an unwelcome signal to the world.

This "ugly American" image played right into the hands of Osama bin Laden and Al Qaeda and their anti-U.S. rhetoric and eventually caused widespread dissension in the U.S. and undermined support for the War on Terror worldwide.

The wide-ranging and greatly expanded authorities incorporated into these two pieces of legislation were approved overwhelmingly by Congress at the time of enactment and reflected the mood and sentiment of the American people. They also underpinned the aggressive actions of the Bush Administration in responding to the unprecedented and unnerving actions by the terrorists on 9/11.

Shortly thereafter, as ongoing military activities in Afghanistan resulted in the capture of suspected Al Qaeda and other terrorists, President Bush signed a Presidential Military Order titled *Detention, Treatment, and Trial of Certain Non-Citizens in the War against Terrorism*. A key passage stated, "I have determined that an extraordinary emergency exists for national defense purposes... this order is necessary to meet the emergency."⁶⁷ The order applied the expansive terms of the AUMF to include, among these non-citizens, members of Al Qaeda or others connected with international terrorism or those who knowingly harbored any of these individuals. It tasked the Secretary of Defense with detaining and trying said individuals and directed those trials to be conducted by the military commission. This novel approach to the disposition of such individuals was deemed necessary because Al Qaeda was not a recognized armed force nor an instrument of legal state power, and because of the presumption that the perpetrators of the savage and murderous acts of 9/11 presented a unique threat.

The U.S. Naval Base at Guantánamo Bay, Cuba (GTMO), which had been in U.S. hands since the Spanish-American War and long a key training locale for the U.S. Navy, was chosen as the primary detention site for suspected Al Qaeda-related terrorists. The rationale for the selection of GTMO as the site to detain and process these individuals was based primarily on a legal opinion that detainees there would be outside U.S. legal jurisdiction and ineligible for all the legal rights (and potential defense attorney stratagems) enjoyed by those on U.S. soil. Also, their status as aliens and "unlawful enemy combatants," the term chosen by the Bush Administration to uniquely identify these people and to distinguish them from prisoners of war, would facilitate potential trials by military commission rather than the U.S. court system of civilian justice.[68]

A precedent for the use of GTMO as a detention site occurred during the 1980s and 90s, when large numbers of Cuban, Haitian, and even some Chinese asylum-seekers were "housed" (detained) there while their cases were considered (outside the U.S. justice system).[69] Thus, when in 2001, the question of where to hold captured accused terrorists arose, the previous use of GTMO put it at the top of the list of potential sites.

The first detainees in the Global War on Terrorism were brought to GTMO on January 11, 2002, opening a new chapter in the rapidly expanding and increasingly complex efforts to deal with terrorists in the wake of 9/11. Over time, GTMO became a lightning rod for criticism of George W. Bush and subsequent administrations. Within two weeks of the first arrivals at GTMO, in a "Tank" session (Joint Chiefs meeting in the Pentagon), which I attended, the service chiefs discussed our unease with the aggressive approach employed by the administration. My notes reflected a strong consensus among the chiefs that we adhere to the customs and traditions of the Geneva Conventions and the Laws of Armed Conflict (LOAC), decrying the "in-your-face attitude" being pushed by the Office of the Secretary of Defense (OSD) and the White House.[70]

It was several months later before we became aware of the use of "enhanced interrogation techniques" at GTMO and other detention facilities. Most of the senior uniformed leadership of the Armed Forces and I consistently advised Secretary Rumsfeld of our strong advocacy for adherence to the standards in the Geneva Conventions and the traditional Laws of Armed Conflict regarding the treatment of detainees. Personally, I was highly skeptical of administration claims of success with "enhanced interrogation techniques." Mindful that U.S. prisoners of war in North Vietnam resisted enemy attempts to extract "confessions" or any other useful information despite months or, in some cases, years of inhumane treatment and extreme torture, caused me to doubt the utility of such methods. Telling the torturer something they want to hear might be the result, but who knows whether it is truthful?

Revelations about the perpetrators of the 9/11 attacks, notably the fact that most of the hijackers were from Saudi Arabia, as was Osama bin Laden, their leader, served to accentuate U.S. government attention on the Middle East. Attempts to understand and explain what motivated these people and why consumed countless hours of study, discussion, and pages of print by government officials, academics, and pundits. Although some intelligence analysts had previously identified Osama bin Laden and others as vociferous advocates of a Salafi Muslim ideology of jihad (literally "striving" or "struggling" in Arabic and, in the case of bin Laden and his cohorts, an armed struggle) against Western as well as secular Arab governments in the Middle East, little was known or understood then about the extent and support for their activities within Saudi Arabia and the greater Islamic world.

Because Osama bin Laden became the personification of terrorism following the 9/11 attacks, some background about him and his prior activities will provide context to better understand his role and that of Al Qaeda (and offshoots) in the challenges that this ideology presented to the world, then and now.

CHAPTER 12

OSAMA BIN LADEN

Born about 1957 to Mohammed bin Laden, a Hadhrami Yemeni who had emigrated to Saudi Arabia and later became wealthy as the founder of a large construction business in service to the House of Saud, and Alia Ghanem, a Syrian Alawite about age 15 at the time of his birth. Raised by his mother, who was quickly divorced by Mohammed after the birth of Osama, and a stepfather in a household with four step-siblings, he grew up in comfortable circumstances like many of his contemporaries from well-to-do families in Saudi Arabia during the 1960s and 70s. One of about 50 of his father's offspring, he benefited from his father's affluence and status in the latter's business relationships with the Saudi royal family. Educated from about age 11 in the Saudi government-funded Al-Thager Model private school with a modern but non-secular curriculum and with a faculty drawn chiefly from other Arab countries, he was influenced by teachers advocating a very conservative, fundamentalist type of Islam common in Saudi Arabia at the time.[71] Recognized as more pious and focused on religion than his numerous stepbrothers, he advocated for a return to the strict practice of the Islamic Faith. He had a fondness for the customs and dress of the era of the Prophet. Attracted to the Muslim Brotherhood of politicized Islamists as a teenager, he was recruited and soon became a member of the organization, according to his childhood friend and fellow "Brother," Jamal Khashoggi, who was later murdered in Turkey, allegedly at the direction of Mohammed bin Salman, current Crown Prince and heir apparent to the throne in KSA.[72]

With the sudden death of his father in a 1967 plane crash, leadership of the Mohammed bin Laden organization was taken over by Osama's older stepbrother, Salem, who assumed the role of overseer of his siblings' education as well as distributor of funds to them from the bin Laden estate and ongoing business operations. An interesting detail is that the King of Saudi Arabia, at the time, Faisal bin Abdulaziz, became the official guardian of Osama and his siblings, a sign of the status and relationship between Mohammed bin Laden and the House of Saud.[73]

Attending King Abdulaziz University in Jeddah for some time before going to work at his now-deceased father's firm, the tall and reserved

Osama bin Laden

Osama shared in the business and recreational activities of the extended bin Laden family. By 1980, and now in his mid-twenties, Osama was married in Jeddah with a growing brood of children. Osama began traveling to other countries while working on various projects at the family firm. He was, by all accounts, religiously strict in behavior, quiet and polite, but still in close communication with his religious mentors and the Muslim Brotherhood.[74]

Meanwhile, Israeli success against Arab forces in the 1967 and 1973 wars and the occupation of formerly Arab-controlled lands, particularly Jerusalem, added to the sense of Muslim grievance, which dates to the collapse of the Ottoman Empire earlier in the 20th century. In fact, during the early 1960s, Mohammed bin Laden was personally engaged in a major reconstruction of the Dome of the Rock Shrine and Al-Aqsa Mosque in Jerusalem and lived there part-time. Resentment against the non-Islamic world intensified with the Soviet invasion of Afghanistan. It became a focal point of interest to Osama and like-minded colleagues.[75]

Support for Muslim entities in Afghanistan fighting against the Soviets came from many parts of the Islamic world, with the Kingdom of Saudi Arabia (KSA) providing significant assistance, albeit secretly, in the form of funds, manpower, and intelligence.

Stepbrother and family patriarch Salem bin Laden had visited Pakistan and Afghanistan many times during the 1970s for business and personal reasons (for example, enrolling two of his younger stepsisters at a boarding school in Peshawar, Pakistan, near the Afghan frontier).[76]

With well-established family, government (KSA), and political-religious (Muslim Brotherhood) involvement in the Afghan-Pakistani region, Osama bin Laden inserted himself into the complex mix of overlapping as well as conflicting interests in 1980, "announcing himself there as a junior philanthropic activist."[77] He was still young, then in his mid-twenties, beginning to actively broadcast his Salafi religious and Brotherhood political inclinations and dispensing money to the mujahideen and other organizations with common interest in the conflict against the Soviets in Afghanistan.

In hindsight, it is clear that Osama had a prominent presence along the Afghanistan-Pakistan border long before 2001. His part-time residency there, frequent travel back and forth between the KSA and the largely ungoverned Pakistani Federally Administered Tribal Areas

(FATA), and across the border to Afghanistan, continued for the duration of the Soviet incursion.

He was serving multiple interests. First, his own in realizing an oft-stated desire to join in the jihad against enemies of Islam (USSR). Also, the family, which wanted to be seen as financially supporting religious causes, used the services of Osama to courier "Zakat" (obligatory Islamic charity) to the needy, most visibly the orphaned and persons displaced by the war. Additionally, by soliciting and then conveying charitable donations from wealthy Saudis to the front lines, he served in a role that supported the clandestine assistance that the Saudi government was providing to the mujahideen. In the latter capacity, he also reinforced the bin Laden family's important image in the Saudi King's eyes. In the process of executing these tasks, he made numerous contacts of various persuasions on both sides of the Afghan-Pakistan border and reinforced his own growing activism as a catalyst for jihad.

About this time, he met another person who was to have a considerable influence on his future direction, Abdulla Azzam, a Palestinian elder in the Muslim Brotherhood who was on the faculty at King Abdulaziz University when Osama was a student there and who set up a presence in Pakistan in support of mujahideen efforts. The older, more experienced, and militant Azzam provided mentorship to Osama, and the two collaborated in establishing training camps and support facilities for Arab volunteers in the war, most notably the so-called "Services Office."[78]

Osama had the money, and jihadist Azzam had connections to key Afghan guerrilla leaders and with ISI (Inter-Services Intelligence). This Pakistani intelligence agency advised and directed much of the counter-Soviet war effort and was also the funnel for most donated funds (both government and private), which enabled the resistance. Osama, now deferentially and obsequiously called "Sheikh," mainly because of his generous distribution of financial resources, began hands-on engagement with the volunteers and groups along the border, proselytizing, advising, and drawing on the construction resources of the bin Laden organization in support of the mujahideen.[79]

The relationship between Osama and the Saudi government in these efforts is murky. The chief of Saudi foreign intelligence then was Prince Turki al Faisal, to whom Osama was well known. Prince Turki was a key interlocutor between the KSA and the U.S., beginning with the Carter Administration and continuing throughout the Afghan-Soviet conflict. Turki, in later years, became the communication link to Osama from the Saudi government in its efforts to dissuade the latter from his increasingly militant activities both in Sudan and Afghanistan. Prince Turki directed Saudi foreign intelligence for more than 20 years, through the entire Afghan-Soviet War and up until a few days before 9/11. He later became Saudi Ambassador to the Court of St. James and then to the United States. I have known him for many years and have met with him several times. I found him to be very sophisticated, highly intelligent, and, to this day, always supportive of the policies of the House of Saud. He, like Osama, spent a lot of time in the region during the decade of the Afghan-Soviet War and no doubt had lots of eyes and ears on the ground. Thus, it is reasonable to believe that there was not much that went on there that was not known to him and relayed to Riyadh.[80]

Although Osama initially directed money in Afghanistan and Pakistan to mostly humanitarian causes, the Saudi government was financing military equipment, mainly through Ahmed Badeeb, a former teacher at Osama's Al-Thager Model School in Jeddah and Chief of Staff to Turki. Each of these people was well-known to the others and collaborated in areas of mutual interest, with Osama in the early years of the war primarily acting as facilitator and courier.[81]

One of the services that he provided was akin to promoting tourism to the war zone for eager Saudi and other Arab youths who wished to demonstrate their Jihadi zeal, but as observers rather than combatants. The short-term visitors to the border areas needed facilities in which to stay, and Osama obliged with the construction and operation of camps, which later in the war progressed to the training of active Jihadi warriors. These endeavors provided Osama with introductions to potential young jihadists that he later exploited as he transitioned to a more active role in the Jihadi cause. This became a point of friction with his ally Azzam, who wanted to be selective in recruiting Arab volunteers for the jihad, whereas Osama openly welcomed everyone.[82]

Nonetheless, the two intensified their cooperation with Azzam, infusing new visitors with his militant view of a worldwide assault against Muslims by unbelievers, with the Israeli incursion into Lebanon in 1982 as an example, in addition to the Soviet invasion of Afghanistan.

During these years, Osama became more militant and eventually heeded a call from Azzam in 1986, moving himself and his growing family (married now to three women and a soon-to-be fourth wife) to Peshawar.[83] He expanded his activities to include funding for weapons as he assumed a more direct role in the war. He was also introduced to a new arrival in Peshawar, Ayman al-Zawahiri, the radical Egyptian, who clashed with Azzam, souring relations between Osama and the latter and later becoming second in command of Al Qaeda.[84]

In addition to purchasing weapons and outfitting Arab forces, Osama began to branch out into Afghanistan with direct matériel and heavy construction support.

One of his first efforts was fortifying an area in Afghanistan's Khost Province near Jaji, across the border from an area of Pakistan known as the Parrot's Beak, where they built an enclave they called the Lion's Den to defend their Arab volunteers against Soviet attack.[85] They imported heavy earthmoving and construction equipment from the bin Laden organization for this effort. The significant extent of these engineering activities had to have been known to Salem and the other stepbrothers.

Later, the construction effort expanded northward into the rugged mountainous area known as Tora Bora, where they enlarged existing caves and other fortifications into hideouts and supply depots for the increasing number of weapons and ammunition flowing into the country. This area and these caves are the same well-known location to which Osama and his Al Qaeda and Taliban allies retreated in 2001 following the American-led attack into Afghanistan in response to the 9/11 assault.

This activity was also well known to and supported by the ISI, which spearheaded anti-Soviet activities during the 1980s, helped sustain the Taliban government in the 1990s, and supported cross-border guerrilla activities which undermined the post-Taliban Afghan government from 2002 onwards. Despite repeated denials by the leaders of Pakistan, it was my experience in dealing with the ISI that they were playing both sides, which undercut much of what the U.S. and our allies were trying to accomplish in Afghanistan.

During post-9/11 U.S. operations there, the Pakistanis had us over a barrel. Because of the landlocked position of the country, the only significant supply lines into Afghanistan ran through Pakistan, where our resupply convoys were routinely subject to extortion and attack by militants.

The Pakistani government insisted on lavish amounts of American financial assistance in exchange for access to the supply routes but turned a blind eye to the convoy assaults and refused our entreaties to provide escorts. My meetings with the then ISI Chief, General Ashraf Kayani, were cordial but frustratingly unproductive. The general was a heavy smoker and spoke in a soft voice, almost a whisper, assuring me of our common goals and interests, which, with good reason, I failed to believe. This double game continued through the complete pullout of U.S. forces from Afghanistan in 2021. The motivation for their behavior, as with virtually every other Pakistani activity in south Asia, is framed in mistrust of India and the belief that the Indians are behind every external action that might be counter to the interests of Pakistan. Control of their back door, that is, Afghanistan, is a top national priority.

As the Soviet-Afghan War wound down and the Soviets announced their intention to withdraw all forces by early 1989, infighting between the many factions of the mujahedin resistance and outside "helpers" (Arab Jihadis) increased. Osama and his collaborators sought to take advantage of the assembled Jihadi to further their confrontation with the non-Muslim West. In a series of meetings in 1988, Al Qaeda was established by Osama, to whom all swore "bayat" (oath of allegiance), and several fellow militants, including two known by their noms de guerre, Abu Hafs and Abu Ubaida (active Arab organizers and military leaders), as the entity to pursue these interests.[86]

The new Arab militia, the foot soldiers for the worldwide campaign, expanded from a nucleus of those drawn to the Afghan fight against the Soviets. Likewise, the initial arms and infrastructure came from the existing stockpiles and facilities. As Osama later explained it, even the name Al Qaeda, "the base," was about the existing training camps built for the Afghan War.[87] The tension between Osama and his erstwhile mentor Azzam, exacerbated by Zawahiri, was broken when the former was killed in an unattributed car bomb attack some months later.[88] About that time, whether due to prodding by ISI, Saudi intelligence, or the pull of family matters, Osama and his family left Peshawar and returned to the KSA, leaving behind resources to keep the newly founded Al Qaeda going.[89]

DECISIONS, DISCORD & DIPLOMACY

As Osama re-immersed himself in family matters in the Kingdom, change was the order of the day. Stepbrother Bakr had become the family patriarch in the wake of Salem's untimely 1988 death in yet another aircraft crash. The family businesses were reorganized into two new entities: the Mohammed bin Laden Company, successor to the original firm, and the new Saudi Bin Laden Group (SBG). The key point is that Osama had a financial stake in both new companies and a cash dividend of millions of dollars. He also inserted himself into the ongoing civil conflict in Yemen, supporting a fundamentalist Jihadi group opposed to the communist regime. The Iraqi invasion of Kuwait and the subsequent arrival of U.S. troops into the Kingdom greatly irritated him as another example of anti-Muslim forces introducing a secular force to oppress the followers of the Prophet.

At some point in 1990, after the Iraqi occupation of Kuwait, as King Fahd related to U.S. Ambassador Chas Freeman in a private conversation, Osama had approached him with a surreal request to use his Arab militia (then a few thousand followers at most) to oust Saddam's forces.[90] A new Jihadi warrior persona was emerging.

Denouncing the American military presence in the Kingdom, his increasingly vocal opposition to Saudi government actions, and his support for jihadis in Yemen did not go unnoticed by the Al Saud. Prince Turki said, "This shy, retiring, and seemingly very reticent person had changed."[91] Osama's passport was taken away from him.

Shortly after the end of the Gulf War in 1991, Osama left the KSA, beginning his self-exile. The exact reason for his exit from KSA and how he accomplished it is unclear, given that his passport had allegedly been seized.

Before this, he had Al Qaeda operatives from Afghanistan secure farms, houses, and other properties in Sudan for him, apparently with money donated by admirers. He had visited Sudan in connection with the family business in prior years and had previously purchased some properties there. In any event, he moved with his wives and children to Khartoum, from where he engaged in increasingly militant pursuits leading to the World Trade Center garage bombing in 1993 and the attacks on two U.S. embassies in East Africa. His alarming activities instigated several attempts by the Saudi government and his family, including a personal visit by his mother, to get him to return to the Kingdom of Saudi Arabia, which he spurned.[92]

By 1996, his escalating public rhetoric and notoriety had become an embarrassment to the government of Sudan, which asked him to "Either keep silent or leave the country."[93] Also, mounting pressure from both the KSA and U.S. governments to expel him from Sudan was brought to bear. He refused to remain silent and decamped for Afghanistan, "…a country for which he had a considerable, almost romantic attachment."[94]

On May 18, 1996, Osama arrived at Jalalabad, Afghanistan, via private jet. Engaged in a brutal civil war, the country was then controlled mainly by the Taliban. This fundamentalist Islamic group espoused many of the same religious and behavioral precepts as Osama. Led by the one-eyed cleric Mullah Omar, recently dubbed "Commander of the Faithful" by a conclave of clerics, the Taliban were in the process of establishing draconian social mores in areas under their control.

But interestingly, Jalalabad and the surrounding area were still in the hands of other mujahideen factions that had been friendly with Osama during the Afghan-Soviet War and which welcomed his arrival. The area, close to Tora Bora, was well known to Osama, who was given a large compound near Jalalabad for his use and facilities in the Tora Bora mountains. Although surrounded and supported by Arab mujahideen and the local warlords, the living conditions were austere. But Osama seemed to revel in the circumstances, comparing the situation to that of the Prophet during his exile.[95]

Several months later, the Taliban successfully secured Jalalabad and its environs. Mullah Omar and Osama evidently reached a satisfactory arrangement. The latter was eventually invited to move to more comfortable and secure accommodation near Kandahar in southern Afghanistan, the heartland of the Taliban, where he resided for several years.[96]

DECLARATION OF WAR

Meanwhile, in the United States, slow to recognize the growing danger posed by bin Laden, intelligence analysts in the "three-letter agencies" began to accumulate and focus on information about him. One of the earliest to appreciate the looming threat was a young analyst named Gina Bennett at the Department of State's Bureau of Intelligence and Research, who authored several classified documents circulated among the agencies.[97]

The first public disclosure that Osama was on the radar of the U.S. government came in the form of an unusually detailed and unclassified Department of State "Fact Sheet" issued in August 1996, soon after bin Laden arrived back in Afghanistan, that highlighted his financial support for terrorist "Afghan Arabs" around the world. Several days later, on August 23, Osama publicly declared war on the United States, issuing a remarkable statement, "Declaration of Jihad against the Americans occupying the Land of the Two Holy Places (KSA)," a lengthy, rambling rant vilifying the U.S. and the ruling House of Saud and entreating Muslims to rise up against the "oppressors."[98] Generally unnoticed in the West at the time, this message was sent to Osama's followers worldwide and used to rally support for the growing armed struggle, and was a message of intent for catastrophic events to come. One of the few U.S. security officials to recognize the coming danger exposed in bin Laden's "declaration" was Ali Soufan, at the time, a young FBI Special Agent in New York, who wrote an illuminating report about it that got the attention of his superior in the Bureau, John O'Neill (killed at the World Trade Center less than a month after retiring from the FBI), but little further response.[99]

In summary, by the time of the 9/11 attacks, Osama bin Laden, though little-known to the American public, had been identified as a significant threat by American intelligence agencies as he perpetrated an increasingly deadly series of terror attacks. A particular challenge for the U.S. in dealing with this problem was that Osama and Al Qaeda were not the traditional state actors for which there were well-established security procedures. Complications included minimal information and understanding about his background and ascent to command a worldwide following of fellow extremists arising out of the shadowy activities in Pakistan and Afghanistan during the war in the 1980s.

Coming from the obscurity of a complex and disjointed boyhood and adolescence, this shy and unassuming student developed a strong affinity for the ultraconservative religious beliefs espoused by 18th-century Sheikh Mohammed Abdul Wahabi, to which he was exposed from an early age. Benefiting immensely from enormous family wealth, which continued to flow to him until at least the mid-1990s, and that he used to fund his terrorist activities, plus connections to the Saudi elite, he nonetheless, except for religious zealotry, remained unfocused until he drifted into the Afghanistan-Pakistan border in 1980. Well known in those days primarily because of the largesse that he conveyed to militant Muslim factions, the "Sheikh" became increasingly radicalized as he assumed an active role in the Afghan conflict.

The extent of his combat activities is debatable. Still, at least in his mind, he became a holy warrior in the battle against the "infidels." Case in point is his role and romanticization of the fighting at Jaji in the spring of 1987 and Jalalabad (Tora Bora) shortly thereafter. Characterized by other accounts as operational blunders and tactical disasters, Osama and his growing publicity apparatus nonetheless highlighted his role as a turning point in the war against the Soviets. He came to be seen as somewhat of a war hero in the KSA.[100] He began to think that his life was unfolding parallel to that of the Prophet as he related events in his life to those in the latter. Initially buying the allegiance and paying the salaries of his Arab recruits and accomplices, his personal piety and frugality enhanced his reputation as he became increasingly vocal in pushing for jihad against "non-believers." This image of himself as an indispensable leader of the modern jihad was reinforced by the adulation of his followers and buttressed by a growing propaganda effort enabled by the Internet and, of course, the money to which he had access.

Although he clearly served a valuable function for the Al Saud during the Afghan War, he quickly wore out his welcome upon his return to the KSA. He went into self-imposed exile in Sudan and then Afghanistan. A review of his rhetoric shows an increasingly anti-American bias, blaming U.S. moral decadence, as demonstrated in dress, movies, and modern technology, etc., and "presence in Muslim lands" as an affront and attack on Muslims. His affinity for political Islam and demands for public adherence to the tenets of Islamic faith had him at odds with Western democracies and the rulers in his native land. His self-righteous stance as the successor to the Prophet, couching his actions and advocacy of violence as a requirement of his interpretation of his religion, attracted like-minded admirers but menaced the rest of the world. He soon launched his war against America by conducting a series of high-visibility terror attacks against the U.S. in the Middle East and

Africa (Riyadh, Nairobi, Dar es Salaam, *USS COLE*), which culminated in the "great event" of 9/11.

There were many indicators that Osama and his Al Qaeda network were planning, funding, and executing lethal terror attacks for at least eight years before 9/11. The U.S. response was clearly ineffective. Several of our allies, specifically KSA, which had a wealth of knowledge about bin Laden and his actions for 20 years, could have been much more helpful rather than stonewalling American requests to share intelligence. Pakistan, recipient of billions of dollars of assistance over the same 20-year period, knew a lot more than it ever shared and abetted Al Qaeda in many ways.

And the U.S. does not have to look far to recognize that some of our actions seriously hindered effective information gathering. To wit, withdrawing (from an over-abundance of caution?) U.S. personnel from key embassies in Kabul and Khartoum during the 1980s and 90s. Without eyes and ears on the ground in these capitals, we were unable to help ourselves in the two countries where bin Laden and his principal associates were residing and plotting.

Of course, it is easier afterward to sift through details brought to light here. However, it seems inexplicable that more forceful actions were not taken against bin Laden.

For its part, the Clinton Administration did launch TLAM (Tomahawk Land Attack Missile) strikes at suspected Al Qaeda basing sites in Afghanistan and Sudan following the U.S. embassy bombings in East Africa, which had been directly tied by intelligence back to Al Qaeda, as had the 1993 World Trade Center garage bombing.[101] But these retaliatory strikes were totally ineffective, and there was no follow-up action aside from the U.S. formally indicting bin Laden and his accomplices for these attacks. More perplexing was the inaction following the October 1990 suicide bombing of the *USS COLE* in Aden, Yemen, another act determined by the lead FBI investigator, Ali Soufan, to have been directed by bin Laden and perpetrated by Al Qaeda.

Part of the answer is likely due to the timing of the contentious 2000 U.S. presidential election and the domestic focus of attention by the senior political leadership.

Osama bin Laden

Another key point was the wearisome, decade-long containment activities in the no-fly zones over northern and southern Iraq, which absorbed activity and resource expenditure by a U.S. military primarily concerned with downsizing and refocusing the post-Cold War defense establishment.

The U.S. intelligence community, although receiving minimal assistance from our Saudi and Pakistani allies, had, by this time, amassed a sizable dossier on Al Qaeda but failed to impress the extent of the threat on the political leadership. Over time, it has also become clear that the CIA and FBI both had independently acquired different key pieces of information, which, if shared with the other agency, would likely have collectively resulted in responses to thwart the 9/11 attack.[102] As illuminated well by Lawrence Wright in "The Agent," a New Yorker magazine piece, "The FBI and CIA have long quarreled over bureaucratic turf, and their mandates place them at odds. The ultimate goal of the Bureau in gathering intelligence is to gain convictions for crimes; for the Agency, intelligence itself is the object."[103] In any event, information was available, and clues were identified, but critical opportunities were squandered.

The incoming George W. Bush Administration was struggling through the process of appointments and policy priorities while getting its feet on the ground in the face of many issues and events competing for its attention. In my experience, it typically takes about six months from the start of a new administration before it has the people in place to become effective in dealing with the full range of challenges. This administration also had a different national security priority, an intensifying focus on Saddam Hussein and Iraq.

Much has been written to rationalize these points, but the bottom line is that we failed to recognize the extent of the danger and act appropriately to forestall the tragic events of 9/11.

CHAPTER 13

WASHINGTON, POLITICS, AND IRAQ AS THE EPICENTER

THE PRESIDENTIAL ELECTION OF 2000 AND THE TRANSITION OF ADMINISTRATIONS

If the intelligence regarding Osama bin Laden and the 9/11 attack was fumbled during the handoff between the Clinton and Bush Administrations, it should be remembered that there were other balls in the air at that time.

First, Bush's razor-thin margin of victory, highlighted by the dramatic, contentious, and even closer election result in Florida, with legal battles quickly escalating to the U.S. Supreme Court, riveted the nation's attention for over a month. The media-hyped controversies over "hanging chads" and political infighting captivated the country with little space for other news.

Meanwhile, small-scale, intermittent exchanges of fire between Iraqi ground forces and Coalition aircraft maintaining the no-fly zones continued. A terrorist bombing attack in Manila killed dozens of citizens, the *USS COLE* attack aftermath was simmering, and natural disasters around the world competed for attention.

Within the U.S. government, the transition process between administrations got underway, nominations to fill key positions in the new administration were announced, and, of course, lots of attention was focused on inauguration day itself.

As the remaining Clinton political appointees wound down their activities in the Pentagon, I received an unusual summons from the Honorable Rudy DeLeon, the outgoing Deputy Secretary of Defense. At the time, I was a four-star Admiral serving as the Vice Chief of the Navy. I knew and worked well with the DEPSECDEF, as he was known within the building, for some time. Rudy advised me that he was passing along his recommendation to the incoming Bush Administration Department of Defense team that I be responsible for a key, incomplete piece of Clinton Administration work. I mention this assignment to illustrate the diversity of tasks to be handled simultaneously: important but for different reasons.

The task to which I was assigned was no surprise. It concerned the Navy Atlantic Fleet Weapons Training Facility (AFWTF), a vast geographic area with thousands of square miles of sea and airspace east and south of Puerto Rico. It had been used for Navy and Marine Corps training since the 1940s. The hub for these training operations was on the island of Vieques, about six miles east of the main island of Puerto Rico.[104] The event that precipitated what by then had become a political firestorm with ramifications far beyond Vieques was the unfortunate death of a civilian Navy employee, wounded by shrapnel from an errant air-to-ground weapon at the live ordnance training area on the eastern tip of the island about two years previously.

A fundamental truth for the military is that success or failure (and survival) in combat, and the risk we ask our troops to shoulder, is a direct function of the preparation we afford prior to commitment. Such skills are highly perishable, and live practice is absolutely necessary. The Vieques training range was critical for pre-deployment training and preparation of Navy and Marine Corps forces. As the irreplaceable hub of the AFWTF, it was the only facility in the entire Atlantic at which our military could conduct realistic, multi-dimensional, live ordnance, combined arms training. Designed to measure, under stress, the performance of people and systems in the maritime combat environment, it was the only range at which live naval surface, aviation, and artillery ordnance fires could be practiced in coordination. Strategically co-located with underwater and electronic warfare ranges, amphibious landing beaches, and maneuver areas, with adjacent deep water sea space, a vast area of low-traffic airspace, and the proximity of a full-service naval base and air station for logistical support activities, the facility offered training opportunities that no separate range or computer simulation could match.

The benefits of simulation to enhance combat performance are significant and far-reaching, with every military activity short of actual all-out war involving simulation to some degree. Technology has not yet produced a mechanism that can simulate the complex, end-to-end series of procedures associated with preparing and launching weapons, then assessing results. Likewise, the handling and use of live ammunition, and the danger, noise, shock, and visual effects associated with the impact of live ordnance, generate a physiological response that simulation cannot replicate. Because simulation falls short of producing an accurate portrayal of actual combat conditions, we cannot replace all live training with simulation.

The Navy and Marine Corps spent years attempting to find a suitable alternative site or one that might be made acceptable, without success. I personally visited more than a dozen sites in the U.S. and abroad in a fruitless search for a replacement.

At the time of the accident, I was the Commander of the U.S. Second Fleet, responsible for Navy operations in that area and the rest of the Atlantic Ocean. In the aftermath of the mishap, Marine Corps Lieutenant General Pete Pace, then the Commander of Marine Corps Forces Atlantic, and I were tasked by the Secretary of the Navy to conduct a study regarding the national security need for the AFWTF and specifically the training ranges on Vieques.

The result of that study was an endorsement of the value and need for these facilities, known as the Pace-Fallon Report. This detailed document became the centerpiece of a political brouhaha in Washington.[105] The saga of what the media dubbed the "Battle for Vieques" spans several years with plenty of material for a separate volume. Much of the controversy that evolved had little to do with the critically important training and readiness of our Armed Forces but much more about political, economic, environmental, and social issues in Puerto Rico, and was rife with unsubstantiated allegations against the Navy.

The Clinton Administration handed the unresolved Vieques issue off to the Bush Administration. This followed an agreement between President Clinton and Puerto Rican Governor Pedro Rossello in January 2000 to hold an unprecedented referendum in 2001 asking voters on Vieques whether the Navy should stay or go. I found myself in the challenging position of designated agent to advocate the Navy and Marine Corps' view of the vital need for AFWTF in the Department of Defense. As we will see, this task soon took on a life of its own. For his part, Rudy DeLeon remained as DEPSECDEF in the new administration until the Senate confirmation of Paul Wolfowitz to that position in March 2001.

WASHINGTON, POLITICS, AND IRAQ AS THE EPICENTER

I'll highlight two related events in the new administration's early weeks. First was another summons to Capitol Hill at the behest of the late Congressman Bob Stump of Arizona, a senior Republican who had recently assumed the House Armed Services Committee chair. The Chairman, who was long-serving, affable, and knowledgeable, knew that I was the DOD point person for the Vieques issue. After a bit of small talk, he delivered a disheartening message: "Admiral, I want you to know how strongly I support your position regarding the need for those training facilities, but you also need to know that I do not have the votes in the House to effect a legislative solution. Your only hope rests with the President. If he will support the Navy, then I think you will be successful, but if he does not, we will not be able to do anything about it up here on the Hill."

Second was a conversation about Vieques that I had with the new Bush National Security Advisor, Dr. Condoleezza Rice, in the White House, soon after she assumed that position. Condi wanted to know why we thought it was essential to maintain that facility's operation. I explained the value of the training ranges as the best and, in some ways, only suitable place to conduct essential training for the readiness of our forces. She intimated that there were strong political reasons for finding an alternative solution. I countered that we had exhausted every proposed substitute without finding a satisfactory site for the critically important training at AFWTF. I understood that she was unfamiliar with the details of the issue and was trying to get up to speed on it. Still, I left that meeting uneasy about the support we would get from the White House.

SECRETARY OF DEFENSE RUMSFELD AND DEPSECDEF WOLFOWITZ

Following the announcement of Donald Rumsfeld's nomination as the new Secretary of Defense, before the new administration's inauguration, I received an unexpected phone call from the former head of the Navy, the late Admiral Jim Holloway. The Admiral, whom I had met and highly respected but did not know well, had been the Chief of Naval Operations and the Acting Chairman of the Joint Chiefs of Staff during the 1970s. His formal name was James L. Holloway III, but we in the fleet, irreverent junior aviation officers at the time, assigned the moniker "Jimmy Triple Sticks" to our much-admired boss. (All aircraft in the fleet are assigned "side numbers," typically painted on the noses of the planes. Aircraft 111 in each air wing was known in aviation slang as triple sticks.) The Admiral invited me to lunch a few days hence at the Alibi Club, a small but exclusive bastion of the Washington leadership elite.

The event was delightful for me; attended by Admiral Holloway, Ambassador, and former Secretary of the Navy J. William Middendorf and several other distinguished persons who had the common attribute of serving in Washington during Donald Rumsfeld's first stint as Secretary of Defense.

Upon being seated at the circular table, Admiral Holloway pronounced, "Fox, here are the ROE (Rules of Engagement, a military term to describe what can be done – or not, in certain circumstances): we will talk, you listen!" He then laughingly explained that those present knew Secretary Rumsfeld well from their prior service with him and thought I might benefit from their experience. He began with the following overview: "Don Rumsfeld and his lovely wife Joyce are a social delight. In fact, Dabney and I look forward to having dinner with them this evening. But as a boss, he can be a real son-of-a-bitch." They then proceeded to share with me the professional and personality traits of Mr. Rumsfeld that they had observed in prior years.

In addition to being a genuinely kind gesture, this luncheon experience gave me a big leg up in my upcoming interactions with the new Secretary of Defense, who proved quite intimidating to many. I was able to share this information with my boss at the time, the head of the Navy, Chief of Naval Operations (CNO), Admiral Vern Clark, and together, we evolved a successful strategy for working with Donald Rumsfeld, with whom we both got along. In his interactions with the Secretary, Vern was persuasive, and his opinions were particularly appreciated.

We learned that Rumsfeld insisted on crisp, to-the-point, no "B.S." information in response to what turned out to be an avalanche of queries on a wide range of subjects. We surmised that we could easily be captured virtually every day in meetings with the SECDEF, so we planned to "tag team" one another and try to split attendance between us rather than CNO Clark attending each time. Our strategy worked, primarily because we delivered (most of the time) good information, well packaged and in a format that pleased the Secretary in response to what became a blizzard of "snowflakes," the moniker attached to his endless stream of questioning memos.

For some period after the Bush inauguration, Secretary Rumsfeld was the only senior confirmed official in the Department of Defense. He wasted no time getting to work, and I remember attending one of his first formal meetings with the Joint Chiefs.

Vern Clark was out of town, as he was for the follow-up discussion the next day. My recall from notes of that face-to-face meeting between the chiefs and the new boss was that it was "stiff" and "awkward." He asked that we get back to him the next day with a short synopsis of what was important to each service and the hard choices. How are they tracking? He then asked, "What shouldn't we be doing?" And commented, "Don't tin cup me without some things to shed!"[106]

The following day, we met with the Secretary in his large (pre-Pentagon reconstruction) conference room, and each service chief spoke in turn in response to the task assigned to him by the new boss. As the junior stand-in among the chiefs, I was fortunate to observe my colleagues and was the last to present, gaining valuable knowledge. The meeting evolved per the script that Admiral Holloway's team had predicted. It was not pretty. But having been forewarned, I prepared a short presentation of only a few viewgraphs in bulletized format, which was to the point and delivered eye-to-eye across the table directly to the Secretary. My post-meeting notes summarized "well received" and "we will be in for a rough ride."

Deputy Secretary Paul Wolfowitz was not confirmed by the Senate to his position until early March 2001 and, as such, could not directly participate in the department's business until then.

Soon after his arrival on the job, I received yet another summons. Mr. Wolfowitz introduced himself and immediately said that he had been informed I was the go-to person from the Navy on the subject of Vieques. He asked for a summary of prior events and mainly focused on the military requirements of the training for the Navy and Marine Corps. I highlighted for him the importance of coordinated land-sea-air live-fire training and the unparalleled scope of the air and sea space adjacent to the live-fire range. He shared that he was aware of the motivation of the prior administration to side with the political leadership in Puerto

Rico against the Navy and our position to preserve the facilities and training there in the face of widespread negative media coverage. He impressed me as reasonably knowledgeable and focused, and he ended our meeting with assurances that the department would stand behind our efforts to retain the facilities. I left his office with renewed confidence and a much more positive frame of mind than after my previous meetings with Congressman Stump and Condi Rice.

As the new Secretary, his deputy, and their growing team within the Office of the Secretary of Defense (OSD) got down to business, some key points regarding their priorities stood out and were reflected in my notes. First, the status quo was challenged on every issue. The previous administration had emphasized the Revolution in Military Affairs (RMA), a proposal for technological and organizational change in the U.S. military after the end of the Cold War and the Coalition's success against Saddam during the Gulf War.

These concepts were also proffered by the late Andy Marshall, longtime Pentagon guru and strategic thinker who was admired by Rumsfeld and with whom he had collaborated during the latter's first tour as Secretary of Defense (SECDEF) and key officials within OSD. The idea was that the structure of the Armed Forces may have been suitable for the Cold War, but that the current global geopolitical situation and the rapid advance of new technological innovations, particularly computers and space-based systems, required changes to the existing organization and procedures.[107]

Rumsfeld wanted a leaner, more agile, and technologically advanced U.S. military. His obsessive focus on RMA and its application to warfighting heavily influenced the subsequent planning for the invasion of Iraq in 2003, driving the troop requirement down to levels that proved insufficient for maintaining security after the invasion.[108] He probed into every detail of service priorities and expenditures. But I also noted less financial scrutiny over programs related to technology applications for little-known but highly classified intelligence and space-based initiatives. There was little discussion because of the restricted classification of these programs, as relatively few of us had access to review them. Meanwhile, many hours were consumed in lengthy debates about programs of significantly lesser cost.

WASHINGTON, POLITICS, AND IRAQ AS THE EPICENTER

One ritual during those early months was an incessant series of meetings, many with Rumsfeld and Wolfowitz in attendance, related to the Quadrennial Defense Review (QDR). This congressionally mandated report, first required in 1997, was due again in 2001. It would be the initial opportunity for the Bush Administration to publicly outline its defense strategy.[109] Despite the seemingly endless discussion, the final report reflected business-as-usual program inputs.

The Secretary intended this report to reflect their new initiatives. It was signed by Secretary Rumsfeld and released in late September 2001 with some hastily included comments reflecting the 9/11 attacks that had occurred only two weeks earlier. Weapons of mass destruction, called CBRNE (chemical, biological, radiological, nuclear, and high-yield explosives), were featured frequently and prominently among the challenges highlighted in the report.[110] In parallel were recurring questions about Iraq and what might be done to counter Saddam Hussein.

VIEQUES: THE RECURRING CHALLENGE

The issue of Vieques remained at the forefront of discussion. I decided to devote several pages here to what may seem like a digression from the subject of the book, because I learned important professional and personal lessons from the experience. Also, some aspects illustrate very well how things really work in Washington.

Little did I know that when Rudy DeLeon first handed the responsibility off to me, it would involve such an enormous amount of time during the entire first half of 2001. Reviewing my notes from then, I found nearly daily entries about meetings and discussions.

I will admit that I became emotionally as well as professionally involved. I often felt that I was getting little to no help from anyone above me in the chain of command, and there were times when I was tempted to just throw in the towel. But I knew how important coordinated live-fire weapons training was to the readiness of our Sailors, Marines, Soldiers, and Airmen. I also had a firm grasp of the details surrounding the Vieques issue.

Let me relate an event to illustrate when I allowed my emotions to overtake prudence and common sense. At one point in this long-running drama, Pete Pace and I were directed to appear before a congressional hearing chaired by Congressman Lee Hamilton of Indiana. As with many congressional hearings, this one was more theater than substance. A parade of witnesses vilified the Navy and Marine Corps for alleged injurious actions against the population on the island. Most of the testimonies were not only unsubstantiated but blatantly untrue. Following a long stream of allegations, the Chairman asked for my comments based on what was said in the hearing room. Succumbing to barely suffused anger, I unwisely offered the following, "Mr. Chairman, in my profession, we deal in facts, and I haven't heard many here today." Congressman Hamilton jumped to his feet, leaned over the hearing table, pointed a finger at me, and said, "Let me tell you something, Admiral. Around here, we deal in perceptions, and the perception is the Navy has not done a good job!" Seething and embarrassed, I bit my tongue and offered no retort.

In a nutshell, this protracted issue was a political football that neither the Clinton nor the Bush administrations chose to squarely confront, seeking to appease political interests while trying to avoid being seen as responsible for shutting down a facility needed for national security. Congressman Hamilton was correct that public perception, fueled by an overwhelmingly negative media bias, was against the Navy, and the latter was too passive in trying to counter it. A group of protesters on the island were emboldened by a diverse group of supporters, including Puerto Rican politicians and allies on the island and the U.S. mainland, compensated lobbyists, environmental advocates, entertainers, and activist clergy, each with different interests, but who championed their common objective, the departure of the Navy from Vieques.

Both principal U.S. political parties also had key members advocating against the Navy in support of parochial political interests. The stated requirements of the Navy and Marine Corps, detailed in the Pace-Fallon Report, were brushed aside with the admonition to find someplace else to train our forces.

One morning, several weeks after that initial meeting with Deputy Secretary Wolfowitz about Vieques, I was working in my office in the Pentagon when the CNO, Admiral Clark, walked in and asked what I had done to provoke Mr. Wolfowitz. I said, "Vern, I don't know what you're talking about." He explained that he had received a phone call demanding that I be fired immediately for insubordination.

Unbeknownst to me, a meeting took place in the White House earlier that day, June 13, 2001, which included Karl Rove, Steve Hadley, Paul Wolfowitz, and the newly confirmed Navy Secretary, Gordon England, to discuss how the Bush Administration could walk away from Vieques. The political background for this meeting was the recently expressed concern, directly to the White House, by Governor George Pataki of New York, who ran for reelection the following year and was confronted with a substantial Puerto Rican and anti-Vieques challenge.[111] Additionally, the President's brother, Jeb Bush, with whom I had worked and admired, was also running for reelection as governor of Florida the following year.[112] In this case, the concern was about the "Hispanic vote" in Florida. Curiously, the influential Hispanic vote in Florida was represented by a powerful bloc of voters with Cuban, not Puerto Rican, affinity. During the meeting, by sheer coincidence, Senator Jim Inhofe, Chairman of the Senate Armed Services Readiness Subcommittee, had placed a phone call insisting on speaking with Karl Rove, then Senior Political Advisor to President George W. Bush. Senator Inhofe evidently lambasted Rove and his political allies for not supporting the Navy and Marine Corps regarding Vieques.[113] After hanging up, Rove apparently asked the group how they thought Senator Inhofe found out about the meeting. Someone offered that it was probably Fallon, as he was responsible for defending Vieques within DOD and was known to have communicated with key leaders on Capitol Hill.

I was incensed upon hearing this and told Vern that I had no advance knowledge of the meeting, nor had I spoken with Senator Inhofe recently about the subject, although from prior meetings, I knew that he was a firm supporter of retaining Vieques and the AFWTF as a training venue. In our earlier meeting, I had previously relayed to Vern that Wolfowitz had offered his full support to retain Vieques. Infuriated, I told Vern that I was falsely accused, but if I was being fired, I was going to confront my accuser face-to-face. Ignoring Vern's advice to not challenge Wolfowitz, I then became insubordinate as I stormed down the hall to the latter's office.

Apparently tipped off to my "visit," I found Wolfowitz's door blocked by Brigadier General John Batiste, his senior military assistant. I walked up to him and said, "John, please get out of the way. I'm going to see the

Secretary." Brushing past him, I went in and confronted Wolfowitz about his accusations, and with the newfound knowledge about the White House meeting and its intent to walk away from Vieques, his about-face from the assurances he gave me in our earlier meeting. I can summarize the next several minutes as a heated and acrimonious exchange between two enraged participants. At some point, John Batiste came in to intervene, but I told him to "Get out!" After a mutual venting of wrath, Wolfowitz and I settled down to a more civil discussion. I denied any prior knowledge of his meeting and of recently speaking with Senator Inhofe or anyone else on the Hill. Still furious that he was not supporting the Navy on Vieques, I challenged him to explain how he justified reversing his position. He had no reasonable answer but said no final decision had been made. I soon learned that this was not the case.

In May 2001, the new Navy Secretary, Gordon England, had been confirmed and brought into the political discussion. Following my blowup with Wolfowitz, I was never included in any further high-level debate on the subject, although I was continually involved in the intra-Navy details about the range and potential training alternatives. Secretary England announced on June 14, 2001, that *HE* had decided for the Navy to cease training at Vieques and that he would ask Congress to cancel the ill-advised referendum established by the Clinton Administration.[114] The placebo offered by England in abandoning Vieques was the recurring admonition to look for alternative training sites.

For his part, President Bush, who was conveniently out of the country when the announcement was made, offered the following: "My attitude is that the Navy ought to find somewhere else to conduct these exercises...these are our friends and neighbors, and they don't want us there."[115] NIMBY (not in my backyard) was alive and well, even though the Navy had purchased the land on Vieques in the 1940s and the bombing range was ten miles from the nearest town on the island. Prior to the tragic mishap, no civilians had ever been injured in the conduct of training there, points missing from the public dialogue. Congressman Stump was prescient in his comment to me months earlier that if the President did not support us, we were finished.

I found it interesting that throughout the entire saga of Vieques, Secretary Rumsfeld remained completely out of the public and intra-DOD discussion, deferring this sticky political wicket entirely, stating in response to a media query on the steps of the Pentagon following the announcement by Gordon England, "The decision has been handled by Deputy Secretary Wolfowitz and the Secretary of the Navy, in whom I have great confidence. I think they are handling it very, very well."[116]

The Navy phased out all operations at Vieques and the AFWTF over the next year and a half and closed the Roosevelt Roads Naval Station on the main island of Puerto Rico opposite Vieques. Roosevelt Roads, the hub of activity for AFWTF, had operated since 1943, with an airfield and deep-water port among its key features. But in the wake of the Vieques closure, the Navy decided there was no need for the extensive facilities, which were turned over to the Puerto Rican government. During the ensuing 20 years, a series of proposals by inept and corrupt local officials have failed to take economic advantage of the former "crown jewel" facility of the Caribbean, which remains unmaintained and undeveloped. Recent Demographic information reveals a declining population on Vieques with an average household income of less than $16,000 per year and a poverty rate above 70%.[117]

Although personally painful for me, this long-running episode offered many lessons. Top of the list at the national level was the relative ease with which a unique and valuable national security resource was lost. Since then, years of searching for equivalent alternative facilities have come up empty, as predicted in the Pace-Fallon Report of 1999. The Navy and Marine Corps have patched together substitute training, but none of it has come close to replicating what was available at AFWTF. Some have argued that the closure was no big deal, that the Navy and Marine Corps still train and deploy forces. The latter part of that sentence is true, but the fact is that the Navy and Marine Corps have not since been involved in a high-intensity combined arms conflict, such as we see now in Ukraine, and which could occur again.

In the political sphere, I watched Presidents Clinton and Bush behave in a profoundly disappointing, similar fashion, talking about the importance of readiness in our Armed Forces but rationalizing decisions to give primacy to political interests and future elections. Likewise, their responsible executive political appointees in both the Department of Defense and the White House, with a better understanding of the military issues, nonetheless subordinated the national interests to the political desires of their bosses.

In hindsight, the Navy and Marine Corps could have taken steps in the past that might have helped enable a different outcome. The first point is an internal issue that I suspect is common in other organizations, particularly government entities. In the Navy, the operational units, in this case, those that use the training facilities, assume that these support activities will be available when needed. The fleets traditionally have little interest in the business side that sustains them, not to mention the surrounding social and economic issues that festered in Vieques.

In fact, the Navy intermittently addressed long-term economic problems and community unrest on the island for decades. The chief instigators of the protests in 1999 were local fishermen who wanted access to the waters around the eastern one-third of the island, which were prohibited because of their proximity to the weapons range. The background was that they had cleaned out the other inshore waters around the rest of the island of most fish species.

During prior decades, the Navy, on several occasions, had convinced Congress to appropriate funds for alternative economic activities on the island, none of which proved sustainable but helped the local economy in the near term.[118] This issue happened again in 1998 when I, the Second Fleet Commander, personally visited the island and saw the disquiet. I went to my boss at the time, the four-star Atlantic Fleet Commander, and opined that we, the Navy, needed to inject some money into the island's economy. Given how poor the people were, I did not think it would take much, a million or two at most, but something to provide a little economic activity. The Admiral rejected my idea, saying, "The Navy doesn't do that!" I thought he was being shortsighted and mentioned that the Navy had been involved in economic activities on the island several times previously. He dismissed further discussion of the topic and told me it was not my business. However, this exchange highlighted the disconnect between various entities in the Navy and, as events would prove, was a missed opportunity.

My number one takeaway from this episode was the importance of information and communication in every aspect of what we do. In this case, disparate groups around the country, with little knowledge or interest in the facts, seized on this issue and made it a cause célèbre, framing it as a David versus Goliath scenario. The Navy and the government, writ large, were slow to respond either out of ignorance about the magnitude of the potential loss of the range or concern about appearances in challenging the outrageous falsehoods spawned by the protesters and their supporters. To this point, in his handoff of the issue to me, Rudy DeLeon suggested that I get some strategic communication help for the Navy, recommending John Rendon, an experienced and well-known public relations expert in Washington.[119] John offered to go down to Vieques and size up the situation for himself, which he generously did at his own expense. He reported back that it would be challenging but winnable if we focused on helping the people on the island economically in the near term and countering the slanders with an aggressive PR program. Unfortunately, there was no desire in the Pentagon to take this issue head-on for the reasons previously cited.

In summary, the lesson in dealing with complex issues was that it is not enough to understand the details, but an aggressive and comprehensive information plan of action is required to inform and influence those charged with important decisions. Even now, two decades after the events in Puerto Rico, false information abounds on the Internet and in books on the subject. Regrettably, despite the ballyhoo of the great "victory" over the Navy, there has been no substantive improvement in the lives of people on the island since the closure of the facilities and the departure of the Navy. As no alternative replacement training for the coordinated live-fire experience of Vieques has been identified, the Navy pulled together a patchwork of the next-best but inadequate exercises, which continue to this day.

CHAPTER 14

MOVING TOWARD WAR IN IRAQ: 2003

Following the 9/11 attacks and even before the retaliation campaign in Afghanistan had run its course, the nascent Global War on Terror (GWOT) began to trend in a new but familiar direction. Iraq was increasingly the subject du jour, with the tempo of discussion and planning increasing throughout 2002. At this time, I was still the Vice Chief of Naval Operations in the Pentagon. How this evolved into the 2003 attack on Iraq is a complex story.

For background understanding, contingency plans for military operations exist in many of the Combatant Commander (COCOM) classified file cabinets. Given the history of trouble and conflict with Saddam Hussein, CENTCOM had just such a plan for a potential attack on Iraq that had been prepared several years earlier when Marine General Tony Zinni was the Commander. It called for a large invasion force of about 380,000 troops.[120]

Just two weeks after the 9/11 attack, on September 26, 2001, President George W. Bush summoned Secretary Rumsfeld and told him to investigate military plans regarding Iraq.[121] Army General Tommy Franks, then CENTCOM Commander and responsible military official, took this direction with disquiet, particularly as he had just been tasked to plan for immediate combat operations against Al Qaeda in Afghanistan. In response to this Iraq tasking, on 28 December 2001, at the Bush ranch in Crawford, Texas, General Franks presented to President Bush, and by video teleconference, to a small group of his top national security advisers, a "commanders' concept" for invasion of Iraq to effect regime change and secure WMD." According to Tom Franks, President Bush concluded the meeting by expressing the hope that war would not be necessary, but then stated, "We cannot allow weapons of mass destruction to fall into the hands of terrorists. I will not allow that to happen."[122]

My observation of events during 2002 was to perceive a duality at work. Two lines of activity operated in parallel in the Pentagon and within the Bush Administration. First was what I would describe as business as usual, in which we went about the processes, meetings, deliberations, and decision-making on a wide range of subjects and issues typically faced in the Department of Defense, including ongoing actions involving Iraq. Recall that we still enforced the no-fly zones over northern and southern Iraq.

But the second undertaking involved the potential of going to war with Iraq. This muted conversation was sometimes overlaid on the first in the normal course of meetings and discussions, but often conducted in more subtle, smaller assemblies. An example of this duality occurred on June 21, 2002, at a Pentagon meeting of the JROC (Joint Requirements Oversight Council- the Vice Chiefs of the services' periodic meetings to discuss DOD acquisition issues) with Secretary Rumsfeld.

Frustrated with what he perceived to be the lack of sound JROC output, conflicting requirements, and questionable metrics, he demonstrated his impatience by asking, "Is there any conceivable way that the JROC could transform to address some of the challenges facing the Department (of Defense)?" But a few minutes later, he segued into a monologue about the undesirability of having to do a reserve personnel call-up (mobilization) before a major military action, as would likely be required for a move into Iraq.[123]

The push to expand the GWOT into an attack on Iraq came from several quarters. First, individuals who shared a common conviction, namely that Iraq, in the personification of Saddam Hussein, was the source of most evil in the Middle East and posed an existential threat to the United States, because of an assumption that he still possessed weapons of mass destruction (WMD). This premise, of course, was later demonstrably disproven.

Second, within the Bush Administration, leading advocates for regime change in Iraq resided within the Department of Defense and at the White House in the Office of the Vice President. The key motivation for this agenda was the firmly held conviction that Saddam was behind or connected to the 9/11 attacks and other recent terrorist activities originating from the Middle East. The already well-documented evidence that Osama bin Laden and Al Qaeda were the real perpetrators of these attacks was discounted by the anti-Iraq lobby, which relentlessly sought linkages back to Saddam from the intelligence community.

DECISIONS, DISCORD & DIPLOMACY

A key recommendation of the National Commission on Terrorist Attacks Upon the United States, better known as the 9/11 Commission, was the creation of a single Director of National Intelligence (DNI) to coordinate the many intelligence entities within the United States.[124] In the wake of intelligence failures that contributed to the 9/11 disaster, the commission determined that the country would be better off with single-point leadership to oversee national intelligence centers and manage the national intelligence program.

Unfortunately, this report was not issued until 2004, with the recommendations implemented the following year. So, the march to war in 2002/03 was fueled by multiple intelligence inputs from different agencies. Under George Tenet's direction, the CIA had the dominant input. Still, even within the Agency, there were many voices with different opinions, particularly on the key issues of whether Saddam retained WMD and potential connections to Al Qaeda. Tenet oversaw the critical erroneous intelligence briefings to Secretary Powell and later admitted to the latter that he had been mistaken.[125]

Also, the shock in the U.S. resulting from 9/11 and the fear that it could happen again amplified concern in the White House. Exactly when President Bush became convinced of the alleged culpability of Saddam and the need for regime change is debatable. A detailed and fascinating description of pivotal individuals and their actions behind the scenes leading up to the invasion of Iraq is contained in journalist Robert Draper's extensively researched and well-documented 2020 book, *"To Start a War: How the Bush Administration Took America Into Iraq."*[126] I can attest to its extraordinary accuracy because of my close observation and involvement in these events.

Deliberation continued to intensify through the year to the point that by mid-summer, I concluded there was a very high likelihood, almost certainty, of a U.S.-led invasion occurring imminently. Consistent feedback from the White House was that no decision had been made. Although this may have been true, I thought this narrative was primarily intended to quell speculation and allow necessary preparations to be completed. Journalist Bob Woodward authored four books about President Bush and the Iraq War. In his final book, Bob recounted that "...General Tommy Franks gave the President a dozen detailed briefings on the invasion plan. Every meeting was about *how* to go to war. There was no meeting to discuss *whether* to go to war. The President had never questioned its rightness, and its rightness made it the only course."[127]

During this period and running in parallel with customary activity, inside the Office of the Secretary of Defense for Policy (OUSD(P)) in the Pentagon was a quiet but vigorous information gathering and analysis effort orchestrated by Wolfowitz and Doug Feith, the DOD Undersecretary for Policy. Wolfowitz had been focused on Iraq for years with an intensity that bordered on fanaticism, believing that Saddam Hussein was an evil force, arch-nemesis of the United States, supporter of terrorism, and should be the number one target for regime change.[128] "Wolfie," as he was irreverently known around the Pentagon, was a true believer in most conspiracy theories involving purported evils by Saddam. He took every opportunity to highlight these ideas to President Bush and senior administration officials. The intelligence community did not share Wolfowitz's zeal in attributing international terrorism, and particularly the 9/11 attacks, to Saddam and consistently pushed back against his theories.[129]

Frustrated with what they considered to be intelligence community foot-dragging on Iraq, Wolfowitz, and Feith, with encouragement from a cohort of like-minded anti-Iraq enthusiasts including John Hannah and Scooter Libby in Vice President Cheney's office, Richard Perle, then chair of the Defense Policy Board, Elliott Abrams, security advisor and later deputy at the National Security Council, Danielle Pletka of the American Enterprise Institute, a conservative think-tank, and others, set up their own separate information processing center in the Pentagon.

Key leaders in this office, run by Abram "Abe" Shulsky, longtime Washington conservative policy advisor and former college roommate of Paul Wolfowitz, were Deputy Assistant Undersecretary of Defense for the Near East, retired Navy Captain William Luti, and David Wurmser, a former Navy reserve intelligence officer. With high-level security clearances and access to similarly classified intelligence information, these three and a few colleagues created their own mini-intelligence analysis center, dubbed the Office of Special Plans (OSP) within Feith's policy office.[130] A common attribute of these people was their background as "policy wonks" with little to no experience outside of academia. The exception was Bill Luti, who earned a PhD in International Relations from Tufts. He was a long-serving, broadly experienced naval officer who did not fit the mold of the others, except for his shared view about Saddam and related conspiracies. I was surprised to learn that he was working in the OSP office.

I knew Bill Luti from his time in the fleet, most notably when he was the commanding officer of *USS GUAM* in 1998, and also his brother Bob Luti, one of my A-6 squadron pilots when I was commanding officer (CO) of VA-65 during the early 1980s. I was impressed with Bill's leadership and performance as CO in *USS GUAM*, which at the time was the oldest, most heavily used, and soon-to-be-retired ship of its type in the fleet. Bill had done a terrific job as CO in challenging circumstances. Before he retired from the Navy in 2001, Bill Luti worked for Vice President Cheney and, earlier in his Navy career, had been assigned as a Navy fellow on the staff of House Speaker Newt Gingrich, so he was well known in Republican political circles.

I began to be concerned when I got wind of briefing papers and presentations in which they were cherry-picking information that fit their view of Iraq and the problem posed by Saddam Hussein. Although he was now retired from the Navy and did not work for me, serving as a politically appointed DASD (Deputy Assistant Secretary of Defense for policy), I requested that Bill meet with me and asked him what he was about. His benign-sounding reply that he was just doing what the Secretary requested struck me as unconvincing and deepened my suspicion. I opined that what he was doing, randomly selecting or discarding information to suit their agenda, was inappropriate and potentially detrimental to DOD and the nation. When we parted company, I did not expect his behavior to change. In fact, it was another example of an agenda at work; this one focused on regime change in Iraq. Bill Luti's OSP gang was basically "cooking the books" to document an alternative view of information and events to justify going to war. But other factors were also at play.

The poster child of the anti-Iraq crowd was Dr. Ahmed Chalabi, an Iraqi ex-pat whose family had fled the country following the 1968 Ba'ath Party coup and takeover that was partially engineered by Saddam. Chalabi was educated in the U.S. at MIT and the University of Chicago, highly intelligent, and an incessant advocate for regime change in Iraq. He was cultured, unusually persuasive, and wealthy from a prior business venture running the Petra Bank in Jordan (after which he was convicted in absentia of fraud).[131] He was of dubious character and integrity, seemingly one step ahead of the law. Still, he nonetheless captured the imagination of the American anti-Saddam advocates, particularly Paul Wolfowitz.

As self-styled head of the Iraqi National Congress (INC), Chalabi was on the payroll of the U.S. Government for years in the role of informant and anti-Saddam activist until dumped by Washington for fraudulently representing his Iraqi role and suspected duplicitous collaboration with Iran.[132] He portrayed himself as the leader of Iraqi exiles who could provide an alternative political leadership in Baghdad once Saddam was removed.

His talent for persuasion was highlighted by persistent advocacy and success behind the scenes on Capitol Hill with congressional passage of the Iraq Liberation Act of 1998 (ILA). Of note, this legislation was drafted by Stephen Rademaker, then a congressional staffer and husband of Danielle Pletka, both of whom would continue to play important behind-the-scenes anti-Saddam advocacy roles. The legislation, signed by Bill Clinton, "Declares that it should be the policy of the United States to seek to remove the Saddam Hussein regime from power in Iraq and to replace it with a democratic government."[133]

This legislation and the impact it would have in supporting the pretext for the invasion of Iraq is another good example of how seemingly unrelated or loosely connected events influence the course of decision-making and policy in Washington. For background, during the autumn of 1998, Saddam, unsuccessful in gaining release from U.N. sanctions, initiated several provocations, resulting in escalated U.S. military actions and added impetus for the ILA. This irritation from Iraq fueled increased suspicion about potential WMD at a time when U.S. policymakers were distracted by the Clinton-Lewinsky political scandal. As the Clinton impeachment hearing in the House of Representatives was nearing a verdict in December 1998, Clinton authorized a long-anticipated four-day bombing campaign in Iraq called OPERATION DESERT FOX, using the ILA as partial justification. The Clinton Administration announced that the strikes were aimed at degrading Iraqi WMD capabilities, which, in hindsight, we know were destroyed well before that time. Nonetheless, the airstrikes were successful in seriously degrading Saddam's air defense capability, and enforcement of the no-fly zones continued. Suspicions regarding Iraqi behavior intensified, and the U.N. inspection process faltered. Charles Duelfer, the deputy head of the United Nations Special Commission (UNSCOM), later said that any progress in Iraq was "done in by the Lewinsky affair."[134]

The ILA Bill authorized the President to provide Iraqi democratic opposition organizations (including, by name, the INC) with wide-ranging assistance and authorized fiscal appropriations. It directed the President to designate one or more organizations that met specified criteria to be eligible to receive financial aid of up to $97 million from congressionally appropriated funds. Thus, armed with potentially substantial resources from the U.S. treasury and bipartisan legislative backing from Congress, Chalabi could wield considerable influence to further his anti-regime agenda.

I only met Chalabi on one occasion, and although impressive in demeanor and language, I was distrustful based on his reputation as a schemer and his self-serving agenda. This opinion was reinforced later by a close colleague within DOD, Mary Beth Long, an Assistant Secretary of Defense, who, years earlier in a civilian capacity, had worked for him at the Petra International Bank in Washington and considered him a fraud.[135] Chalabi was a strong advocate for two proposals that I thought were ridiculously unlikely to succeed, but which he pushed and were warmly received by the anti-Saddam lobby.

First, he advertised that he would put together a group of Iraqi ex-pats, the so-called Free Iraqi Forces (FIF), to be armed and trained by the U.S., and that would then lead the military assault on Baghdad to depose Saddam. The idea that this group of mostly middle-aged men, the majority of whom had not lived in Iraq for years and had no prior military experience, was going to be the vanguard of an invasion was ludicrous.

Second, the idea that invading U.S. forces, a foreign occupying army with him in the van, would be warmly welcomed by the population of Iraq, many of whom certainly feared Saddam but almost all dependent on his socialist state for their well-being, seemed highly unlikely. We discovered that the "welcome" afforded the attacking American forces was decidedly unfriendly.

Chalabi was intimately involved in many aspects of the run-up to the war in 2003, including the dissemination of information about supposed WMD in Iraq by later discredited informants. He went into Iraq soon after the invasion and joined the Iraq Interim Governing Council, overseen by Paul Bremer's Coalition Provisional Authority (CPA). He later served in several ministerial positions in the Iraqi government but left incomplete work and a cloud of suspicion behind him in every endeavor in which he engaged.[136]

Another significant factor in the march to war was two successive United Nations Weapons Inspection teams established by U.N. Security Council resolutions following the 1991 Gulf War. Intended to verify the elimination of Saddam's WMD programs, first UNSCOM operated from 1991 to 1998, headed by Swedish Ambassador Rolf Ekeus and his deputy, American Charles Duelfer. Succeeded by the United Nations Monitoring Verification and Inspection Commission (UNMOVIC) 1999-2003, led by another Swedish diplomat, Dr. Hans Blix, were stymied in their work by the Iraqis and some UN member countries that authorized their establishment, including the U.S. Eventually, having found no operative WMD, UNSCOM and UNMOVIC concluded that Iraq had, in fact, destroyed the vast majority of its WMD, although admitting that Iraq did not fully comply with all the obligations required by the U.N. resolutions. Before being withdrawn just before the start of the invasion in 2003, both Iraqi and Bush Administration leaders disparaged Blix and his Commission.[137] Saddam wanted ambiguity about WMD to deter potential attacks, and the Bush Administration had decided to disbelieve the evidence.

As 2002 progressed, Rumsfeld and Franks went back and forth numerous times in discussions about a potential attack on Iraq, the latter becoming increasingly frustrated with SECDEF's direction to reduce the size of the attacking force and the incessant barrage of questions from Doug Feith and the DOD policy gang. Franks was also disappointed at the policy divisiveness among the political appointees, particularly the Deputy Secretaries of Defense and State, observing, "On far too many occasions, the Washington bureaucracy fought like cats in a sack."[138]

Planning at CENTCOM increased in intensity, and on June 3, I attended a "Tank" (conference room where Joint Chiefs meetings take place) session with Franks as he discussed some detailed options for war in Iraq. My notes revealed, "Tommy doesn't want to be seen pushing this plan to go to war." I also knew that he had already briefed the President at least twice and that an executable OPLAN (operations plan) was taking shape. My notes highlighted the unanswered question, "What is the *casus belli*?"[139] Indeed, other sources report that Bush received a dozen detailed briefings on the invasion plan from General Franks in the months leading up to the war.

Over the next several months, I received unexpected hospitality from Paul Wolfowitz. Despite our blowup over Vieques the previous year, we maintained a proper relationship in the day-to-day activities in the Pentagon. Mindful of his unrelenting advocacy for regime change in Iraq, I was surprised to receive an invitation to join him alone for dinner one evening at a Chinese restaurant in downtown Washington. He picked me up in his armored SUV, and we enjoyed a pleasant meal in a back corner of the restaurant with a security guard as a buffer from other diners. The discussion quickly turned to Iraq as the Secretary worked to persuade me of the evils of Saddam and the need for regime change. Curious why I was singled out for this special lobbying effort, I surmised that he knew I was skeptical of the agenda he was promoting and that I was not shy about expressing my opinions. I recall agreeing with him that Saddam was a real problem, but I was unconvinced about the need to invade. This one-on-one dinner engagement was reprised several months later at a different restaurant. I wondered, but never confirmed, whether others may have received similar DEPSECDEF attention.

The 2002 National Security Strategy (NSS), issued on 20 September 2002, revealed a new emphasis on preemption that was first articulated by President Bush in a June 2002 speech at West Point. In the new document, preemption, defined as the anticipatory use of force in the face of an imminent attack, was expanded to include preventive war. The strategy envisioned the potential of using force without evidence of an imminent attack, "… taking anticipatory action to defend ourselves even if uncertainty remains as of the time and place of the enemy's attack."[140]

At another "Tank" session with Secretary Rumsfeld on August 7, shortly before the release of the new NSS, it was clear that Iraq planning had proceeded into a comprehensive OPLAN, but that a *casus belli* for potential war in Iraq had not yet been established. The discussion focused on the merits of preemptive self-defense versus going to the U.N. for justification.

I offered an unsolicited proposal to the Secretary, opining that I saw a quick military arrival in Baghdad but that the real problems would be in the post-hostilities phase of the operation (phase IV in military speak). I further offered that this would require a significant "whole of government" effort involving other nonmilitary entities. If he were interested, I would happily help lead such an effort in Washington. The response was immediate and sharp, "No, that's not your business. That's State's (Department of State) problem."[141] In retrospect, this was the biggest issue with the operation, confirming Colin Powell's Pottery Barn warning to President Bush, "If you break it, you own it."[142] Interestingly, Rumsfeld later insisted that the DOD be in charge of the entire operation, including phase IV. Actual planning for this part of the invasion began very late. It was only a fraction of the effort that went into the actual attack on Iraq.[143]

The critical issue of the number of troops required for the invasion was shaped by two different views of how the operation might unfold. On the one hand, the size of the force eventually employed was heavily influenced by Secretary Rumsfeld, who favored a smaller force in a fast operation to get in and get out of Iraq quickly, as his abrupt dismissal of my suggestion on the post-hostilities phase demonstrated. The counter view was that substantial forces would be required to maintain stability until the country became self-governing again. Chief of Staff of the Army General Eric (Ric) Shinseki was publicly berated by Rumsfeld and Wolfowitz for suggesting that several hundred thousand troops would be required for the post-hostility phase in Iraq in response to a question at a congressional hearing in February 2003. I observed in several meetings that Ric had already been taking flak for what Rumsfeld considered going too slowly in transforming the Army from the traditional division-centric organization to the leaner, faster Brigade Combat Team (BCT) concept, which was successfully employed later in Iraq.[144]

As the likelihood of invasion ramped up, the focus of the regime change advocates was on the threat of WMD. Extensive efforts were underway to pinpoint if, what, and where through intelligence sources. The business of intelligence is gathering information and then, through analysis, attempting to determine the veracity of the information and how, if ever, the myriad pieces fit together into a coherent story. Recall my involvement seven years earlier in Jordan with the defection of Saddam's family members. The son-in-law, Hussein Kamal al-Majid, former head of the organization overseeing Iraqi weapons programs, admitted to UNSCOM and the intelligence agencies that although the Iraqi WMD programs were maintained for some time after the 1991 Gulf War, they were subsequently halted and materials destroyed. Nonetheless, in 2002, the pressure was on to document existing WMD in Iraq, and the focus zeroed in on biological weapons (bio).

In 1999, an Iraqi émigré had surfaced in Germany offering information in exchange for asylum. He claimed to have been an engineer at a plant that designed mobile biological laboratories in Iraq. German intelligence passed the information to the U.S. agencies, which were initially excited about this revelation. However, the German BND (German Intelligence) agents became suspicious when trying to corroborate his story. Eventually, they decided he was lying, had fabricated the tale, and dropped the defector (strangely but accurately code-named "Curveball") as a source in September 2001. However, the story this source concocted, even though debunked and later proven untrue, was too good to pass up for those looking for reasons to invade Iraq. Uncorroborated reports circulated in U.S. intelligence and policy circles, citing the "Curveball" story.[145]

In September 2002, in another "Tank" session with Secretary Rumsfeld, it appeared that the searchers for a "smoking gun" had struck gold, in fact, a trifecta! An intelligence briefer described an alleged nexus of activity near Khurmal, Iraq, at which alleged indicators of Al Qaeda, Iranian, and Iraqi representatives were in the presence of a bio-weapons facility, possibly the mysterious mobile trailers described by the infamous "Curveball." If this report were accurate, seemingly all the evil actors were linked.

A discussion ensued about what this all meant and what we might do about it. I suggested that a SOF (special forces) team be inserted with detection devices to ascertain what biological material was there, so we might have proof. Rumsfeld quickly dismissed my proposal as far too risky for the people involved. I later mused that six months after this, it was not too dangerous to send more than 200,000 troops into Iraq![146] The possibility was then offered to launch a Tomahawk Land Attack Missile (TLAM) strike at the site, followed by the collection of air samples either by human or mechanical means. That idea was also rejected. After the invasion of Iraq, it was discovered that the mobile "bio laboratories" were, in fact, mobile helium facilities for weather balloons.[147]

Moving Toward War In Iraq: 2003

I departed that meeting, dejected at being rebuffed but also with the feeling that the march to invasion was well underway and unlikely to change course. My rationale for offering these suggestions was that up until this time, the "evidence" advanced to support both the Saddam-Al Qaeda connection and the allegations of WMD, of which I was aware, was circumstantial and not convincing. This supposed nexus of bad actors seemed an unexpected opportunity to potentially confirm the assertions. At some point during this time, I recall having a conversation with Vern Clark in which we asked one another whether we really believed that the information being put forward added up to the conclusions the OSD Policy briefers assumed. We were both unsure. But at another meeting in the Tank on September 28, 2002, the Secretary stated that the department needed to shift to a war footing and that the services should submit their reserve mobilization requests to him within two weeks.[148]

With armed conflict increasingly likely, we had much to do inside the U.S. Navy to prepare the fleet for combat. The two key issues were overall readiness and, as a subset, the need for an increased inventory of PGMs (precision-guided munitions). For background, throughout the 1990s, following the end of the Cold War, the naval force structure was steadily reduced from the high-water mark of the late 1980s. The exodus of people, ships, and aircraft from the active fleet was helpful in the near term, as we could choose to retain the best people and the highest quality equipment. But readiness has three critical components: people, material assets, and proper training. Our immediate challenge was ensuring the people were trained, and the material assets were positioned for ready access.

The second issue of precision-guided munitions surfaced in the mid-1990s as the fleet transitioned from reliance on unguided ordnance to weapons matched to the new technology targeting and delivery systems, particularly in recently introduced aircraft. The illuminating event for me in this regard was the short conflict in the Balkans in 1995, in which the precision air-to-ground munitions employed by CVW-8 was precisely opposite the percentage when I commanded the air wing during DESERT STORM four years earlier. A key factor in this change was the proliferation of newer aircraft with infrared and laser aiming devices and new "buddy bombing" tactics in which F-14 Tomcats and F/A-18 Hornets coordinated weapons delivery and guidance. In Bosnia,

DECISIONS, DISCORD & DIPLOMACY

94% of the ordnance was precision-guided compared with only 6% during DESERT STORM.[149] These newer munitions, although more accurate and thus fewer required, were more expensive, and we were starting from very low inventory levels. Much effort was directed to successfully addressing both issues, and by the time the conflict began in early 2003, the Navy was at unprecedented high levels of readiness, and weapon inventories were adequate and growing.

In November 2002, I was preparing for a Thanksgiving visit with our forward-deployed forces in the Middle East. My son Bill was assigned to an F-14 Tomcat fighter-bomber squadron onboard *USS ABRAHAM LINCOLN*, then in the Arabian Gulf. His aircraft carrier and Battle Group ships were scheduled to return to their home ports before Christmas. But as Vern Clark and I discussed the matter, it seemed prudent to advise the leadership in the Gulf that their deployment would be extended as a conflict in Iraq seemed probable, in which case carrier-based air support would be crucial.

Following several stops visiting sailors at shore facilities in the region, I flew aboard *LINCOLN*, flagship for the afloat forces in the Gulf, arriving on Thanksgiving Eve. I was in familiar surroundings and happy to reconnect with my son and Rear Admiral John Kelly, the commander of the afloat forces, and my former Chief of Staff, when I commanded U.S. Second Fleet.

Following an address to many of the crew and air wing personnel in the hangar bay of the carrier, John and I sat down alone to discuss the readiness of his Battle Group. He was pleased with his high readiness and morale assessment, which I concurred with based on my observations of the last several days. I then told him in strict confidence our view from Washington that we appeared to be on course for war. Given our trust in the high state of readiness of his forces, we wanted them to remain on station in the Gulf and expected they would play a leading role if we went to war. Thus, he needed to understand they were unlikely to return home on time and should assume they would be in combat sometime soon. John was genuinely surprised and asked when I thought the war would begin. Replying that officially, and as we were still hearing from the White House, no decision had been made, but I estimated within a couple of months.

MOVING TOWARD WAR IN IRAQ: 2003

Following a discussion about operational details and support, I told John to assume they would remain in the region until the invasion began or it was decided not to carry it out. Given the extension of their deployment, I asked him if I could help facilitate a preferential port visit. Without hesitation, he replied, "How about Perth, Australia?" A visit to that port, coveted by fleet sailors, involved a transit across the Indian Ocean and back again and would require concurrence from the operational chain of command and the Australian government. As it turned out, both agreed, and the crew of *LINCOLN* and its air wing enjoyed warm Australian hospitality over the Christmas holidays. Departing to begin what was assumed to be a transit back to her homeport in San Diego, the ship reversed course and returned to Fremantle, the port of Perth, in early January for two weeks of maintenance and last-hour training ashore before returning to the Gulf for the commencement of hostilities.

As 2002 wound down, General Franks began to submit his requests for forces to be moved into the theatre. Although in advance of an announced decision to go to war, the force flow into the Middle East began the slow but steady buildup necessary to prepare for the invasion.[150] Many political activities, including Secretary of State Colin Powell's infamous speech to the U.N. Security Council laying out the U.S. case at the behest of President Bush, were yet to occur, but events were moving inexorably toward war. According to my notes from the debrief of a cabinet meeting at the White House on 13 December 2002, a key point of the purpose of that meeting was to reinvigorate efforts to focus on the coming war.[151]

CHAPTER 15
THE 2003 INVASION OF IRAQ: WHY IT HAPPENED

In mid-March 2003, the "shock and awe" invasion of Iraq and march to Baghdad began. Advocates for the attack celebrated the rapid military advance of Coalition forces and the fall of Saddam's regime in only three weeks. The euphoria faded quickly, however, as trouble began almost immediately, with a slow realization that this war would drag on for many years.

The run-up to the invasion illuminated many processes, behaviors, political pressures, and other factors that occur in the determination and execution of national security policy. In this case:

- Saddam Hussein's murderous domestic policies and belligerent attacks against his neighbors, including the use of chemical weapons of mass annihilation, had inflamed world opinion and firmly established his position as a pariah. His well-documented past attempts to acquire nuclear and biological weapons also generated intense suspicion and fear and an ardent desire to be rid of him.
- An influential and well-connected coterie of political policy advisors in the U.S. with a long-standing animus toward Saddam was convinced of the need to change the regime in Baghdad and gained ascendancy in the Administration of George W. Bush. This vocal lobby for ousting Saddam pointed to and echoed the 1998 Iraq Liberation Act, overwhelmingly passed by Congress during the Clinton Administration.
- The devastating attacks of 9/11/2001 traumatized the population of the United States to its core and motivated President Bush to undertake strong initiatives to prevent a recurrence. Concern about the terrorist threat spawned enhanced domestic security measures and an aggressive preemptive national security strategy. The President was mindful of the post-Cold War "sole superpower" status and unrivaled military capabilities of the U.S. and saw himself as a bulwark of democracy against threatening authoritarian regimes

and wanted to export democracy, his "freedom agenda" to other nations, including Iraq.[152]

- Long-standing no-fly zone military containment measures implemented following the Gulf War were expensive, resource-intensive, and perceived to be ineffective in altering Iraqi behavior, as were extensive U.N.-agreed economic sanctions.
- Osama bin Laden, perpetrator of the 9/11 attacks, had gone missing, but his Al Qaeda organization was still active and threatening. A widespread but unsubstantiated assumption of collaboration between Al Qaeda and Saddam was deep-seated among some Bush Administration policy advisors and generated widespread anxiety.

Intelligence information, as always, was often inconclusive and contradictory. Agencies and their patrons competed for the ear of policymakers. Skepticism and firmly held beliefs among some advisors resulted in alternative analysis and "alternative facts." At the end of the day, the President accepted what turned out to be faulty intelligence and used it to buttress his strongly held opinion. I found it ironic a couple of years later, in February 2005, as I met with Secretary Rumsfeld in his office before going out to assume command of USPACOM, when he sternly warned me not to believe half of what I heard from the intelligence community. Indeed, he stated, "They are often wrong."[153]

Disparate agendas were pushed by extra-governmental actors like Ahmed Chalabi, who sought to reestablish his personal and familial position of influence in Iraq but needed a U.S. invasion to facilitate his ambitions. Competing policy advisors often fought among themselves but pressurized the decision-making environment.

Two successive U.N. weapons inspection teams attempting to verify the elimination of WMD in Iraq were abused by conflicting political agendas, yet had concluded and reported that no WMD remained before the invasion. The Bush Administration declined to endorse their findings. Later, when the U.S. military was unable to find any WMD following the 2003 invasion, yet another inspection team, titled the Iraq Survey Group (ISG), was tasked with the search. After a futile hunt, the ISG, led by Charles Duelfer, previously the deputy head of UNSCOM, confirmed to President Bush that no WMD were found.[154]

General Franks, the military commander responsible for the Middle East, did what he was asked to do: draw up and then execute a plan for the invasion of Iraq. The Joint Chiefs of Staff were charged with offering our best military advice to the Secretary of Defense and the President. They were skeptical of the rationale but went along with the plan when asked by the Secretary. The problem with this is that, however well-structured the plan might have been, not enough thought was applied to the long-term strategic implications of this preemptive attack on Iraq.

For his part, the unworldly Saddam Hussein, addicted to power and obsessed with insecurity, brought about his own demise by trying to be too clever. Although eventually destroying his WMD stocks, he nonetheless continued to attempt to deter Iranian and U.S. adversaries by public equivocation, evasive responses to the U.N. weapons inspectors, and signals that he might still possess these weapons. His doublespeak was interpreted by the Bush Administration as proof that he still retained those weapons.

President George W. Bush took responsibility for the invasion, and rightly so, as he memorably characterized himself as the "Decider." The combination of factors listed above, seized with his "freedom agenda" and his own determination to be seen as strong in the face of political and security challenges (with Saddam's failed attempt to assassinate his father, former President George H.W. Bush, as a possible added incentive), motivated his decision.

A recently published memoir by longtime Swedish diplomat and former head of UNSCOM, Ambassador Rolf Ekeus, adds further intrigue to the decision to invade Iraq. As recorded in his book "Iraq Disarmed," Ambassador Ekeus recounts an event in January 1998 at a dinner held at the U.S. Supreme Court building to which he had been invited by the late Justice Sandra Day O'Connor. Ostensibly a social event at which he was asked to play piano, he "…realized that the event had a far different purpose than music."[155]

In attendance were former President George H.W. Bush, sons George W. and Jeb, and their spouses, and several other prominent members of the former Bush Administration. This event occurred shortly before George W. Bush announced his presidential candidacy. Following dinner, Bush Sr. called Rolf aside and, in the presence of his son, George W., asked for the ambassador's assessment of Iraq's destruction of WMD and Saddam's intentions. Recounting, "George W. seemed interested in the latter, but was clearly displeased when I said that UNSCOM had been successful and Iraq no longer held banned weapons of mass destruction,"[156] Ambassador Ekeus related that Bush Sr. noted his sons' increasingly skeptical demeanor, pulled at his arm, and said, "now listen to what Rolf says, the U.N. has removed all prohibited weapons."[157] Ambassador Ekeus related that the son grew less interested in the conversation, even though former National Security Advisor Brent Scowcroft joined and supported the account of the removal of the WMD. This anecdote reinforces the idea that President George W. Bush had long considered removing Saddam from power in Iraq.

Saddam was indeed deposed, but almost every assumption made before the invasion was incorrect. Implications and fallout from this decision still reverberate around the world.

Recently, former longtime (2006-11) Iraqi ambassador to the U.S., Samir Sumaidaie, opined that George W. Bush's attempt to create a U.S. democratic model in the Middle East in its image turned out "as far as you can imagine from that objective." The result, he said, "was catastrophe."[158]

CHAPTER 16

LEARNING THE ROPES: PREPARING FOR USCENTCOM

Still serving as Pacific Commander, I returned to Washington in mid-January, got up to speed on current events in Central Command, and prepared for congressional confirmation hearings. Although there were still many balls in the air at Pacific Command, I knew I needed to get ready for CENTCOM quickly, as the administration sought my Senate confirmation hearing as soon as possible. Soliciting views on Iraq from all sides, I asked for assessments from each intelligence agency (CIA, NSA, DIA, etc.) because they had fields of specialization and analysts with unique areas of expertise. I invited people around Washington with diverse experiences and opposing views to share their opinions. Searching for perspective, I also read everything available.

One thing that quickly became apparent was the intensifying partisan political divide within the U.S. over the Iraq War, which was, with rare exception, straight down the aisle between Republicans and Democrats. I sensed that I would have to be very careful in dealing with the Hill, partly because both sides, in their most extreme views, were pushing agendas that I thought were guaranteed to be detrimental to the country. On the Democrat side, the objective was to end the war immediately and just get out of Iraq; some Republican members wanted to "win," whatever the cost. Both sides seemed oblivious to the long-term danger to American interests in pursuing either of those avenues. At the subsequent Senate hearing, from the questions I was asked, it was obvious that the inquisitors wanted to put me in a box of being either for or against the newly announced "surge" and, by extension, the war.

My preparation "to-do" list was lengthy. Still, with limited time, I had to prioritize topics and the number of people I could see. An immediate advantage was having previously established personal relationships with most senior U.S. military personnel and leaders in the intelligence agencies. Another edge was a small group of mentors, advisors, and savvy individuals across the personal and professional spectrum, in whom I had high trust and confidence to provide candid and accurate assessments of key individuals and situations. Many years ago, I learned how difficult it was to receive honest appraisals, particularly about other people, but how valuable such assessments were.

General John Abizaid, my predecessor and, at that time, the serving USCENTCOM Commander, was generous in quickly arranging a team of staff officers who provided me with briefings about the current situation and key activities at CENTCOM. I found the orientation helpful but troubling in that it revealed several issues contributing to, rather than ameliorating, the overall challenging situation in the Middle East. My immediate reaction was that most of the effort at CENTCOM was focused on Iraq, but generally rubberstamping whatever the U.S. commanders requested. It seemed that Afghanistan was a secondary area of interest, but the briefings revealed some troubling issues of which I was unaware, many having to do with NATO nations' reluctance to allow proper employment of their troops and related chain-of-command matters.

The third major item was a revelation of the considerable extent to which the staff was engaged in planning for potential military conflict with Iran. This was perplexing given that we were already at war in both Iraq and Afghanistan, and the extensive Iran contingency planning was dilutive and diverting attention from the existing conflicts. I was aware of frustration in Washington about Iran's bad behavior in the region and specific malign activities inside Iraq, chiefly in providing lethal projectiles to Shia militia groups for use against Coalition forces. Actions to counter Iranian influence were collectively known as "Contain, Protect, Deter" (CPD),[159] but extensive contingency planning was also underway.

My overall appraisal of the situation was of somewhat unfocused activity across a broad spectrum of operations with too many "priorities." For instance, the mission statement alone included ten tasks far greater than could reasonably be pursued as priorities.

General Colin Powell was invaluable in providing a detailed appraisal of the personality traits, agendas, and modus operandi of key George W. Bush Administration members. His extensive experience in Washington and as the most recent Secretary of State in that administration was invaluable. Likewise, crucial was the keen insight of several of my diplomatic colleagues in the Pacific, particularly ambassadors Frank Ricciardone, Kristie Kenney, Chris Hill, and Frances

Cook, in assessing major international issues as well as key individuals in the Department of State.

Among the very first people with whom I met was Secretary of State Condoleezza Rice [Condi]. We had known one another for several years, first when she was the National Security Advisor to President Bush, and later after becoming Secretary of State. There were also many interactions involving matters in the Asia-Pacific during my time as Pacific Commander.

Condi hosted me at a lengthy one-on-one meeting in her office, during which she shared key points about activities and her leadership team in the countries of the USCENTCOM area of responsibility. She emphasized the importance of making progress in Iraq as the number one priority of the Bush Administration and offered her experienced assessment about a host of other issues in the region. I was grateful to receive her extensive analysis. Still, I was surprised by one of her recommendations in response to a comment I made about the unhelpful contribution of Iraq's neighbors. She advised avoiding discussion of Iran or Syria with President Bush.

I was pleased to learn of an initiative led by retired USAF General Joe Ralston with our NATO ally, Turkey, regarding the problematic issue of the Kurds and their periodic hostile cross-border activities. Kurdish behavior in the multinational area (Turkey, Syria, Iraq, and Iran) of the region in which they lived was often problematic. An ongoing Kurdish insurgency inside Turkey had the latter threatening a retaliatory incursion into Iraq, which was being used as a safe haven by the insurgents. Such a move would have been sure to anger the Baghdad government and add to the woes there. Learning that the U.S. had taken a diplomatic initiative to address the problem was encouraging.

Regarding Turkey, let me illustrate the constant political churn in Washington and an example of how seemingly small, unrelated events often impact other policies and endeavors. About this same time, the new Speaker of the House of Representatives, Nancy Pelosi, with a significant Armenian heritage population in her congressional district, had introduced and was energetically pushing a symbolic congressional resolution to affirm as genocide the 1915 massacre of Armenians by Ottoman Turks. The Turks admitted many Armenians were killed during that period a century earlier, but objected to the term "genocide."

Learning The Ropes: Preparing For USCENTCOM

They were furious at this initiative and threatened countermeasures that might directly undermine U.S. operations in Iraq, then highly dependent on extensive logistical support through Turkey. Speaker Pelosi's controversial resolution continued to swirl in Washington for the next six months, contributing unnecessary friction to bilateral relations at a sensitive time, eventually being neutered by a lack of political support in the House during my tenure at CENTCOM.[160]

Meanwhile, Iran and Syria were directly contributing to the bloodshed in Iraq by actively supporting destructive insurgent operations. I recalled Condi's advice to not mention either of these countries in the presence of President Bush. But Syria was facilitating ready access for terrorists, serving as a waystation for Sunni Al Qaeda volunteer fighters from around the world seeking to infiltrate Anbar province in western Iraq, following well-established "rat lines" into Ramadi, Fallujah, and Baghdad. For their part, the Iranians were arming and training the Shia militias, specifically with explosively formed penetrator projectiles (EFP), lethal weapons used against American armored vehicles. Both countries were enabling and encouraging the sectarian Shia-Sunni violence then ravaging Iraq.

When I asked why I should avoid Iran and Syria, she said the President had a negative opinion of both governments and their activities, and that I would be asking for trouble by raising the subject with him. Nonplussed, I queried her about what seemed an obvious need to address the behavior of both entities, given their activities and negative influence on the situation in Iraq. She advised focusing on military activities in Iraq and that my "meddling" beyond the borders of Iraq would not be seen as helpful. I opined that, as the regional commander with responsibilities beyond just Iraq and Afghanistan, I was certain that improving the situation in Iraq would eventually involve the other two countries. She cautioned me again about bringing up the subject with Bush.

Some months later, I chose to disregard this advice, as I considered the issue too important to ignore. Even then, I was never given permission by the White House to engage with the Syrian military, nor were my comments about Iran viewed favorably in Washington. In hindsight, engagement with the senior Syrian military leadership might have led to a different outcome than the situation during the past decade and a half of civil war and ISIS chaos in Syria.

Further preparing for my CENTCOM duties and following discussion with several key interagency leaders, including Deputy Secretary of the Treasury Bob Kimmitt, Deputy Secretary of State Richard Armitage, the late Dr. Tony Cordesman, the well-regarded security analyst from the Center for Strategic and International Studies (CSIS), National Security Advisor Stephen Hadley and others, I concluded that a novel approach in Washington might help our efforts in Iraq.

Contacting Steve Hadley at the White House, I offered the following background and proposal. Given that little time was left on the political clock to achieve a turnaround in Iraq, the best chance of success would be a concerted, all-hands effort across the spectrum of military, political, economic, and information activities. The just-announced "surge" in military forces could be complemented by a "surge" in these other areas of national capability.

Based on my initial discussions with the aforementioned leaders and others, it was clear that U.S. government departments other than DOD were struggling to provide the focus, particularly the people, to complement the military resources being dedicated to the effort in Iraq. For example, the Provincial Reconstruction Teams (PRT), which were comprised of military and civilian experts established across the provinces throughout Iraq (and Afghanistan) to augment stability and security, were having difficulty making progress. The foremost problem was the lack of civilian personnel with the requisite qualifications to staff these teams. Ideally, people with expertise in a wide range of political, economic, and engineering skill sets would be identified in the U.S. and sent to join these teams to advise and help the Iraqi people recover, reconstruct governance, and create infrastructure in their provinces.

Yet the U.S. was not mobilized on a national emergency war footing, such as during World War II, and the government departments were not identifying and providing the desired civilian expertise. In the initial PRTs, personnel shortfalls were filled by military people, but many lacked the required expertise. Back in Washington, there was ample finger-pointing but little progress in providing the necessary people.

My proposal to Hadley was to establish a civilian "czar," Special Assistant to the President, reporting through the National Security Advisor but with direct access to the President at the cabinet level, to

LEARNING THE ROPES: PREPARING FOR USCENTCOM

coordinate interagency support for the war effort and empowered to direct compliance. Hadley's initial reaction was one of surprise but interest, as he certainly understood the need, and he said he would get back to me after he thought about it. Although I wanted to characterize the position as overarching and powerful, I later regretted my choice of the word "czar." The exigency was real; however, the term carried many negative connotations. Yet the tag had been affixed.

Several days later, we reconnected to discuss the proposal. Hadley asked me if I knew who might be a good fit for this assignment. I suggested retired USMC General Jack Sheehan as a person who was deeply knowledgeable and experienced in the ways of Washington, in addition to his extensive military and interagency expertise. Importantly, Jack was a no-nonsense, straight-shooting leader who got results. He replied that he did not know him and would like to check with his connections and then get back to me.

I had already taken the initiative to contact General Sheehan and asked him if he would consider doing this. Protesting that he was busy and suggesting there were others better suited, he eventually agreed to be considered after I had twisted his arm with the rationale that, having already signed up for what was probably a "no-win" situation myself, I needed all the help I could get. He was, in my view, the ideal candidate.

Steve Hadley got back to me the next day, commenting, "Wow, this guy has quite a reputation and a strong personality." I replied, "That's exactly what we need." I suggested that Steve speak with him and get a firsthand impression. Several days later, after bugging him about moving forward on this issue, Steve called me to say that he had spoken with General Sheehan, whom he found "impressive," but that he might be "too strong" a personality, given the sensitivities of the Washington bureaucracy. I replied that we needed a strong, bureaucratically fearless leader to get the required action. He said he would get back to me, but nothing happened for weeks while the White House dithered. Initially willing to be considered for the position, General Sheehan grew tired of being kept in limbo. He eventually vented his frustration publicly, writing an op-ed published by the Washington Post entitled "Why I Declined To Serve."[161]

This revelation embarrassed the administration, particularly as General Sheehan took the opportunity to blast the Bush

Administration's Iraq policy, stating in part, "There is no agreed-upon strategic view of the Iraq problem or the region." Probably because of this, the administration shortly thereafter announced the nomination of Army Lieutenant General Doug Lute as an assistant to the President and Deputy National Security Advisor to coordinate interagency affairs supporting war efforts in Iraq and Afghanistan. I lamented to Steve that I knew Doug Lute as a good guy from his service on the Joint Chiefs of Staff as the J3 (Operations), but that he would not have the clout to get the results we needed.

Although Doug went on to other senior positions, including Permanent Representative (Ambassador) to NATO, his appointment to the NSC as the "War Czar" (as characterized by the New York Times)[162] achieved no appreciable results during my time at CENTCOM. He was too junior, still an actively serving military member, and frankly, not tough or experienced enough to overcome the resistance of the entrenched Washington bureaucrats.

An upshot of my aggressive attempts to facilitate desired actions in Washington was a call from Defense Secretary Gates to stop engaging directly with Hadley at the White House. This was a pointed first warning that the administration was sensitive about and did not appreciate activity by me outside of the "military lane." As Pacific Commander, I was used to engaging with and coordinating activities throughout the U.S. government, usually informing my boss (Secretary Rumsfeld) after the fact unless I sensed it was a sensitive issue. Given the intense focus on Iraq by the administration, it was forewarned that my every action would be closely scrutinized.

An early meeting was held with then-Lieutenant-General Dave Petraeus, which was a first for both of us. We discussed the situation in Iraq as we understood it. Dave briefed me on the work that he had recently done at Fort Leavenworth regarding counterinsurgency doctrine in conjunction with Lieutenant Generals Jim Mattis and Jim Amos of the Marine Corps that resulted in a document known as the U.S. Army/U.S. Marine Corps Counterinsurgency Field Manual (FM 3-24)[163]. We agreed that a change in tactics in Iraq was necessary. It seemed to me that the surge would provide additional manpower. But Dave and his team in Baghdad would have to decide how best to employ them along with the other troops already in Iraq. I understood that he planned to implement his newly refined counterinsurgency tactics and

LEARNING THE ROPES: PREPARING FOR USCENTCOM

concurred with this approach, although I noted the added dimension of sectarian strife in Iraq differed from textbook insurgencies.

I admit I was puzzled by the fact that the Army and Marine Corps had to seemingly reinvent counterinsurgency doctrine, given that these types of operations were a significant component of past U.S. military activity, particularly in Vietnam and other places in the world, and not that long ago.

My experience in the Navy was planning and training for a wide range of military endeavors, even though they might not be the most likely military missions required. The facts were that many types of warfare expertise had been needed at different times and probably would come up again sometime in the future. Prudence dictated a good understanding and at least occasional training in these areas. However, in the face of what evolved into an insurgency in Iraq during the past three years, our ground forces had seemingly forgotten all about how to do this type of activity. That was inexcusable, but good that Dave Petraeus and Jim Mattis spearheaded efforts to revive this competency.

Assuming a successful confirmation by the Senate, it appeared that Dave would relieve General George Casey in Baghdad in about a month, mid-February 2007. I was likely to be about a month behind him, not being able to leave PACOM and take over at CENTCOM until mid-March, so he would have the advantage of being in place to begin his employment plans well before we could discuss them together, given the sensitivity of Senate confirmation. I understood that until confirmed, I could not engage in any activity or discussion within CENTCOM, particularly about current or contemplated operations. Still, I was eager to see what Dave would recommend once he was in command.

In our first meeting, he impressed me as quite self-assured and reserved, but he did not share much about his thinking and intentions. He seemed a little wary of me, possibly given my Navy background or his prior Army-centric service. He did not solicit my opinions about our upcoming work, which was an unexpected and puzzling fact, particularly as he would report to me as his immediate superior and the high-stakes endeavor we were about to undertake. His penchant for not involving me in his thought processes or planning would continue in our new responsibilities unless he wanted something.

DECISIONS, DISCORD & DIPLOMACY

In hindsight, I was remiss in not appreciating the relevance of several factors in play during this timeframe. Already previously aware of the close relationship between Dave and retired General Jack Keane and alerted by Secretary Gates that the President had selected Dave as ground commander in Iraq before I was even approached about command of Central Command, I should have assumed the possibility of an alternate communication link that bypassed me.

Another factor was the reality that ongoing responsibilities at Pacific Command and preparation for the short-notice turnover of that command to Admiral Tim Keating precluded time for any serious study of Iraq operational matters. As events unfolded, Dave Petraeus arrived in Iraq in early February. He immediately engaged in discussion and planning of tactics and operations. In fact, with the arrival of the first surge brigade, the next subordinate operational commander in Iraq, Lieutenant General Ray Odierno (also in communication with Jack Keane), had already initiated the redeployment of forces in and around Baghdad to secure neighborhoods and the population.[164] Thus, the two senior ground commanders in Iraq were on the same page in the tactical employment of forces, engaged in intimate dialogue regarding ongoing and future activities, and the employment of the surge brigades.

I was entirely out of this loop until I arrived in Baghdad in late March 2007, assuming, incorrectly as things turned out, that I would be involved in the decision-making. That train had left the station, and I found it challenging to insert myself into the already underway Iraq planning and execution process. After I assumed command, Dave's staff quickly perceived my numerous and detailed questions as objecting to their unfolding new force employment scheme, mainly when I wanted to see and understand the rationale for the countless additional troop requests forwarded to my headquarters from Petraeus's staff.[165] We started poorly.

Nonetheless, my pre-confirmation search for knowledge, good ideas, and perspective spanned the spectrum of opinions. I occasionally received unexpected input, some good, some less so. In the first category, a meeting with former Senator and Secretary of Defense Bill Cohen was beneficial in expanding my horizons beyond Iraq and Afghanistan. Secretary Cohen shared his knowledge and experience about other countries in the region, mainly in the Gulf area, providing great insight regarding their priorities, concerns, and capabilities.

Learning The Ropes: Preparing For USCENTCOM

I would also highlight my observation that the late Dr. Tony Cordesman of CSIS provided consistently accurate and valuable analysis and recommendations about the situation and events in Iraq and Afghanistan. For example, his assessment of the situation in early 2007, in which we were fighting for time for political and economic progress in Iraq, was absolutely correct. I often recall his good advice about military action: "Beware of tactical victories at the cost of long-term stability."[166] Even now, almost two decades later, as I worked on this manuscript, Tony provided an insightful analysis of the Russian invasion of Ukraine up until his recent untimely death.

Another useful discussion was with Ambassador Dawn Liberi, my former classmate at the National Defense University, about 15 years earlier. Dawn had an extensive and successful career with the United States Agency for International Development (USAID). Particularly noteworthy was her prior assignment as the USAID Mission Director in Iraq, responsible for the country's multibillion-dollar economic development program in 2005–2006. Not only was she familiar with a vast amount of current detail about Iraq, but her big-picture understanding of the many nonmilitary aspects of governance and the economy caused me to significantly broaden my thinking about what might be possible in Iraq and Afghanistan. Later that year, I was able to "borrow" her from USAID as a special advisor at CENTCOM to help in Afghanistan.

An interesting discussion occurred when I followed some advice to solicit the views of one W. Patrick "Pat" Lang. Clearly a contrarian, Lang was a retired Army intelligence officer with counterinsurgency experience in Vietnam and, more recently, a commentator on Middle Eastern affairs. He impressed me as someone who held himself in high regard, but somewhat peevish and prickly. He was critical of current military activities in Iraq and of the Bush Administration's Middle East policies in general. Despite the negatives, some of his information and suggestions validated the recommendation to meet with him. First, his detailed description of the various armed militias in Iraq, their leaders, and their objectives was the most comprehensive I had heard to date. Second, he reinforced my idea about establishing a relationship with Syria. He opined that the Syrians were frustrated at the lack of communication with Americans, particularly Syria's military leaders, who wanted to engage us in discussion about the future. Pat was also eager to discuss Iran and the potential for U.S. military action there.

I distinctly recall downplaying that idea, pointing out that two ongoing "hot" wars in Iraq and Afghanistan gave us more than enough challenge. Later, he falsely alleged that I told him that "there would be no attack on Iran on my watch," a statement that I never made but was attributed to me through Ray McGovern in a blog discussion of Bush Administration Iran policy.[167] This is an example of the ongoing background chatter in the D.C. blogosphere, of questionable veracity but attention-getting, nonetheless.

CHAPTER 17

SENATE ARMED SERVICES COMMITTEE CONFIRMATION

My confirmation hearing before the Senate Armed Services Committee occurred on 30 January 2007 in Washington. It followed Dave Petraeus's hearing before the same body by a week. His questioning allowed me to get an advanced peek at the thinking of the various senators on the committee, as I expected much the same line of questioning. Dave was confirmed several days later and cleared to head off to Baghdad.

A little background on confirmation hearings. The process by which senior political appointees and military officers are confirmed follows strict adherence to law and protocol. Individuals are nominated by the White House in the name of the President to be considered for high-level positions requiring Senate confirmation in accordance with the Constitution. For senior military officers, the services prepare a lengthy background document on the individual, his or her biography, and service history. A list of questions from the Senate requiring mandatory answers, mainly regarding financial and potential conflicts of interest, must be submitted concurrently. Additionally, another list of questions prepared by the senators regarding the specific nomination and the details about the possible area of upcoming service must be answered with particular attention, as they often contain policy and other sensitive political issues. The committee must receive these documents in writing at least a day in advance so that the committee members and their staff can review them and prepare questions to be asked orally during the hearing.

I was familiar and experienced with congressional hearings of one type or another, having served in senior positions for many years and being called to testify about different matters. Confirmation hearings often receive special scrutiny by the committee because of controversial or particularly sensitive nominations. One needs to be careful not to assume confirmation either by comment or actions, including any contact or activity in the assignment for which nominated.

After the hearing, the committee will vote on whether to forward the nomination to the full Senate for confirmation. Unless the nomination is contentious, the process will typically be completed in several weeks. However, in some situations, occasionally unrelated to the individual appearing for confirmation, individual senators may put a "hold" on the nomination until the political or other procedural issues are resolved. Although rare, there are instances in which the nomination is never put forth for confirmation by the full Senate.

Although one can never be certain, I did not anticipate serious issues with my confirmation in part because the recent years of my service seemed to be favorably viewed by senators from both parties. Additionally, I was acquainted with most committee members from previous testimony or meetings with them in Washington or elsewhere.

Prior experience and common sense suggested pre-hearing courtesy calls on the committee Chairman, Senator Carl Levin, and ranking minority member, Senator John McCain, and a few other key members from both parties out of deference and to get a sense of what was on their minds.

Preparation for the hearing included studying key topics, briefings by the CENTCOM staff regarding current activity, and drafting answers to the specific questions the committee members had submitted to me. I preferred to provide a summary of the priority issues and my views about them "for the record," along with written answers to the questions posed by the committee. Rather than read this lengthy text during the hearing, I offered a short opening statement. I requested that my written testimony also be accepted for the record, being personally put off when anyone sat in front of me reading text previously handed to me, and which I had received or could read myself, preferring knowledgeable but unscripted responses as more useful and persuasive.

The background for this hearing was complex. The U.S. had been at war in Iraq for four years and in Afghanistan for five and a half years. As already mentioned, the U.S. population was polarized along political lines, with the Democrats wanting "out" of Iraq and the Republicans wanting to "win" (or at least not withdraw, perceived as an acknowledgment of failure). Three weeks earlier, in a nationally televised address to the nation, President Bush announced the "New Way Forward,"[168] which he characterized as a new strategy for Iraq. Key elements of this "surge" plan were an increased U.S. force of five combat brigades (about 20,000 troops), soon followed by three-month tour extensions for the troops already in Iraq. Additionally, he planned their renewed emphasis on Iraqi security force participation and eventual ownership of security in Baghdad and the provinces, plus increased focus on economic recovery and Iraqi governance. The response to the announced change was predictably positive or negative down the political fault line.

It was noteworthy that before the President's decision, he considered two assessments with different recommendations. First, the Iraq Study Group Report, titled "The Way Forward-A New Approach,"[169] a study mandated by Congress earlier in 2006, was a bipartisan effort that included many well-known figures on the panel. There was something for everyone in the final report, which included a whopping 79 policy recommendations. It considered three courses of action in the near term but did not specify which should be pursued. In essence, the options discussed were (1) pulling the troops out, (2) continuing as is, and (3) increasing troop strength. But the panel did not recommend the last option, having been told by Army leaders with whom they consulted that it would not be feasible due to an already overstretched military. Furthermore, the panel assumed that U.S. forces would be withdrawn by 2008.

A second report, undertaken on its own initiative by the American Enterprise Institute (AEI), was entitled "Choosing Victory: A Plan for Success in Iraq."[170] The effort was spearheaded by Dr. Frederick Kagan and retired General Jack Keane, who strongly favored a troop increase. This latter report from the AEI was the course chosen by the President. But the two reports were used to buttress each side of the political divide, liberally (and selectively) quoted before the hearing.

It was obvious to me that my number one task as Commander CENTCOM would be to facilitate the success of the new plan announced by President Bush. I struggled, probably more than I should have, mentally defining the new "strategy." In my view, President Bush announced not a strategy but a redoubled commitment to succeed in Iraq by providing additional forces (the surge).[171]

My assessment was that this new force allocation was not likely to change the situation on the ground unless operationally and tactically employed differently. At the start of 2007, and for much of the prior two years, our forces had been working out of Forward Operating Bases

(FOBs), from which they conduct raids and clearing operations, then withdraw back to the FOB. I knew that Dave Petraeus wanted to change that construct, as did I, and employ ideas from his newly released Army/Marine Corps Counterinsurgency Field Manual. Dave and his subordinate commanders had to figure out how this would be implemented once he got to Baghdad. I did not know at the time of the hearing, nor did I expect to learn much detail until Dave and his generals decided on an operational employment plan.

As mentioned, this new employment of troops operating from combat outposts (COP) inside the neighborhoods under the direction of Generals Odierno and Petraeus was well underway when I arrived at CENTCOM. In hindsight, the tactical redeployment of forces achieved security in Baghdad. But my absence from the initial discussion established a precedent that I found almost impossible to overcome as time went on.

We should be mindful of the human dimension of war. I want to relate an event from the day before my confirmation hearing. Traveling to San Antonio, Texas, for the dedication of a unique facility at Brooke Army Medical Center called the *Center for the Intrepid*,[172] I was joined by JCS Chairman General Pete Pace and Senate Armed Services Committee members Senators John McCain and Hillary Clinton. The establishment of this installation adjacent to the Brooke Army Hospital is a heartwarming story illustrative of some exemplary Americans' patriotism and philanthropic endeavors.

The project was initiated with the late Zachary Fisher, co-founder of Fisher Brothers (a New York construction and real estate firm), who, during his lifetime, responded to military members in need. Zach and his late wife, Elizabeth, established the Fisher House Foundation to build temporary residence facilities at military hospitals worldwide where families can stay free of charge while a loved one is in the hospital. More than 90 of these temporary lodging "Fisher Houses" have been constructed and are operated by the foundation. After Zach and Elizabeth passed away, Zach's nephew, the late Arnold Fisher, and the latter's son, Ken, assumed the foundation's leadership.

Appalled by the growing number of severely wounded service personnel from the wars in Iraq and Afghanistan, many with life-altering burns and injuries requiring limb amputations, Arnold Fisher

SENATE ARMED SERVICES COMMITTEE CONFIRMATION

decided to act. He spearheaded the construction and creation of the *Center for the Intrepid*, financing the entire $50 million structure with private donations through the Intrepid Fallen Heroes Fund. Their vision was to build a state-of-the-art rehabilitation facility to treat military amputees and burn victims.

At the dedication ceremony, Arnold Fisher proudly emphasized that the entire undertaking was completed by his volunteers in record time without any government or public assistance. As he famously quipped, "We don't want government money. I can build these things in half the time at half the cost and twice the quality as the government."[173]

The Intrepid Fallen Heroes Fund followed this achievement with another massive private philanthropic effort to build the *National Intrepid Center of Excellence*, a peerless facility to treat military service members suffering from traumatic brain injuries adjacent to Walter Reed National Military Medical Center on the Navy medical campus at Bethesda, Maryland.

This emotional dedication ceremony, with many wounded service members in attendance, certainly focused my attention on war and the inevitable casualties that would result on my watch. I resolved on the spot to do whatever it would take to get the job done responsibly and as quickly as possible.

The confirmation hearing itself unfolded without surprise after some initial disruption caused by the "pink ladies," a group of anti-war protesters, formally named Code Pink, which had become a fixture at congressional hearings and other events around Washington concerning anything to do with the wars. I found it interesting that, in the course of comment and questioning by the senators, almost all the issues I would have to eventually address were mentioned in one way or another.[174] This demonstrated that the senior leaders knew the necessary big-picture decisions and actions. Although they had divergent opinions on what to do. Much of the attention was focused on Iraq, with some interest, particularly from Senator McCain, on Afghanistan. A few comments and questions involved Iran, but little mention was made of the other two countries in the CENTCOM area of responsibility. Recurrent comments from the Democrat members highlighted quotes from other congressional testimony that there was "no military solution" and only a "political solution" could resolve the conflict. Although not commenting on those specific statements during the hearing, I was acutely aware that there could not be a political solution, which I fully supported, unless the military put an end to the chaos being experienced in Iraq.

The employment of additional forces using counterinsurgency tactics, sometimes dubbed "Clear, Hold, and Build,"[175] was intended to provide security and facilitate a political solution by Iraqi leaders. I winced at the repeated emphasis on required complementary interagency support to the military effort, knowing that I had failed in my initial attempt to convince the White House of the urgent need to pressure the bureaucracy in this regard. We needed that Czar!

Another criticism that struck true was reference to equipment shortfalls and inadequate protection against deadly IEDs and EFPs, which were taking a heavy toll on our troops. In that regard, I thought about a farewell review I had attended in Alaska a few months earlier to send off the fourth brigade of the 25th Infantry Division to Iraq. This unit was composed of paratroopers, lightly armed, and headed for a part of Iraq that was particularly dangerous and where they would be vulnerable to these lethal weapons.

An issue raised by several senators was the subject of "benchmarks" applied to both Iraq and Afghanistan. The Bush Administration, with much prodding from Congress, had established a series of measures intended to demonstrate progress in a host of areas, military, political, and economic, by the respective governments in Baghdad and Kabul. In the minds of Congress, the benchmarks would become the standard measure of the success or failure of the administration's new "Policy." It became a liberally applied cudgel during the rest of the year that kept me busy as internal political issues in both countries repeatedly delayed achievement of these benchmarks, which were front and center at every subsequent congressional hearing.

The gist of my testimony was: "What we have been doing in Iraq has not been working, and we need to change." Left unsaid was precisely how we intended to do this, for which I needed proposals from General Petraeus once he got on station.

During the hearing, Senator McCain characterized the situation in Iraq as "dire" and further stated that the surge was "the last opportunity to salvage Iraq." I concurred with his opinion and was eager to initiate a plan of action to effect security and stability in that country. Immediately following the hearing, I flew back to Honolulu to resume my duties as Commander of Pacific Command, not expecting any drama. But I was in for a surprise.

Entering the office the next morning, my executive assistant, Navy Captain (later 4-star Admiral and Commander U.S. Southern Command) Craig Faller, said that Senator McCain was on the phone and wanted to speak to me. Puzzled, I picked up the receiver and was blasted with a torrent of angry and generally unprintable words expressing unhappiness with the previous day's hearing. As he had not directed any particularly irritating comments to me during the hearing, I was perplexed but recalled that he had left shortly after offering his remarks and a couple of questions.

Absorbing this tirade for a minute or so, I understood the thrust of his irritation, an opinion that I was not forceful enough to support the President's surge initiative. He then added his dissatisfaction that I did not specifically outline a plan of action for Iraq. Concluding with the comment, "If I had known you would have acted this way, I would never have supported your nomination," he abruptly hung up the phone. Unsettled, I was handed a one-page letter faxed to me from Senator Lindsey Graham containing more of the same disgruntlement. I put two and two together and concluded that Senator Graham, a close political ally of Senator McCain, although not expressing any notable irritation toward me at the hearing, was behind the double-barreled rhetorical blasts. I told Craig Faller to arrange an airplane to go back to Washington immediately (a ten-hour trip) and to call Senator McCain's office, informing his EA that I would like to see the senator first thing in the morning. When informed that McCain would not be available the next morning, I told Craig to tell him that I was coming back anyway and I would wait at his office until he could see me.

John McCain and I had a long history going back to the time when he was a prisoner of war in North Vietnam. In the last year of his captivity, 1972-73, I was the Navy liaison to his first wife, Carol, and his family, then living in Orange Park, Florida, a few miles from my home at the time. During the late 1970s, we were both back in Navy aviation squadrons and crossed paths occasionally. In the late 1980s, Doug McCain, Carol's son, whom John adopted as a young boy, was a naval aviator and A-6 pilot in a squadron at Naval Air Station Oceana in

DECISIONS, DISCORD & DIPLOMACY

Virginia Beach, Virginia, working under my command. Doug was a good pilot, eventually leaving the Navy to fly with commercial airlines. John, then a senator, and I communicated during this time. Finally, during my time at Pacific Command, we lived in the Pearl Harbor quarters that had been occupied by John's mother, Roberta, while he was a POW, a fact that he reminded me of several times with the admonition to make sure the quarters were kept in good shape.

Arriving back in Washington the next morning, I went over to John's Senate office, and the two of us had an animated private conversation of the type sometimes seen in naval aviation. My key point, which he eventually conceded, was that I was not about to opine to the Committee exactly what was planned in Iraq until (if) I got the job, talked with Petraeus in Baghdad, and had a cohesive operational plan. I could not endorse the President's "new strategy" for Iraq until we figured out what that really was. The dispute settled; we parted on good terms. My nomination to USCENTCOM was confirmed by the Senate a week later on a voice vote with no dissent.

The tension in Washington, exemplified by this episode with John McCain, would, unfortunately, be all too typical of my time in CENTCOM. I sometimes thought this "rear-guard" action was more challenging than the two wars.

CHAPTER 18
COMMANDER USCENTCOM 2007-08

My assumption of command of USCENTCOM occurred on March 16, 2007, at MacDill Air Force Base in Tampa, Florida, when I relieved General John Abizaid with Defense Secretary Bob Gates presiding. With no time to spare, I immediately got to work familiarizing myself with the staff and functions at MacDill headquarters. I was fortunate to inherit several highly competent senior staff officers already serving at CENTCOM. In particular, the Deputy Commander, Vice Admiral Dave Nichols, with whom I had worked several times previously. I knew that I would not be able to retain him for long, as we were both in the Navy, which would break a long-standing precedent against officers of the same service in the top two positions. Army Major General (later General and Commander, United States European Command, USEUCOM) Mike Scaparrotti headed operations, and Air Force Major General (later Lieutenant General) Rusty Findlay was director of policy and plans; both were standouts. I brought a few members of my personal staff with me from USPACOM.

One of the first observations was the immense size of the staff, fully one-third larger than Pacific Command, even though there were almost twice as many countries in the PACOM area of responsibility (AOR), plus the vastly larger geographic area. Not one who believes that bigger is necessarily better, my suspicions were quickly confirmed as I walked around and chatted with individual staff members at their workstations, finding many nonessential or redundant activities. At this juncture, we needed people in Iraq and Afghanistan, not on bloated stateside staffs.

As many of the commanders from throughout the AOR were in town to attend the change of command ceremony, I took advantage of their presence by convening a commanders' conference that first afternoon on the job. Most of the key people, except, understandably, Dave Petraeus, were able to attend. In addition to meeting many of them for the first time, I received quick updates from their perspectives and views on priority tasks.

Repeating an idea used successfully in my first days at PACOM, I invited several percipient one-star officers or civilian equivalents of diverse professional backgrounds, about a dozen, to remain for another day. Also, including a few key staff members in the discussion, I wanted the group to review the existing CENTCOM mission statement and priorities with me and to share my vision for the way ahead with them.

As previously mentioned, the existing CENTCOM mission had a dozen priorities. Given these competing issues, how could anyone be the absolute priority? The objective of this drill was to re-baseline the strategic guidance by inviting out-of-the-box thinking from the diverse group of participants and, in the process, to get buy-in. As these people were all part of the process and agreed (verbally) with the result, they became advocates when they returned to their assignments throughout CENTCOM.

The final product was a typed single page, double-sided and creased into a trifold, which included a cover page, a several-paragraph message from me as Commander, and my guiding principles for expected behaviors. The inside of the trifold contained the important statements of Vision, Mission, and five Major Focus Areas, starting with Iraq and Afghanistan. This key guidance was intended to be reviewed annually, with the major focus areas varying from time to time based on assigned tasks and changes in the regional security situation (see below).

**COMMANDER
U.S. CENTRAL COMMAND**

Strategic Guidance

Vision, Mission, Principles, and Major Focus Areas

16 April 2007

Message from the Commander

An organization needs a clear vision and understanding of mission in order for all members to efficiently and effectively coordinate activities. It is important that we understand what we are about and how we achieve objectives.

The mission statement reflects the vastness of our AOR and the complexity of our task; the vision statement, our aspirations for the future; and the principles, the way we do business. The Major Focus Areas may vary from time to time in accordance with changing priorities but reflect those areas of major effort in staff activities.

When you refer to this document remember that first and foremost, we are warfighters. Do not allow administrative process or institutional mechanism to lead us astray from excellence and primacy in warfighting.

Remember that we are focused on operational objectives but the way we conduct daily business with our people and those of other organizations, partners and allies is very important.

This summary of our strategic plan is the collective result of work from the entire staff. I challenge each of you to actively support the efforts initiated by this plan. Take initiative and act now! I am counting on you to make it work and need your full support.

William J. Fallon
Admiral U.S. Navy

Guiding Principles

Establish an environment which

- Promotes integrity, teamwork, trust, and accountability
- Recruits and retains high caliber people
- Demands mutual respect and professional behavior
- Emphasizes speed, agility, and prudent risk taking

Instill a culture that

- Is results oriented
- Plans collaboratively
- Encourages innovative thinking and challenges assumptions
- Empowers subordinates and encourages decentralized execution

Provide solutions with

- Options based on analysis and data
- Maximum return on investment
- The most efficient and effective joint force

COMMANDER
U.S. CENTRAL COMMAND

VISION

A combatant command directing, integrating, and employing ready, credible military capability in peace, crisis, or war to advance U.S. interests as a partner in pursuit of a secure, stable, and prosperous region.

MISSION

US Central Command, working with national and international partners, promotes development and cooperation among nations, responds to crises, and deters or defeats state and transnational aggression in order to establish regional security and stability.

MAJOR FOCUS AREAS

Set conditions for stability in Iraq. Strengthen the Government of Iraq (GOI) by working with regional, international, and interagency partners to develop emerging institutions while conducting operations with Iraqi Security Forces to reduce violence and transition security responsibilities to the GOI.

Expand governance and security in Afghanistan. Working with International Security Assistance Force (ISAF), conduct operations that provide security, stability, and maturing governance to the people of Afghanistan. Through Combined Security Transition Command-Afghanistan (CSTC-A), continue to mature and grow the Afghanistan Security Forces.

Degrade violent extremist networks and operations, with defeating al-Qaeda the priority. Use all available methods to build regional and international momentum for moderate behavior while eroding support for violent extremist ideology. Defeat irreconcilable extremists.

Strengthen relationships and influence states and organizations to contribute to regional stability and the free flow of commerce. Work with allies and partners to build capacity and set conditions for regional security and prosperity.

Posture the force to build and sustain joint and combined warfighting capabilities and readiness. Anticipate future operational needs and position well trained and ready forces to respond as needed.

CHAPTER 19

IMPORTANT VOICES AND INTERESTS

FIRST VISITS IN THE REGION – 2007

I looked forward to visiting my new area of responsibility, especially Iraq, to experience the situation firsthand. We left on that first trip within a week of my arrival at CENTCOM, with stops scheduled for Iraq, Afghanistan, and seven other countries in the region.

Describing some contemporary activities, events, and relationships with countries in the Central Command area of responsibility is essential to better understanding the big picture. Although Iraq and Afghanistan consumed most of my time and effort that year, many factors in other nations impacted the two wars. But unrelated activities were also crucial to regional security and the United States. Leaders in most of these other countries were eager to establish a relationship with the CENTCOM Commander as another avenue of communication with Washington.

My area of responsibility spanned a vast geographic area, and the relationships between these countries and the United States were important to regional security. As always, personal connections are critical to building trust. Several leaders had been in their positions for years and enjoyed close relationships with my predecessors. Some had very good ideas and suggestions. I did not engage in relationship-building with these leaders just because it was protocol to do so, nor was I trying to supplant our diplomats.

Over the years of my service, I learned the enormous benefit of building trust through personal relationships. The leaders often appreciated my taking the time to visit them in person and solicit their opinions. Having a personal connection with someone offers an invaluable opportunity to link and address the inevitable issues, problems, or surprises when they arise. It was also an opportunity to see and learn firsthand without intermediaries. My lament was the lack of time to pursue, to greater depth, some of these relationships and to be able to act on the advice offered.

DECISIONS, DISCORD & DIPLOMACY

BAHRAIN

The stop in Manama, Bahrain, home of the U.S. Fifth Fleet and Commander U.S. Naval Forces Central Command, Vice Admiral Kevin Cosgriff, an old friend and colleague, was an important visit to our longest-standing ally in the region. The first U.S. Navy support facility was established at the port of Mina Salman during World War II, officially known as the U.S. Middle East Force since 1948. My meeting with King Hamad al-Khalifa, accompanied by U.S. Ambassador William Monroe, reaffirmed mutual respect and common interests. I also visited with the Commander-in-Chief of the Bahraini Defense Forces, Crown Prince Salman. The U.S. has been the historical beneficiary of unwavering support from the Bahrainis during times of calm and crises in the Gulf and maintaining that good relationship was very important to me.

QATAR

Doha, site of the Central Command Forward Headquarters and the largest and most important U.S. airbase in the Middle East, Al Udeid, would become my home away from home over the next year. Owing to vast oil and natural gas resources, the transformation of Doha from the dusty, unimpressive desert town of my first visit in 1991 to the sleek, ultramodern capital of 2007 was astounding. Our U.S. ambassador, the Honorable Chase Untermeyer, a longtime acquaintance, alerted me to bruised feelings among the Qatari leadership before our first meetings with the Emir, His Majesty Sheikh Hamad bin Khalifa al Thani, and his well-known and larger-than-life Minister of Foreign Affairs, Hamad bin Jassim al Thani.

The White House was particularly unhappy that the Al Jazeera television channel, based in Doha and supported by the royal family, often broadcast stories critical of U.S. activities in the region. The White House also received an anti-Qatari whispering campaign from their resentful (of the upstart Qataris) royal neighbors in Saudi Arabia and the UAE. As Chase and I discussed the issues, we found ourselves in complete agreement that, notwithstanding grievances, Washington seemed insensitive to the extensive and irreplaceable support we received from Qatar to enable our military activities in both Iraq and Afghanistan.

Important Voices And Interests

In my meeting with Sheikh Hamad, whom I found astute and cordial, he came to the point, asking why many of his efforts did not seem to be appreciated in Washington. I replied, "Your Majesty, I do not think that is the case." He said, "No, you are wrong," and relayed a list of perceived slights to me. He went on to highlight actions he took that he thought were in line with American values and priorities in the areas of women's rights, healthcare, and the education of his people. He followed this up with a discussion regarding the media, observing that his neighbors dislike Al Jazeera because it tells the truth about events in their countries. He continued, stating that Al Jazeera was the only television network in the region that could exercise free speech.

Before our meeting, Sheikh Hamad requested my assent to allow his daughter, Sheikha Al-Mayassa, a recent Duke University graduate, to be present, saying, "She needs to learn." This daughter's mother, Sheikha Moza, the influential consort of Sheikh Hamad, had demonstrated an unusual, for Arab royalty, high-profile public role in spearheading initiatives in education and health, not only for her country but also for less fortunate people around the world. I readily agreed to her presence.

The next day, I met with Sheikh Tamim, who became ruler of Qatar after the abdication of his father, Hamad, in 2013. At the time of our acquaintance in 2007, he was only 26 years old but worldly and eager to learn. Mindful of his father's request for me to get to know him, we had a far-ranging discussion about matters in Qatar and the region and were quickly on the same wavelength. Tamim was also mentored by General Hamad al Attiyah, the Qatari Chief of Defense, with whom I also began close professional relations and friendship.

Kuwait

During a short stop in Kuwait City, I was briefed by Chargé Matthew Tueller before meeting with Chief of Defense General Fahad Ahmad Al-Amir, to whom I took an instant liking. Fahad was down-to-earth and no-nonsense; he was a man who stood out among Arab military leaders by actively engaging in professional conversation and inviting his key junior staff officers to participate in meetings that the two of us held together to broaden their perspectives. He also privately advised that senior Syrian military officers were anxious to meet with me. Fahad disclosed, "I have a farm in Syria near Damascus and know these Syrian generals well. I would be pleased to be an intermediary if this would be useful to you." This offer was music to my ears as I was convinced such a relationship would be helpful in Iraq. And this was precisely why I had pushed back when Condi Rice warned me not to mention or engage with the Syrians or Iranians. Alas, my effort to gain approval for this initiative, which I carried up the chain of command through Secretary Gates, was rebuffed by President Bush himself, as Condi had predicted. It is interesting to speculate what might have been different with Syria in later years had a relationship been developed.

My meetings with the affable Amir of Kuwait, the late Sheikh Sabah al Jaber Al-Sabah, and his son, Defense Minister and head of the important Amiri Diwan, Sheikh Nasser Sabah, were salient because of the critical dependence of our forces on Kuwaiti ports and supply bases for the effort in Iraq. The Amir kindly stated, "I know you are a busy man with many responsibilities, but if you could reduce the size of the military footprint here, it would be helpful." I knew there were political challenges with opposition members in the National Assembly. I had the consolidation of U.S. bases in Kuwait on my "to-do" list. We did follow-up to downsize the number and the visibility of our forces in his country.

Meeting with Sabah Al-Ahmad Al-Jabbar Al-Sabah, Amir of Kuwait, and ministers, Kuwait City, May 2007

Important Voices And Interests

Jordan

The Honorable David Hale, U.S. Ambassador to Jordan, met me on arrival in Amman and provided helpful background information about the king, challenging internal political and economic issues, and several helpful Jordanian initiatives involving Iraq. The Chief of Defense, General Khalid al-Sarayeh, and I covered many items on his pre-meeting discussion list, many of which were mutually supportive. He was an exceptionally gracious host then and on many other occasions. I often traveled through Amman to change aircraft enroute to Iraq.

My prior interaction in Jordan in 1995 had been with King Hussein, the long-reigning monarch who passed away in 1999. His son and the current leader, King Abdullah II, was friendly and always exuded high energy. We met previously when I was Commander of Pacific Command and enjoyed an easy-going relationship. King Abdullah had extensive military training and experience, some in the United States, where he also attended graduate school at Georgetown University. He was a qualified special forces commando who enjoyed an easy rapport with his troops and often engaged with them, even as king. On the spur of the moment, he invited me to fly with him in a Black Hawk helicopter out to a desert training area, where we spent several hours observing and in dialogue with his troops.

His brother Prince Faisal, also U.S.-educated and well-known internationally, was a good complement and helper to the king, with whom I would also engage. But Abdullah was clearly the man in charge.

The king exhibited an easy-going demeanor on every occasion, despite many issues and pressures weighing on him. He was particularly beneficial to the U.S. as an interlocutor with other Middle Eastern countries and, at the time, one of the few Arab leaders who had a positive relationship with Israel. His support of training initiatives for Iraqi forces in Jordan was uniquely helpful, as was his training of Palestinian police destined to patrol parts of the West Bank.

In our first meeting, he jokingly complained, "Half of the population of Baghdad is living in Jordan, and they are pushing housing prices through the roof. Many Jordanian families can't afford to live here anymore." This was a consequence of his open-door policy for Iraqi refugees, mostly Sunni, trying to escape the turmoil in their home country.

With HRH Abdullah II, King of Jordan, observing a military field exercise in the Jordanian desert, August 28, 2007.

Gracious gestures such as this policy placed an increasingly challenging burden on the king to maintain domestic stability in the face of political and economic pressure. Tension between his native Bedouin people and a large resident Palestinian population that had fled the turmoil in Israel years earlier was mounting. Despite these challenges, Abdullah continued to spearhead efforts at reconciliation between Israel and the Palestinians, as well as between Iraq and its neighbors, for which I was very grateful.

KINGDOM OF SAUDI ARABIA (KSA)

Hosted by Major General Rhett Hernandez, Chief of the U.S. Military Training Mission (USMTM) in Saudi Arabia, and Chargé Mike Gfoeller, I received background briefings from the Embassy Country Team and USMTM leaders. The largest and traditionally most influential country in the Gulf region, KSA, had a worldwide impact because of its oil reserves, national wealth, and the Gulf Cooperation Council (GCC) leadership.

IMPORTANT VOICES AND INTERESTS

Having previously met Crown Prince and longtime Defense Minister Sultan bin Abdulaziz al Saud when I was assigned to Riyadh 15 years earlier in 1992, facilitated our cordial meeting and discussion of three main topics; first, Saudi-U.S. relations with which he was pleased, principally because U.S. forces were not then based in KSA; second, Iraq, in which he was highly displeased with the U.S. invasion of 2003 and continuing chaos; and third, Iran, which he considered the biggest strategic challenge in the region. Regarding Iraq, he reiterated several times what he said he had told every American leader since he learned about the pending invasion. Namely, it was a big mistake and should never have been undertaken.

Regarding Iran, Sultan asked what I planned to do about the challenge from across the Gulf. I asked, "What would you like me to do?" He did not have a particular recommendation but emphatically stated, "Do not start another war."

My meeting with the KSA Chief of General Staff, General Saleh al-Muhaya, a leader of Saudi forces during the Gulf War, was less than satisfactory. First, he reiterated the complaints about the U.S. invading Iraq in 2003, stating, "This was a huge mistake. The situation is worse now than with Saddam." Next, he expressed unhappiness that the U.S. was not conducting large-scale joint military maneuvers with the Saudi army. I tried to explain that we just did not have forces available for training exercises, given the enormous manpower demands in Iraq and Afghanistan. I said, "When we can get our troops out of Iraq and reset the force, we will do our best to make them available for the exercise program." He was unsatisfied with this answer, but I had no other options, so we moved on.

Later in the year, when I hosted a meeting of the Gulf area chiefs of defense (CHOD) in Tampa, he was notably the only senior attendee openly inhospitable toward the new Iraqi Chief of Defense, General Babaker Zebari.

I found the King, His Majesty Abdullah bin Abdulaziz al Saud, fascinating. Our first meeting, in which he was accompanied by a large retinue of princes, advisors, and other notables, began awkwardly, primarily due to the large crowd in attendance and translation challenges. However, we soon fell into an animated conversation on various topics. He continued the oft-stated refrain about the inadvisability of invading Iraq in 2003 and his ignored warning to President Bush on the subject. But he then treated me to a discussion of his views on people, specifically leaders in the Middle East. Offering advice on how to deal with challenges, he pointed out the concern he had about the leadership in Iran and the danger, in his view, that the regime in Tehran posed to the region. He advised caution, stating, "Do not let them become more powerful." But also counseled, "Do not start another war." He further suggested that I be wary of the Maliki (Shia-led) regime in Baghdad and his perception of bias against Sunni tribes in Iraq.

We then segued into a lengthy discussion about religion, which was discomforting to many of his entourage, judging by their body language. In fact, one of his advisors soon came up and whispered to the king what I assumed was an opportunity to disengage and end the audience. King Abdullah waved him away and invited me to remain and continue the discussion. He then began a long monologue about God and the fact that people seem to have forgotten about our common origins and a proper fear of God if we do not act in ways prescribed by the prophets. I concurred that we would all be held accountable for our actions, to which he wholeheartedly agreed.

In a surprising admission, he shared the challenges of changing behaviors in the Kingdom. One of his initiatives was advocating for moderation in the heretofore strict application of behavioral norms enforced by the Mutawa (religious police). But the king said he was mindful of the dangers of dictating rapid change in his conservative culture lest it be reversed when he was gone. I left that meeting grateful for the opportunity to discuss matters of substance with a leader of vision and a keen understanding of God and mankind.

EGYPT

The final stop on this trip was in Cairo, Egypt, where my escort was the exceptionally competent U.S. Ambassador, Frank Ricciardone, with whom I worked closely in the Pacific when he was our ambassador to Manila. Frank and his team's detailed briefings and information before my visit were first-rate and particularly valuable given the complex relationship between Egypt and the U.S.

I was mindful of the history, particularly the wars with Israel and the initiative of former President Anwar Sadat and his Israeli counterpart

IMPORTANT VOICES AND INTERESTS

Menachem Begin, in establishing the Peace Accords between those two countries.

(L-R) Hon Francis Ricciardone, U.S. Ambassador to Egypt, me, Field Marshal Hussein Tantawi, Minister of Defense, and General Sami Enan, Chief of Armed Forces of Egypt, Cairo, April 2007

My Egyptian host was the Minister of Defense, the late Field Marshal Muhammad Hussein Tantawi. In office for more than 15 years at my arrival in 2007, he was widely recognized as the most powerful man in Egypt after the president, whom he served with intense dedication and loyalty. He became a good friend and trusted colleague. Speaking of his long service and the constant challenge of difficult situations, he told me, "I get on my knees every day and pray to God to end this duty, but I remain in the job, as I know I must do as my president asks." Field Marshal Tantawi later served his country as de facto head of state during the difficult government transition in the wake of the Arab Spring protests in 2011-12. And he, in my opinion, was singularly responsible for holding the country together.[176]

With Field Marshal Tantawi, Cairo, April 2007

My first meeting with Egyptian Minister of Foreign Affairs, the Honorable Ahmed Ali Aboul Gheit, a distinguished and long-serving diplomat, was engaging and entertaining. Having been forewarned that the minister was an avid historian and exceptionally knowledgeable of naval history, I was not surprised when I was quizzed straightaway about a few U.S. naval battles. In this case, I knew the answers to the questions about history, and we had an enjoyable discourse about several events.

Getting down to business, Minister Gheit displayed an intimate grasp of regional policy and the history of U.S.-Egyptian relations. The conversation then took an unexpected tack as the minister declared, "Admiral, you have been to Egypt many times and know Egyptians well. It is disrespectful that some in your country deride and ridicule us as ignorant and backward. We are proud people with a long history. You have been in our houses; you know we have a large, well-educated middle class. We expect to be treated with dignity and respect." I knew he was referring to recent statements by U.S. congresspersons and in the media opposed to continuing military assistance to Egypt, as had been agreed at Camp David. I replied, "I understand and agree with you, and

IMPORTANT VOICES AND INTERESTS

I will do my best to collaborate with Ambassador Ricciardone to provide a complete picture of the viewpoints from Cairo."

My first meeting with Egyptian President Hosni Mubarak, then in office for 26 years, occurred at his surprisingly modest two-story villa at Sharm el-Sheikh on the Sinai Peninsula. We sat on the second-story covered sun porch overlooking a golf course for a relaxed discussion with the affable president smoking a cigar. I made a note to myself to bring a couple of fresh cigars with me on my next visit, which we enjoyed together.

Mubarak began with the now familiar litany about what a blunder it was for the U.S. to invade Iraq, saying, "I told President Bush this would be a huge mistake, but he didn't listen, and now we have this ongoing mess in Iraq." I opined, "I cannot do anything about past decisions, but I am trying to pick up the pieces and could use your help." He asked, "How can I help?" I explained that, as I saw it, Prime Minister Maliki in Baghdad was under tremendous internal political pressure and suffered from a lack of credibility with other regional leaders that undercut his stature inside the country. He received no recognition or respect from other countries. I told Mubarak I understood the Sunni concerns about the Shia-dominated Maliki government. Still, I thought it could be a big morale boost for Maliki, and it would help his credibility with his own Sunni population if another Sunni leader reached out to him.

I asked, "Mr. President, could you invite Maliki to Egypt? I do not believe he has to stay overnight or go anywhere; just meet with you for a discussion." "We have already invited him," was his reply. I said, "No, not an official invitation through diplomatic channels, but a call from you personally, as I think it would be well received and help to normalize things." He was not enthusiastic but said he would think about it. Before the end of April 2007, he did exactly as I had asked. At Mubarak's personal invitation, Maliki flew to Egypt for a short meeting, receiving widespread media coverage and a favorable reaction inside Iraq.[177]

REFLECTIONS

The return trip to Tampa allowed me a few hours to think about what I had just seen during the previous two weeks. First, decisions regarding Iraq and subsequent actions had continuing repercussions in the region. They affected virtually everything else in every country I visited. Without exception, each of the leaders engaged me in open and frank discussions, and each expressed dissatisfaction with the U.S. decision to invade Iraq. But the die had been cast, and the next several months in Iraq would determine the future of that country and have an immense impact on the region.

Afghanistan was suffering from insecurity and neglect compared to the focus on Iraq. Success, if measured in long-term stability and potential economic improvement, was possible, but the security situation and the complex relationship with Pakistan would have to be addressed quickly.

I was impressed with the keen attention to U.S. actions, the complexity of issues, and good and bad interrelationships among the other countries I visited. Certainly, problems, issues, and behaviors were not aligned with Washington's desires and priorities. But there was a wealth of knowledge and experience available among the leaders of these other countries if we could find a willingness and devote the time to engage with them. I was unsure about the Bush Administration's reaction. Still, I was determined to do as much as possible to elicit cooperation and support from the other countries for the Iraq situation and the region's general well-being. Competing priorities and time available would shape the immediate future. The clock was moving quickly. I was also mindful that I had not yet seen two-thirds of the countries in my area of responsibility.

CHAPTER 20

BEHIND THE POWER CURVE IN IRAQ

FIRST TRIP TO IRAQ AND THE REGION - MARCH 2007

Map courtesy of U.S. CENTCOM

On the eve of departure, I took stock of the state of affairs as I perceived them. Although comfortable understanding the current situation, I felt "behind the power curve" in aviation parlance because my full-time job at Pacific Command in the six weeks following the Senate confirmation kept me busy. Flying directly from Honolulu to the Tampa headquarters with no time off allowed, I had only a few days for transition with John Abizaid and his staff before his departure. In my mind, I compartmentalized the new command responsibilities geographically in order of priority: Iraq and Afghanistan, followed by the other countries and issues.

Undoubtedly, Iraq was President Bush's priority and, by extension, the rest of the administration's. In typical Washington fashion, once decisions were made, in this case, the new military commanders chosen and the direction to execute the surge of additional forces, it was assumed that the job was underway. However, just as it would take almost 5 months to get all the surge forces in place in Iraq, I could not immerse myself in the new job until late March 2007.

By this time, Dave Petraeus was in place in Baghdad for six weeks, promulgated his counterinsurgency guidance,[178] and received detailed briefings on the distribution of forces and implementation plans from Lieutenant General Ray Odierno, Commander of Multinational Corps Iraq (MNC-I). I was not part of these discussions or actions. This reality set the tone for what followed: decisions often made by the team on the ground in Baghdad, with Dave Petraeus advising me after the fact.

Given the time delay in my arrival at the job, it made no sense initially for me to try to restart the planning process, particularly as I was in concurrence with the counterinsurgency emphasis and the focus on establishing security among the population as the first order of business. However, during my tenure at CENTCOM, I was increasingly frustrated by the difficulty in trying to insert myself into the operational and strategic decision-making, as Dave and his team had become quite acclimated to acting on their own, for example, the forthcoming decision about the post-surge force drawdown.

Again, to make the point, politicians in Washington and the media continued to refer to the surge as a change in strategy when, in reality, it was an allocation of additional resources to the war in Iraq. The factual change in operations occurred on the ground in Iraq beginning in early 2007, with a revised focus on population security using counterinsurgency tenets rather than the previous emphasis on turnover of security responsibility to Iraqi forces and a quick drawdown of U.S. troops. Iraqi assumption of security and American combat force drawdown were clearly the desired end state, but this was not achievable until security was established in the country. General Odierno and his team in Baghdad were already planning and implementing this shift of focus when General Petraeus arrived to provide his leadership, guidance, and additional emphasis.[179]

Despite some media reports to the contrary, I fully supported these efforts. Nonetheless, as CENTCOM Commander, I was acutely mindful of the limited time available to show results. Given the extraordinary pressure on our personnel and the simultaneous need for rotational forces in Afghanistan, I was skeptical about the ability to sustain the surge for very long. The latter point became a source of great friction between me and General Petraeus, who was focused solely on Iraq, in contrast with my responsibility for Afghanistan and the rest of the theatre in addition to Iraq.

The change in operational and tactical strategy in Iraq was coming none too soon, as February and March 2007 saw the highest number of attacks of all types (small arms, rockets, bombs, etc.) against Coalition forces since the war in Iraq began in 2003. Specifically, there were close to 250 attacks per day recorded by U.S. forces in Iraq in early 2007.[180] Additionally, the death toll among Iraqi civilians, primarily due to the sectarian strife and ethnic cleansing efforts instigated by the Sunni and Shia militias, continued at near-record-high numbers (about 2,500 per month).[181] These statistics reinforced the political clamor against the President's bold but risky decision to increase forces in Iraq, although the directed changes were only beginning to be implemented.

For me, there was little doubt that U.S. forces would incur escalating casualties as the tempo of operations increased and more troops began to establish combat outposts among the civilian population in most Baghdad neighborhoods.

Near-term challenges were highlighted when I received a telephone call from General Petraeus the day after he assumed command in Baghdad. He relayed a report of an astonishing and disheartening event that he witnessed at a welcoming dinner in his honor hosted by U.S. Ambassador Zalmay Khalilzad the previous evening. Among the invited guests were Iraqi Minister of Defense Abdul al-Qadir al-Obeidi and Speaker of the COR (Iraqi Parliament) Mahmoud al-Mashhadani. These key government leaders, Sunni politicians, got into an acrimonious debate, which escalated until Mashhadani abruptly got up and stormed out of the dinner.[182] This incident illustrated the friction and mistrust prevalent in the administration of Iraqi Prime Minister Maliki and the obstacles to progress we would encounter.

To make things more concerning, on the eve of my first arrival in Baghdad on 23 March, Iranian Revolutionary Guard Corps (IRGC) operatives seized 15 Royal Navy sailors from a British ship, HMS Cornwall, which had been conducting contraband checks of merchant ships in the Gulf and carried them off to Tehran, where they were held captive for several weeks.[183] Iranian speedboats were also engaging in provocative harassment tactics in the vicinity of U.S. Navy warships. These activities at sea were complementary to increasingly lethal IRGC Quds Force (a branch of the IRGC primarily focused on anti-Western military activities) sponsored attacks by Shia militias against U.S. forces in Iraq. The Iranians were supplying their surrogates in Iraq with a variety of weapons, including deadly EFPs, a type of rocket that was particularly effective against our armored vehicles, causing a sharp increase in casualties.[184] This activity again highlighted a point I previously tried to make with Secretary of State Rice about the need to engage Iran (and Syria) to be successful in our efforts in Iraq. It was my observation that activities originating from and directed by Syrian and Iranian authorities were directly contributing to the battlefield challenges in Iraq and should be addressed with these two countries.

In summary, when I assumed command of CENTCOM, I climbed aboard an already fast-moving vehicle in a complex environment fraught with political, diplomatic, and military challenges. At this point in time, I could not change what had already happened since the ill-considered decision to invade Iraq. Still, my commitment was to affect the current and future situation. Specifically, my goal was to set conditions to end the war in Iraq as quickly as possible on terms that would facilitate the best chance for long-term stability in that country. It was clear to me first that establishing security in Iraq was the prerequisite for any possible political success with the Maliki government in Baghdad, and second, it really did seem like our last opportunity.

One of the first lessons I absorbed in the earliest days of my military career was to note and understand the geography and weather in any area of operations. Iraq was illustrative, as these factors often influenced our activities. About six hundred miles from south to north, the topography where our forces operated is mostly flat desert or dry floodplain agricultural areas. The climate is generally pleasant during the winter but oppressively hot and dry during the summer, with daytime temperatures typically well over 100°F. Rainfall is sparse, usually occurring in winter, and snow is negligible except in the northern mountains. Dust is pervasive during the warm months, with occasionally severe sandstorms precluding most movement. The dry soil has the consistency of talcum powder. It permeates everything from engines to clothing, exacerbated by our extensive use of tracked vehicles, resulting in dense clouds of choking dust. The occasional rains transform the dust into a thick layer of gooey mud, precluding movement except on paved roads. This adverse environment was oppressive to our troops, especially during the long, hot, and dry summer.

Logistic support throughout Iraq was provided primarily by wheeled land vehicles delivering matériel from our support bases in Kuwait. The truck convoys followed Iraqi Highway One, dubbed MSR (Main Supply Route) Tampa by our forces, snaking from the Kuwait border north, some 350 miles to Baghdad and beyond. An early stop in my familiarization was a visit with the drivers and their escorts as they described the treacherous trips up and down this Highway, running a gauntlet of ambushes and roadside bombs to deliver essential supplies to our people. I was shown an interesting array of improvised cabin protection for the mostly unarmored vehicles. I immediately recalled my brother Bob's description of almost identical steps (stacked sandbags, steel plates under the seats, etc.) to protect himself in his USMC truck on the perilous trips up Vietnam Route 1 some 40 years earlier.

A significant number of our casualties in Iraq occurred while moving supplies up the MSR Tampa highway. Several weeks later, while flying in a helicopter near Baghdad, I viewed a vast open-air supply depot stretching ¼ of a mile and composed entirely of stacked pallets of bottled water. Each of these pallets was brought by truck from Kuwait. I was astonished that we were still trucking all our water on this dangerous, manpower-intensive, and time-consuming land route four years into this conflict. Compact reverse osmosis technology to provide fresh water has been used on ships and in many other places worldwide for decades. The direction to investigate alternative sources of fresh water was immediately forthcoming. I also suggested to our logistics folks the potential of a "twofer" in having Iraqi businesses supply the water, thereby providing desperately needed jobs. In hindsight, this situation should have been remedied earlier in the conflict. Many standard procedures, particularly logistics, were fertile ground for innovative thinking. However, inefficient and costly processes persisted.

As my U.S. Air Force C-17 transport aircraft began a steep descent into Baghdad International Airport (BIA), avoiding the potential of a man-portable missile attack, I thought to myself that I was offering a fresh set of eyes to the war in Iraq. I certainly had no land battle experience, but I had seen a lot of challenging situations with people around the world. And I had the big picture regarding politics back home, resource availability, but only a finite amount of time to make a difference.

General Petraeus met me at BIA, and we flew by helicopter to his headquarters at the nearby sprawling base known as Camp Victory for a series of briefings. Afterward, we shared a meal with his senior leadership at his quarters. Two dominant conflicts coincided. First, Iraqi insurgents, both Sunni (primarily Al Qaeda and allies) and Shia (principally Iranian-allied and supported militias), were attacking Coalition (primarily U.S.) forces. Second, both Sunni insurgents and Shia militias were attacking each other, or more precisely, targeting the civilian populations of the opposite religious persuasion. There was a bit of chicken-or-egg discussion about the origins of the Iraqi-on-Iraqi violence, but the typical characteristics were Sunni vehicle bomb attacks in crowded Shiite areas and Shia death squads seizing people off the streets or going house to house in attempts to purge Sunnis from mixed neighborhoods. Both deadly attack modes had to be blunted.

We knew that new operational concepts were being deployed in and around Baghdad. Specifically, U.S. forces, bolstered by the first surge brigades and other realigned units led by Lieutenant General Ray Odierno, were joining forces with Iraqi troops led by Iraqi Lieutenant General Qanbar of the newly formed Baghdad Operations Command.[185] The plan was for both forces to establish joint combat outposts in various Baghdad neighborhoods and remain there as visible security signals to the civilian population. These security actions were intended to curtail insurgent activities and thus enable Iraqi political leadership to establish a credible representative government that the population could trust and support.

Iraq, in March 2007, continued to be a dangerous country. Camp Victory, a vast facility with a secure perimeter and many structures, including several of Saddam's palaces, plus buildings that originally housed members of his family and senior officials, was a lucrative target for the insurgents. The sound of explosions, particularly at night, was routine, usually distant, but occasionally an incoming rocket or mortar, launched by one or another of the various warring factions, would detonate on the base. Hence, there were protective barriers around most of the structures, and personal protective gear was standard procedure when outdoors.

My travel around Iraq was typically by helicopter in those days, as the threat levels were very high. Flying low and fast, employing random evasive maneuvers, and accompanied by protective helicopter gunships was standard procedure as the helos were subject to occasional attack by enemy guns and missiles. Driving on the roads, particularly some of the high-visibility highways around Baghdad, such as "Route Irish" between BIA and the heavily fortified Green Zone, home to the American Embassy and most of the Iraqi government offices, was sometimes like transiting a shooting gallery of roadside bombs, small arms, and rocket-propelled grenade fire.[186]

When staying overnight in Iraq, usually for several days, my small traveling staff and I would sleep in the JVB (Joint Visitors Bureau), one of the former Saddam palaces at Camp Victory taken over by the U.S. military. The large and garish "palace" had been converted for various uses, including troop billeting, a mess hall, meeting rooms, and communication facilities. General Petraeus' personal quarters were in another smaller former Hussein family "palace" a short distance down the road. Dave kindly allowed me to use a small workout weight room next to his bedroom after I had gone for early morning trots (only about half the distance of Dave's legendary six-mile morning jaunts).

The typical routine would be to attend Dave's daily BUA (Battle Update Assessment) briefing and then huddle with his senior leaders at Al-Faw Palace, the immense and gaudy former Saddam facility (complete with moat), converted to house the headquarters and staff for MNF-I (Petraeus) and MNC-I (Odierno). I would then travel, usually by helicopter, to the various subordinate headquarters and troop outposts in Baghdad or other locations around the country, dismounting to travel by vehicle or on foot around the cities, towns, or neighborhoods. These tours, known as "battlefield circulations," to interact with our troops in their combat outposts, sometimes included nearby "market walks" if feasible, to give me a sense of the atmospherics among the civilian population. These frequent visits with our troops all over Iraq were, I am sure, a nuisance to Dave and his subordinate commanders, but were essential to my up-to-date understanding of the situation. They also demonstrated my keen interest in our people and their well-being.

General Ray Odierno accompanied me to most places on that first 5-day trip into Iraq, providing candid, helpful observations and assessments and introducing me to the Coalition and Iraqi military commanders in all parts of the country. Many were leaders already known to me; some had previously collaborated with me in the Pacific. We were constantly on the move, pushing hard to enable me to get to as many places and meet with as many key people as possible while taking measures of the security situation all over the country.

After an office call with U.S. Ambassador Zalmay "Zal" Khalilzad, I first met with Prime Minister Nouri al-Maliki, including other key Iraqi government ministers and officials in his administration. Over the next several days, I was also introduced to and spoke with Deputy Prime Minister Barham Salih and the three-person Presidency Council, consisting of President Jalal Talabani, Vice Presidents Tariq Hashemi and Adil Mahdi. Other important introductions were to Defense Minister Abdul Qadar Obeidi al-Mufraji and Minister of the Interior Jawad al-Bulani. These last two men had the security portfolios of the Iraqi military and police, respectively. Abdel Qatar became my principal Iraqi interlocutor in Iraqi Armed Forces security matters.

I also met with several Coalition military commanders and ambassadors, including the British, Korean, and Polish contingents. A lengthy discussion and dinner with Lieutenant General (later General and Commander in Afghanistan) Stan McChrystal at his headquarters at the Balad Airbase got me up to speed on the extensive and critically important work of his Special Operations team and their nightly battles against insurgents. Meeting with Lieutenant General Marty Dempsey (later my Deputy Commander at CENTCOM before becoming Army Chief of Staff then Chairman JCS), commander of the effort to train and equip Iraqi security forces, I left with a good sense of where we stood and what was possible.

Dave Petraeus reintroduced me to British Lieutenant General Graeme Lamb, the Deputy Commander of Multinational Forces in Iraq and the person leading the effort at reconciliation among the warring Iraqi factions, which we all considered essential to restoring stability in Iraq. At dinner in Graeme's quarters in the Baghdad Green Zone later that evening, we were interrupted by the detonation of incoming rockets landing nearby.

The security situation in late March varied by location in Iraq. When viewed from a helicopter, one would see columns of smoke rising from areas around the capital and occasionally in other parts of the country. The rattle of small arms fire, punctuated by explosions, was commonplace on the ground. One of the most feared sounds was the heavy detonation indicative of a nearby IED blast. During a visit to a joint security outpost in central Baghdad, soon after I arrived in Iraq, the stop was cut short by just such an attack on a vehicle belonging to the brigade hosting me. Regrettably, casualties resulted from that attack, but fortunately, my helicopter, loitering nearby, was available to evacuate several of the severely wounded soldiers.

On subsequent trips, I would periodically visit our medical trauma facilities, particularly the CSH (Combat Support Hospitals) in Baghdad and at Balad Airbase.[187] The prompt and professional intervention provided to our wounded by the military medical teams saved many lives. I recall an evening at Balad while visiting an on-duty medical team when word came of inbound helicopters bringing three or four soldiers severely wounded from an EFP attack on their vehicle. Doctors and nurses went to work immediately, triaging and then surgically addressing the wounded men.

In the case of one horribly wounded trooper, my observation was that this man could never survive his traumatic injuries. But the medics, who happened to be part of an Air Force team that night, would not give up. They performed near-miraculous work and stabilized the patient well enough to enable him to be flown out to a comprehensive facility in Germany that very night. Later, I would locate this individual at Walter Reed Medical Center in Bethesda to verify his survival. The rapid intervention of our highly skilled medical personnel on the battlefields saved countless lives, especially those who could be evacuated quickly to the CSH for initial treatment.

Another important foray on that first visit was a flight to Erbil, the capital of Iraqi Kurdistan, for a visit with the Korean Coalition forces holding down security in relatively quiet northeastern Iraq. From there, I flew to a meeting with the influential Massoud Barzani, president of the Kurdistan region of Iraq. He initiated a fascinating dialogue and an introduction to other key leaders from Kurdistan, including his nephew, eventual successor, and current president, Nechirvan Barzani.

The final swing on that first trip was to the southern area of Iraq, stopping at Basra for meetings with British Major General Shaw, the Coalition commander in southeast Iraq, to discuss security in that area. Later that day, I flew by helicopter from Basra to Camp Bucca, the U.S. detention facility located in an isolated desert area just north of the Iraq-Kuwait border. Insurgents apprehended by U.S. forces were confined there.

As we approached Camp Bucca, the helicopter pilots reported some trouble on the ground ahead, and we were asked to delay our landing at the facility. While circling overhead, I could see several columns of smoke rising from structures inside the camp, suggesting the installation might be under attack. After several minutes, we were cleared to land and met by the installation commander and staff, who explained the situation.

By way of background, Camp Bucca was, at that time, by far the largest U.S.-run detention facility in Iraq, the other being Camp Cropper, both successors to the infamous Abu Ghraib, the site of the prisoner abuse scandal several years earlier. With almost 20,000 prisoners incarcerated at that time, Bucca was situated in a desolate area and considered reasonably secure due to its remote location and security measures in place. Given the sinister history of the previous main detention facility at Abu Ghraib, I wanted to look at it myself.

We discovered that the smoke we witnessed that day resulted from inmates setting their living quarters, constructed primarily of wood, ablaze as part of a widespread protest and riot instigated by troublemaking prisoners complaining about their confinement and security procedures in the camp. The situation upon my arrival was still tense, with heavily armed U.S. guards confronting protesting prisoners.

The physical layout of the detention facility consisted of about a dozen outdoor barbed-wire, fenced compounds with enclosed sleeping structures. The numerous contiguous but fenced stockades were used to limit the number of detainees in each compound. The facility had undergone several expansions as the number of incoming prisoners increased with the surge.

I saw the situation that day as particularly ominous for several reasons. First, my discovery that given the manpower shortages in Iraq, the vast majority of the guards and security personnel were not trained detention officers, such as military police or similar civilian backgrounds, but an assortment of multiservice, mainly reserve, support personnel without relevant experience and minimal training. The guards were armed and nervous, fearful of a mass assault by the detainees, and prepared to open fire if prisoners attempted to storm the fences. Second, it was obvious to me that there were far too many detainees in each compound, and little attempt was made to differentiate among the prisoners. We later learned that many detainees were not hardened insurgents but people who were swept up in Coalition raids and mixed in with some of the most notorious jihadists in Iraq, a surefire breeding ground for future trouble.

The security force at the camp impressed me as well-meaning and diligent, but ill-prepared for the task they were being asked to execute. Also, they were inundated by the rapidly increasing number of detainees, a consequence of the aggressive new security operations being implemented by General Petraeus.

I immediately placed a secure telephone call to Secretary of Defense Gates to inform him of what I had just seen and to alert him to the potential of significant bloodshed and unintended consequences should there be another riot. My recommendation was the immediate dispatch of detention-experienced military police units to oversee camp operations and an expeditious review of the physical facility with an eye to expansion, better security, and improved living facilities. The situation was under control at the time of my departure several hours later, and eventually, my recommendations were implemented. The detention facilities and programs were soon vastly improved with the arrival of USMC Major General Doug Stone to command Iraq detention operations.

DECISIONS, DISCORD & DIPLOMACY

IMPRESSIONS FROM THE FIRST VISIT TO IRAQ

Absorbing what I had seen and heard during visits to most areas of the country gave me lots to think about. Changing the overall dismal security situation, I observed, would not be easy. Still, there were enough signs for me to be cautiously optimistic. Generals Dave Petraeus and Stan McChrystal had their hands full, and it was clear to me that the burden was almost entirely on the U.S. forces. The remaining Coalition forces (the U.K. was the major troop contributor, but several other countries also participated), except for SOF (Special Operations Forces) operating with Stan's Special Operators, were looking for the exit door from Iraq. Most of the Iraqi units were not yet dependable enough to operate on their own.

The new troop employment concept was beginning to take effect in Baghdad. As expected, the number of live-fire security incidents and casualties increased. The third of five surge brigades was moving into position. Coalition unit boundaries were adjusted to take advantage of the new troop arrivals. The insertion of U.S. forces by Ray Odierno and his subordinates into the embattled neighborhoods of Baghdad was being resisted, often fiercely, by the entrenched and heavily armed insurgent and militia forces. The continuing carnage from IED and EFP attacks on our vehicles demanded a solution.

On a positive note, the "awakening" of predominantly Sunni tribes in Anbar province to stop supporting the insurgents and to join Coalition forces in resisting Al Qaeda was beginning to mushroom into a significant factor in battling the enemy.[188] The deeply suspicious Prime Minister Maliki and his Shia-dominated government had not yet embraced the awakening, owing to its overwhelmingly Sunni tribal roots. But the movement was spreading, including now some Shia tribes, as the population sought to assist in improving security. As I saw it potentially playing out, western Iraq could become inhospitable to Al Qaeda, and the flow of insurgents from Syria might be stanched. A win!

Stan McChrystal's Special Operations Forces (SOF) were stepping up the level of activity against insurgents and their bomb factories in the areas around Baghdad. Stan was perfecting a combined intelligence and immediate execution effort that became the best-integrated operation of this type I have ever seen. Enabled by the expanding full-time presence of the conventional surge forces in the neighborhoods, virtually an "anvil" under the SOF "hammer," the operations were increasingly effective in disrupting the enemy and removing some of the worst insurgents from the battlefield.

My initial observation of the Iraqi infrastructure was that it was ineffectual. Government services at the national, provincial, and municipal levels were nonexistent. Electricity was spotty and generally available for only a few hours daily. Municipal water and sewage systems, dependent upon sketchy electrical power, were unreliable. The availability of food and other essentials like cooking oil, formerly provided throughout the country by Saddam's socialist regime, was problematic. Fuel availability, particularly gasoline for private and business vehicles, was hamstrung by erratic output from the sole operating refinery at Baiji, then extortion and corruption within the delivery system by militias. The population, accustomed to these basics provided by the government, now expected the occupying U.S. forces to furnish them and were incensed at the failure to deliver. This was yet another reality unforeseen by, or assumed away, in the decision to invade Iraq.

Underlying these issues was the pervasive lack of legitimate employment opportunities. During Saddam's time, the state aligned with the socialist governing ideology and provided most jobs. The lack of work and the physical danger of people being out and about had brought the economy to a standstill. Employment as members of the state security forces on multiple levels had been a mainstay. Still, Paul Bremer's Coalition Provisional Authority (CPA), with its de-Ba'athification initiative, had effectively barred Sunnis from this line of work. The Maliki regime continued discrimination along ethnic lines for those seeking government-funded positions.[189]

At issue was whether the Maliki regime would step up to provide the kind of unbiased governance on which people of all persuasions around the country could rely. Restoring government services was hampered by corruption and lethal activities in Shia-dominated ministries. The underlying U.S. assumption for the surge and aggressive efforts to enforce security was to provide time and space for the Iraqi leaders to assume leadership and provide good governance. The continuing fractious relations between Sunni, Shia, and Kurd politicians did not augur well for the future of Iraq.

CHAPTER 21

THE CONUNDRUM: AFGHANISTAN AND PAKISTAN

AFGHANISTAN, MARCH 2007

As our plane circled to land at Kabul airport, I reflected on my last visit there as PACOM Commander a little more than four months earlier, in November 2006, and wondered what would be different. The mountains to the north, particularly the majestic and towering Hindu Kush, were still snow-covered. From the air, the land seemed peaceful and silent. The scenery was stunning, and I was eager to engage with the Afghan people, whom I recalled as decidedly tribal in culture but curious and friendly.

Upon landing, I found the airfield little changed from my last visit, hosting commercial and military activities in adjacent facilities. Most of the U.S. military air footprint was at Bagram Airfield, about 40 miles north of the city. Although security was heavy, the atmosphere in Kabul was decidedly less tense than Baghdad.

Pre-arrival briefings and study offered a mixed view of security depending on where one might be in the country. For several years following the 2001 defeat of Al Qaeda and their Taliban hosts in Afghanistan, relative peace had endured, allowing economic progress and a more democratic governing system under the leadership of President Hamid Karzai.

But by 2005, with U.S. attention focused on Iraq and only a small Coalition military footprint in the country, security began to deteriorate. The remnants of Al Qaeda and the Taliban, which had melted into the population or fled across the rugged and porous border into Pakistan, took advantage of opportunity and began returning to Afghanistan, aligning with tribal allies, and ramping up attacks on U.S. and Afghan Security Forces.

During the spring and summer of 2006, the Taliban launched a series of surprisingly large attacks in Helmand and Kandahar provinces in the south of the country.[190] At the time of my return, there were occasional roadside and suicide vehicle bombings in Kabul and sporadically in other major cities around the country, which primarily targeted military personnel but, increasingly, civilians as well. Coalition and Afghan Security Forces were reporting daily attacks by insurgents, particularly in the southern and eastern parts of the country. I wanted to see for myself.

(L-R) With then Colonel (later General) Mick Nicholson, CO of 3rd Brigade Combat Team/10th Mtn Division, and Major General (later General) Rod Rodriguez, Commander CJTF-82 and 82nd Airborne Division. Jalalabad, Afghanistan, April 2007

The geography of Afghanistan was a key determinant of military operations. The country is mostly mountainous and arid, with a landmass about the size of Texas, spanning nearly 600 miles north to south and east to west. The spectacular landscape, with flat deserts in the southwest rising to almost 25,000 feet in elevation at the sublime Hindu Kush in the northeast, is harsh, and the weather is severe. Summer temperatures are well over 100°F, with long, cold, and snowy winters in the mountains.

By long tradition, the tribal "fighting season" (military conflict at some level occurring for centuries) is severely constrained by weather.

It typically begins after the snow melts in the spring and continues until the onset of the following winter.

Infrastructure around the country was primitive, with few paved roads other than the "Ring Road," a highway that encircled the central mountainous area and connected the major cities. Coalition military forces usually moved by fixed-wing transport aircraft and helicopters.

Most of my time was spent in Kabul, meeting senior American and key Afghan leaders. My host was U.S. Army Major General Bob Durbin, Commander of the Combined Security Transition Command-Afghanistan (CSTC-A), the critically important organization charged with planning, organizing, advising, and training Afghan Security Forces, both the Afghan National Army (ANA) and Afghan National Police (ANP).[191] Bob had led CSTC-A since its inception about a year earlier. I found him to be sharp, detail-savvy, and keenly perceptive. His small, unpretentious headquarters, Camp Eggers in downtown Kabul, was where I would stay whenever I visited Afghanistan. The compound was surrounded by a concrete wall and guarded gates, but the second-floor bedroom and shower in the modest apartment I occupied were overlooked by the civilian house next door, with neighbors occasionally providing entertainment in the form of Afghan music. Security concerns, at this time, were not near Iraq's elevated level.

My first meeting was with U.S. Ambassador Ron Neumann, a career foreign service officer (FSO) who was about to complete a two-year tour as our senior diplomat in Kabul. He was uniquely acquainted with Afghanistan, having also spent time there when his father was the ambassador in Kabul during the late 1960s and into the 70s. An astute observer of the situation, the ambassador had been advising Washington of the deteriorating circumstances but receiving little response. His key messages to me were that security was deteriorating as the Taliban presence increased, forecasting a tough year militarily, and to remember the Afghan mindset, "foreigners come and go." He intimated that the government would, therefore, be inclined to make a political deal with the Taliban, a homegrown Afghan entity, which to me seemed reasonable.

The ambassador and I then went to the palace for my first meeting with President Hamid Karzai, with whom I immediately resonated favorably. He impressed me as confident and well-tuned-in to his surroundings. I sensed an immediate difference in command and personality from the Iraqi leader Maliki, whom I had just met in Baghdad. For example, during the Afghan meeting, Karzai took a phone call from a provincial governor, then called one of his ministers and provided specific guidance to the latter on a couple of issues.[192] There was no doubt who was in charge.

But something else happened during our first meeting that presaged the unfortunate reality of a steadily deteriorating relationship between Karzai and a succession of U.S. Ambassadors, which I believe was a key factor in the strategic failure of our mission in that country. It was triggered by a lengthy monologue from Ron Neumann about his view of the situation in Afghanistan. It struck me immediately as strange and inappropriate, and glancing at Karzai several times, I detected a similar reaction. Elaborating on this observation, Ron Neumann was relieved as ambassador a couple of weeks later by another career FSO, Ambassador William B. Wood, who, unlike Ron, had no prior experience in the region, having focused most of his career in Latin America. Bill Wood arrived in Kabul after a lengthy tour in Bogotá, Colombia. Karzai later shared privately with me his assumption that Bill Wood was sent to Kabul primarily to focus on drug issues (poppy cultivation and processing into illicit opium and heroin), an opinion with which I concurred.

Reinforcing these thoughts was a revelation several weeks later that a small fleet of MI-17 helicopters was being modified by the U.S. with spraying equipment for poppy eradication purposes.[193] Shortly thereafter, on my next trip to Kabul, Karzai pulled me aside and privately displayed his dismay with this initiative, asking me: "Do they not understand that for many of the small farmers in Afghanistan, this is currently their only source of income? We will work on solutions for this, but we cannot allow their livelihood to be taken away without an alternative in place."

I understood his rationale and was able to divert the MI-17s for Afghan military transportation instead of poppy eradication. This repurposed initiative was not received well by some in Washington who thought the war on drugs should be the top policy priority in Afghanistan. In line with Karzai, my opinion was that, notwithstanding the negative contribution of drug profits to corruption, more important considerations should be addressed, such as Afghan governance, the economy, and training Afghan Security Forces.

(L-R) Afghan President Hamid Karzai and Abdul Rahim Wardak, the Defense Minister of Afghanistan

Bill Wood was succeeded two years later as ambassador by Karl Eikenberry, a retired Army Lieutenant General who, while in uniform, had previously served two tours in Afghanistan and worked with me at Pacific Command. I viewed Karl as an Asian expert with a principal focus on China, where he also served as defense attaché in Beijing. However, undoubtedly a result of his extensive time in Afghanistan, Karl demonstrated shrewd insight about the country and its people, advising me on an earlier 2006 visit to Kabul that the critical needs of the country prioritized economic development over military matters and that the complex ethnic and tribal relationships were little understood and appreciated by outsiders. His fraught relationship with Karzai was exacerbated by the alleged leaks revealing uncomplimentary comments about the latter and Ambassador Eikenberry's dim view of the Obama-era Afghan "surge" policy.[194] In summary, a succession of complex personal relationships and mutual antipathy undercut top-level attempts to encourage and assist Karzai to improve governance and stability in Afghanistan and, over time, severely eroded trust between Washington and Kabul.

With appropriate training, security in Afghanistan was intended to be in the hands of the ANA under the direction of the Ministry of Defense and the ANP under the Ministry of the Interior. I met with both these ministers and, on subsequent visits, was regularly engaged with Minister of Defense Abdul Rahim Wardak, an ethnic Pashtun like Karzai and a former mujahideen leader during the war against the Soviets. Wardak was affable, seemed competent, and often hosted me for dinner at his house when I was in Kabul. He was a frequent visitor to and had a second home in the United States, where his sons were residing following college studies in the U.S. Although we subsequently had disagreements about the composition and direction of the ANA, we got on well. But I was concerned about corruption, notably when one of his sons secured a logistics contract worth hundreds of millions of dollars to move U.S. equipment in Afghanistan.[195]

Unsettling was my meeting the following day with U.S. General Dan McNeil, newly arrived (about a month earlier) Commander of International Security Assistance Force (ISAF), the U.N.-mandated organization established in 2001 to enable the Afghan government to provide effective security in the country. NATO had taken leadership of this force in late 2003, gradually expanding it in scope and size (in part as contributing nations backed away from or declined participation in the Iraq Coalition) until, at the time of my arrival, it had a sizable presence of about 30,000 personnel deployed throughout the country.[196]

As I worked my way around Afghanistan and met with the various military commanders, I had a better appreciation for the complexity of the responsibilities and the convoluted chain of command. There were several overlapping mission areas for United States forces. ISAF, already described, included U.S. participation, and at that time, was U.S.-led by McNeil, but he did not report to me, the Commander supposedly responsible for all U.S. forces in the region. Instead, General McNeil reported up the NATO chain of command to Brussels. However, the U.S. troops in ISAF, commanded at that time by Major General (later General and Commander of USAFRICOM) David "Rod" Rodriguez, also Commander of Regional Command (RC) East, were my responsibility.

DECISIONS, DISCORD & DIPLOMACY

CSTC-A, under Major General Durbin, previously described, did report directly to me and, at that time, was composed of U.S. personnel, also under my responsibility. A third mission area was the continuation of OPERATION ENDURING FREEDOM (OEF), the still ongoing Global War on Terror (GWOT) initiated in Afghanistan against Al Qaeda and the Taliban following the 9/11 attacks on U.S. soil in 2001. The personnel in this mission area also reported to me in their task of continuing the pursuit of Al Qaeda and its supporters. This activity was conducted chiefly by Special Operations Forces (SOF), partly by troops reporting directly to me and partly by other forces working for me through Lieutenant General Stan McChrystal, then focused on operations in Iraq but with part of his force operating from Bagram airbase in Afghanistan. If this seems confusing, it certainly was, and as I discovered, it diluted our security efforts in Afghanistan.[197]

The meeting with General Dan McNeil, the ISAF Commander, whom I had known for about 10 years since he was a Brigadier General with the 18th Airborne Corps, was eye-opening. He provided me with a comprehensive and discouraging view of the security situation throughout Afghanistan. Again, he was the top NATO commander, but I did not report to NATO and was not officially in his chain of command. Nonetheless, Dan outlined his frustration with the lack of support from the NATO leadership and the underwhelming performance of many of the NATO troops assigned to him, primarily due to "national caveats" (employment limitations imposed on forces by political leadership in the various "providing" countries). An example of the chain of command obstacles was the fact that Dan had to run any request through the Allied Joint Force Command (AJFC) in Brunssum (Netherlands) before it could be presented to the Supreme Allied Commander in Europe (another American General, John Craddock), the top NATO military officer, for action. The AJFC was well-meaning, but the Commander was a career logistics officer with little understanding of the realities of the Afghan battlespace.[198]

Dan provided an excellent briefing on the deteriorating security situation on the ground, walking me through each of the geographically oriented NATO regional commands. His area of greatest concern at the time was RC South, the British-led area that was coming under increasing pressure from the resurgent Taliban. He also highlighted the deficiencies in the well-intentioned Provincial Reconstruction Teams

THE CONUNDRUM: AFGHANISTAN AND PAKISTAN

(PRT), established around the country to assist local authorities with security, governance, and reconstruction, but which were undermanned, especially on the civilian side. I promised to get smarter about the details, stay in close contact with him, and do whatever I could to assist and support him.

A SPECIAL CASE: KORENGAL AND PECH RIVER VALLEYS

An area of Afghanistan to which I paid particular attention and tried to visit on every trip was the rugged, forested, mountainous area of Nuristan and Kunar Provinces, East of Kabul, along the Pakistan border. Part of RC East, the American sector of responsibility, the area was a likely conduit for Al Qaeda from Pakistan with their Taliban and other tribal allies. It has been a focus for U.S. commanders since 2005.[199] I also had a personal interest in this area as the Navy SEAL son of longtime friends had been killed there in a complex ambush in June 2005, along with 18 other SEALs and Army Special Operations troops.[200]

The region was spectacularly beautiful but nearly roadless, with small villages, mainly along the Kunar, Pech, and Korengal River valleys. Our troops occupied small outposts scattered in the mountains above the river valleys; the only way in or out was by helicopter. The theory was that our soldiers' presence would be disruptive to the insurgents. But on each successive visit, I became less convinced of the wisdom of the operations. Our forces were spread thinly and isolated, under almost constant attack, regularly absorbing casualties, living in wretched conditions, and assigned to the 15-month-long combat tours required to sustain simultaneous operations in Iraq and Afghanistan.[201]

The tipping point for me was the discovery that most of our soldiers on extended duty in these outposts had been prescribed drugs for lengthy periods by military doctors to help them cope with the anxiety and stress of their environment. I shared my dismay at the latter with General George Casey, then Army Chief of Staff, in early January 2008,[202] but by that time, retaining the "outpost strategy" had become a tenet with many of the U.S. and Afghan military leaders. It would be almost two more years before new U.S. leadership in Afghanistan, recognizing the high cost and futility of these operations, finally shut down the outposts and pulled our troops out of those mountains.[203]

Presenting then 1st Sgt (later Command Sgt Major) John Mangels, 10th Mountain Division, the Silver Star Medal for valor in combat. Pech River Valley, Afghanistan, April 2007

CIVILIAN CASUALTIES

A serious live-fire incident in Nangarhar province, located between Kabul and the Pakistan border, which resulted in the deaths of innocent Afghan civilians, occurred on March 4, 2007, shortly before I assumed command of CENTCOM. President Karzai was understandably furious at the report of about two dozen killed or wounded Afghans. I soon realized the profoundly negative consequences whenever the deaths of Afghans were caused by U.S. forces. This would be a recurring issue during my time at CENTCOM and a key factor in the outcome of events in Afghanistan.

The reported perpetrators in this incident were from a small Marine Corps unit known as Marine Special Operations Company Foxtrot (MARSOC-F), a newly organized entity on their first overseas deployment. A vehicle-mounted patrol from the unit was subjected to an IED attack while transiting a town near the Pakistan border. While no serious injuries were incurred by the Marines, they were evidently rattled by the explosions, assumed they were under attack, and started firing, killing or wounding many civilians.

When initially informed by Army Major General (later Lieutenant General) Frank Kearney, Commander of CENTCOM Special Operations (SOCCENT), I requested a speedy investigation to determine what happened. Based on the results of the initial inquiry into the event, Frank recommended that the unit be redeployed out of Afghanistan and sent back to the U.S. I concurred. Subsequently, this event became very controversial, particularly inside the Marine Corps, and it was highly embarrassing. It was later politicized by a U.S. Congressman who wrongfully accused General Kearney of scapegoating the Marines. The latter was eventually fully cleared by a DOD investigation.[204] Given this chaotic introductory event, complementing my initial days in Afghanistan, I appreciated how different it was from Iraq regarding the population and the security environment.

AFGHAN SECURITY FORCES

My introduction to the Afghan Security Forces, specifically the ANA, came through Minister of Defense Wardak and my initial meeting with the Chief of Staff and Commander of the Afghan National Army, General Bismillah Kahn Mohammadi. "BK," as I called him, was an ethnic Tajik, veteran mujahideen fighter in the war against the Soviets, as were Wardak and Karzai, the latter both ethnic Pashtuns.

I was impressed with BK from the start because of his grasp of detail, big-picture view, and very rational assessment of priority needs for the ANA. As I soon learned, Karzai and Wardak shared grandiose but impractical expectations about what the U.S. could or should do for the ANA in terms of equipment and training. BK was much more pragmatic and thoughtful. He was eager to get me out in the field to see his people in action and to show me his Panjshir Valley homeland in the mountains north of Kabul. He later escorted me on a pilgrimage of sorts to see the final resting place of his mentor and hero, Ahmed Shah Massoud, "The Great Massoud," a famous mujahideen guerrilla leader from the Soviet War, assassinated by Al Qaeda in September 2001 while leading his forces against the Taliban.[205]

Throughout that trip to the Panjshir Valley, BK demonstrated a keen understanding of ground combat operations and tactics as we toured several sites and battlefields from the Afghan-Soviet War. I found it noteworthy that despite numerous attempts spanning many years, neither the Soviets nor the Taliban were able to conquer the Panjshir until the Taliban took control of it during the final disastrous U.S. withdrawal from Afghanistan in 2021.

Departing Kabul near the end of that first visit to Afghanistan, we flew to the Bagram Airfield, a critical facility that, among other things, provided the only fixed-wing (A-10/F-16 aircraft) quick response combat support for the entire country. It was also the base from which Stan McChrystal's forces staged assaults. While there, in addition to meeting with Stan, I had a good discussion with Major General Rod Rodriguez, the U.S. Commander of RC East. From both commanders, I learned that the next stop on my itinerary, Pakistan, was the source of their greatest headache.

The relationship between the governments of Pakistan and Afghanistan is complicated and rife with competing interests. In addition to some of the most challenging terrain in the world along an ill-defined and disputed border, historic tribal areas, particularly Pashtun and Baloch, overlap the two countries. The tribes do not recognize any political borders. Historically, warring tribes from Afghanistan have found haven in the loosely governed tribal areas of western Pakistan. Having fled across the border after being defeated in 2001, Al Qaeda and the Taliban had returned to staging areas along the border, conducting incursions into Afghanistan and then retreating into Pakistan for safe haven when pursued by U.S. or Afghan forces.

Key takeaways from that visit to Afghanistan were: First, regarding dedicated resources (both military and civilian), this area of operations was clearly seen in Washington as secondary to events in Iraq. For example, the U.S. had only one combat brigade (from the 82nd Airborne Division) operating then. In contrast, General Petraeus had 20+ brigades in Iraq.[206] Second, while not as insecure as Iraq, the situation was deteriorating and complicated by the multitude of "cooks in the kitchen" in the form of military and civilian entities from dozens of well-meaning countries.

THE CONUNDRUM: AFGHANISTAN AND PAKISTAN

As I verified on this and later visits around Afghanistan, many security assistance and nation-building activities were uncoordinated. The confusing chain of command complications also increased the challenge. Compounding these issues was the continuation of tactical operations with rising civilian casualties in a changing security environment.

In hindsight, the American shift in focus to Iraq and the subsequent invasion of 2003 undercut initial good work in Afghanistan and was the primary factor contributing to the eventual disastrous failure of the U.S. engagement in that country. This reality, exacerbated by our fundamental unfamiliarity with the culture and customs of Afghan society, positioned us on the road to tragedy. Two decades of political, military, and economic mistakes, compounded by ignorance of historical lessons, corruption, and lack of political will, offset the many tactical successes and laudable achievements of U.S. and Coalition forces serving in Afghanistan.

PAKISTAN

Next stop on this trip was Islamabad, Pakistan, for meetings with the senior military leadership and President Pervez Musharraf. As intimated earlier, Pakistan has long had an outsized influence on events in Afghanistan. Fresh from my discussions in Kabul and at Bagram, I was eager to get the view from the Pakistani side of the border. Predisposed to doubting the extent to which Pakistan was helping the security situation in the region, I reserved my opinions and requests, planning to listen before speaking.

With high confidence based on my previous tour of duty at Pacific Command, I knew the top strategic security issue in Islamabad was India. I understood that Pakistan's engagement with Afghanistan was framed in the relationship between India and Pakistan. Ever since the withdrawal of the British from the Indian subcontinent in 1947, relations between the two countries have been marked by suspicion, hostility, and periodic conflict. Large armies were maintained by both sides along the border, equipped with nuclear weapons. Inferior in size, population, and economic capability, Pakistan was incessantly fearful of Indian encirclement; hence, the intense focus on a friendly or at least neutral Afghanistan. The atmosphere between Pakistan and India is always tense, with periodic forays by insurgents, mainly from Pakistan, often resulting in bloodshed in attempts to instigate larger conflict.[207] The situation is long overdue for a settlement, yet to be realized. Let me relate a pertinent anecdote.

About a year earlier, on an official visit to India in my capacity as Commander of Pacific Command, I was invited by the Indians for a rare firsthand look at the Line of Control (border) between the two countries in Kashmir, the beautiful northernmost region on the Indian subcontinent. The visit was not announced nor publicized. However, shortly thereafter, an opinion piece appeared in a newspaper in Pakistan. The author revealed that Admiral Fallon of Pacific Command, as a guest of the Indian military, had recently visited the Line of Control in "Indian-occupied Kashmir." The author then speculated that the Admiral might have suggested to the Indians that they should consider reducing the size of the large military force on the border to improve India-Pakistan relations. He then speculated that someday in the future, the Commander of Central Command might visit Pakistan and suggest a similar reduction on the Pakistani side of the border. And there I was! That this article appeared at all was more interesting because this was precisely a point of discussion I had with the Indian leaders, and there was no public disclosure whatsoever in India. Events on the border obviously draw scrutiny. I also raised this issue of Pakistani troops on the border during my visit to Islamabad.

Discussions with Pakistani leaders inevitably began with professions of shared common objectives in the region, specifically stability, security, and growth of good governance. They would then decry insurgent activity within Pakistan emanating from the same Afghanistan-Pakistan border region that they were trying to address while lamenting the difficulty in working in their Federally Administered Tribal Areas (FATA) adjacent to the Afghan border. These areas had traditionally been loosely governed, semi-autonomous, and provided a buffer zone for the rest of Pakistan. The leaders would then mention other "issues" with the Afghans, highlighting, on that visit, a claim that two Baloch insurgents wanted for terrorist activity within Pakistan were being harbored in Kabul.

In addition to stressing the need for better Afghanistan-Pakistan cross-border cooperation, I had another high-priority item for discussion. To support our forces in Afghanistan, we were almost totally dependent on one tenuous supply network for major items such as parts, ammunition, and fuel. These critical supplies came over land by truck from Karachi through the mountains and narrow passes into Afghanistan, but were frequently subjected to ambush and attack by various groups within Pakistan. Allegedly, the work of "insurgents" but just as likely to be that of criminal elements, the uncertainty of delivery and mounting costs were serious concerns. Of note, at this time, the U.S. was providing Pakistan with between $2.0 and $6.0 billion per annum in "Coalition Support Funds."[208]

The two key meetings on that first trip were with the Director-General of Inter-Services Intelligence (ISI), Lieutenant General Ashfaq Parvez Kayani, and the President of Pakistan, General Pervez Musharraf. The U.S. ambassador position in Islamabad was open pending the arrival of newly nominated Ambassador Anne Patterson, so my host was the Chargé, Peter Bodde, and my escort, Major General Ron Helmly, Director of the Office of the Defense Representative – Pakistan (ODRP), the senior U.S. military person in the country, who also worked directly for me.

General Kayani had the appearance right out of central casting and a well-deserved reputation as the powerful and mysterious head ISI spy. A chain smoker with a barely audible voice, he had been leading ISI for almost three years. He was widely understood to be the individual who called the shots regarding Afghanistan. His organization was considered the most powerful institution in the country, and it had an outsized influence over domestic and international relations.

During the Afghan-Soviet War, it coordinated most of the assistance to the mujahideen, establishing relationships with most of the Afghan tribal and guerrilla leaders, including Al Qaeda and the Taliban, which endured until the time of my arrival. It was clear to me that ISI had and would insist on a continuing seat at the table in any discussion about security in Afghanistan. Kayani was reserved but hospitable, later hosting me at a small dinner at his home. But I never expected to hear the whole story about anything.

The first meeting with President Musharraf was friendly and relaxed. I found him welcoming and congenial. Our relationship got off to a good start. I had a personal message for him from President Bush that the latter asked me to deliver privately. I had already advised the chargé, so he left us alone. President Musharraf and I withdrew to a smaller office, where I delivered the message and received his reply. We then continued our discussion on a variety of matters. To break the ice, I noted that he had just returned from attending an Arab summit. To my knowledge, he was the only non-Arab at the gathering, so I asked him how it had gone. He laughingly replied that it was a typical gathering of Arabs. They tried to cut separate deals with him, and no one trusted anyone.

Shifting to Afghanistan, I decided to dig into the heart of the security matter. I pointed out the fractious relationship with Kabul and the growing issue of cross-border insurgent activities in Afghanistan from the FATA. He admitted his dislike for Karzai, but when I pressed him, he agreed that having a better relationship between the two leaders made sense. He said he would reach out to Karzai and suggest they get together, which they did a couple of weeks later in Ankara. He also indicated they might jointly host a tribal *jirga* to encourage cooperation among the tribes. But he also asked for my help in convincing Karzai to send back the two Baloch terrorists that he was protecting in Kabul.

I suggested he continue the dialogue with India, which he did, and some small steps toward reconciliation followed. After my meetings in Islamabad, I felt encouraged that we had made some progress that might help the situation in Afghanistan.

CHAPTER 22

IN THE CROSSHAIRS

THE MOST CHALLENGING MONTHS IN IRAQ

Ten days after returning from that first trip to the CENTCOM Theatre, I was headed back to Iraq and Afghanistan in mid-April. En route, I stopped in Washington to update the Joint Chiefs with impressions of my first visit to the war zones. Then, I called on several congressional leaders at their request.

Occasionally, members of Congress would impart their recommendations or views regarding operations or topics in the theater. One unhelpful idea proffered by Senator Joe Biden, then Chairman of the Senate Committee on Foreign Relations, was for us to encourage the Iraqi government to accentuate federalism in the country along ethnic lines in regions of majority Sunni, Shia, and Kurd populations. Although long supported by the Kurds, this proposal would emphasize sectarianism and be diametrically opposed to our initiatives for reconciliation and cooperation to end the ethnic conflict in Iraq. It was also passionately resisted by the central government in Baghdad.[209]

I was anxious to return. In Baghdad, I would rendezvous with General Petraeus, who would be hosting a delegation from Washington headed by Secretary Bob Gates and the Chairman of the Joint Chiefs, General Pete Pace, who were also eager to see the situation firsthand. The Secretary and his party would only be on the ground for about 24 hours, including an overnight stay in Baghdad, so the schedule was packed to enable them to meet with as many key leaders and see as much as possible during that brief period.

After a quick stop at the Marine Corps headquarters near the restive city of Fallujah in Anbar province, the Washington visitors returned to Baghdad for briefings by General Petraeus and his staff. Next morning, following a visit to one of the joint security stations in Baghdad, we met with the new U.S. Ambassador Crocker. Then, we called on the Iraq Presidency Council, followed by a visit with Prime Minister Maliki. The tone of the meetings was amicable, with no unexpected revelations or new contentious issues. Participants knew the surge was still unfolding as new troops entered Iraq and the Baghdad Security Plan was in its early days. Secretary Gates urged the prime minister and the other Iraqi leaders to move quickly on the many political and governance issues that still needed resolution and implementation.

Recognizing the need to include more than just the military aspects in his counterinsurgency plan, Dave Petraeus quickly assembled a brain trust of advisors, even pre-dating his arrival in Iraq. This group, christened the Joint Strategic Assessment Team (JSAT), composed of military and diplomatic members, provided major input to the Joint Campaign Plan (JCP), the blueprint Crocker and Petraeus followed to implement the counterinsurgency effort in Iraq.[210]

During this and my subsequent several visits to Iraq, I tried to get to many separate places throughout the country to have the best possible understanding of the situation. During April, May, and June, as the full increment of surge forces were deployed, the level of combat activity increased, culminating with OPERATION PHANTOM THUNDER in the second half of June. This long-planned operation by General Odierno's troops, primarily in the "Baghdad Belts," semi-rural areas surrounding the central areas of the city, was meant to cut off the flow of insurgent forces into the city and facilitate the "clear" and "hold" operations that were already underway.[211] The enemy resisted, intense combat often resulted, and U.S. casualties increased, peaking in May and June (with 126 and 101 deaths respectively) 2007.[212]

To limit insurgent movements in the city and facilitate control of individual neighborhoods, General Petraeus had his troops construct blast-proof walls, installing sections of concrete ten to 12 feet high that helped partition the city to enable the clearing operations within the neighborhoods. This maze of obstacles cut into the ability of the sectarian death squads to go about their lethal business. Another result of these barricades was the disruption of vehicular transit, as drivers were forced to navigate through multiple checkpoints surrounded by high walls. This eventually had a positive impact on reducing the deadly vehicle-borne IED (VBIED) traffic.

Despite objections from some Iraqi residents and politicians, there was no doubt about the effectiveness of these barricades in isolating troubled areas and facilitating security.[213] In my opinion, this maze of walls was one of the most helpful steps in reducing violence, as it created numerous small zones in which our troops could operate against the insurgents. Over time, insurgent activity declined, stability was established, and security was improved and enforced. As more troops from the surge were added, U.S. and Iraqi security forces expanded their control of the Baghdad neighborhoods. OPERATION PHANTOM THUNDER then shifted the principal focus to the "belts" around the city that harbored the bomb factories and staging areas of the sectarian killers. But in the meantime, tough weeks of heavy combat and casualties ensued.

In early April, U.S. Marine Sergeant Major (SgtMaj) Jeff Morin assumed duties as my Senior Enlisted Advisor. I had selected him for that assignment at USPACOM just before my departure, but he graciously agreed to a change of orders to accompany me to CENTCOM. Jeff was whip-smart, combat-experienced, affable, fearless, and possessed keen powers of observation and deduction. Given my desire to understand as much of the combat situation on the ground as possible, but recognizing that as a four-star officer, I could not visit each frontline unit or go into every combat outpost, Sergeant Major Morin became my extended eyes and ears.

Determined and relentless, he managed to get into every neighborhood in Baghdad and later into the Baghdad Belts, relaying his detailed observations and assessment, an invaluable complement to the battlefield reports I received through the chain of command. Jeff would move around and embed with U.S. forces in each brigade area within MNF-I, visiting the bases and joint security stations and patrolling with the soldiers and Marines. His ability to talk with the troops and observe their activities while in combat enabled real-time understanding of the situation on the ground. He also joined several of Stan McChrystal's operations. He later went on patrol with Iraqi special forces as they began to assume responsibility for security. Jeff was particularly impressed with the skill and effectiveness of the Special Operations troops and the respect they demonstrated when dealing with the population, despite their typically kinetic missions.

One of his early observations was the differences between units and areas of responsibility regarding weapons posture and the willingness to engage (or not) with local populations. These attitudes and actions were critical to successfully implementing the counterinsurgency strategy. I asked him, "Sergeant Major, how are things really going in Baghdad?"

He said that conditions were difficult, we were making progress, but in his view, some of the troops "just didn't get it" (that a key objective of the counterinsurgency approach was to get the population on our side) and "didn't know why they were there." Often, this was because many of these troops had been in Iraq earlier in the war in more offensive mission circumstances and were inclined to be more aggressive with their weapons.[214]

Jeff proposed a practical remedy, suggesting that the more junior leaders in the combat units at squad and platoon levels participate in the counterinsurgency indoctrination that General Casey and then General Petraeus had initially set up at Camp Taji for more senior leaders.[215] I passed all this information on to Dave, who indicated he had not previously received these points from his subordinate chain of command.

During the next several months, Jeff noted an overall improvement in attitudes and actions at platoon and company levels. He also reported the benefits of having our troops embedded in the same neighborhoods for extended periods with the local populations. The growing level of trust and confidence that U.S. forces would not abandon the areas to insurgents and sectarian militias helped convince the people to cooperate and collaborate with us. This was the key objective of the new employment strategy, and it was working.

Soon after my immersion in Iraq, a tantalizing tidbit of information came to my attention. It seemed that Prime Minister Maliki frequently had a late evening visitor, sometimes the last appointment of the day/night, a female confidant. Digging into this a bit, I was fascinated to discover that the woman, Dr. Basima al-Jadiri, had an unusual and unique background. Coming from humble origins as a Shiite in Sadr City, she studied statistics and then physics at university during the Saddam era, becoming an expert in missile technology and radar; even more unusual because, in addition to being Shia, she was a single woman.

A Sadrist member of Parliament with Maliki, she became part of his inner circle when he was appointed prime minister. Maliki soon established an organization called the Office of the Commander-in-Chief (OCINC) to help coordinate national security policy, but that, in reality, was functioning as a sectarian screening filter for key jobs and appointments to try to keep the military, long prone to play a key political role in Iraq, firmly under his control.[216]

Dr. Basima became an important leader in that operation. Later, in June 2007, she became the deputy in an organization entitled Implementation and Follow-up Committee for National Reconciliation (IFCNR), the delightful-sounding title of an organization that, unfortunately, was not helpful, particularly at inception. When, in the summer of 2007, I initially asked Dave Petraeus if he had met her, he replied in the negative.

Intensely curious about her potential influence on events in Iraq, I arranged to meet with her and her IFCNR colleague, Dr. Safa al-Sheikh Hussein (later Maliki's deputy national security advisor). Stylishly attired in a colorful hijab headscarf and heels, Doctor Basima impressed as self-assured, intelligent, and certainly un-intimidated by the otherwise all-male environment. We had a very useful conversation in which I emphasized the need for progress with the reconciliation of Sunni Iraqis so that they could achieve employment at the earliest opportunity, a step that would be helpful to the country in many ways. She replied that her team was working hard in this direction.[217] Although officially the deputy in her group, she took the lead in the discussion. I came away from that meeting with the impression that she was someone with whom we could work to accelerate the reintegration process in Iraq. Unfortunately, I did not have more time to build that relationship, and it did not seem to be a high priority with anyone else in Baghdad then.

The one person who found the time to engage Doctor Basima was Emma Sky, the British-born political advisor to General Ray Odierno, who successfully interacted with her to the advantage of Coalition forces in Iraq. Sky, an Oxford graduate in "Oriental Studies" (study of the Near and Middle East), was often compared with Gertrude Bell, her famous British predecessor, Iraq expert, and key advisor to the British rulers, previously mentioned in this book, who preceded her in Iraq by a century. Sky was later able to intercede with Dr. Basima on behalf of the Coalition to accept Sunni Awakening volunteers, tribesmen who had defected from Al Qaeda, into the Iraqi army, a notable success.[218]

A point often overlooked in international affairs is the critical role of translators when working with people who are not fluent in other languages. In Iraq, I was particularly well served by two people. First, Mr. Sadi Othman, a tall, amiable Palestinian who grew up in Jordan, was educated in the U.S. and became a naturalized American citizen. Already working for our embassy and General Petraeus as a contract employee when I arrived in Baghdad; he had previously worked for Dave as a translator and cultural advisor during his earlier tours in Iraq. Sadi, my usual translator for meetings with key Iraqi officials in and around Baghdad, was superb as a translator and advisor and in his ability to build relationships, particularly with his Iraqi interlocutors.

With translator "Betty" and Prime Minister Nouri al-Maliki, Baghdad, Iraq

My other translator was a female U.S. citizen who preferred to go by the pseudonym of "Betty," also a contract employee working out of General Petraeus' office. She accompanied me all over Iraq, typically wearing the same body armor as the rest of us. When not attired in a battle helmet, her red hair, piercing green eyes, and pale skin was a focus of interest and attraction for most Iraqis. Thoroughly fluent in Arabic, she had a unique ability to simultaneously translate from one language to another, typically without missing a single word. Although of Irish descent, she had spent her childhood in western Saudi Arabia, immersed in the local Wahhabi culture and practice of Islam before attending college in the U.S. Her linguistic abilities were phenomenal, but on the advice of Sadi, I was cautious in the presence of senior Shia that the Sunni bias of her upbringing did not influence the discussion.

As the surge continued to increase the flow of U.S. forces into Iraq and the combination of the expanding troop presence in Baghdad and the more aggressive Special Operations, mostly nighttime raids, pressurized the enemy, the latter struck back. The weapon of choice was typically the IED, which continued to exact a dreadful toll on life and limb. Although our troops used increasingly up-armored vehicles in their travels, mostly modern Jeep-like machines designated HMMWVs but called "Humvees" in Pentagon-speak, the enemy kept pace by increasing the size and lethality of the explosives. Not a new problem in Iraq or Afghanistan, response to the issue was prioritized with the formation of an organization by former Defense Secretary Rumsfeld in 2006. Christened with a moniker that could only have originated in the Pentagon, it was called the Joint Improvised Explosive Device Defeat Organization (JIEDDO).[219] But this was not a joking matter! Sparing little effort and money (billions of dollars were expended), the task force focused most of its resources on surveillance and electronic countermeasures against the increasingly sophisticated IED bombs. My concern with this effort was that it seemed to be one step behind an enemy who was constantly innovating and addressing our countermeasures.

One approach was initiated by the Marine Corps in adapting vehicles used by the South African military, which seemed more successful in protecting their soldiers. These new vehicles, called MRAPs (Mine-Resistant, Ambush-Protected), were slowly winding their way through the acquisition system. Very few of them had been delivered to Iraq at the time of my arrival at CENTCOM. Fortunately for many of our soldiers and Marines, Secretary Gates, upon learning of the MRAP, made it his personal priority to get the Pentagon bureaucracy to deliver these vehicles. Often reciting his attention-getting mantra, "Every delay of a single day costs one or more of our kids his limbs or his life," Secretary Gates was unrelenting in pressurizing the "system" to eventually deliver the vehicles.[220] Thanks in considerable measure to his efforts, the number of deaths and serious injuries dramatically decreased as the vehicles eventually arrived and were put into operation in Iraq. For a detailed description of the institutional resistance to what should have been an obvious battlefield requirement and how he overcame it, see Secretary Gates's memoir "Duty." We all owe him a debt of gratitude.

Eager to help in any way possible, I thought my newly arrived "outside eyes" might notice opportunities that could be overlooked in the pressurized atmosphere of Baghdad. I wondered if any low-hanging fruit might be plucked to assist the ongoing kinetic military efforts. I recalled that in December 2006, President Bush had entertained a visit from Ayatollah Abdul Aziz al-Hakim, a prominent Shia cleric and the leader of the recently renamed Islamic Supreme Council of Iraq (ISCI).[221] He also served as head of the initial provisional government of Iraq installed by CPA head Paul Bremer, prompting me to ask Petraeus and Crocker if they had conducted any direct outreach to him. "Not yet," was the reply. So I asked Ryan Crocker, as this was more in his political lane, if he would accompany me to see Hakim, assuming the latter would agree to meet. With Ryan's blessing, we went about trying to arrange the meeting. I had several motivations for this request. First, Hakim's political party, ISCI, appeared to represent about 20% of the Shia population. The name change to ISCI from its former title of Supreme Council for the Islamic Revolution in Iraq seemed to signal a step in the desired political direction. More importantly, the ISCI armed militia known as the Badr Brigade, with lots of support from Iran, was a major perpetrator of the sectarian violence sweeping Iraq. Success would be if Hakim could be persuaded to assist in reducing the killing and take positive steps to cooperate in governance with the Maliki regime. If he declined, I could not see us being any worse than we were then.

Subsequently, the request was accepted, with an invitation to meet at Hakim's residence in a compound in central Baghdad on May 12, 2006. Accompanied by Ambassador Crocker, Sadi, my EA, Captain Craig Faller, and a small security detail, as Baghdad was still a dangerous place, we drove across a Tigris River bridge in a motorcade. Upon arriving, we left all our weapons and personal protective equipment outside in the hallway at my request. We entered a reception room where the Ayatollah sat in the middle, at the end of two lines of chairs separated by about 15 feet. Ryan Crocker invited me to take the first position on the right, nearest the Ayatollah.

The reception from our host, Hakim, was formally correct but chilly, eclipsed by the contemptuous glares from his ISCI colleagues seated across the room from us. I immediately noted that the individual closest to Hakim's left was the leader of the ISCI military arm, Badr Brigade chief Hadi al-Amiri. We had not met before, but his image and distasteful reputation were well known.

I began addressing Hakim with his honorific title, "Saeed, we ask for your assistance to end the sectarian violence and to collaborate with other parties toward an acceptable political solution for the benefit of the people of Iraq." He deflected my request by reciting the well-known challenges to stability and security in the country. Appealing to the high esteem in which he was held and his influence among his followers, I repeatedly requested his engagement in the reconciliation process in Iraq. The gist of his response was to state that there were so many things out of his control that he could do nothing.

Frustrated, I looked at Hakim and said, "So I guess we just give up our efforts and say *Inshallah* (It is all in God's hands)?" Although admittedly irreverent in my remark, I could tell immediately by looking into his eyes that he got the point. Hadi al-Amari then jumped to his feet, shouting, "Blasphemer!" and appeared to be reaching for a weapon in his clothing. Hakim motioned for him to sit down, and the conversation, without further ado, became noticeably more amicable.[222] Following a hospitable serving of chai (tea), our discussion covered several useful topics.

Hakim personally escorted me out, inviting me to return and to share a meal with him at the next visit. He also said, "I want you to meet my son Ammar soon." Hakim did not appear particularly robust during our meeting. Ambassador Crocker said he was rumored to be in ill health. In fact, only four days later, Ryan informed me that Hakim had requested assistance arranging a medical consultation in America. Flying to Houston on April 16, doctors there confirmed that he was suffering from inoperable lung cancer.[223] Abdul Aziz al-Hakim subsequently went to Tehran for treatment and died there two years later without recovering.

His son, Saeed Ammar ai-Hakim, appeared to be the chosen successor. The son invited me to visit later that autumn of 2007, back in the same residence as the earlier meeting. We had a pleasant and wide-ranging discussion that began, "My father said he wanted me to meet with you." Ammar later disclosed that he had something he wished to show me and led me outside to the garden behind the residence.

Declaring, "I wish to honor my father and to bring him pleasure in his illness," he proudly displayed a newly completed *Mudhif*, a house wholly fabricated of marsh reeds, traditionally constructed for thousands of years by the marsh Arabs of southern Iraq, his father's ancestral people. The structures, like the one that Ammar showed to me, are typically used as gathering places for meetings, weddings, and funerals. It was an impressive edifice, and he was delighted with his handiwork.[224]

Ammar and I maintained a good relationship. Although a young and relatively inexperienced cleric, he took over leadership of ISCI and later founded another political party of mostly younger people with a much more open agenda and membership than most Iraqi parties.[225] Although admittedly, there were many other factors in play in Iraq at that time, I believe that this outreach to the Hakims helped tamp down the violence.

Interrupting this visit to Iraq and other countries for a few days at the end of the month, I returned to Tampa to prepare for and host a meeting of USCENTCOM Coalition partners that President Bush planned to attend in person. For background, several years earlier, my predecessors at CENTCOM established office space for representatives from the many countries that chose to join the Coalition in the War on Terror (GWOT). The workplace for the representatives, dubbed the "Coalition Village," was located near our headquarters at MacDill Air Force Base in Tampa. Only a tiny fraction of these countries participated meaningfully in Iraq. Still, the Coalition was seen as a helpful way to keep countries informed and have some affiliation with CENTCOM. Dave Petraeus flew back to be there for the meeting and to update the delegates on the situation in Iraq.

President Bush arrived, and after a separate meeting with General Doug Brown, Commander of U.S. Special Operations Command, and me, the President addressed the representatives of the Coalition. His speech was a pep talk, thanking the countries' emissaries for their participation in the GWOT, outlining the new counterinsurgency effort in Iraq, about which he said, "We are seeing some signs that give us hope," and cited a few examples of progress. He restated his commitment to "winning the fight in Iraq." Also, he invited their continued participation in Afghanistan's security and stability efforts.[226]

IN THE CROSSHAIRS

VIGNETTES FROM IRAQ 2007

Returning to Iraq, I resumed my quest for information at the grassroots level to enable a better understanding of the situation. The historic book market on Al-Mutanabbi Street in Rusafa, in central Baghdad, was highlighted on the list of sites to visit. Situated on the east side of the Tigris River near the city's geographic center, Mutanabbi, named after a 10th-century Iraqi poet, was well known in the Islamic world as "The Street of the Booksellers." Revered as a center of learning and culture for over a thousand years, the neighborhood was filled with small shops and street-side stalls containing books of every size, shape, and content. Unfortunately, the crowded neighborhood of shops with significant historical and cultural value attracted the attention of Al Qaeda terrorists, who detonated a powerful car bomb on the street in March 2007, killing dozens of people and wounding scores more.[227]

When I visited a couple of months later, signs of the devastation were still quite apparent in shattered buildings, blackened walls, bloodstains, and widespread debris. With a large security contingent from Colonel Jeff Banister's Second Brigade of the Second Infantry Division preceding and following me, I slowly walked through the streets, stopping to chat with the help of "Betty" in some shops that had reopened despite the horrific destruction all around.

At every turn, local Iraqis pleaded for assistance in restoring essential services and an end to the sectarian violence.

Walking out of that neighborhood, now under the watchful eye of our troops and turning onto a nearby, larger street, we passed the Shabandar Café. Looking in through the open doors of that "chai (tea) house," as our troops called them, I saw that it was filled with civilian Iraqi men, and I made a spur-of-the-moment decision to walk inside. Removing my battle helmet and accompanied by "Betty," I motioned, despite their objections, for the heavily armed and now shocked security detail to remain outside.

As the new center of attention, I surveyed the room and was invited in English to sit at a table with three men who shifted their seats to make room for me. An English-speaking gentleman, who I am sure had no idea of my identity but surmised that I was a senior officer, questioned, "Sayyid, can you bring peace to our city?" Accepting a cup of tea proffered by a waiter and not answering him directly, I said I was there to help but wanted to hear their concerns.

As the crowd pressed around our table and Betty translated into Arabic, my host continued, "This part of the city has been the center of Iraqi culture for hundreds of years." Motioning to his two friends, he introduced one as a Shia school teacher, another as a Kurd businessman, and himself as a Sunni professor. "We have been friends for many years, and we used to meet here every week, but now only rarely because it is so dangerous." He said, "General, we are of different backgrounds and beliefs, but remain good friends. If only we citizens could be left alone without the politicians and their gunmen, we could return the city to what it used to be. Please help."

Recognizing that his request was a tall order, I offered to try, but they could help by spreading their personal reconciliation to others. He continued, "Since the bombing, we have had no electricity or water here. Can you help with this?" Not that I needed reinforcement of that last point, but on my way out the door, a woman ran up to me, crying hysterically that she could not care for her children because she had no food or utilities.[228]

Several months later, on another walkabout in Baghdad, I intentionally revisited the café and was quite surprised that the three gentlemen were there again at the table. I was warmly greeted, "Sayyid, welcome back! Please have some tea with us. As you can see, things are getting better now." In fact, they were correct. By the fall of 2007, security had improved significantly in Baghdad. On the day of my second visit, the street pavement was torn up as new water and sewer lines were being installed.[229]

I still recall the impression these men made on me amid the ugly chaos that enveloped Baghdad in the Spring of 2007. Just ordinary citizens caught up in war, but not succumbing to dreadful sectarian violence. They knew that the cause of their problems was man-made, and the key culprits were Iraqis, Saddam, and the squabbling politicians of that day. But it was another reminder of how unlikely the American invasion of 2003 would really "fix" things. Further, it reinforced that, along with the essential prerequisite of physical security, which was being imposed in Baghdad by U.S. troops, parallel efforts to improve governance, civilian infrastructure, and economic development, then woefully inadequate, were required if victory were to be achieved. It seemed apparent that we (the U.S.) could not accomplish these tasks soon and that the Iraqi government had to step up quickly.

Shortly thereafter, on a swing through northern Iraq, I asked to see the sprawling oil refinery at Bayji, the only functioning facility of its kind in the entire country.

My first impression was of disorder as we drove through the ill-maintained and shabby infrastructure en route to the headquarters building. One of the lures attracting me to this place was a story that the Iraqi manager was still on the job, doing his best to run the day-to-day operations. Indeed, Director-General Dr. Ali M. al-Obaidi, a petroleum engineer attired in a suit and tie, warmly bade me welcome despite the stifling heat and lack of air conditioning. Outlining his efforts to continue production despite the woefully poor infrastructure and regular attempts at sabotage by the insurgents, he said, "We must increase output because we are the only source of fuel for the country." I silently admired his courage and tenacity but doubted that he could even maintain the plant in operation, given the day's circumstances. I was wrong. He and his team surprised me by keeping the facility in commission through the worst security problems and beyond.

During the meeting, a young U.S. Army Captain assigned to provide security for the refinery outlined the dysfunction he discovered and his plan to fix it. He explained, "Admiral, tanker trucks are arriving every day from all over the country to take fuel back to their cities and towns, as this is the only supply source south of the Kurdish area. When we arrived, the situation was chaotic, with the drivers fighting to position themselves first to pick up the gasoline. We have now established order."

As I soon learned, the Captain had completely understated his leadership. In fact, this young officer had not only forced the truckers to line up in an orderly manner by requiring them to drive through a self-designed and constructed mini-maze of barricades enroute to the loading platform. He also established a schedule in which provinces throughout Iraq were assigned specific days of the week for fuel pickups to reduce the congestion at the refinery. It was an amazing demonstration of initiative and leadership.

But my surprises that day kept coming.

On our way out of the administration building, the Captain asked if I would congratulate some of his soldiers for exemplary performance. I said, "Sure, what did they do?" He proceeded to explain that earlier that very day, while processing incoming Iraqi workers through the gate of the facility, they recognized by sight an individual who was a key insurgent leader long sought by our forces. They identified him by referencing a sheet containing mugshots of the most wanted people.[230] Each of these soldiers was subsequently recognized appropriately for their performance. My lasting impression was of our good fortune to have such soldiers serving our country.

On another swing through the Baghdad neighborhood of Kadhimiya, I encountered something important that changed a previously held opinion. By way of background, in 2006, Mr. Paul Brinkley served as a Deputy Undersecretary of Defense. He was in charge of a task force for business and stability operations in Iraq. The objective was to restore business activities and employment opportunities by providing resources and direction to the moribund private sector. This economic activity was meant to complement the ongoing military operations in recognition that the latter alone would not be enough for us to succeed in Iraq.[231]

I will confess that coming into the job at USCENTCOM, while applauding the initiative, I was highly skeptical of this endeavor and thought it was a colossal waste of money. My thinking was that most business enterprises in Iraq were state-owned in accordance with Ba'athist socialist central planning and grossly inefficient. The idea that we would pump money into these businesses to continue more of the same seemed foolish.

I toured a newly restarted factory that was taking locally grown cotton, a commodity in ample supply at nearby warehouses, and turning it into finished products. However, for puzzling reasons, this factory resumed its two preinvasion product lines, which were gauze bandages on the one hand and military web belts on the other. At that time, I saw an immediate need for the former, but not so much for the web belts. Another striking impression was the lack of mechanization, exemplified at the start of the production line by a group of about a dozen men pulling raw cotton out of bales by hand and placing it on conveyor belts. While recognizing the employment value of the factory, the lack of urgency, efficiency, and valuable results reinforced my firmly held prior opposition to funding these endeavors.

But on the way out of the door, I was accosted by an Iraqi civilian speaking in an animated voice that "Betty" quickly translated as imploring me to see his nearby factory. Walking a short way down the street, we came to a bakery, a large facility with a half-dozen conveyor belts, all inactive at our visit. He spoke through the translator, "Sir, this is the largest bakery in Baghdad. We provided bread for people all over the city. But now I can only run one production line because I do not have the money to buy all the needed materials and generators to power my machines." Walking around, I saw flour and other material stocks alongside several idle hands. He then offered a telling comment that captured my attention. "Sir, you know the city is racked with violence. One of the reasons is that there is no work, and so the young men will accept payment from the terrorists to facilitate their evil deeds. If I could reopen my factory, we could get them off the streets and give them jobs. And we could help feed many people in need."

Later that day, a converted skeptic following the enlightening encounter with the bakery owner, I fortuitously encountered Paul Brinkley at Camp Victory. Describing what I had seen, I encouraged him to support the bakery and other grassroots initiatives that could put people back to work. Of course, not all the projects were as compelling as the bakery. Still, that business owner was correct in his assessment of the situation and the potential to improve things in Baghdad if he could get his plant back in operation.

During the summer of 2007, roughly coinciding with the U.S. surge, the country of Georgia redeployed troops from Baghdad to southern Iraq to fill in for British forces that had consolidated at Basra airfield. The Georgians set up their main base at Al Kut and deployed their forces along the Iraqi border with Iran.[232] Dave Petraeus was appropriately focusing the surge assets in and around Baghdad, where the brunt of the fighting was occurring. But the Georgians were occupying some key terrain in an area where Iran was providing Shia insurgents with arms and ammunition, smuggled across the border into southern Iraq and then to the Baghdad area.

During one of our weekly video teleconferences, I mentioned to President Bush that, in addition to particularly lethal EFPs, the Iranians were providing their Shia militia collaborators with the big (240mm) rockets that were raining down on the Baghdad "Green Zone" (site of the U.S. Embassy and Iraqi government offices) and other Coalition facilities. The President asked, "How big are these rockets?" I responded, "About 15 feet long." Astonished at the large size, he said, "Well, how do they get into Iraq?" When I told him, "They're smuggled in on trucks from across the Iran border," he was surprised. I explained that cross-border commercial traffic was not well screened and that the Iranians often hid them in other cargo.

On a visit to southern Iraq, I made it a point to stop in Al Kut and meet with the Coalition partner Georgian brigade commander. This sharp leader, confident in demeanor and professionalism, was eager to demonstrate the capability of his soldiers. I told him we were grateful that he volunteered to move his troops into this challenging area of the country. "The Iranians are smuggling deadly weapons across the border into the hands of the militias, and I need you to cut the supply routes."

The Georgian Colonel then produced a map of the road network through the provinces of southern Iraq. He had appropriately noted the large marshy areas that constrained traffic to the roads and had already figured out good places to interdict illicit traffic. He said with a broad smile, "We will do it!" He was good at his word, and his tough, disciplined soldiers did an outstanding job. I was impressed with their performance and the subsequent visit with their troops along the Iran border. These troops also understood the counterinsurgency priority of careful interaction with the local population to get them on our side. Assisted by only a handful of U.S. Special Forces soldiers, the Georgian brigade was the only significant Coalition force along the border from Basra to the outskirts of Baghdad, a distance of almost 300 miles.

While in the south of Iraq, I made another visit to Camp Bucca. A dramatic change in the situation with detainees, then numbering about 20,000, was underway at the direction of the newly assigned Commander of Detainee Operations in Iraq, Major General Doug Stone, USMC, an experienced reserve officer mobilized for this assignment. Doug brought a tremendous breath of fresh air with a new vision and a series of initiatives to revitalize and avert the pending disaster with detainees. Concisely, he recognized that the increased number of Iraqis being held by our surge forces was saturating the detention facilities and that many of those pulled off the streets were not hardened insurgents.

To reduce the growing number of detainees, he came up with a reasonable way to distinguish between the potentially innocent and the "irreconcilables," as Petraeus dubbed them. The goal was to release some of the corrigible.

Dave and his troop commanders initially resisted his efforts because they feared having bad actors back on the streets. But Doug Stone persisted and inaugurated a system in which a three-person team of U.S. officers and senior enlisted soldiers screened the detainees one at a time in a trial-like process to determine their innocence, delinquency, or real culpability. If deemed not a terrorist, detainees could be released on probation under the responsibility of a senior leader in their hometown or neighborhood. Even General Petraeus himself participated in one of the screening sessions. This process significantly reduced the number of people in detention, and the recidivism rate was quite low.[233]

Doug Stone later initiated religious education processes directed by volunteer Iraqi clerics to counter the insurgent propaganda being circulated by zealots in the camps. He also began basic education and training programs to provide life skills for detainees as they reintegrated into their communities.

Unfortunately, before Doug Stone's arrival, hard-core extremists in the camp were successful in proselytizing and converting some detainees to their cause with disastrous future results. One of the most notorious, best known by his pseudonym, Abu Bakr al-Baghdadi, a former detainee at Camp Bucca, joined fellow inmates initially as a member of Al Qaeda and later led the renamed "Islamic State" (ISIS) on its murderous rampage in Iraq and Syria. Released from the camp in late 2004, he completed doctoral studies in religion. He became the spiritual advisor to ISIS before being appointed "emir" and leading the infamous group.[234]

Summarizing the experiences and observations of those early months of the surge, I recognized the painstakingly practical work of Generals Petraeus, McChrystal, Odierno, and their troops. I was honored to serve with them. Complemented by the tireless work of Ambassador Ryan Crocker, the active, perceptive, and frank-speaking chief diplomat, our team in Baghdad was, to borrow a phrase from Dave Petraeus, "All in."

But the situation on the ground remained dangerous and violently hostile to our forces and the ordinary citizens of Iraq. Overall, civilian deaths were declining from recent elevated levels. Still, U.S. casualties were, as we expected, reaching new record high levels (more than 100 U.S. personnel killed in action in both May and June 2007). Hints of progress emerged from areas around Baghdad where U.S. troops had moved into and remained in the newly walled-off neighborhoods.

Being briefed by then Captain (later Colonel and Asst. U.S. Attorney) Joshua Kurtzman, 2nd Battalion, 327th Infantry Regiment, 101st Airborne Division. Samarra, Iraq, December 2, 2007

On the other hand, I had heard and seen enough to know that Iraqi police were not helping and were a major contributor to the bloody street violence abetted by the egregiously sectarian Maliki government. The Iraqi army, beneficiaries of extensive U.S. training and equipping efforts, was expanding. But with rare exceptions (special forces), the Iraqis were still combat ineffective.

The continuing frustration was the demonstrated unwillingness and ineptitude of the Iraqi government to provide effective leadership and basic services for its population. U.S. support, advice, and demands were generally for naught as virtually zero progress was made by the Maliki government to improve the country's political, economic, and safety conditions. It was clear that the security improvement was courtesy of the U.S. surge and counterinsurgency focus on population protection. But, enforcing security with an occupying army was counter to historical precedent and unsustainable without significant Iraqi political and military participation.

I was filled with admiration and respect for our troops and encouraged by the examples of resilience and basic human goodness on the part of some Iraqi citizens. However, the essential importance of establishing effective Iraqi governance remained for long-term stability, enabling conditions for a drawdown of U.S. forces.

CHAPTER 23

PLANNING AHEAD

Given the tenuous security situation, the high number of U.S. casualties since the start of the surge, and the lack of progress on governance by the Maliki government, I was increasingly concerned about the future of our operations in Iraq. I began to seriously consider what options we might have. The fraught political situation in Washington increased in intensity, with most Democrat politicians demanding an end to what they considered a failed endeavor. This was even before the last of the five "surge brigades" arrived on the ground in May 2007, not allowing time for them to have an effect. I sensed some progress in Baghdad as our forces imposed security in the neighborhoods where we had sufficient forces. Still, it seemed to be almost all due to U.S. efforts. The Iraqi army was mostly ineffectual, and the police were proving to be thoroughly infiltrated by Shia militias, often counterproductive to our efforts. And despite many prompts by the U.S. to spur action, the Maliki government was simply not moving forward effectively in governance, reconciliation, or economic progress.

In reviewing my notes, I found no less than five occasions between April and June of 2007 that Secretary Gates inquired about when and how we might effect a future drawdown of our forces. By this time, I had already agreed to a request by Dave Petraeus to commit additional troops to the surge, specifically the CENTCOM theater reserve (the only remaining in-region but uncommitted ground force), the 13th Marine Expeditionary Unit (Special Operations Capable). This force of about 2000 Marines and their equipment, embarked on Navy amphibious ships, was disembarked in Kuwait beginning on 31 May 2007, then sent to Anbar province to augment the surge as part of OPERATION PHANTOM THUNDER.[235] To quote a famous 1980s TV beer commercial, we were now "out of Schlitz" regarding any available additional troops.

The Secretary was appropriately prodding us to think ahead beyond the surge. I was mindful that, in addition to the surge brigades, the tour lengths for all U.S. troops had been extended from 12 to 15 months, and this, on top of what, for many soldiers, were multiple tours in the combat zones. While Dave Petraeus regularly requested additional forces

Planning Ahead

beyond those surge brigades, the Army staff in Washington implored me to stop further requests, as they repeatedly said they were out of combat-deployable people. And, of course, I was aware of the badly under-resourced ongoing conflict in Afghanistan.

As I was forming opinions about the contemporary Iraq situation and how and when to propose structuring a drawdown and eventual handover to Iraqi security forces, I wanted an additional outside view, unbiased by those working the day-to-day problems, which excluded Petraeus, me, and our staffs. Seeking the best-experienced minds I could find, I asked their respective bosses at the time to lend me Rear Admiral James "Sandy" Winnefeld, then awaiting assignment as the new Commander of the U.S. Sixth Fleet in three-star rank, and Dr. Thomas "Tom" Bowditch (a retired USMC Colonel) at CNA (Center for Naval Analyses) for about two months.

Both had previously collaborated with me, Sandy as my executive assistant in the office of the Vice Chief of the Navy several years earlier, and Tom as my Plans and Policy leader at Pacific Command in Honolulu. Each was gifted with extraordinary intellect, intuition, and discernment, and was a "big picture" thinker. They were also well-versed in the ways of Washington and attuned to the contemporary political situation. My charge to them was to visit Iraq to observe conditions, probing and evaluating as much of the situation as reasonable. The objective was to enable me to better assess where we stood at that time. And, based on their observations, to gauge the likelihood and time required to establish sufficient security to achieve the President's goal of a functioning democracy in Iraq, able to provide security for itself.

I had formed my preliminary assessment but was curious to see if our views were consistent. Later that summer, our collective judgments formed the backbone of my report responding to a Joint Staff and Secretary of Defense query regarding the recommended way ahead in Iraq. But meanwhile, I was acutely mindful that time was not on our side.

Arriving in Tampa in late May 2007 for background briefings by the CENTCOM staff, they accompanied me on my next trip to Iraq in early June. We attended the daily briefings at MNF-I HQ and visited several commands together before my departure and travel to other countries in the region. They remained in Iraq for another week and went back for a follow-on visit about a month later. I had advised Dave Petraeus of their mission in advance and asked for his assistance in arranging access to as many places and people as reasonable.

Although skeptical that there was some hidden agenda at work (there was not), he provided help and later met with Admiral Winnefeld for a debrief after their work. General Petraeus was not happy that anyone other than himself would have recommendations for the way forward in Iraq. Furthermore, some of Dave's staff incorrectly concluded that I was sending Sandy and Tom Bowditch as "spies" and that they were minimally helpful.[236] But also, trouble was brewing in the chain of command from another direction.

In our initial discussion, Secretary Gates stated that the White House had already selected Dave Petraeus as the new ground commander for Iraq. As previously mentioned, I was concerned about the possibility of an alternate channel of communication bypassing me at CENTCOM. Recall that retired Army General Jack Keane, whom I consider a friend, was a longtime mentor to Dave, instrumental in saving his life years earlier in a training mishap, and championed Dave for the Iraq Commander job with the White House, Gates, and Pace. I also assumed that Jack had proposed my name to relieve John Abizaid at CENTCOM in the same circle. A suggestion he probably later regretted.

Even before I took command at CENTCOM, Petraeus had invited Keane to come out to Iraq in what became monthly visits to the battlefields for observation, advice, and then information provided to Bush and Cheney, bypassing the chain of command.[237] I admired Jack Keane when we worked together as service Vice Chiefs in the Pentagon. He was a highly effective combat-experienced leader with a deep understanding of ground military matters who cared fiercely about the U.S. Army and its reputation.

But my concern was that his reports and advice directly back to Washington, however well-intended, not only circumvented the chain of command of those charged with responsibility for the lives and well-being of our troops but was without accountability. Bypassing the chain of command was well understood by military officers as an unacceptable adulteration of the established order of responsibility and accountability. Observation and disclosure of opinion in public was one thing often dispensed at that time by journalists, think-tank pundits,

PLANNING AHEAD

and other "experts." Still, it was quite another to provide one's opinions directly to the Commander-in-Chief without informing those actually accountable: myself, Secretary Gates, Chairman Pace, and the Chief of Staff of the Army.

I raised my concerns with Dave Petraeus, who said he was only soliciting advice and experience from his mentor, which was fine with me, but not when I discovered these opinions were passed directly to the White House. Sharing my unease with General Pace and Secretary Gates, I told them that the Keane visits were no longer welcome and must stop. Jack and I had a direct conversation in which he objected strenuously to my denial of permission. But I could not countenance what I considered direct interference in the "Chain." Admiral Mike Mullen, who succeeded Pete Pace as Chairman of the Joint Chiefs, later confronted Jack and made it clear that we considered him way out of line and that he was to stay away from Iraq. However, not long thereafter, I received a call from Washington relaying word from Secretary Gates, following intervention from the White House, to rescind the restriction on Keane's visits.[238] So much for the chain of command.

CHAPTER 24

A NEW FRONT IN THE IRAQ WAR

As the blistering hot temperatures and pervasive Iraqi dust of mid-summer 2007 complicated the operational environment for our troops, things were warming up on another front. I became increasingly aware of friction among myself, Dave Petraeus, and with various Bush Administration entities in Washington.

To recap my thoughts from the start of the year, I remained convinced and supportive of the need to change our tactical employment of forces if we had any chance of leaving Iraq better than we found it in 2003. To completely withdraw, as some in Washington desired, would be an unmitigated disaster. President Bush's surge was a gamble, but a one-time, and likely our last opportunity, to reverse the losing security situation of 2006.

For many reasons, spurred by political events in Washington and Baghdad, we would soon need to begin turning security over to the Iraqis and withdraw the bulk of our combat forces. I understood that a prerequisite for a successful drawdown of troops would be establishing a responsible government in Iraq. But basic safety on the streets would be required. Accordingly, our troops strove to establish security through their new and continuing physical presence in the neighborhoods, the blast-proof protective walls they were erecting, and the unrelenting pursuit and elimination of extremists.

As the responsible Combatant Commander and regularly prompted by Secretary Gates, I was thinking ahead, assessing conditions, and planning for the eventual turnover of security responsibilities to the government of Iraq. Not that Dave was not aware of the same thing, but he was wholly immersed in the operational execution of his plans. Dave and some of his staff thought I wanted to just turn things over to the Iraqis and leave. In their view, this was the same plan as the failed strategy of the prior year.[239] In fact, their assumption was not true.

We, all involved in the war, understood that we would eventually turn responsibility over to the Iraqis. Still, I knew well that if we did not impose better security in Baghdad, there would be no functioning Iraqi government. I was 100% supportive of these efforts. I was left to question most of the details because I was not included in the operational planning as it developed, but rather briefed about it after the fact, as if I were just another visitor to Baghdad.

My skepticism about the unending avalanche of requests for more personnel in Iraq was a key point of contention. Dave and I had several heated discussions on this topic as he was adamant that he needed additional "boots on the ground" despite the increased capabilities of the new Army Brigade Combat Team structure. At one point, I recall highlighting to him that brigades equipped with the new Stryker high-mobility wheeled combat vehicles, although slightly fewer in number of assigned people than previous infantry brigades, provided vastly increased flexibility and firepower.

Dave would likely have received what he desired if the resources had been readily available without competing needs, such as Afghanistan or the critical deficit of available Army troops. A pointed comment in a recently released book by a former Vice Chairman of the Joint Chiefs of Staff illustrated the issue. "Indeed, sometimes it seemed as though commanders in the field felt as though any request should be approved as an entitlement, no matter the cost or impact."[240]

On one occasion, my frustration boiled over. I sarcastically suggested to Dave that if he was desperate for additional troops, he should stop by the Base Exchange at Camp Victory and move the soldiers there selling big-screen TVs into the field.

Also understandable, from my view, was the solidifying push by Dave and his staff to extend the surge as long as possible to increase the time available for a convincing demonstration of Iraqi governance. As Sandy Winnefeld and Tom Bowditch queried U.S. field commanders for their opinions regarding time before Iraqi security forces could take over, suspicions developed that leaving Iraq was my priority.[241]

To me, notwithstanding the complex political environment of Washington and Baghdad, the most important long-term objective of the turnover of security to the Iraqis, assuming that we could establish it with the surge, was to put in place an abiding mutual security relationship between the U.S. and Iraq, which I thought was essential. This would require, first and foremost, trust in the minds of the Iraqi leadership, many of whom were still suspicious of our long-term intentions regarding their country. I assumed this could be facilitated by us to "show some leg" and then withdraw a small part of our forces as soon as security conditions would reasonably enable it. Nonetheless, in June 2007, we were making progress with security. But the jury was still out regarding the success of our new counterinsurgency tactics, inspiring the required improvement in Iraqi governance.

Although, as previously mentioned, Secretary Gates had regularly asked about drawdown plans, at some point in late June, about the same time that Dave began advocating to extend the surge as long as possible, the Secretary went silent on this issue.

After returning from Iraq and exchanging views with Winnefeld and Bowditch, I went to Washington to meet with Secretary Gates on June 29.

Offering my assessment of the situation in Iraq and sharing my thoughts on the way forward, I opined that progress was being made in security due to the valiant work of our troops, though at a high cost in casualties. But better governance on the part of the Iraqis was almost entirely lacking. I heard no disagreement about continuing our activities to train and equip the Iraqi military and prepare them to assume responsibility for security in their country. And that we would begin the withdrawal of our combat forces as the Iraqis were judged prepared to shoulder that task. The big issue was the timing and the conditions for this responsibility transfer.

An ever-present concern of mine was the stinging memory of the humiliating U.S. abandonment of support for South Vietnam because of congressional mandates in the 1970s.[242] I was eager to preempt, if possible, a similar situation with Iraq, which I saw as a very real possibility in the wake of the upcoming Petraeus/ Crocker testimony scheduled for September.

I made no secret that I wanted to lean forward as the security situation improved in Iraq. In other words, proposing a drawdown schedule to preempt a congressionally mandated political ultimatum. The Secretary listened to my report but did not share his opinion, contrary to the assertion in his memoir that he disagreed with me at that time. It later became clear that he had aligned with the White House and Petraeus on extending the surge and that I was the odd man out.

A New Front In The Iraq War

My notes, and those from a subsequent staff meeting on July 10 with Winnefeld, Bowditch, and another key member of our team, Marine Corps Colonel Ron Johnson (later Brigadier General and USMC deputy for operations) reflect our understanding that Petraeus wanted to press on with as many forces on the ground for as long as possible, as well as a comment by President Bush during a video teleconference (VTC) with me, Gates, Petraeus, et al. on the previous day that "we will stay the course."[243] But our CENTCOM leadership discussion indicated we felt that in late June and early July, Gates was still open to more flexibility regarding the timing and extent of the initial drawdown of forces.

The strategic challenge at that time was the question of the readiness and willingness of Iraqi security forces and the Maliki political leadership to assume responsibility for their own country in the near term. Ron Johnson, with extensive combat experience on the ground in Iraq, was doubtful. As Tom Bowditch summarized it, "We're back where we started. We can't get off the Tiger. Can't leave and can't stay."[244] The principal point of disagreement was whether maintaining the bulk of the surge forces on the ground longer in Iraq would lead to real reconciliation and political progress in Baghdad sometime soon. Petraeus clearly thought it would; we at CENTCOM did not.

I could soon sense the change in the atmospherics from Washington. But the issue would not come to a head again until August, when the Chairman of the Joint Chiefs of Staff, on behalf of the Secretary, sent a request to both MNF-I and CENTCOM soliciting our inputs on the future long-term U.S. security posture in Iraq. The timing of the request for this information was driven by the much-anticipated congressional hearing, which featured testimony by Dave and by Ryan Crocker, scheduled for early September.

Meanwhile, the security situation noticeably improved in July 2007 and continued through August. This was a direct result of the population-focused activities of Dave's conventional forces in and around Baghdad, the spread of the Anbar Awakening through the tribes, and the increasing effectiveness of Stan McChrystal's JSOF forces.

My personal indicator of progress was based on visits to the battlefields in Diyala province, just north of Baghdad, which had become the epicenter of insurgent activity and fierce resistance to the American initiative to clear the "Baghdad Belts" with OPERATION PHANTOM

THUNDER. The climactic battles took place in and around Baqubah, a city of several hundred thousand people, occupied and savagely defended by Al Qaeda using myriad IEDs placed throughout the city. The U.S. effort was led by Colonel Steve Townsend and his 3rd Brigade Stryker team and Colonel Dave Sutherland and his 3rd Armored Brigade from the First Cavalry Division.

In my view, these heroic efforts had finally broken the back of the worst of the insurgent activities against U.S. forces and the Iraqi population. But to be sure, security was still tenuous, reversible, and unsupported by Iraqi political progress. The clock was running quickly, and our conundrum was exacerbated by the inability to tell how or which way the political winds would blow in Washington and Baghdad. Tom Bowditch highlighted our dilemma, "We broke this country, yet we do not have the time or the resources to fix it properly because of the intractable demons we have let loose. Everyone we talked to seems to understand that, except no one is ready to say pull the plug."[245]

CHAPTER 25

THE SURGE WAS SUCCESSFUL, BUT THEN WHAT?

CONTROVERSY OVER THE WAY AHEAD IN IRAQ

With the September 2007 date for the congressional appearance of Crocker and Petraeus drawing closer, anxiety was increasing in Washington, Baghdad, and at CENTCOM HQ in Tampa. The assignment before the two principals appeared straightforward: respond to congressional tasking for an update on the war's progress, specifically the surge, after their six months on the job. The expected questions would be: First, a progress report on security and what the Iraqi government was doing to take advantage of the surge. Second, what would the Ambassador and the General recommend going forward, particularly about American presence and troop strength in Iraq? But the background was complex, with myriad issues and challenges at every level of military and political chains of command. Not surprisingly, the views depended on where one sat and one's perceived priorities.

As the CENTCOM Commander and Petraeus's immediate superior in the chain of command, I had an input into any decision on the way forward. Whether my judgments and recommendations would be of consequence or affect the future course of events was yet to be determined.

My approach to command has always been to learn as much as possible about the situation, solicit the views of my subordinate commanders and my staff, then leverage my experience to make decisions based on the priority of the issues and the available information. The politically charged atmosphere surrounding Iraq issues and the reluctance of Dave Petraeus to include me in his planning put a premium on my having the correct information to inform upcoming decisions.

This brings us back to the reasons for sending Admiral Sandy Winnefeld and Dr. Tom Bowditch to Iraq. I needed another perspective to reinforce or invalidate my assessment of the situation and the strategic way ahead. These two professionals had peerless gifts of perception and analysis and intimate knowledge of strategy and politics from a military point of view. And importantly, they were not beholden to me or any other interested parties, as they were outside the chain of command. Contrary to several published accounts, including the Army War College history of *The U.S. Army in the Iraq War Volume 2 Surge and Withdrawal, 2007-2011*,[246] I was not opposed to the surge itself, nor were they sent with the mission to build a case for withdrawing U.S. surge forces from Iraq. They were, without any predetermination by me, to assess the situation and provide their recommendations to me on the strategic way forward to help me have the best possible understanding of the complex situation and make good decisions. As requested, they traveled extensively in Iraq and the Middle East, asking probing questions at every level. They also met with the various agencies around Washington that were connected to the war effort. As they completed the task, they prepared a short briefing to highlight their findings and recommendations for me. I personally and privately shared their preliminary assessment with General Petraeus in Qatar during the mentioned CENTCOM commanders' conference. Then I asked Winnefeld and Bowditch to share the details with Petraeus in Baghdad, which they did several days later, before returning to the U.S.

The meeting on July 17, 2007, with General Petraeus, as recorded in the meticulously detailed notes of Tom Bowditch, was not well received by the General, who reacted angrily and demanded they convey several pointed messages to me, the gist of which was his displeasure that anyone other than himself, and his personal staff, might propose a way ahead in Iraq, warning against "going behind my back" to the Secretary of Defense. He was dismissive of their assessment, stating, "Believe me, he (Fallon) knows nothing about my AOR," and "Tell your boss get out of MNF-I business." Further, "we need to concentrate now on today's fight, get the 'now' done, then in mid-January or so we can evaluate where we are. We don't see any real reductions (force levels) until the end of 2008 at the earliest."[247]

This acrimonious outburst, directed at Winnefeld and Bowditch but intended for me, untidily but accurately summed up dilemmas for me at two levels. First, the idea, vehemently expressed by General Petraeus and firmly held by Jack Keane and others, that I should not be involved in Iraq military planning and policy was an inappropriate proposition for the CENTCOM Commander and unacceptable to me.

THE SURGE WAS SUCCESSFUL, BUT THEN WHAT?

At this point in time, in the summer of 2007, we had been at war in Iraq for more than four years, with nearly 4,000 Americans already killed and almost 20,000 wounded. As the Combatant Commander accountable for all the military personnel in the AOR, including General Petraeus, it was my duty and responsibility to be directly involved in decisions regarding their lives. General Petraeus' position at this time was likely influenced by his informal but privileged information link to President Bush via General Keane. That unofficial connection bypassed the chain of command. It reflected the idea that Petraeus was reporting directly to the President and thus accountable only to him. Indeed, as Tom Bowditch reported, "It is crystal clear to me watching this little drama (the meeting with Petraeus) that these guys in Baghdad do not have the slightest interest in what Admiral Fallon thinks."[248] Not surprisingly, this is precisely how it played out. At that time and now, I reflected on that first conversation with Secretary Gates when he offered me the job at CENTCOM, and I asked, "Why me?" And his reply, "We need a strong and experienced Combatant Commander [to interact with Petraeus]."

My second dilemma, while understanding and supportive of Petraeus' focus on the near-term tactical situation, was that I saw the need to craft a way forward to put the U.S. in the best possible long-term strategic position in the region. This would mean an internally stable Iraq, closely aligned in an enduring partnership with the U.S. and able to play a stabilizing regional role, particularly given the hostile neighboring regimes in Iran and Syria. This connection would be the most important legacy the U.S. could leave behind from our intervention in Iraq, an arrangement reassuring to the GCC (Gulf Cooperation Council) allies and beneficial to the Iraqis.

The disagreement between Petraeus and me has been framed as his resistance to my allegedly wanting to "end the surge" and quickly handing over security responsibility to the Iraqis. Petraeus stated this proposition: "He (Fallon) wants to pull back and turn it all over to the Iraqis, which we tried before,"[249] and that was later in published accounts by his staff.[250] Ironically, the stated vision at every level, from President Bush down to the on-scene commanders in Iraq, was precisely this: for the U.S. to establish security as soon as possible, resume turning responsibility over to the Iraqis, and draw down our forces. The issue was the timing and extent of the drawdown and turnover of responsibility. There was no doubt in my mind that Petraeus's duty was to proffer that critical first on-scene assessment and recommendations *up the chain of command* to the President, with the intermediate commanders reviewing and leveraging their experienced views and consideration of larger theatre issues and imperatives besides those in Iraq. That is not the way things played out.

Although Petraeus did not include me in his thinking, discussion, or planning before his decisions, I shared with him the evolving assessment and recommendations that Winnefeld and Bowditch prepared for me. My intention was not to "go around him," although as his immediate superior, I was not obligated to get his endorsement. Part of the motivation for sharing thinking at the CENTCOM level was my understanding that he wanted to extend the surge indefinitely or for as long as he could, which, in my view, was infeasible. Mindful of the extended 15-month individual combat tours in Iraq, we could not just continue the current troop levels until we were *certain* that the security situation was beyond reversion, particularly given the Maliki regime's ongoing lack of progress toward good governance.

In summary, given the significantly improved security, we at CENTCOM proposed a *prudent time-based withdrawal plan*. In contrast, General Petraeus insisted on a strictly *conditions-only* withdrawal. I was keenly aware of the hard-earned security progress in Iraq that Petraeus and his troops had achieved at high cost and had no intention of squandering those gains by an ill-considered drawdown decision on my part. On the other hand, a pure, "conditions-based" decision would leave the initiative in the hands of an indecisive Iraqi government when we needed to capitalize on our success. As to mission change, it was time for more *enabling* potential Iraqi success than *imposing* security with our forces. Indeed, in this dynamic and rapidly changing situation on the ground, it had become clearer to me that we were moving from counterinsurgency to more of a peace enforcement mission; this became more apparent over the next several months.[251]

Given the many uncertainties in this equation, I thought we would have to take some prudent risk in at least announcing our intention to begin the force drawdown soon. This would induce the Iraqis to take greater responsibilities and, more importantly, show them that we seriously intended to withdraw our combat forces and partner with them in a long-term security arrangement. I knew the Iraqis were already hyper-focused on their "sovereignty" (sensitivity about inviolate

THE SURGE WAS SUCCESSFUL, BUT THEN WHAT?

national boundaries and political decision-making free of outside influence) and desire to run their country without U.S. "hands on the steering wheel." Petraeus initially saw this modest risk as intolerable. As we witnessed, the situation in Iraq played out to reduce that risk over the next six weeks, leading up to the highly anticipated congressional appearance.

Indeed, looking ahead, I saw the internal Iraqi political infighting and bureaucratic foot-dragging as a major obstacle to reaching an agreement with the Maliki government on just about anything. In many ways, we were trying to do the impossible in Iraq in 2007: recover from disastrous chaos and insecurity, impose Western political and governing standards, and turn over responsibility for these areas to the Iraqis. At the same time, we were effectively controlling almost every aspect of life in Iraq, hence further provoking their sensitivity about "sovereignty." All this within the context of an American public and Congress increasingly intolerant of our continuing engagement in that country.

The next major event for me was a 90-minute meeting back in Washington on July 25th with the Joint Chiefs of Staff in the "tank" (Joint Chiefs briefing room). At the Joint Chiefs' request, the briefing was for me to provide a current assessment of Iraq and explain my view of the way forward. The Chairman, General Pete Pace, Vice Chairman Admiral Ed Giambastiani, and the service chiefs were in attendance. The meeting began with a lengthy discussion about an article by the journalist Michael Gordon, then in Iraq interviewing Petraeus' team, which appeared in the *New York Times* the previous day.[252] The article revealed details about the Petraeus-Crocker Joint Campaign Plan (JCP) blueprint for operations in Iraq, "foresees a significant American role for the next two years," and was clearly meant to set the stage for the upcoming congressional hearing.

As an aside, an interesting opinion attributed to one of Petraeus' inner circle staff members in that article stated, "… in spite of any battlefield success the surge might have, if the Iraqi government and the various sects and groups do not come to an agreement on sharing resources and power and reconcile to stop the violence, then the surge assumption basis is invalid, and we will have to re-look the strategy."[253] As we now know, this is what happened in 2008-9. The military surge prevailed, but the political complement did not; we left Iraq, and the country soon descended into chaos again. There was no re-examination of the strategy, and we failed to agree to a lasting strategic compact with Baghdad.

I provided a briefing to the JCS that was essentially the assessment and recommendations of Winnefeld and Bowditch, who also attended and with whom I fundamentally agreed, adding my personal observations and comments, particularly on the way forward.[254] The Joint Chiefs were aware of the divergent opinions between Petraeus and me, the incessant demand by Petraeus for additional forces, and the back-channel connection to the President. I found agreement in the JCS with my assessment of the current situation in Iraq that security was improving. Still, there was little movement on the political and reconciliation front.

Most of the JCS's interest was in the potential troop drawdown proposal. I outlined the draft presentation I shared with Petraeus and noted his vehement non-concurrence, aversion to a drawdown timeline, and insistence on only "conditions-based." My proposal was to draw down the USMC 13 MEU and one of the Army brigades by the end of 2007, with four more brigades out by summer 2008, leaving us with 15 Army brigades in-country at that time, which is where we started the surge, having now extended it for a full year. This plan would leave Petraeus another five or six months with all the surge brigades in place. I reminded the group that the 13th MEU was the CENTCOM Theatre reserve, which I agreed to loan to Petraeus for three months, expiring in September. Which would be fortuitous, as their departure could signal the start of the larger drawdown.

The Vice Chairman then mentioned a *new* Petraeus proposal, just received, which was more in line with what I had briefed for the initial drawdown and reflected a change from Petraeus' original intention to defer the drawdown. It had not been shared or sent through me for comment. General Pace then proposed a desire to reconcile the two "plans" and announced his intention to have the JCS issue a formal Planning Order to CENTCOM and MNF-I, the goal of which would be to provide a single detailed proposal back to Washington before the congressional hearing. The Planning Order would request recommendations and comments for three potential scenarios: security conditions strongly improve, conditions deteriorate significantly, or a middle-of-the-road scenario where things continue as they were. The Planning Order also included a list of about a dozen questions requiring

THE SURGE WAS SUCCESSFUL, BUT THEN WHAT?

detailed responses in specific areas of JCS interest. Among other things, it specified a concept for long-term military support for Iraqi security forces, a plan for detainee transition, proposed rules of engagement for U.S. forces in support of a long-term security posture in Iraq, and contractor support proposals.

In hindsight, although leaving the tank session with the verbal concurrence and preference of the chiefs for a combination of a time and conditions-based drawdown, I did not get the sense that the chiefs were prepared to play a future significant role in the details of the road ahead. General Pace voiced concern about the need to try to condition the President to entertain alternatives that might not be strictly in line with what we expected Petraeus to propose. To his great credit, Pete Pace worked hard over the next month to broker a compromise between Petraeus and me on the drawdown plan.

In addition to Iraq, where the outcome was critical to our country's military and political future, I had parallel ongoing planning efforts as the theatre commander. Of particular importance was the newly discovered nuclear reactor in Syria and the soon-to-be executed OPERATION MOUNTAIN SHADOW in Tora Bora, Afghanistan.

The previously discussed JCS Planning Order was issued a few days later, on August 1, and the staff in Tampa went to work preparing responses to the many questions and requests for information contained in it.

For his part, Petraeus ignored the Planning Order, providing no input to me regarding the response, focusing instead on his upcoming testimony to Congress, including his recommendation to continue the surge focus on population security. In the end, he would also propose the possibility of a conditions-based commencement of a drawdown of forces, which, as it turned out regarding timing, was remarkably close to what I originally proposed based on the Winnefeld-Bowditch recommendations. Despite this, tension remained.

The essence of my response to the JCS Planning Order, in addition to providing detailed answers to the many questions, was an outline of how I suggested we transition our military structure in Iraq in anticipation of a long-term security agreement between our countries. The questions proposed in the Planning Order were all forward-looking. My interpretation of comments expressed by the JCS during that tank session in Washington was that the idea of the Planning Order might be a useful means to get Petraeus and me on the same page. I sent a draft of my response to the document to Petraeus, who declined to endorse it. He was focused exclusively on the near term. He wanted nothing to do with anything that might divert attention from the current JCP (Joint Campaign Plan) in Iraq and his upcoming congressional testimony.

Those weeks in August 2007 were a whirlwind for me. We were approaching the climactic point in Iraq with an intense debate about how to frame our strategy going forward and key decisions about the drawdown of forces. In the middle of these discussions, I returned to Washington to obtain President Bush's approval for the Tora Bora operation. My busy travel schedule that month included Afghanistan, a meeting with King Abdullah in Saudi Arabia, a first visit in many years by a senior U.S. military officer to Lebanon, then in turmoil, and a lengthy live prime-time television interview on Al Jazeera in Doha, the first for a U.S. military officer. The purpose of the latter was to counter the prevalent negative media narrative with a positive view of the improved security situation in Iraq. Near the end of the month, I was back in Baghdad to get a personal update before meeting with President Bush again a few days hence. While in Iraq, I sat down with Petraeus to narrow our differences regarding future policy proposals.

In a nutshell, I wanted to take advantage of what I firmly believed was his short-term success in achieving security by accelerating the transition of security responsibility to the Iraqis and beginning our drawdown of forces. I found Dave to be cautious and conservative. He did not want to risk any backsliding in the security situation, which I understood. But I was focused on what I considered the bigger issue, the long-term security situation in the country and our evolving relationship with the Iraqi government. At that time, we were still in charge of the country, not only providing security but directing or overseeing everything else, while the Maliki Administration procrastinated and deferred all the hard political decisions. In my view, we needed to make them take responsibility. I thought we had a window to do that, having established vastly improved security in the country. It was imperfect, but security was moving in the right direction. It seemed reasonable to assume that it would continue to improve, and we would still have the preponderance of the surge force available in Iraq for the remainder of the year. As Dave and I went through the mechanics of discussing the proposed drawdown, we really were not that far apart on dates. A principal difference was the mission change to transition security to the Iraqis. I wanted it sooner, Dave later.

Following several video teleconferences with Petraeus, General Pace, and the Joint Staff attempting to refine and mesh an agreed approach to the President, it was back to Washington for me. On August 31, I met with the President in the situation room, and the Vice President, Gates, Rice, Hadley, and Pace were in attendance. Crocker and Petraeus presented their proposals via video teleconference from Baghdad. By this time, Dave and I had reached an agreement on the basic plan, but I remained convinced we should accelerate the turnover of security and the drawdown. In a couple of briefing slides I sent to the White House the night before, I outlined my view of why faster was important and noted the downside of extending the large U.S. military footprint in the country. A principal factor in my mind was that a big presence would continue to attract the lethal attention of Al Qaeda, still active despite diminished capability, inflicting more casualties on our troops, now their primary target. We would also provide an enduring excuse for the Iranian-aligned politicians and militias seeking the complete removal of any U.S. presence in the country. My slides created a fuss in the White House, and Pete Pace asked me to modify them to a less aggressive stance.

The meeting lasted for several hours, mostly consumed by a dialogue between the President (from Washington) and Petraeus and Crocker (from Baghdad). Following this discussion, the President asked for my view. I told him I supported the proposal but believed we could and should entertain more prudent risk by accelerating the timelines. Given his prior experience as a fighter pilot in the Texas Air Guard, I tried to explain my position to the President with an analogy from aviation. "Mr. President, envision yourself in a dogfight in which you were being pressed by an opponent on your tail at the six o'clock position." "So, what do I do?" asked Bush. "To turn the tables, you could take some risk by abruptly slowing your aircraft and then executing a high-G barrel roll, forcing your opponent to overshoot, ending up in a position in front of you, now giving you the advantage," which I demonstrated with my hands. "So, take a little risk, thereby reversing the situation, ending the encounter with a victory."[255]

Whether the President understood my aviation metaphor, I am not sure. Still, it was certain he did not want to accept any more risk and elected to go with Dave Petraeus's more conservative approach to drawdown timing and mission shift. In addition to trying to accelerate the transition, I sensed that the Maliki Administration would view the slow drawdown as an excuse (ours) to keep us in Iraq. It could also become an obstacle in the upcoming discussion about a long-term security arrangement and a SOFA (Status of Forces Agreement) affording legal protection to U.S. forces remaining in Iraq.

Some media members were hyperventilating in public during this lead-up to the Crocker-Petraeus congressional appearance, with stories based on snippets of fact but mostly conjecture. A *Washington Post* headline on September 9, the day before the first hearing commenced, blared, "Among Top Officials, 'Surge' Has Sparked Dissent and Infighting," citing alleged competing "plans."[256]

PRESIDENT BUSH TRIP TO AL-ASAD, IRAQ

A few days later, I flew back to Washington and joined Secretary Gates on his C-17 transport aircraft for a flight to Iraq. Landing at al-Asad airbase in Anbar province on August 3, we joined General Pace, Ambassador Crocker, Generals Petraeus and Odierno, awaiting the arrival of President Bush and Secretary Rice, who were coming for an unannounced visit to Iraq. It was an opportunity for the President to see the whole Iraqi leadership in person, Prime Minister Maliki and the Iraq Presidency Council (Jalal Talabani, Adil Mahdi, and Tariq al-Hashimi), and the President of the Kurdish region, Masoud Barzani. But the principal reason for the trip was to meet with Sheikh Abd al-Sattar al-Rishawi, the leader of the "Anbar Awakening,"[257] and his fellow tribal sheiks, along with the governor of Anbar province, Maamoon Sami Rasheed al-Alwani, and the provincial governing council leadership.

The meeting was remarkable in several respects. First, it was indicative of the success in improving security in the country. The presidential arrival, in the huge blue and white painted B-747 Air Force One (think lucrative target), landing at an airfield that until quite recently was under frequent rocket and mortar attack by Al Qaeda and their insurgent allies, was a visible testament to the turnaround. Second, the actual meeting in a building on the airfield was conducted in a relaxed and congenial atmosphere with open engagement by attendees representing each of the major Iraqi sects, Shia, Sunni, and Kurd, and the critically important group of Sunni tribal leaders from Anbar who were instrumental in turning the tide against Al Qaeda with the "Awakening." Third, it was an opportunity that I am sure Bush relished to personally spur the political process to obtain action on Iraqi governance.

In an initial "pull-aside" meeting among the Americans, Bush asked Crocker, "Can you say we will be successful? ... that the basic instincts and desires of people for good will prevail?... We know there is a deep desire in people for peace." Crocker replied, "We can be successful... but this was not just a regime change, it was a revolution." Following some back-and-forth about the details of recent events and the fragility of the security situation, Bush said that he did not like that "It could all come off the tracks." Crocker concluded, "The Iraqis (here in Anbar) were the first to see the Al Qaeda caliphate and rejected it."[258]

When the full complement of Americans and Iraqis was together, Bush opened with congratulations and an admonishment to "get moving" with political progress to match the security improvement. "It is important to give confidence to the Iraqi people and their U.S. supporters... we want a long-term strategic partnership." And "I brought the American leaders to show respect and to encourage your leadership." The President was fired up and played the role of cheerleader, noting, "We all have the same God." And "I came to salute your courage!"[259]

The Iraqi political leadership was welcoming and magnanimous toward one another. Prime Minister Maliki gave a practical assessment of the situation and offered, "Thanks for the sacrifices of the U.S. Armed Forces to prevent a civil war." He proclaimed the Bush strategy successful and that he was determined to pursue reconciliation, adding, "We cannot allow failure." After kudos and stressing the need for national reconciliation, Tariq al-Hashemi said, "Some of the population doesn't trust and has misgivings." To which Bush replied, "Can you, as leaders, put misgivings aside? Can you put the people together for the common good?" As the leaders loosened up, they highlighted their issues and priorities within Iraq. Barzani proclaimed, "No more dictators... we need a unified position, not regional interference," a thinly veiled shot at Maliki's authoritarian bent. Adil Mahdi, pushing for openness in political discussions, added, "As a former runner, it is most important to know how to finish."

The Anbar governor and the sheiks were vocal in stating their complaints and needs, but conciliatory overall in dialogue with their colleagues from Baghdad. Sheikh Sattar, respected by all for his leadership in the "Awakening," opined, "The former regime (Saddam) was not Sunni but anti-Sunni, anti-Shia, and anti-Kurd. They served Saddam Hussein's family." He expressed hope that the Americans would stay with them and prevail. In closing, he offered, "Don't listen to the media, Mr. President."[260]

In a most unfortunate turn of events, Sheikh Sattar was assassinated by Al Qaeda only 10 days after this meeting.[261] Anbar Governor Maamoon al-Alwani, alleged to have survived more than 30 assassination attempts, proclaimed, "Our tomorrow starts today." In summary, that meeting was a visible measure of the success of the military surge, providing optimism and encouragement in advance of the upcoming congressional appearances.

CROCKER AND PETRAEUS CONGRESSIONAL TESTIMONY SEPTEMBER 2007

The adage that "timing is everything" certainly applied to this near-term lead-up to the much-anticipated Washington appearance of Crocker and Petraeus, who were successful in satisfying Congress in September and enabling President Bush to claim a policy "win" in Iraq for the short term.[262] Several factors contributed to this success. First, the continued outstanding work of Generals Petraeus, Odierno, and McCrystal and their troops to improve the security situation, as demonstrated by the meeting at al-Asad Airbase and the significant decline in attacks around the country, which had now shifted security substantially in favor of U.S. forces. Second, the critically important contribution of the Anbar tribal "Awakening," in which they flipped allegiances from supporting the insurgency to allying with us against Al Qaeda. The third major factor was the decree on 29 August by the firebrand cleric Muqtada al-Sadr for his potent Shia militia, the "Mahdi Army," to stand down and cease attacks on U.S. forces for six months.[263] Al-Sadr was opposed to the U.S. military presence in Iraq and was a persistent agitator since 2003. Although living in Iran at the time, he

THE SURGE WAS SUCCESSFUL, BUT THEN WHAT?

had incited his followers, supplied with deadly Iranian munitions, into armed attacks against U.S. forces. His cease-fire decree, partly due to U.S. military pressure on his militia, was timely and most welcome. Thus, by the date of the congressional hearings, the security situation in Iraq had improved decidedly.

On September 10, 2007, Crocker and Petraeus testified at the much-anticipated Joint Hearing before the combined House Committee on Foreign Affairs and Committee on Armed Forces. Then, the following day, they made a similar appearance, delivering the Crocker-Petraeus Report before the Senate Committee on Foreign Relations. Just before the hearings, a group opposed to the U.S. presence in Iraq organized a public protest campaign that included a full-page advertisement in the *New York Times* attempting to smear General Petraeus in an outrageously ugly and personal attack.[264]

Shrugging off these affronts, the Ambassador and the General provided highly credible and convincing testimony regarding the surge's success and the current situation. They announced their recommendations for the future, including the imminent drawdown of the USMC MEU and an Army brigade before the end of the year, as well as the transition to Iraqi assumption of responsibility for security. Of note was the final of 13 slides that General Petraeus presented in his congressional testimonies. It was a graphic portrayal of his "Recommended Force Reductions/Mission Shift" over time. It matched my proposal through the summer of 2008, with unspecified further drawdowns to be "conditions-based."[265] These two American patriots deserve major credit for their unselfish service to their nation and, specifically, their extraordinarily successful leadership in turning around the security situation in 2007 Iraq.

However, in the absence of any other enunciated long-range plan, the emphasis on a conditions-based drawdown became the de facto U.S. strategy for Iraq, essentially open-ended, without fixed responsibility for the Iraqis.[266]

CHAPTER 26

LONG-TERM U.S. SECURITY POSTURE IN IRAQ

The success of the Crocker-Petraeus testimony before Congress provided some political breathing room in the U.S. to shift focus to some longer-term planning. My response to the JCS Planning Order entitled "Long-Term Security Posture in Iraq" offered a vision for the future of Iraq based on a list of assumptions regarding the improving security situation and continued U.S. engagement in Iraq. It outlined what I thought the strategic framework and objectives should be. Then it went into some detail about the actual construct of the post-surge U.S. military presence in Iraq. The latter envisioned what I called the "Two Pillar Construct." Pillar One would be a security assistance command led by a military officer reporting to the ambassador in Baghdad, like those we had established in other countries, to provide training, education, technology transfer, military sales, and other traditional forms of support. The command would work closely with the Iraqi military to enhance its capability and sustain its needs.

I envisioned this command, nominally entitled Office of Military Cooperation – Iraq (OMC-I), as a logical successor to the existing and previously described MNSTC, then primarily focused on training the Iraqi army. The proposed new entity would be structured to provide a full range of support and assistance to the host nation, Iraq. A few weeks later, General Petraeus sent a message signaling his support for this new initiative.

The second pillar, anticipating a continued drawdown of U.S. forces and a parallel reduction in headquarters and rank structure, would be a non-permanent presence of significantly reduced U.S. combat forces led by a JTF Commander, taking over from General Petraeus or his successor later during the post-surge drawdown. This transitional force, with fewer assigned combat troops than the current 20 brigades, eventually on the order of 50,000 troops, was envisioned as a quick response force to back up the Iraqi military should support be needed for security and to provide special capabilities, such as intelligence, airlift, medical, and fire support that were not yet mature in the Iraqi army.

LONG-TERM U.S. SECURITY POSTURE IN IRAQ

This force could assume missions subject to a joint Iraqi-U.S. agreement. As the transition of responsibility objectives were achieved, the missions would be scaled back and finally eliminated. Eventually, with mutual U.S. and Iraqi agreement, this force would be withdrawn. Additional information was provided in my response to CJCS, including many of the details required to answer the CJCS Information Requirements (questions) included in the JCS Planning Order.

This second pillar of my proposal, with a downgraded headquarters rank structure in addition to the troop drawdown, was far too forward-leaning for the Bush Administration, which declined to even consider it, although it might have been immensely helpful in concluding a long-term security arrangement.

Many details in my response to the JCS Information Requirements were later adapted. Still, the cornerstone proposal for the "two-pillar" approach was not. In hindsight, although the proposals were classified at the time, and I intentionally avoided affixing dates to a timeline, I believe neither Bush nor Petraeus wanted any discussion that might reveal the scope and speed of a future drawdown. As a result, it was ignored.

DIPLOMATIC EFFORTS TOWARD A LONG-TERM AGREEMENT

Highlighting the urgency to establish future plans was the looming deadline on U.S. and Coalition forces' authority to operate in Iraq, which was based on U.N. Security Council Resolution (UNSCR) 1723, scheduled to expire on December 31, 2007, later extended "one last time" by UNSCR 1790 to 31 December 2008.[267] With the mandate for the U.S.-led multinational force presence in Iraq expiring, we faced many new, mostly political challenges. As it became clear that security was dramatically improved by the autumn of 2007, political infighting within the Maliki government intensified.

In the U.S. view, the necessary steps to take advantage of the improved security were, first, progress on reconciliation between Shia and Sunni factions. Efforts in this area were thwarted by strong opposition from Iran, which pushed its Iraqi surrogate Shia militias to resist reconciliation, which was made worse by Malik's sectarian bias and his fear that the "Ba'athists will return" if he provided concessions to the Sunnis.

This issue was illustrated at the al-Asad Airfield meeting and by the proliferation of Sunni tribes participating in the "Anbar Awakening," who rightly expected compensation and to be included in the Iraqi security forces. Maliki resisted these requests, again fearing a political power shift back to the Sunnis. The second issue was the need to decentralize political decision-making from Baghdad to the provinces, especially regarding finances. The third major point of contention was oil revenue, the financial lifeblood of the country, and the need to achieve a fair apportionment among the competing interest groups. Particularly adamant were the Kurds, with President Barzani demanding a proportional percentage for the people of the northern Kurdish provinces based on the size of the population.

The security situation in Iraq continued to gradually improve through the remainder of 2007. Noteworthy advances occurred in the historically troubled areas of Anbar and Diyala provinces. Two memorable, contrasting scenes from Fallujah in Anbar are etched in my mind. The first was a battlefield reconnaissance with the Marines in mid-summer 2007. Heavy fighting still raged in the city as the Marines fought to recapture it, for the third time, from Al Qaeda and their allies. As we dashed to the shelter of a forward command post in a partially destroyed building, I noticed several armed Iraqi men in civilian clothes running up the street to our left. Grabbing the sleeve of my escorting Marine major, I pointed and said, "Uh oh, better check your flank here." He chuckled, "No worries, Admiral, these are our guys. See, they are all wearing the same armbands." This was my first-person introduction to the tribal awakening "Sons of Iraq" in action. The combined Marine and tribal force soon liberated the city again. Still, it was a shambles of debris from the fighting, and the population was nowhere to be seen.

The difference was astonishing on a return visit to the city seven months later. The streets had been cleared of debris, reconstruction was underway in many places, the civilian population had returned, and I was walking around without weapons or body armor. The central market was crowded, and when I saw that the gold merchants had returned to display their wares openly, I turned to my escort and said, "Seeing this tells me things are getting back to normal."[268]

LONG-TERM U.S. SECURITY POSTURE IN IRAQ

But progress on the political front was glacially slow to nonexistent. Security improvements allowed the Iraqi political side to continue squabbling with less pressure to resolve their many disputes. Frustration on this point was evident from bottom to top on the American leadership side. My notes from the October 29 video conference with the President recorded that he was "pissed at the lack of political progress in Baghdad."[269] In my view, the Iranians were exercising the leverage they had with their surrogate militias and their supporters in the Shia-dominated Maliki Administration in opposing anything and everything that could be beneficial to the U.S.

I was and remain convinced that the only real hope for a successful end to the U.S. intervention was concluding a long-term security agreement with Iraq. Although it was previously discussed, this effort picked up momentum following the September congressional testimony. The first detailed public declaration was a document dated November 26, 2007, co-signed by Bush and Maliki, entitled *Declaration of Principles (DOP) for a Long-Term Relationship of Cooperation and Friendship Between the Republic of Iraq and the United States of America*. (See it at the end of this chapter).[270] This agreement was appropriately focused on high-level principles divided into three "spheres:" political, economic, and security. The agreement stated, "...bilateral negotiations shall begin as soon as possible with the aim to achieve, before July 31, 2008, agreement..." Events were off to a good start.

However, shortly before this public declaration, Secretary Gates shared with me the decision by Secretary Rice to appoint Ambassador Robert Loftis to head the State Department negotiating team. This appointment made sense as Loftis headed the Department of State Bureau of Political-Military Affairs. I did not know him personally, but I was acquainted with his background, particularly his prior negotiation of basing rights and terms of our access to and use of facilities in Central Asia. Loftis's service and career had been splendid, but I saw this decision as problematic.

I responded to Gates with my view that this appointment, given his background as a basing access and Status of Forces Agreement (SOFA) expert, would likely result in a focus on the details rather than the broad scope of the necessary agreements, and that this would be the wrong approach in dealing with the Iraqis given their hypersensitivity to sovereignty and the other nationalistic baggage accumulated over the past several years.[271] Particularly mindful of past Ottoman, British, and American occupation and their consequences, the Iraqis were intent on ruling themselves as a sovereign state.

My perspective was moot as Gates told me it was the Secretary of State's business, not mine. The key point that I tried to make, unsuccessfully, was that a long-term security arrangement with Iraq should have been designed from the start with a focus on strategic issues as enunciated in the November "Declaration of Principles," rather than the details, particularly in areas of extreme Iraqi political sensitivity like the SOFA. In fact, the administration went forward negotiating two related agreements, a Strategic Framework Agreement (SFA) and the previously mentioned SOFA, but one that differed substantially from traditional SOFAs, notably including an expiration date, "...authorization for military operations, the establishment of a withdrawal timeline, and the creation of committees to implement the agreement."[272]

As an illustration, I will relate a conversation with the Iraqi National Security Advisor (in three Iraqi Administrations, 2005-09). Dr. Mowaffak al-Rubaie and I spoke at an event for another purpose that we both attended in Manama, Bahrain, in October 2007. Our conversation illuminates the sensitivity to Iraqi sovereignty. Dr. (Neurologist) Rubaie was Maliki's confidant and close advisor and played a key role in U.S.-Iraq negotiations. He highlighted areas of particular interest in the upcoming discussions between our two countries, citing, among others, the need to minimize public U.S. military visibility as security improved. He mentioned the heavy military escort for senior officials like me when transiting streets and highways around Baghdad. I told him that once Iraq assumed responsibility for its own security, those U.S. escorts would disappear, as this was a task that they would assume. He said, "I do not believe it. You will insist on continuing this practice." I disagreed and told him that when I traveled to other countries, the host nation assumed the responsibility for my protection. He was unfamiliar with how this worked and was in denial, so I brought him over to the Bahraini Minister of Defense, who also attended the reception, and asked him to explain to Rubaie how Bahrain provides security. "We take full responsibility for his safety and security anywhere he goes in the country, and all of the security personnel are Bahraini." I added, "Only one U.S. security person travels with me in plain clothes."[273] This interest in micro-management of mundane procedures reinforced my impression of how difficult the upcoming negotiation task would be, not to mention the big issues involving legal protections for U.S. service personnel and civilian contractors.

Rubaie and I enjoyed a courteous, professional, and personal relationship with regular dialogue throughout my tenure as Commander CENTCOM. During one trip to Baghdad, he invited me to dinner at his home to enjoy the Iraqi national Dish of "Masgouf," which he prepared himself. The masgouf fish, from the Tigris River, is considered a delicacy in Iraq, and this event, at which I was the only guest, was quite an honor. But I had to redeem myself from a social faux pas when I first saw the fish and exclaimed, "It looks just like a carp from back home." A befuddled Dr. Rubaie retorted, "It is not a carp; it is a masgouf." Appropriately chastened, I watched as he and a helper prepared and baked the fish on an open fire. It was delicious, but it still looked like a carp to me!

Other senior officials in the Iraqi government were anxious to solidify a long-term security arrangement with the U.S. as soon as possible,[274] particularly the leadership of the new Iraqi Armed Forces. The defense minister (2006-10), General Abdul Qadir al-Obeidi, and Chief of Defense (2004-15), General Babaker Zebari, were particularly keen to remain close to U.S. forces. Both had extensive professional experience in the Iraqi army during Saddam's regime but ran afoul of the dictator and were jailed and then exiled for speaking out against him. Judged trustworthy in the post-Saddam era, they were installed in the two highest positions in the Iraqi military, later working with General Petraeus and his team during the surge. Babaker was a Kurd, and Obeidi was a Sunni. To the U.S. leadership, their diverse backgrounds were a good omen for a potentially integrated and effective new Iraqi army. Unfortunately, despite their longevity in the Maliki Administration, they lacked influence outside the Army in the Shia-dominated government.

By the end of 2007, as serious discussions about the future relationship were underway, Obedi asked to chat with me privately. "Admiral, I need your help to ensure we get American equipment, particularly armored vehicles and aircraft, for the Iraqi Armed Forces." He noted they would be willing to finance the expensive U.S. equipment. Indeed, by this point, the Iraqi government was paying most of the cost to outfit the Iraqi Armed Forces. I was a bit surprised by his request, mindful of American gear's high cost and complexity. He explained, "We cannot maintain this high-technology equipment on our own. We will need continued U.S. help for training and support. If we buy the equipment from you, your technicians will come with it. This is good because it is a way to keep you close to us."[275] I am sure his comments were sparked by his recall of the Iraqi army during Saddam's rule, when most of their equipment came from the Soviet Union and, with it, a heavy Russian presence, maintenance, and operational support. I got the point and was also mindful of the benefit of compatible equipment if Iraq became a partner in regional security.

BLACKWATER CONTRACTORS

No sooner had the drama of the congressional hearings passed than an event occurred in Baghdad with profound negative implications in the U.S. and for our work in Iraq. By way of background, given all the military tasks on the plate of General Petraeus and the limited availability of combat troops for other missions, the protection and escort of our diplomatic and other civilian personnel was assumed by U.S. government-funded contractors.

A key role in this vital support mission was provided by Blackwater Security Company, founded a decade earlier by former U.S. Navy SEAL Erik Prince. Operating in Iraq since 2003, the company was first hired to provide personal security support for Paul Bremer, the head of the Coalition Provisional Authority (CPA). This personal protection mission, staffed by heavily armed civilian personnel, most with former U.S. military backgrounds, used armored ground vehicles as well as helicopters in the conduct of their missions. The Blackwater role in Iraq was expanded the following year with a contract from the U.S. Department of State to provide protective services for diplomatic and related personnel throughout Iraq.[276] They did essential tasks in a very demanding and hostile environment, highlighted by an ugly incident at Fallujah in 2004 by Iraqi insurgents involving the capture, mutilation, and murder of four Blackwater contractors on a logistics mission.

I had known Blackwater CEO Erik Prince for years since his companies provided excellent training services for the U.S. Navy. The role of his company in Iraq and Afghanistan, among many places around the world, was to provide essential security services at a time when our uniformed military members were overtaxed. As his company worked for the Department of State, his people did not come under Dave Petraeus' jurisdiction but coordinated their activities with our military command in Baghdad.

On September 16, 2007, while providing security for State Department personnel attending a meeting near al-Nissour Square, close to the diplomatic "Green Zone" in downtown Baghdad, a deadly incident occurred with worldwide repercussions. The event was triggered by a bomb-rigged vehicle explosion, among the most common but deadly events in Iraq, at Nisour Square. The blast prompted the Blackwater security team to prepare to escort the State Department personnel back to the safety of the Green Zone.

Exactly what happened in the ensuing chaotic minutes has been reported in widely varying accounts, but regrettably, more than a dozen Iraqi civilians were killed, and a larger number injured.[277] Prime Minister Maliki and most of the Iraqi populace were outraged, and he ordered Blackwater operations in the country terminated. The event was sensationalized in the media, and the U.S. Congress reacted along typical partisan lines, with Democrat leadership demanding a wide range of investigations and punitive actions. Erik Prince became the new poster person of the anti-war crowd, with criminal and civil legal proceedings against his company continuing for more than a decade. Later, Prince would become enmeshed in controversy resulting from his messianic zeal and involvement in dubious international security activities.

In the immediate politicization of the Nissour Square incident, the term "contractors" took on a universally negative connotation as all companies working with government contracts were lumped together and assumed evil, regardless of task or function. This cynical view of contractors emanated from the civilian casualties that resulted from the Baghdad incident and an opinion that advocates for armed intervention in Iraq were profiting financially from the conflict. In fact, most contractors had nothing to do with security, nor were they connected to Washington insiders, but provided a wide range of mainly logistical and other administrative services, freeing military personnel from these support functions.

At my level, the fallout from this incident was twofold: First, back in Washington, the relative calm following the Crocker-Petraeus testimony evaporated into recriminations and renewed demand to immediately pull all forces out of Iraq. Second, to impose more work on General Petraeus, sorting out how to exercise oversight of all the contractors working in Iraq, while also continuing his fight against the insurgents. This event would result in more obstacles on the Iraqi side as we tried to negotiate long-term security agreements with the Maliki government. It became a focal point for Iraqi complaints about the U.S. presence.

Meanwhile, on the plus side, Petraeus and I worked through our differences together, and except for one incident a few weeks later in Bahrain, we worked in tandem for the balance of my time at CENTCOM.

DETAINEES

A good news story that evolved from that inauspicious first visit to the main insurgent detention center at Camp Bucca early in my tenure at CENTCOM was the remarkable pivot achieved under the leadership of Major General Doug Stone.

In less than a year, he turned the camp from a ticking time bomb of overcrowded, festering discontent into a detention center that effectively segregated hard-core evildoers from a much larger population of less nefarious transgressors and innocents swept up with the bad actors.[278]

In addition to instituting the previously mentioned detainee hearings to identify the corrigibles and reintegrate them into their communities, General Stone undertook a camp-wide effort to rehabilitate willing detainees using mullahs to counter the radical proselytization of Al Qaeda and its allies. He also began an extensive education process in basic life skills to prepare detainees for reintegration into Iraqi society. I was elated with the results of his incredible dedication and resourcefulness and eagerly tried to assist him in lobbying for congressional funds to continue his good works. At one point, he put together an impressive briefing for Chairman Murtha of the U.S. House Appropriations Committee. This resulted in the necessary funds to continue his exemplary programs at Camp Bucca.[279] Never one to rest on his laurels, he volunteered to go to Afghanistan to help us with detainee operations in that conflict zone. I made it a point to stop at Camp Bucca on my final visit to Iraq in 2008 to see the latest examples of progress and to thank him for his remarkable achievements in an unenviable position.

NEGOTIATIONS DRAG ON

Negotiations on the SOFA and SFA, soon led on the U.S. side by Ambassador Ryan Crocker and Brett McGurk of the NSC, proved even more protracted and painful than initially feared. Progress was hindered by the sheer volume and intricacy of issues, large and small. An indication of the scope and complexity of the challenge was illustrated in advance by the fact that it took me 30 pages in a condensed, bulletized format to respond to the Joint Chiefs' Planning Order of August 1, 2007. This response to a dozen questions, each pertinent to aspects of any long-term security agreement, reflected only the initial U.S. concerns about issues that had yet to be resolved.

On the Iraqi side, the spectrum of unresolved internal problems related to any U.S. force drawdown and consequent turnover of security reflected local and national concerns. External pressure, none of it helpful, was ratcheted up by Iran, which used every tactic imaginable to thwart the proposed U.S.-Iraqi agreement. Progress was slow, missing the original July 2008 deadline, as internal Iraqi dissension proved frustrating for the U.S. negotiators.[280] For example, spurred on by Iran, most Shia parties sought the total ouster of the U.S. military presence, but Maliki, recognizing the danger of a complete withdrawal, wanted an extended U.S. presence.

Finally, on November 17, 2008, on behalf of both the U.S. and Iraq, Ambassador Crocker and Iraq Foreign Minister Zebari signed two documents: (1) *The Strategic Framework Agreement for a Relationship of Friendship and Cooperation Between the United States and the Republic of Iraq* [281] and, (2) *The Agreement Between the United States of America and the Republic of Iraq on the Withdrawal of United States Forces from Iraq and the Organization of Their Activities During Their Temporary Presence in Iraq,*[282] thereafter called the SOFA in shorthand. The latter agreement contained the military and security details, including the withdrawal of U.S. combat forces from all Iraqi cities and villages by June 30, 2009. Critically, the agreement also pointedly required the departure of *all* U.S. military personnel from the country by December 31, 2011.

Already retired when this document was signed, I recall being astounded at what I considered U.S. acquiescence to an incredibly shortsighted, remarkably naïve, and ill-considered demand by the Iraqi government. President Bush traveled to Baghdad and, with Prime Minister Maliki, signed the agreements on December 14, 2008, brushing aside an assault by an angry Iraqi journalist who tossed his shoes at the President. With only a few weeks remaining before the turnover of administrations to President Obama, Bush hailed the agreement as a great achievement. Instead of providing appropriate conditions to extend and protect a small residual U.S. military presence, the SOFA mandated the withdrawal of *all* U.S. military personnel and self-expired at the end of 2011.[283]

After a recent discussion with our long-serving, consummate ambassador and principal negotiator, Ryan Crocker, I came to understand the rationale behind what, in its wording, seemed to be a recipe for disaster. According to Ryan, the backstory was that he and both Bush and Maliki saw the need for a long-term residual military presence in Iraq. However, as the negotiations dragged on and the clock kept moving, the desire on the part of the administration to have an agreement in place before President Bush left office was pressing. How many troops remained in Iraq, where, and for how long, was yet to be resolved. The decision was to "kick the can down the road" and establish an end date for the U.S. military presence well into the future with the expectation that it would be easier to reopen negotiations later and conclude an agreement once most of the U.S. forces were already out of the country and "normalcy" had returned to an Iraq without the overbearing U.S. presence.[284]

But circumstances did not play out as envisioned.

In the final bitter turn of events in the eight-year saga of the U.S. military intervention in Iraq, relied-upon assumptions again proved to be invalid, and important decisions did not achieve the desired results. The new Obama Administration, with its principal focus on domestic affairs and a President who had campaigned to get U.S. troops out of Iraq, declined to negotiate a new "SOFA" to extend the U.S. military presence there. The decision was taken to let the accord expire. All U.S. troops left the country, and the arduously negotiated agreement terminated on December 31, 2011. The long-sought goal of a stable, secure, and contributing partner in regional security vanished.

Long-Term U.S. Security Posture In Iraq

In hindsight, the troop surge in 2007 dramatically reduced the level of violence in Iraq and improved security in the near term. But in retrospect, in that hard-won security window, the U.S. negotiated our complete withdrawal without preserving the desired benefits of a long-term security arrangement and force presence. After the U.S. withdrawal in 2011, chaos returned to Iraq in less than three years with the appearance of the bloody "caliphate" of ISIL (Islamic State of Iraq and the Levant) or Daesh, as it was known in the Middle East, the genocidal successor to Al Qaeda. Absent any U.S. military oversight and assistance, the Iraqi military collapsed, ISIL overran most of western and northern Iraq, and the country returned to turmoil with thousands of additional lives lost. Eventually, the Obama Administration decided to redeploy U.S. forces to Iraq to help stabilize the situation and defeat ISIL. In some respects, this return was a rerun of those painful days in 2006-07.

DECISIONS, DISCORD & DIPLOMACY

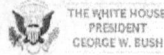

THE WHITE HOUSE
PRESIDENT
GEORGE W. BUSH

CLICK HERE TO PRINT

For Immediate Release
Office of the Press Secretary
November 26, 2007

Declaration of Principles for a Long-Term Relationship of Cooperation and Friendship Between the Republic of Iraq and the United States of America

In Focus: Iraq

As Iraqi leaders confirmed in their Communiqué signed on August 26, 2007, and endorsed  White House News
by President Bush, the Governments of Iraq and the United States are committed to developing a long-term relationship of cooperation and friendship as two fully sovereign and independent states with common interests. This relationship will serve the interest of coming generations based on the heroic sacrifices made by the Iraqi people and the American people for the sake of a free, democratic, pluralistic, federal, and unified Iraq.

The relationship of cooperation envisioned by the Republic of Iraq and the United States includes a range of issues, foremost of which is cooperation in the political, economic, cultural, and security fields, taking account of the following principles:

First: The Political, Diplomatic, and Cultural Spheres

1. Supporting the Republic of Iraq in defending its democratic system against internal and external threats.

2. Respecting and upholding the Constitution as the expression of the will of the Iraqi people and standing against any attempt to impede, suspend, or violate it.

3. Supporting the efforts of the Republic of Iraq to achieve national reconciliation including as envisioned in the Communiqué of August 26.

4. Supporting the Republic of Iraq's efforts to enhance its position in regional and international organizations and institutions so that it may play a positive and constructive role in the region and the world.

5. Cooperating jointly with the states of the region on the basis of mutual respect, non-intervention in internal affairs, rejection of the use of violence in resolving disputes, and adoption of constructive dialogue in resolving outstanding problems among the various states of the region.

6. Promoting political efforts to establish positive relationships between the states of the region and the world, which serve the common goals of all relevant parties in a manner that enhances the security and stability of the region, and the prosperity of its peoples.

7. Encouraging cultural, educational, and scientific exchanges between the two countries.

Second: The Economic Sphere

1. Supporting Iraq's development in various economic fields, including its productive capabilities, and aiding its transition to a market economy.

2. Encouraging all parties to abide by their commitments as stipulated in the International Compact with Iraq.

3. Supporting the building of Iraq's economic institutions and infrastructure with the provision of financial and technical assistance to train and develop competencies and capacities of vital Iraqi institutions.

4. Supporting Iraq's further integration into regional and international financial and economic organizations.

5. Facilitating and encouraging the flow of foreign investments to Iraq, especially American investments, to contribute to the reconstruction and rebuilding of Iraq.

6. Assisting Iraq in recovering illegally exported funds and properties, especially those smuggled by the family of Saddam Hussein and his regime's associates, as well as antiquities and items of cultural heritage, smuggled before and after April 9, 2003.

7. Helping the Republic of Iraq to obtain forgiveness of its debts and compensation for the wars waged by the former regime.

Long-Term U.S. Security Posture In Iraq

8. Supporting the Republic of Iraq to obtain positive and preferential trading conditions for Iraq within the global marketplace including accession to the World Trade Organization and most favored nation status with the United States.

Third: The Security Sphere

1. Providing security assurances and commitments to the Republic of Iraq to deter foreign aggression against Iraq that violates its sovereignty and integrity of its territories, waters, or airspace.

2. Supporting the Republic of Iraq in its efforts to combat all terrorist groups, at the forefront of which is Al-Qaeda, Saddamists, and all other outlaw groups regardless of affiliation, and destroy their logistical networks and their sources of finance, and defeat and uproot them from Iraq. This support will be provided consistent with mechanisms and arrangements to be established in the bilateral cooperation agreements mentioned herein. 3. Supporting the Republic of Iraq in training, equipping, and arming the Iraqi Security Forces to enable them to protect Iraq and all its peoples, and completing the building of its administrative systems, in accordance with the request of the Iraqi government.

The Iraqi Government in confirmation of its resolute rights under existing Security Council resolutions will request to extend the mandate of the Multi-National Force-Iraq (MNF-I) under Chapter VII of the United Nations Charter for a final time. As a condition for this request, following the expiration of the above mentioned extension, Iraq's status under Chapter VII and its designation as a threat to international peace and security will end, and Iraq will return to the legal and international standing it enjoyed prior to the issuance of U.N. Security Council Resolution No. 661 (August, 1990), thus enhancing the recognition and confirming the full sovereignty of Iraq over its territories, waters, and airspace, and its control over its forces and the administration of its affairs.

Taking into account the principles discussed above, bilateral negotiations between the Republic of Iraq and the United States shall begin as soon as possible, with the aim to achieve, before July 31, 2008, agreements between the two governments with respect to the political, cultural, economic, and security spheres.

President of the United States of America
George W. Bush

Prime Minister of the Republic of Iraq
Nouri Kamel Al-Maliki

###

CHAPTER 27

SOMETHING NEW EVERY DAY

A BUSY PART OF THE WORLD

With millions of people living and interacting in this vast region, interesting events were the daily norm. Following are a few highlights from 2007.

SOMALI PIRATES

An issue that I inherited at CENTCOM was the ongoing problem of piracy centered on the waters around the Horn of Africa, near the failed state of Somalia. For several years, heavily armed pirates operating from small boats would range offshore from the Somali coast, boarding and then capturing merchant and fishing vessels, bringing them into Somali waters, and holding the crews and cargoes hostage for ransom. The waters near the Horn of Africa were heavily trafficked by Suez Canal shipping and fishing vessels from around the world. These dastardly activities resulted in many deaths of crewmen and high insurance rates for shippers.

Early in my time at CENTCOM, Vice Admiral Kevin Cosgriff, the Commander of U.S. Naval forces in the region, and I discussed this issue. I asked him to look for opportunities to do something about the problem. In mid-May, Kevin called me and reported, "Boss, it looks like we have a situation that might be a chance to deal with the pirates." I eagerly listened as he gave me a synopsis of the situation: "We have an opportunity coming up in the next week or two as we conduct a turnover of maritime forces in the region. An amphibious ready group with embarked Marines, the 13th MEU, is inbound from the Pacific, as is the aircraft carrier *JOHN C. STENNIS* Strike Group. Additionally, the aircraft carrier *NIMITZ* Strike Group is already in the area. We would have plenty of firepower, and currently, there is only one hostage vessel anchored along the shore. If you could arrange to have some Navy SEALs made available to take down the pirates on that hostage vessel, the Marines from the MEU could destroy the small pirate boats along the beach. We would put these guys out of business for quite a while."

I decided to act, recognizing a rare opportunity to remove the pirate vessels and send a strong message of deterrence. Telling Kevin to quickly put a detailed plan together, I called Secretary Gates, explained the situation, and asked for clearance to execute the plan if I approved it. "Mr. Secretary, in addition to our overwhelming force, current intelligence indicates that most of the vessels used in this piracy are now in the same area along the beach in Somalia. The living quarters for their families are nearby but away from the beach. I believe the SEALs could be dropped by helicopter to rescue the hostages on the vessel. The Marines could lay waste to all the shipping using their attack helicopters and Harriers. We should not have to put anyone on the ground. And I would expect minimum risk to families or other innocents." He asked a few questions and said, "I will get back to you after checking across the river (the White House)."

The Secretary called me back and said, "No. They did not like the idea of more military action in addition to the two wars." Although appealing the decision, it was quickly evident that my reclama was unsuccessful, so I reluctantly called Kevin. I told him to stop the planning process. I never ascertained whether the denial of permission came from the President himself or the NSC, but I assume that Gates spoke with Hadley at a minimum. At the time, I mused about Washington's reluctance to approve an action that probably resonated well with most of the world, and at the same time, they were ratcheting up tension with Iran.

In my view, this pop-up opportunity was minimal risk with a high probability of success and at a low cost, as our assets were readily available. But it proved too much for the Washington leadership to take upon themselves. I quickly moved on as there was much to do. Regrettably, this was a lost opportunity that may have precluded the continuing acts of piracy in the area, including the seizure of the U.S.-flagged cargo ship *Maersk Alabama,* less than two years later. In that incident, the captain of the ship, Richard Phillips, was taken hostage but ultimately rescued by Navy SEALs who killed the pirates. As we know, only a movie resulted, no solution.[285]

DECISIONS, DISCORD & DIPLOMACY

BACK TO AFGHANISTAN AND CENTRAL ASIA

Returning to Central Asia, I revisited Afghanistan and Pakistan and took the first opportunity to visit the neighboring countries. My decision to meet with the leaders of these nearby states was primarily in the context of the current situation in Afghanistan, which I was convinced in advance could be improved with their cooperation. Surprised by the decidedly negative opinion of the Karzai government and Afghanistan, I probed to understand the rationale. I quickly uncovered the two principal drivers of those opinions.

First was the influx of drugs, primarily heroin grown in Afghanistan and transported through their countries, enroute to illicit world markets, which invited corruption and potential addiction among their populations. The second issue was overall disdain based on their experience during the Afghan-Soviet War of the 1980s. Each of the other "'Stans" had been part of the USSR during the war, and many in the populations of those countries had participated directly on the side of the USSR. They were also mindful of the humiliating defeat and withdrawal of Soviet forces from the conflict.

In any event, I saw the potential for assistance to our efforts in Afghanistan. I was mainly motivated by the precarious supply lines that we inherited. Aware that the majority of our material support was coming through the one overland road network via Pakistan, constantly under attack or sabotage, I was eager for alternatives. Discussing the matter with Army Major General Ken Dowd, our logistics chief, I was astonished to discover that we only had a few days' fuel and ammo reserves in the country. Most personnel and some high-priority cargo came in by air through Kabul or Bagram airfields, often after the transport aircraft stopped to refuel at Ashgabat airbase in Turkmenistan or Kyrgyzstan. But the fuel, most ammo, and bulk items had to pass on roads through the Khyber Pass from Pakistan. An alternative fuel line from the north was now near the top of my priority list.

Each of the other five neighboring "stan" countries to the north of Afghanistan had been a Republic in the former USSR and was governed by an autocratic, corrupt, former Soviet "strongman" with little regard for human rights. Although blessed with abundant natural resources and other advantages, they nonetheless struggled to maintain viability as independent nations outside of the pervasive influence of Russia, on which they were still economically dependent. China was also aggressively seeking to extend its influence in the region. I decided to try to engage with the leaders of these nations, not only to boost our chances for success in Afghanistan but to offer a U.S. alternative to Russian and Chinese hegemony.

KAZAKHSTAN

A vast country four times the size of Texas, Kazakhstan is by far the largest nation in Central Asia, straddling the continents of Europe and Asia. Stretching from the Caspian Sea in the west to China in the east, its vast steppes link Russia with the rest of Central Asia. About 19 million people are primarily ethnic Kazakh and predominantly Muslim, like the rest of Central Asia. Inheriting a massive stockpile of nuclear weapons upon the declaration of its independence from the dissolving USSR in 1991, it voluntarily denuclearized and returned all nuclear weapons to Russia during the 1990s.

My initial meeting with President Nursultan Nazarbayev, who ruled Kazakhstan for almost three decades, at the capital, Astana, was cordial, as were relations between the U.S. and his country, the economically and politically dominant nation in Central Asia. Subsequent meetings with the defense minister and senior military leaders placed me in familiar surroundings. I had met and worked with many of these men as Deputy Commander of U.S. Atlantic Command during the previous decade. This relationship, an outgrowth of the NATO post-Cold War Partnership for Peace (PFP) initiative, centered on the formation of what was originally called the CENTRAZBAT (Central Asian Battalion), including troops from the U.S., Kazakhstan, Kyrgyzstan, and Uzbekistan working together to develop regional security and cooperation.[286] On the order of Nazarbayev, it was dissolved and succeeded in 2000 by KAZBAT (Kazak Battalion), intended to conduct peacekeeping and humanitarian assistance missions.

The KAZBAT deployed hundreds of troops to Iraq beginning in 2003 in support of Coalition operations, focused on non-combat but essential de-mining operations. While in Kazakhstan on that first visit, I met with members of the KAZBAT, who had recently returned from Iraq, and was honored to present military decorations to several for their performance.

DECISIONS, DISCORD & DIPLOMACY

Also, on that first trip, I became aware of the pervasive presence of pro-Russian propaganda in television programming beamed from Moscow. Russian was the common language throughout Central Asia; almost all television broadcasts originated in Russia.

In Central Asia, except for Afghanistan, which had some radio but almost no TV coverage, television was the most common mass communication medium. Upon my return to Washington, I suggested to Secretary of State Rice that the single most useful and least expensive thing we could do to help our long-term interests in Central Asia would be to operate a Russian language satellite channel devoted to public diplomacy to beam accurate messaging into that region.

A recent reorganization of the former U.S. Information Agency (USIA) and its subordinate Broadcasting Board of Governors (BBG) into the State Department resulted in another federal entity, dubbed the U.S. Agency for Global Media.[287] Whatever the name, the purpose remained. I thought it would be inexpensive to maintain strategic influence through nonmilitary means. Unfortunately, no action was taken, and today, we see that Russian sway in the region is even more pervasive than it was a decade ago.

Several months later, on a subsequent trip to Kazakhstan, I encountered an example of the persistence of bad behaviors from the corruption of the Soviet era. Flying into the capital of Astana in my U.S. Air Force crewed C-40 (Boeing 737-type aircraft) on a chilly, blustery, and rainy day in early November, the crew advised of an upcoming change to winter weather. Later, looking out of the hotel window early the next morning, I beheld a scene of horizontally blowing snow. The flight crew left for the airport with a recommendation to delay by an hour to allow them to prepare the aircraft. Carefully navigating the slippery roads, we arrived to find the airfield shrouded in clouds and snow. Our plane was encased in ice from the now-frozen rainfall of the previous evening, topped with a thick layer of snow. The pilot said we were stuck because the airport crew told him they had no deicing fluid. But having observed a Lufthansa civilian airliner being deiced on a distant part of the parking ramp, I knew differently.

It happened that I had a brand-new young aide, Navy Lieutenant Mike Nordeen, fluent in Russian, with us for his first trip. I directed Mike, with the copilot in tow, to go out and find the major-domo in charge of airfield operations and to ask this person what it would cost to get the aircraft deiced. Mike returned shortly and reported that the quoted fee was $10,000 in cash! Knowing that this outrageous sum could be (and was) reclaimed by our embassy staff, I told him to pass along that we would pay if the deicing truck were immediately dispatched to our aircraft. Less than 10 minutes later, that truck pulled up with the demand for payment up front. I said, "Only when the job is done." I then asked the aircrew to display the cash as an incentive. The deicing crew went to work and completed about 80% of the aircraft surface before the process stopped; they had run out of deicing fluid! After another 20 minutes had passed, I sent Mike out to find the "boss man" and tell him that unless the job was completed, he would see no cash, and we would report the event to the national authorities. A few minutes later, another truck arrived, and the process was completed. Mike paid in $100 bills (several rejected as "too worn") in exchange for a signed receipt (for the embassy) and quickly took off for our next destination.[288] This process was a Russian-Soviet legacy.

KYRGYZSTAN

My entry into Kyrgyzstan was through the air base at Manas, near the capital of Bishkek. Our U.S. Ambassador at the time was Marie "Masha" Yovanovitch (later famously recalled when serving as ambassador to Ukraine in connection with an ugly political scandal). She was a very competent diplomat, on top of the events in Central Asia. My arrival there came during a critical point in relations between the U.S. and the host country.

Controversy surrounding the shooting and death of a civilian contractor at the Manas base by U.S. Air Force security personnel in December 2006 had soured relations with recently elected President Bakiyev.[289] This event followed a previous incident involving the nighttime ground collision between a commercial Altyn Air TU-154 airliner, rolling down the runway on takeoff, which clipped a just-landed but not yet fully clear U.S. Air Force KC-135 tanker aircraft. The crash resulted in fire, but miraculously, no casualties to the occupants of either aircraft.

These events played into ongoing heavy diplomatic pressure from Russia and China exerted upon the government of Kyrgyzstan, seeking to evict U.S. forces from Central Asia. I was aware of an upcoming

Shanghai Cooperation Organization (SCO) meeting scheduled for August 2007 in Bishkek. This organization included Russia and China, in addition to Central Asian countries, and was used by the former to reassert influence and diminish U.S. clout. In addition to hosting the leaders of these countries, President Bakiyev was under pressure from them to demonstrate his independence from outside (U.S.) influence. He later took advantage of this situation to demand increased lease payments from the U.S. for the facilities. Ambassador Yovanovitch had her hands full as the country also had severe economic problems and political unrest.

Fortunately, I was previously acquainted with the Minister of Defense, General Isakov, and his assistant, General Oruzbayev, and we renewed our cordial bond. With good military-to-military relations, we had at least a foundation of trust to maintain the precarious air logistics link into Afghanistan. Access to the air base was critically important as there was no other facility near Afghanistan through which we could stage troops and other support personnel. This visit reinforced my decision to closely examine relations with the Central Asian leaders.

TURKMENISTAN

Ashgabat, the capital of Turkmenistan and the first place I visited in that country, is fascinating in several respects. Geographically, it sits near the southern border of the vast, sparsely populated, arid, and mostly flat desert country, just north of a low mountain range near the border with Iran, and astride the ancient Silk Road from China. The central part of the city is filled with immense, predominantly white marble monuments featuring unusual architectural designs, the brainchild of former "President for Life" Niyazov, also known as "Turkmenbashi" (leader of all Turkmen), who ruled from the 1991 declaration of independence from the USSR until he died in 2006. My staff dubbed it "The City of Oz" after the movie version of *The Wonderful Wizard of Oz* because of its many peculiar structures. Although the city has a population of about one million, people were rarely seen in or about most of these spectacularly eye-catching buildings.

Turkmenbashi ruled with an iron hand and established strange rules, laws, and edicts. He published a two-volume book called the *Ruhnama* (Book of the Soul in English), which came to be known as the Little Green Book in the manner of Chinese Chairman Mao's Little Red

Book. These tomes, Niyazov's version of the history and culture of Turkmen, were mandatory reading for citizens until his death. More importantly—for me at the time—Turkmenistan has enshrined a statement of "permanent neutrality" in national and foreign policy in the nation's Constitution. The practical result is that the government is extremely cautious in relationships with other countries.[290]

My meeting with President Gurbanguly Berdimuhamedov, who had assumed power following the death of Niyazov only a few months before my visit, began awkwardly as he seemed tense and nervous. Loosening up as we proceeded, he related an incident that had just occurred involving his powerful Iranian neighbors. Complaining that the Iranians were already testing him by stopping payment for the natural gas they were receiving through a pipeline from Turkmenistan, he said, "I asked why they were not paying the agreed price, but I received no response. I then directed that we turn off the gas supply. The Iranians very quickly resumed payments." Impressed that he responded resolutely to the pressure, I got the message that, although new to the job, he was not a pushover. "Fair enough," I thought. "He is learning quickly.'

Nonetheless, I had several requests for President Berdimuhamedov that might have pressured his implementation of the neutrality issue. The first concern was the U.S.'s use of the airfield at Ashgabat for emergency refueling of cargo aircraft en route to Afghanistan. In some cases, the logistic resupply flights using the northern route across Europe and Russia found themselves critically low on fuel on the way into Manas and Bagram airfields. My predecessor had negotiated this concession from Niyazov, but the conditions for use were quite restrictive, including emergencies only and a prohibition on aircrews from disembarking, requiring them to immediately refuel and continue the flight, regardless of other conditions.

I also sought permission to use the airfield at Mary, a large former bomber base in the days of the USSR, a couple of hundred miles closer to Afghanistan, for similar emergency refueling purposes. This airfield was better positioned for that purpose. The President said he would take these issues under consideration.

The most important request was this: "Mr. President, we are working hard to try to improve the security situation in Afghanistan, and I need your help to get fuel supplies into that country. If you could provide the urgent support needed by road or rail, we would happily pay you for the material." To my satisfaction and surprise, he soon began work on an upgrade and extension of an existing rail line to connect about ten miles across the Afghan border, providing the alternative supply line we so urgently needed.[291]

TAJIKISTAN

The Republic of Tajikistan shares a long and, at that time (2007), tightly controlled border with its southern neighbor, Afghanistan. On my first visit to the capital of Dushanbe, I learned from Ambassador Tracy Jacobson that the country endured frequent electrical blackouts resulting from political disputes with its neighbor, Uzbekistan, on whom it relied for most of its electrical power, and that mistrust between countries was common in Central Asia.

Acutely aware that military power alone was unlikely to deliver the long-term security we sought, one of the principal reasons for my engagement with Central Asian countries was to encourage cooperation in areas of mutual benefit. Electrical power was at the top of the list because of the scarcity of electricity in Afghanistan and western Pakistan and the enormous potential of hydropower in Tajikistan and Uzbekistan. Ambassador Dawn Liberi, whom I had borrowed from USAID, led an initiative with representatives of these countries to establish a common framework. Despite high interest, we were not able to get agreement on a workable way ahead.

Another reason for my specific interest in Tajikistan was the outsized role those Tajik ethnic personalities, such as General Bismillah "BK" Khan, the Chief of Defense, and Amrullah Saleh, the intelligence chief, played within Afghanistan. Historically, the legendary warlord and former Minister of Defense, Ahmad Shah Masoud (aka "The Lion of Panjshir" and "Great Masoud"), assassinated in 2001, was widely revered.[292]

The Tajik President, Emomali Rahmon, came to power in 1992 following a brutal civil war in the aftermath of independence from the USSR that devastated the country and claimed the lives of an estimated 100,000 people. Already leading his country for 15 years when we first met, Rahmon—as of this writing—still ruled in 2025. In doing my pre-visit homework, I discovered that he had served in the Soviet Navy when he was a young man. I believe that mentioning our common naval heritage surprised Rahmon. Still, it proved a good entrée into a relationship that was enlightening and helpful to me.

The Tajik President wasted no time in highlighting the drug problem across the border and expressing his general dislike and unhappiness with the Afghan neighbors. I pushed back at this, extolling the potential benefits of expanded trade, highlighting the nearly completed and U.S.-funded $40 million bridge linking the two countries over the Panj (historically known as the Oxus) River.

Although I missed the official opening ceremony, attended by Presidents Karzai and Rahmon, I was soon back in Dushanbe to lobby the trade issue.[293] Having been informed by Karzai and U.S. Ambassador Wood that, although completed and open to traffic, the bridge was carrying minimal trade, I discovered that the Tajik authorities were restricting transit to only a few hours a day. Raising this issue with Rahmon, I was pointed in the direction of the Chairman of National Security, General Adburahimov. The latter was another persona straight out of central casting; a former KGB operator who looked like a Hollywood thug and acted the role to perfection.

Visiting the general in his office, I inquired why he was restricting bridge access, "Your president told me that he is in favor of allowing traffic all day, but that you control the operating hours. Why the restrictions?" He blamed the Afghans: "They do not screen people, and smugglers are bringing drugs into our country." I opined, "Well, then you screen the people when they come over to your side of the bridge." We repeatedly went back and forth for some time, but in a respectful manner, and at the end of the conversation, he told me that he would see what he could do. Soon thereafter, our U.S. ambassador in Dushanbe, Tracy Jacobson, informed me that the operating hours on the bridge had been expanded to daylight hours.

During our trade discussion, Rahmon invited me to come with him and visit the strategic Wakhan Corridor in the eastern part of the country bordering Afghanistan and China. In addition to highlighting the area's spectacular beauty, he said, "You will see active exchange between Tajikistan and Afghanistan. Do you know what they are trading?" Having no idea, I asked, "Please tell me." He said with a laugh,

"Everything is Chinese. Both sides are exchanging Chinese goods, and only the Chinese make money!"

Mentioning the dispute about electrical power with neighboring Uzbekistan, I asked for his view on this matter. He said, "Karimov (president of Uzbekistan) is a very difficult man. He thinks he is the boss of Central Asia." I opined that if the countries cooperated with one another, particularly regarding Afghanistan, we would all be in a better place and offered to meet with Karimov. He said, "Good, maybe you could help. But I recommend you see me before you see him because I know him well and can give you some helpful information. But do not go directly to Tashkent from Dushanbe, or he will suspect that we are collaborating, and it will not be good." All this suspicion has deep roots.

UZBEKISTAN

Several months later, after overcoming persistent resistance from Washington, I finally went to Tashkent to meet with Karimov, traveling a circuitous route that included an intermediate stop to receive Rahmon's advice. The Tajik President said Karimov "knows the world," thinks himself smarter than the neighboring leaders, and is the natural "capo." He suggested I speak to him about sharing water and electrical power with neighbors, but to stay away from sensitive human rights issues. He cautioned that whatever was said would be reported "directly to Moscow as a debriefing to Putin." He "talks long and wide" and "does not like interruptions;" therefore, I should be prepared for a lengthy meeting and "do not drink much coffee before the meeting!"

I was eager to meet the Uzbek president because it had become clear that he was Central Asia's most influential (although certainly not the most admired) leader with the potential to influence cooperation among the countries. And we were still looking for alternate supply routes into Afghanistan.

The reluctance of the administration to allow my meeting with Karimov stemmed from Uzbek security forces' violent suppression of demonstrators in the city of Andijan in the Fergana Valley in 2005. Seen by human rights advocates as proof of Karimov's autocratic repression of civil liberties, key members of Congress supported sanctions against his government.[294] Secretary of State Rice, aware of my desire for a meeting, which was also enthusiastically encouraged by Richard

Norland, our U.S. ambassador in Tashkent, but sensitive to the congressional pressure, deferred the meeting several times until finally assenting.

In the immediate aftermath of the 9/11 attacks, the U.S. sought overflight and aircraft basing rights in Uzbekistan (also Tajikistan and Kyrgyzstan) due to the proximity to Afghanistan and a lack of any nearby U.S. facilities. Karimov quickly granted use of the old Soviet airfield at Kashi-Khanabad (K2). However, relations between Uzbekistan and the U.S. later soured after the 2005 Andijan incident and the resulting congressional outcry. Extremely sensitive to the criticism from Washington, Karimov indignantly canceled the rights to the airfield and expelled U.S. forces from the country.[295] Despite an intense effort by Ambassador Norland to improve the situation, relations were still stagnant when I arrived on the scene.

My meeting with President Islam Karimov was another one of those unforgettable, once-in-a-lifetime events with a larger-than-life character and well-deserved reputation as a bully. Our aircraft's arrival in Tashkent was delayed until midafternoon due to severe weather, but once on the ground, Ambassador Norland told me that the Uzbek president wanted to see me immediately. It had already been a long day, and mindful of Rahmon's warning about lengthy meetings, I tried, to no avail, to postpone the event until the next day. The audience was held in the "White Palace" building, which housed the office of President Karimov, a structure that, from the outside, looked like the White House in Washington. The immense meeting room held a huge table where Karimov and I sat on opposite sides. The only other people present were Dick Norland, my EA, Craig Faller, and the translator. I had never been to a meeting where the principals were seated as far apart as I recall, about 15 feet across a table.

Karimov, who ruled Uzbekistan for 25 years, began the meeting by inquiring, "Why did it take you so long to come see me?" Not waiting for a reply, he launched into a lengthy discourse that included an opinion (typically critical) on virtually every regional leader. He highlighted the region's political, economic, and military issues, focusing on Afghanistan. Revealing keen insight, he noted the fraught personal relationship between Musharraf and Karzai, observed that, in his view, the U.S. was now "occupiers" and asked, "Can the U.S. prevail?" I knew immediately that I was talking with someone broadly interested and informed.

I encouraged his monologue, reinforced by his firm grasp of detail, because I found his insight interesting and educational. Turning to the strained U.S.-Uzbek relationship, he passionately objected to the personal criticism he had received from members of Congress. He vehemently denied killing "innocent demonstrators" in Andijan, claiming that he was facing "Islamist extremists" who were trying to overthrow the government.

Noting the apparent difference of opinion between the President and his critics, I opined that I could not do anything to change the past and had no desire to debate the issue with him, but was focused on the present and improving relations between our two countries.[296] Highlighting that, in addition to my Commander-in-Chief, I had an obligation to the 535-person legislative branch of my government, some of whom were quite upset at the perception of human rights abuses in Uzbekistan. Mindful of his well-known authoritarian reputation, I suggested that actions on his part to dialogue with nongovernmental organizations regarding the treatment of his citizens could be helpful to perception and, in turn, to him.

The conversation changed and became about religion and its internal role in governments and international relations. It was fascinating. Several hours into our discussion, Karimov remarked that he wished I had come sooner to see him, stating, "I like you because you understand things." Changing gears again, he surprisingly asked, "So what do you want? Do you want access to K2 again? If you want the base, you can have it." I thanked him for his offer and said, "No, I don't really need that base right now, but we may need other help with Afghanistan." He said, "Okay, if you need access in the future, just let me know."

Following our meeting, Ambassador Norland asked me to join him the next morning for a breakfast discussion with a representative of the International Committee of the Red Cross, Mr. Raffaello Mueller, who had been in Tashkent for weeks, unsuccessfully petitioning the Uzbek government to see Karimov about civil rights issues. Reluctantly agreeing, I was treated to a lengthy breakfast monologue from Mueller decrying Karimov's civil rights abuses and bad manners in not meeting with him. I replied that, having raised these issues with Karimov the previous day, there really wasn't much more that I could do. A few days later, I received a phone call from Ambassador Norland with the surprising news that Karimov summoned Mueller to a meeting the day after I left Tashkent. Several weeks later, following negotiations in Uzbekistan, the ICRC resumed detention visits. Some of my messaging may have been effective!297

When I called Secretary Gates and told him about Karimov's offer to reopen the base, he was also pleasantly surprised. Although we did not need the immediate use of that facility, the positive dialogue from our meeting provided the foundation to encourage Uzbek participation in what became known as the Northern Distribution Network (NDN), the alternative supply route into Afghanistan that was ultimately established.298

OTHER EVENTS IN CENTCOM, SUMMER 2007

Attempting to get my head and those of my other senior commanders out of the tactical morass of Iraq, I decided to hold a commanders' conference in mid-July at CENTCOM forward HQ, Camp As Sayliyah, near Doha, Qatar. The conference was attended by all three- and four-star General and Flag Officers in CENTCOM, and we had strategic discussions about several issues in the region. Dave Petraeus flew down from Baghdad and spoke in detail about matters in Iraq, as did Stan McChrystal, who also discussed the situation in Afghanistan from his perspective. Dave stated that he and his staff were working on a plan for the way forward for Iraq and revealed his intention to forward the details to CJCS Chairman Pace before the congressional hearing in September. But he did not mention coordinating or sharing the plan's details with me. The "working in parallel" business was beginning to grate on me.

U.S. SECURITY ASSISTANCE TO THE PALESTINIAN AUTHORITY

An item to which I had paid little previous attention before that meeting was raised by Army Lieutenant General Keith Dayton, who had an unenviable job. While operating from our U.S. Consulate General office in Jerusalem, he was tasked to train Palestinian security forces on the West Bank. His official assignment was United States Security Coordinator for Israel and the Palestinian Authority. This position was created by the U.S. Department of State in the wake of what was known as the Roadmap for Peace Agreement, an initiative by the George W. Bush Administration.[299] It was an outgrowth of the previously agreed 1993 Oslo Accords, another of a long series of U.S. attempts to resolve the Israeli-Palestinian conflict.

General Dayton's primary task was to organize and train an indigenous security force of Palestinians with the expectation that they could assume responsibility for security in the West Bank. In this way, it might be possible for the Palestinians to credibly establish law and order there and preclude the periodic forays into that territory by the Israeli military. As Israel was part of U.S. European Command (EUCOM), it was technically not in my area of responsibility. However, Keith was getting no help from EUCOM or the Israelis, and the Palestinian issue was an item of great concern with most of the Arab countries in CENTCOM.

I decided that, in the best interest of the people in that region, and in my own small way, to support yet another attempt to facilitate better relations between the Arabs and the Israelis. Acceding to his request for assistance, I offered to function as a go-between or in any other useful manner to facilitate his mission. King Abdullah of Jordan was conspicuously supportive of this effort. When I asked him for help on my next visit to Jordan, he said, "Of course, if you can get funding, we will provide people and the facilities." Financial support was made available from the U.S. and some other NATO countries. Training has been conducted for many years at the Jordan International Police Training Center near Amman, Jordan.[300]

Alas, results from this initiative have been mixed, primarily due to halfhearted support and bureaucratic obstacles by both Israel and the Palestinian Authority, and violence on the West Bank continues to this day.

NUCLEAR REACTOR IN SYRIA

Although issues in Iraq were clearly on center stage that summer of 2007, several other events competed for my attention and required continuous decision-making. One long-running drama, the details of which were highly classified for many years, concerned the secret construction of a nuclear reactor near Dier al-Zor, Syria, also known as al-Kibar.

This facility, modeled on the North Korean reactor at Yongbyon and built mainly with North Korean assistance, was likely intended to give the Syrians a nuclear weapons capability. Construction had evidently been ongoing for some time before intelligence analysts realized the project's true nature, hiding in plain sight in the sparsely populated desert area of eastern Syria along the Euphrates River.

Although the facility was not yet completed, planning was initiated to destroy it before it became operational. Brought to my attention in April by CIA chief Mike Hayden, the issue of what, if anything, to do about it was a topic of ongoing attention at the highest levels of the U.S. government throughout the summer of 2007.[301] I was involved because Syria was part of the CENTCOM area of responsibility, and any military action would have been executed through me. Also, highly classified intelligence from another country, later identified as Israel, demanded the utmost sensitivity in any discussion.

Without going into detail, I can confirm that we looked at several options, including ground assault and aerial bombardment. I quickly found myself turning to the superbly talented and versatile Commander of the Special Operations Forces (SOF), Lieutenant General Stan McChrystal, for operational advice. He was in Iraq, operating on-scene for several years, directing critically important work against Al Qaeda and the Iranian-supported militias. Loath to pull him away from what was already more than a full-time job, we discussed options. Stan said, "I can make some planners available who have technical expertise."

I decided to set up a planning cell at CENTCOM headquarters in Tampa and welcomed his people. Eventually, in September 2007, Israeli aircraft attacked and destroyed the facility. However, official confirmation did not come until more than a decade later.[302] Discussion and planning for potential U.S. options consumed many hours over several months.

BACK TO TORA BORA, AFGHANISTAN

During July 2007, intriguing intelligence snippets began to filter into the headquarters regarding a potential Al Qaeda return to their former mountain redoubt at Tora Bora. This information presented several dilemmas leading to a series of important decisions. First, recall that Osama bin Laden was still at large, whereabouts unknown. We knew that his last known location was in that area of eastern Afghanistan along the border with Pakistan, and the idea that his adherents might be preparing to stage a comeback focused my immediate attention. That border area was becoming increasingly restive with a rise in Taliban and allied Afghan militia attacks against Afghan and NATO security forces. The geography of isolated, sparsely populated Tora Bora was daunting: high, rugged mountains, few roads, and an open door across the mountains to the ungoverned frontier area in Pakistan, a safe haven for the insurgents. I had few nearby military assets at my disposal.

As previously mentioned, the command-and-control structure in Afghanistan was complex and often confusing. In this instance, an operation against Osama bin Laden's forces would fall into the category of counterterrorism under OPERATION ENDURING FREEDOM (OEF). It would be my responsibility as the CENTCOM Commander rather than a NATO operation under General McNeil. Fortunately, the on-scene forces in eastern Afghanistan at that time were American, a brigade of the 82nd Airborne Division led by then Major General (later General) Rod Rodriguez, who, as Commander of Combined Joint Task Force 82, reported directly to me in his National Command Element hat.

This setup offered nearby assets for a potential operation that would be strictly U.S. and not NATO, although Rod was devoting most of his work at the time in support of NATO. But I immediately recalled that Rod had already shifted a battalion of his troops to the southern area of Afghanistan at General McNeil's request to bolster our NATO allies there. His remaining forces were spread over a vast area of eastern Afghanistan. A significant military operation would require additional troops.

Despite any operational challenges it might present, I considered this an issue of the highest importance, as the actions of Osama bin Laden and his zealots were what started the terror war more than a decade previously. Tora Bora became my priority focus for several weeks, notwithstanding Iraq, the Syrian nuclear reactor, and other issues in Afghanistan.

A key challenge was again the geography in remote, mountainous, landlocked eastern Afghanistan, just as it had been in 2001 during the initial assault on Al Qaeda. But this time, we had a few facilities near the potential scene of action from which we could stage forces, particularly the air base at Bagram and the nearby base at Jalalabad. As we attempted to refine the intelligence to pinpoint what was going on as best we could, I had to decide who to put in charge of this operation. Given the lack of any numerically significant nearby U.S. military capability, I assumed this would have to be a joint operation, pulling together whatever forces could quickly be made available from all the services worldwide.

The ongoing conflicts in Iraq and Afghanistan already tied up the senior military leadership in CENTCOM. I was reluctant to ask for someone from the outside who was not already familiar with the area, particularly as I assumed action would need to be taken very soon. There would be little time to bring someone new up to speed. Also, this was clearly going to be a land-focused operation. I quickly decided to go back to my ace, Lieutenant General Stan McChrystal, and appointed him the Joint Task Force Commander using his TF-714 designator.

Stan was familiar with the area; some of his Special Operations Forces were also operating in eastern Afghanistan, he knew the other ground commanders likely to be involved, and I trusted him unequivocally to offer sound recommendations and make good decisions. The obvious drawback was his almost full-time focus on battling the insurgents in Iraq from his post at the Balad Airbase north of Baghdad.

As Stan worked with the other CENTCOM land, air, and maritime component commanders in developing his eclectic plan of attack, I briefed Secretary Gates on what was becoming a complex and worldwide effort to quickly pull together appropriate forces to act on the intelligence information. Considering what I told him, he said, "You will need to come back and brief the President to get his approval."

On August 3, 2007, I went to Washington and briefed President Bush at the White House with his national security team in attendance. The intelligence at the time was consistent but still sketchy about the number of potential participants and the purpose of the purported gathering of Al Qaeda leadership and their allies at Tora Bora. "Mr. President," I began, "I think we have a rare opportunity to capture or eliminate key Al Qaeda leadership and, at a minimum, to deny them use of their former sanctuary. We have forces that are familiar with this area and have detailed plans to seal it off, particularly with respect to the 'back door' into Pakistan. The plan includes troops from the 82nd Airborne,

Special Operations Forces, Air Force, and Navy tactical air support, and with your permission, B-2 bombers to covertly begin the operation by hitting known cave complexes and other key nodes." I went through several graphics and briefing slides, noting that the force was scalable based on what we found once it commenced. I advised him that the area's proximity to the Pakistan border would almost certainly entail aircraft penetration into Pakistani airspace. We discussed that point, and I said, "Again, with your permission, I would like to notify President Musharraf concurrent with executing the operation." I also told him that I would need to temporarily pull some Special Operations troops and equipment out of Iraq for use during the operation, which I did not anticipate taking more than a couple of weeks. Needless to say, when I briefed Dave Petraeus on this, he was not happy. Following questions and answers from the President and some of his key advisors, I asked permission to launch the operation during one of the next several nights when we had all the pieces in place. He said, "Okay, permission granted."

As I gathered my materials and prepared to leave, I said, "Mr. President, you might want to know something else. I have an interesting photograph just taken up in those mountains." Before I could continue, President Bush, not missing a beat and demonstrating his keen intuition, said, "Don't tell me you're going to show me a picture of a tall guy in a turban and vest?" I replied, "How did you guess?" and handed him a fuzzy photo of a figure resembling Osama bin Laden in mufti. He laughed and said something like, "I don't believe it, but it would be your lucky day."

With the President's approval, we finalized planning as the forces prepared to move into position. After giving the order to execute OPERATION MOUNTAIN SHADOW, I called Ambassador Anne Patterson in Islamabad, Pakistan, outlined what would unfold, and asked her to reach out to President Musharraf. I asked her to advise him that we had an operation about to be conducted entirely within Afghanistan, but along the border. I wanted to inform him of the likelihood of aircraft potentially spilling into his airspace, which I was certain would occur as they maneuvered during the operation. Anne later reported that he appreciated the heads-up.

The B-2 bomber aircraft were launched from a base outside the region well before the start of the ground operation, with a long distance to travel to reach their targets. They had already been in the air for several hours when I received a critical intelligence update. The gist of the latest information was that the scope of the planned Al Qaeda gathering and the number of people involved was much less than initially anticipated.

I had two concerns: first, the acute sensitivity of President Karzai to civilian casualties, and the potential for the same with a heavy bombing attack. Second, using the B-2s was a rare occurrence that would generate intense international scrutiny. Their contribution, in what now appeared to be a low-payoff operation, could compromise their potential use in future operations. Accordingly, I decided to cancel the B-2 participation and turn them around in mid-flight. In hindsight, I still believe that was the correct decision, although it disappointed the Air Force bomber crews. To the credit of the people involved, particularly the Air Force crews, everyone kept their mouths shut at the time, and their participation in the operation remained secret for many years.[303]

To summarize, the remainder of the operation was conducted effectively, with minimum casualties. Several camps and facilities in and around the Tora Bora cave complexes showing recent use were discovered, along with several Al Qaeda suspects apprehended or eliminated. Thousands of our assembled troops and support forces were soon released to resume their prior duties. Although very well executed, the operation was a disappointment in that no key leaders, including Osama bin Laden, were captured. I was pleased with the execution by our people, the leadership of General McChrystal, and particularly with the cooperation and collaboration of the forces working together. The scope and speed of the operation were not lost on the insurgents, and it certainly kept them off balance for the near term. President Karzai was also pleased with our initiative.

CHAPTER 28

AFGHANISTAN: THE BEST OF INTENTIONS

WORKING TOWARD A BETTER FUTURE

The uptick in activity at Tora Bora was only one facet of a busy year in Afghanistan. Incidents of violence were increasing in many of the provinces, traditionally peaking during the summer "fighting season." The intelligence analysts offered a variety of reasons, unsurprisingly, as the country's culture, history, politics, and current circumstances were complex.

From my perspective, the key contributing factors were first, the long-standing tribal and, to a lesser extent, ethnic differences; second, the traditional preference and practice of governance at the local and provincial levels versus the strong central government favored by Western nations, and third, systemic and enduring corruption, fueled mainly by cash from opium cultivation.

Overshadowing these factors and everything else in the recent history of Afghanistan was the U.S.-led post-9/11 attack on Al Qaeda that ousted the Taliban and turned the country upside down. After initial progress and improved circumstances in almost every aspect of Afghan domestic life, interest and attention dwindled as the U.S. focused on Iraq. This was the reality we inherited in 2007.

The insurgency in Afghanistan was largely homegrown and rekindled by the once-vanquished Taliban. In hindsight, I underestimated the extent to which the Taliban regrouped and infiltrated into the provinces from 2006 onwards, aggressively asserting influence with the population and opposing Coalition forces by military force with increasing frequency. Interestingly, except for Pakistan, other neighboring countries were wary and non-supportive of destabilizing actions in Afghanistan.

On the other hand, Pakistan, highly desirous of a weak and non-threatening neighbor, encouraged factionalism and allowed easy access and safe haven in its largely ungoverned Federally Administered Tribal Area (FATA) along the Afghan border. The Pakistanis assiduously

AFGHANISTAN: THE BEST OF INTENTIONS

worked both sides of the equation, allowing the U.S. access to Afghanistan at a high price but at the same time abetting internal strife to keep the central government weak.

A vastly greater amount of attention and resources from Washington was devoted to Iraq when I took command at CENTCOM. It was quickly apparent that the situation would not change appreciably anytime soon. Nonetheless, I noted several things about Afghanistan that, if nurtured properly, could lead to a much better outcome than the 2007 situation in Iraq. First and foremost, we were still widely seen as helpful by most of the population, bringing assistance rather than military oppression.

Indeed, "In 2005, 83% of Afghans expressed a favorable opinion of the United States – unheard of in a Muslim nation."[304] These opinions were still favorable, at 65% in early 2008.

Although afflicted with centuries of instability and conflict, usually due to external military incursion, I found the Afghan population generally cohesive, long-suffering, and self-sustaining. Uppermost in my mind was the often-heard but unheeded lesson that these people, however primitive by Western standards, were intolerant of foreign military occupation. Therefore, we needed to be as unobtrusive as possible while trying to facilitate their governance, not ours.

As I thought about the "big picture" in Afghanistan, I was mindful of what Major General Karl Eikenberry said in 2006 when he was the senior U.S. military officer in Kabul and on his second tour there. I visited some of my USPACOM troops who were then assigned to Afghanistan. He said, "They (leadership in Washington) have this all wrong. The priority here should not be more troops. What these people need is water, electric power, roads, and help with agriculture."[305]

This was the same message I received from Dawn Liberi, my advisor at CENTCOM on loan from USAID. These were not military-focused tasks. Sure, we in the military were doing what we could, but this business of "nation-building" was fundamentally an endeavor best undertaken by civilian experts. Of course, they needed security and stability to conduct their functions, and that was the Afghan situation in 2002 and 2003 before the U.S. turned its attention to Iraq.

As a counter to those who object to the concept of nation-building, I believe it is worth noting that the U.S. has been helping people in other countries around the world for many decades, particularly since the end of World War II. Although a small part has been done by the military, historically, the vast majority of assistance, be it political, economic, food, health, and other person-to-person help for fellow human beings, has been done by civilians or nonmilitary entities of the U.S. government, for example, USAID, U.S. Information Agency, the Peace Corps, and so forth. In Afghanistan, the first major dam constructed for agricultural irrigation and electric power at Kajaki on the Helmand River was funded and built by Americans in the 1950s and later expanded with electric power-generating turbines installed in the 1970s.[306] Assistance to other countries has been a long-standing and admired feature of American engagement in the world.

Back to Afghanistan in 2007, beginning at the top with President Karzai. I perceived him as steeped in Afghan culture and tribal roots yet comfortable in Western mores. For example, he told me several times that he was inclined to interact with his people through traditional tribal meetings to understand their opinions and exchange views. Indeed, as noted earlier, he and Musharraf jointly attended and spoke at just such a Jirga in Kabul attended by Afghan and Pakistani tribal leaders a few days before my arrival for a regularly occurring visit in mid-August 2007. He was also sophisticated, with a keen understanding of how things worked in Western societies, and he seemed to transition easily between the two cultures.

The Afghan government included members of all the major tribes and ethnicities: Pashtun, Tajik, Uzbek, and Hazara. Although friction was inevitable, my interaction with the leaders indicated that most were pragmatic and savvy. I soon observed that a similar blend of backgrounds and professionalism was apparent in military leadership. I resolved to do all we could to facilitate the training of a competent national security force for Afghanistan. This was easier said than done, with as many obstacles coming from the U.S. as from Afghanistan. There were competing opinions about what to do and how to do it. Still, as the Commander responsible for this task, I quickly made decisions about the way forward, rejecting the tendency to imitate U.S. organizations and procedures.

To this last point, the size, structure, equipping, and training of the Afghan National Army (ANA) was a point of contention in both Kabul and Washington. In the U.S., I was lectured regularly by members of

AFGHANISTAN: THE BEST OF INTENTIONS

Congress on substantially increasing the size of the Afghan army as quickly as possible so that the ANA could assume security for themselves and relieve us of the responsibility and the need for military forces in the country. This was also the view of the administration. However, the reality on the ground, well-documented by Special Inspector General for Afghan Reconstruction (SIGAR) John Sopko during the many years of our engagement in Afghanistan, was often quite different and more complex than the official view in Washington.[307]

Arriving as the CENTCOM Commander in 2007, I inherited as staff Army Major General (later Lieutenant General) Bob Durbin, succeeded by Major General (later General) Bob Cone of the Combined Security Transition Command-Afghanistan, both competent officers, as my on-scene commanders in Kabul. They were directly tasked with the organization, training, and equipping of the ANA. A key point here is that the USA was footing almost the entire bill for everything to do with creating and training an indigenous Afghan security force, to the tune of some $7 billion in FY 2007 alone.[308] The nascent Afghan economy generated little revenue and was still almost totally dependent on the contributions of donor nations.

Back in 2001, at the Bonn Conference on Afghanistan that ratified the accession of Hamid Karzai as president and made available initial financial resources to the Afghan government, a decision was made to establish what became the ANA, with the goal of some 70,000 troops. By mid-2007, the size of the force was only about 50,000, with slow progress being made toward a higher number.[309] In addition to paying for everything from Afghan salaries to the operation of their equipment, the U.S. also did the bulk of the training. Although some of our allies were helping in training the ANA, this mission was hamstrung primarily by the lack of trainers from the U.S. due to the prioritization of people to the war in Iraq. The trainers, insufficient as they were, came primarily from the U.S. Army National Guard, as few regular, active-duty troops were available.

On my first visit to Kabul, Bob Durbin shared his plan to grow and train the Afghan military (ANA) and the Afghan National Police (ANP). My immediate reaction was that the objective number of troops was too high, given the many challenges of enlisting soldiers into their all-volunteer force and the slow pace of training, dictated mainly by the lack of available U.S. instructors.

DECISIONS, DISCORD & DIPLOMACY

By then, the objective number had already been raised to 120,000 troops, with a pending request to go even higher to 135,000 men. After listening to Bob's details about the existing challenges, I told him, "I will not support a target number higher than 120,000, and I believe even that is going to be a stretch." Bob did not reclama, admitting that the numbers seemed daunting, but he was under pressure from all sides to grow the ANA with the idea that they would take over security in the country as soon as possible. He said, "Minister (of Defense) Wardak is also pushing hard for these increased numbers."

Bob then had one of his subordinate U.S. Air Force generals brief me on their plan for the Afghan Air Force. After listening to the presentation, I thought, "What are these guys thinking?! This is totally impractical." My objections were straightforward. The idea that we would equip the Afghans with modern American aircraft such as the C-130J transport, Blackhawk helicopter, and F-16 fighter aircraft struck me as immediate non-starters.

Although this proposal would share compatibility and modern capability with U.S. forces, there was no way the Afghan Air Force could adapt to operate these machines for years, if ever. "Generals, not only would we have to start a training program that would take years to show results, but the cost of these machines, added to the already under-resourced fiscal challenge, is totally unrealistic." They were surprised, but I continued, "More importantly, the idea that the Afghans could maintain and operate these machines would be impossible without full-time contractor support, costing untold additional millions of dollars."

Directing them to scrap that plan, I decided on a new one: "I want you to put your team to work and find us some available MI-17 helicopters and AN-26 transports and forget the fighter aircraft for now." My reasoning was simple: the Afghans already operated both these Soviet-designed and built machines that, although dated, were rugged, easy to maintain, and fly. "I will direct the CENTCOM staff to collaborate with you to try to find some of these aircraft, which would be much less expensive to refurbish and put into operation than new U.S. aircraft."

In fact, in less than six months, both aircraft types were located and reconditioned; a squadron of helicopters in the UAE and several AN-26/32s (updated AN-26s) in eastern Europe.[310] Of course, there was whining from several quarters, including members of the U.S. Congress who objected to spending funds on non-U.S. equipment. Once they received them, the Afghans wasted no time putting these newly acquired machines to work. I was pleased to observe many instances in which they used the aircraft on their own initiative to move troops and supplies around their country. However, after I departed CENTCOM, illogical reasoning prevailed, and the U.S. re-equipped the Afghan Air Force with modern, but unmaintainable on their own, American aircraft.[311]

Shortly thereafter, in a meeting with Defense Minister Wardak, he objected strenuously to my decision to limit the size of the ANA. I told him, "Mr. Minister, six years have already gone by since the authorization for a 70,000-man army, and the force level is still only about 50,000. More importantly, there has been great difficulty finding volunteers who are literate, which I think is essential to the new ANA." He retorted, "During the Soviet War, most of our mujahideen were illiterate, and we did very well. This should not be an obstacle to enlarging our army." I replied, "It was different then, as you were defending your homeland against a foreign invader with widespread support from the population. Now, the challenges are mostly internal and more sophisticated. I think literacy should be a fundamental requirement. Already, our trainers are spending much of their time on literacy training, and it is going slowly. And remember, the U.S. is paying for all of this. We need to get more results for the dollars."

Later, I had a similar conversation with Karzai, who supported Wardak's appeal for a larger ANA. I knew these Afghan leaders had been hearing from U.S. congressional visitors that we should push to grow the size of Afghan Security Forces more quickly. My sober assessment of the unlikelihood of achieving these unrealistic goals dampened their enthusiasm, at least when I was at CENTCOM. But soon after I left the job, the target numbers grew substantially. The results from this vastly expanded but less capable force were evident later in the contribution to the abysmal performance of the ill-prepared and poorly motivated ANA/ANP in the eventual collapse of the Afghan government.

Karzai did not belabor the point with me as I explained my rationale for a reasonably sized, competent, professional force. However, he did ask me for support in the hardware area. "Admiral, just think if we had a few F-16s and they did a flyover during our next national day parade. What a great morale boost that would be for our people!" Smiling, I demurred. "Mr. President, I understand, but this is not at all realistic." He got the point and never brought the subject up again.

I quickly decided to seek additional troops, not to enhance the ISAF security mission but to bolster the insufficient numbers engaged in trying to train the Afghan Security Forces. Long since leaving that assignment at CENTCOM, I have maintained this view as much more likely to achieve the desired result of a reasonably stable and secure country than the policies subsequently followed to vastly increase outside troop levels in Afghanistan. In the end, it became clear that those policies had failed.

Regarding the need for trainers to instruct the Afghan Security Forces, I received no help from Washington. I explained to Secretary Gates that my top need was for trainers rather than more combat troops, but Iraq was the priority, and I was told none were available. Finally, working on my own, later in the year, I called General Jim Mattis, newly commanding U.S. Joint Forces Command, asking for his help. Jim called me back and reported, "Fox, I think we found something that can work." He identified a Marine battalion he felt could be deployed to Afghanistan early the following year (2008). He said he could make it happen if I could get permission from Gates. I called the Secretary and connected with him on his aircraft while he flew home for the Christmas holidays. I said, "Mr. Secretary, I think we have a short-term solution to the Afghan trainer challenge," explaining that Jim and I had worked out a deal if he would bless it. He directed me to submit a formal request after the holidays, which was approved.[312]

Reinforcing the idea of emphasizing quality over quantity was also my experience in the field, observing the ANA. On one occasion in mid-August, I witnessed an operation briefed in eastern Afghanistan by a *kandak* (brigade about 600 men strong) of the ANA 203 Corps. This *kandak* was partnered with U.S. troops of the 82nd Airborne Division and was incrementally assuming more responsibility; first by observing an operation run by the Americans, next by jointly planning and then briefing with the Americans, and lastly by planning, briefing, and conducting an operation by themselves. I was there for that culminating event.

While watching a group of junior and mid-grade Afghan officers working together on their own, planning details of the operation, I was struck by two things: First, I noticed the mix of different ethnic backgrounds as these officers worked closely to get the job done. Second, I could not help but contrast this team's initiative, cooperation, and enthusiasm with what I had seen in Iraq.

And third, as the briefing began, I was surprised that the Afghans did the entire event independently without American assistance. I noted that this was not just an exercise briefing but a detailed combat plan that would be executed in the field, opposed by the Taliban and their allies.

U.S. Army Colonel (later Brigadier General) Marty Schweitzer, overseeing this operation, introduced the briefing. "Sir, this is Major General Abdul Khaliq, ANA, commanding the 203 Tandar (Thunder) Corps. His First Kandak (brigade) has planned, and he will brief you on OPERATION "Khyber," and then conduct the operation in Khost Province this week." The briefing, despite some language challenges, was comprehensive and professionally done. I was impressed with the level of detail, down to the seemingly mundane but essential business of food and water resupply.

At the end, a soldier in fatigue uniform without discernible rank insignia stood up and gave the Afghan troopers an emotional and inspiring pep talk in the Dari language. I leaned over and asked the U.S. Colonel, "Is this man the *kandak* commander?" He replied, "I don't know him, sir." My translator picked up most of what he said: an awe-inspiring motivational speech with a bit of a religious overtone. I was eager to meet this gentleman who introduced himself as Nassib. It turned out that he was a mullah, loosely assigned to the ANA 203 Corps. He spoke some English, so I asked him about his talk. He explained, "Sir, my responsibility is for cultural affairs and the morale of our soldiers. It was important for me to remind them that what they're doing is for their families, their country, and for Allah. They should pray for His blessing and to be strong."

I later connected my CENTCOM Chaplain, Father Jim Danner, with Nassib to learn more about his position and see if we could assist in expanding this exemplary role. Over the next year, Father Jim was able to help the Afghans to formalize a broader role for their mullahs in the ANA with support from the U.S. I was pleased to learn that with the assistance of some American friends, General Nassib, by then the chief mullah in the ANA, was able to safely escape with his family during the debacle of U.S. withdrawal from Afghanistan in August 2021.[313]

Several weeks later, I was invited back to Khost by Arsala Jamal, the governor of the province, to a meeting he was hosting for 12 of his local governors (tribal leaders). I said little through an interpreter, "I want to encourage Governor Jamal and you other leaders to continue with this good work because I believe it's a wonderful example to the whole country of Afghanistan." But I listened and observed a lot. It was obvious that some tribal leaders were unhappy with our presence and asked when we were leaving. In fact, one Afghan argued with the governor and stalked out of the meeting. The majority of the attendees seemed cooperative and appreciative of our assistance.

The Provincial Reconstruction Team (PRT) operating in Khost was particularly well led by Navy Commander Dave Adams, and they engaged with the local population. The partnership between the soldiers of the 82nd Airborne, led by Colonel Schweitzer, the PRT, the provincial leadership of Governor Jamal, and the local security forces was exemplary and the best I had seen anywhere in Afghanistan, and much better than any place in Iraq at that time. The entire experience in Khost was quite encouraging and gave us a hint of what might be possible if we focused on the correct issues. The U.S. soldiers did not obtrusively lead with their weapons but with their actions when partnering with the civilian leadership in the province. In my observation, this was a terrific example of successful counterinsurgency at work. It was also a case in point that individual actions can make all the difference in the world.

In Khost Province, we were fortunate to have exemplars in key leadership positions on both the U.S. and Afghan sides. Even more remarkable was the progress in counterinsurgency, given the location of this province along the Pakistan border in rugged terrain that traditionally had been dominated by the Taliban. I left there pondering how it might be possible to capture this model of excellence and export it throughout the rest of the country.[314]

On another trip to a remote part of Afghanistan, I saw more good governance and cooperation with a PRT. The occasion was a visit to Bamiyan province in the north-central mountains to meet with the first female governor in the country, Habiba Sarabi, a medical doctor by education and training, returning after the ouster of the Taliban and agreeing to serve in government. That impoverished province, home to mostly ethnic Hazara people, as was Dr. Sarabi, was the site of the famous Buddha statues in caves that were destroyed by the Taliban.[315] I asked the governor, "What do you need?" She explained that spring floods had destroyed a bridge on the only road connecting the province to Kabul, and "the people have been waiting for this bridge for three years!" I directed the senior Coalition officials there to find a way to help her. I suggested a temporary military pontoon bridge to allow people to cross the river.

Later, on a walking tour of the main town with only one kilometer of paved road and viewing the remnants of the Buddha statues with Dr. Sarabi, I noted the admiration and respect her people had for the governor and the good relationship with the PRT headed by Coalition troops from New Zealand.

Dr. Habiba Sarabi, the first and only female governor of Bamiyan province, Afghanistan, with famous caves in the background. Buddha statues carved in the caves about 2000 years ago were destroyed by the Taliban in 2001.

Unfortunately, all was not goodness in Afghanistan, which was not a surprise to me, given the history and complexities of this nation, with an even larger population than Iraq. In addition to the challenges of trying to train and equip the ANA, the large, roughly 30,000-troop NATO military contingents of ISAF, despite their well-intentioned presence in the country for security purposes, brought with them as many problems as solutions.

After NATO took command of ISAF in 2003, the size and scope of the operations in Afghanistan progressively increased as the force expanded its presence from Kabul through the remainder of the country by late 2006. The primary mission was to provide and maintain security, but from 2006 on, this gradually entailed more intensive combat, particularly in the southern and eastern parts of the country. As Taliban and other insurgent attacks increased, the hostile environment resulted in more casualties and escalating caveats (political restrictions on military operations) by the participating nations. From my first encounter with ISAF Commander General Dan McNeil, who bluntly stated, "I need help," it was challenging to figure out how to effectively employ these forces.

Let me offer an example from a personal experience several weeks earlier in northern Afghanistan at Mazar-i-Sharif in Balkh Province. Recall that this was the site of the successful turning point in the 2001 Coalition military effort to oust the Taliban and Al Qaeda from Afghanistan. I planned to spend most of the day there visiting with the governor of the province, then the ISAF in RC North, commanded by the Germans, the Afghan ANA 209 Corps, and the Swedish-led PRT. The first meeting, with Governor Atta Mohammad Nur, a former commander in the Northern Alliance against the Taliban, began with a very blunt question from the governor, "What is ISAF doing here?" As I prepared to reply, he said, "You are not helpful to the people of this province." When I asked him to please explain, he continued, "There are thousands of soldiers here, but they just live in their camps and do not do anything for the people; they don't protect them, they don't help them with their daily lives," and then tellingly he said, "and they don't even have any money for us to build things or buy things." And further, "they just get in the way. They drive their big military vehicles down the roads and force our people out of the way, making them angry."[316]

Recognizing the impossibility of explaining the voluntary nature of the ISAF troop contributions and the myriad caveats applied to them, I invited him to provide me with a concise list of practical tasks, and I would see if I could help.

Afghanistan: The Best Of Intentions

Meeting next with the Swedish-led PRT, an eager, outgoing group anxious to do anything useful but severely constrained by political restrictions, commonly known as "caveats,"[317] and glimpsing the large, boxy troop transport vehicles parked in their camp, I better understood what the governor was talking about.

At the RC North Headquarters Camp, I was hosted by Brigadier General Josef Blotz, the commander of the German-led ISAF force in north Afghanistan. He was affable, knowledgeable, and engaged. He took me on a tour of his facilities and introduced me to his people. During a one-on-one conversation over dinner in his mess hall, I asked him how long he had been in command of RC North. He replied, "I have been here for three months." Assuming he would be there for a year, I asked him, "Based on what you have seen, what do you have in mind to accomplish for the rest of the year?" He replied that he didn't have much time left, "I have to leave in one month."

When I looked at him quizzically, he explained that they were on rotational six-month tours of duty in Afghanistan that included a period of home leave on the front and back ends, leaving an actual tour of duty only about four months in-country. He said, "I now know enough to be useful here and asked my superiors to let me remain for a year, but my request was denied."[318] He struck me as sincere but professionally embarrassed and frustrated. This was one of the realities in Afghanistan.

Another issue that loomed larger and severely impacted events in Afghanistan was the challenge of civilian casualties. The previously mentioned incident involving the U.S. Marine MARSOC company in March 2007 was only the tip of the iceberg for me in confronting a problem that persisted to a degree or another for the entire U.S. engagement in Afghanistan. Most of the cases involved errant air strikes. Given the relatively small number of Coalition troops trying to cover a vast area, airpower was our greatest force multiplier and often the only backup support for our soldiers engaged with the enemy. The insurgents operated close to the population and frequently used the people for cover.

Despite the almost exclusive use of precision-guided ordnance, there were times when various factors, including human error, weather, faulty intelligence, computational mistakes, and malfunctioning systems, resulted in fatal unintended consequences. As most incidents involved urgent close air support for Coalition or Afghan soldiers, we instituted a comprehensive, sometimes painful set of procedures to question assumptions and minimize risk. Despite continuous attention and a requirement to elevate permissions following a strict set of rules, occasional errors resulted in loss of life.

This issue was arguably the most contentious and difficult topic of discussion with President Karzai. Exasperated, he asked me, "Why can't you stop this? It is turning the people against us." In hindsight, his prescient warning pinpointed one of the most significant factors in the deterioration of Afghanistan's political and military situation.

In summary, notwithstanding some heroic efforts by thousands of dedicated American and ISAF Coalition allies working closely with Afghan partners, the security situation in Afghanistan deteriorated steadily. Undone by inconsistent attention to issues large and small, imprudent overreach, corruption, and the presence of large numbers of foreign troops in a historically hostile culture, the best of intentions failed to achieve the expanded mission set of nation-building in Afghanistan. Once again, the notion that long-term security and stability can be achieved and maintained without cooperation from the civilian population was demonstrated to be ephemeral.

CHAPTER 29

NEW ISSUES, NEW DECISIONS

OTHER CENTCOM MATTERS

Issues regarding Iraq continued to dominate activities through the end of 2007 and into the following year. But events in other countries within my area of responsibility demanded attention and decisions.

Recognizing the utility of the CENTCOM Coalition Conference that I hosted in May at Tampa and President Bush addressed, and at the urging of General Petraeus, I decided to reprise that event with another Coalition Conference, but at Manama, Bahrain, in October 2007. This would be an opportunity for General Petraeus to detail the progress being made in Iraq and for us to rally our partners to continue their assistance until the job was done. We were able to answer questions and conduct a series of bilateral meetings with senior diplomatic and military leaders worldwide.

One other initiative resulted in a "first" for CENTCOM in January 2008, when I decided to host a CENTCOM Chiefs of Defense (CHOD) Conference in Tampa, sending an invitation to a meeting of the senior military officers from each country (CHODS). This was a venue that I inherited and used quite successfully in Pacific Command in my prior assignment as the Commander there. The idea was to bring the senior military leaders together to engage in issues of common interest, to foster mutual support and cooperation, and to allow me to exchange ideas and solicit support for our various initiatives. There were a few administrative challenges, like finding a venue to meet since CENTCOM headquarters had no appropriate facilities, and we faced an unexpected dilemma. It dawned on us late that English was not universally understood, so we needed a common language as a baseline. There were two distinctly different groups of countries. The first centered around the Arabian Peninsula, which is almost entirely Islamic and speaks Arabic. The second is also mostly Islamic but speaks Russian as the common language of Central Asia. Splitting the group and having two conferences solved the language challenge and allowed more focus on separate issues of common interest to the Gulf countries and the Central

Asian states. The newly appointed U.S. Chairman of the Joint Chiefs of Staff, Admiral Mike Mullen, addressed the group and met most attendees for the first time.

One especially rewarding aspect of that meeting was the gracious welcome and inclusion that each CHOD displayed toward General Babakir Zebari of Iraq.[319] This embrace was no small thing, as most participants harbored deep suspicion and mistrust of the Iraqis, given recent events. The initiative worked well, but my only regret was that I was not in office long enough to capitalize on the bonds of cooperation and trust established among the senior military commanders in the region.

IRAN

One meeting on the sidelines of the Coalition Conference that resulted from an earlier chance encounter stood out in my mind: a one-on-one discussion with the Australian ambassador to Iran, Greg Moriarty. Given that there had been no diplomatic relations between our two countries since 1979, my guidance from Washington precluded any direct contact with Iran. As we had no other links and little real intelligence or information, I was always eager to learn as much as possible about what was happening in Tehran. Before my introduction to Ambassador Moriarty, the only reliable information about Iran came from the ruler of Oman, the late Sultan Qaboos, who maintained good relations with the U.S. and Iran and supported me in many ways throughout the region.

Greg Moriarty was gracious and helpful, going out of his way to provide me with his up-to-date views and the thinking of the Iranian leaders, at least as he understood them. I expressed my frustration: "Washington can seemingly do only one thing at a time, and that would be Iraq," and as I explained, "I have been prohibited from any engagement with the Iranians." He confirmed several of my assumptions: "Iran is caught in its own hubris and insecurity, controlled by the hardliners who want to retain power." He caused me to chuckle when he relayed Iranian views of the U.S. and its allies as a "coalition of the stupid" and that the allies were "poodles of the U.S."[320]

There was some U.S.-Iranian communication at sea in the routine course of naval activities, plus several incidents of dangerous maneuvering by vessels of the Iranian IRGC, resulting in warning shots being fired by U.S. vessels during my time as CENTCOM Commander. To reduce the likelihood of any unintended consequences of an incident at sea, I drafted a proposal for Ambassador Crocker to present to the Iranians during a meeting in turbulent but neutral Baghdad with his Iranian counterpart. The presentation explored establishing formal communications procedures between U.S. and Iranian maritime forces that might be utilized in mutual encounters under defined circumstances. This proposal was one of several points of discussion at a meeting designed primarily to discourage Iranian support for Shia militias in Iraq. There were no follow-up meetings, and nothing came of the proposal.[321]

The only face-to-face interaction of a non-operational nature between the U.S. and Iran occurred in early September 2007 in Geneva, Switzerland, during the annual Global Strategic Review conference organized by the London-based International Institute of Strategic Studies (IISS). The event provided, in the words of panel moderator David Ignatius of the Washington Post, a "chance encounter" between Vice Admiral Kevin Cosgriff, Commander of U.S. Naval Forces Central Command, and Iranian Professor Seyed G. Safavi, Director of the London Academy of Iranian Studies and brother of the erstwhile commander of the Iranian Revolutionary Guard Corps (IRGC), General Yahya Rahim Safavi. The latter, the protagonist of malicious Iranian activities in Iraq, spent ten years directing terrorist activities around the world. He had been relieved of IRGC command only a few days before that conference. According to the conference record, Cosgriff and Safavi offered "tempered assessments of the current state of affairs between their two nations."[322]

BACK TO AFGHANISTAN AND PAKISTAN

In November 2007, I was back in Islamabad for meetings with General Kayani and President Musharraf, primarily to talk about cross-border issues and ongoing problems with insurgents from the Federally Administered Tribal Areas (FATA) of Pakistan crossing into Afghanistan. There had been several ugly incidents along the border earlier that year, including Pakistani Frontier Corps militiamen shooting and killing an American officer following a meeting between U.S. and Pakistani soldiers.[323] Tensions had been rising along with the increasing number of kinetic incidents involving U.S., Pakistani, and Afghan soldiers and insurgents.

Anne Patterson, a sharp and experienced career diplomat, had taken up her position as our U.S. Ambassador to Islamabad, and we got on well together. Pakistan had been roiled in domestic turmoil for most of the year. Musharraf suspended Chief Justice Chaudhry and was pressing corruption charges against him. There was clearly no love lost between the two. During an earlier session I had with Musharraf, he exclaimed, "This guy is running around acting as if he were the president!"[324]

Other presidential rivals, Benazir Bhutto and Nawaz Sharif, had been negotiating for their return to Pakistan from exile, posing an issue of great political concern to Musharraf. Before we met with Musharraf, the ambassador and I received word that the Pakistani president was considering suspending the Constitution and assuming extraordinary powers beyond constitutional limits. Ambassador Patterson and I received messages from Secretary of State Rice and Secretary Gates, respectively, directing us to try to convince Musharraf to reject declaring emergency rule.

The three of us met on the morning of November 2, during which it seemed likely that he was resolved to enact such a rule. We took a break for lunch, and following that, I asked to see him alone. During our one-on-one session, I advised him not to do it. I related my experiences in the Pacific with two other countries that went through coups. I related, "Things typically do not turn out the way you want, with unforeseen complications forcing affairs down different paths." He responded, "What do you want me to do, step down? Resign?... there would be chaos... who would become the president?... what would they do?" He then lapsed into a period of self-reflection. "I'm very proud of the progress we've made in this country. Look at the economy. It is so much better than before my time." He continued, "I have made some mistakes," and then recounted an earlier conversation in which I asked him why he did not take decisive action in the "Red Mosque" incident, where insurgents had barricaded themselves and engaged in a shootout with police. He admitted that he "should have done something sooner."[325]

New Issues, New Decisions

It was clearly an emotional time for him, and I left that meeting convinced he would follow through with this plan. He had often repeated, "I have no choice."

As the ambassador and I climbed into our vehicle for the return trip to the embassy, I opined that we needed to get on the phones right away and tell Washington to "stand by for action." Connecting on secure telephones with our respective bosses, Secretaries Rice and Gates, we explained the situation as we understood it. Secretary Gates asked me, "When?" "Very soon," I replied, "probably within 48 hours."

The next day, November 3, Musharraf suspended the Constitution, fired the Chief Justice again, and announced emergency rule. Subsequently, Benazir Bhutto, who by then had returned to the country, was assassinated in December 2007, plunging the country deeper into turmoil. Less than a year later, Musharraf resigned from the presidency and went into exile.[326]

Although failing to dissuade Musharraf from his extra-constitutional foray, I had more success in a different conversation with him regarding Afghan-Pakistan border security. On previous visits to the border and in discussions with our forces assigned there, I observed that each of the three entities purporting to have the same objectives, the U.S., ANA, and Frontier Corps (Pakistan army) elements, occupied separate outposts in the vicinity of the border. The open spaces in between, traversed by insurgents but also personnel from the three security forces coming and going to their outposts, were often scenes of misidentification and gunfire, some resulting in casualties.

If we could get the security forces to work together, sharing the same border outposts and communicating with respective higher headquarters, there would be less likelihood of mistaken identification and casualties. Musharraf agreed, and I got concurrence from Afghan President Karzai and Minister Wardak.

On a subsequent trip to Nangarhar province, I visited one of the first joint outposts under construction near the "Torkham Gate" entry to Afghanistan, just west of the Khyber Pass. It was at the Afghan-Pakistan border on the road from Peshawar, Pakistan, to Kabul.[327]

At the November 2007 meeting with Musharaf, I again urged him to invite Karzai for a personal meeting to diffuse the border tensions, reminding him that Karzai had hosted him earlier in the year in Kabul. He acted on my suggestion, hosting Karzai the following month in Islamabad.

Pakistani President Pervez Musharraf (on right) ushers Afghan President Hamid Karzai (on left) into a joint press conference in Islamabad following a 26 December 2007 meeting.

In my discussion with President Karzai, he again raised the issue of civilian casualties, which we continued trying to minimize. As most of the unintended victims were the result of airstrikes, my "go-to" officer to manage this challenge was USAF Lieutenant General (later General and Commander Pacific Air Forces) Gary North, who did a terrific job as the Commander of AFCENT (U.S. Air Forces Central Command) and the Air Component Commander for CENTCOM. He was a reliable and trusted officer, and our friendship was based on our prior service together in Pacific Command. Gary was diligent, resolute, and dependable in dealing with other challenges, particularly airspace control over Iraq, which was always a contentious issue with General Petraeus.

One of the most challenging issues during that time, in late 2007 and early 2008, was related to the previously discussed matters. Specifically, the cross-border insurgent and terrorist activity conducted mostly by

New Issues, New Decisions

Pashtun tribesmen with allegiances to the Taliban or various warlords in the border area. One of the more interesting aspects of this activity was that various insurgents targeted not only Afghanistan and the Karzai government but also Musharraf and his government in Islamabad. The actual terrain that offered the best sanctuary for all the militants was in the FATA area of northwest Pakistan, just across the border from Afghanistan. These semi-autonomous tribal areas are immune to Islamabad's control for many reasons too complex to explain here.

When I speak of the border, I refer to the Durand Line, named after the British diplomat who demarcated the border between Afghanistan and British India in 1883.[328] This currently internationally recognized line (2007 and now) was inherited by Pakistan after its independence from Britain in 1947. However, the line divides both Pashtun and Baloch tribal areas, whose members reside on both sides of the border, and, as a result, remains unrecognized by Afghanistan.

In a discussion I once had with Musharraf about problems along this porous "border," he indignantly asked, "Do you want me to build a fence? I will be happy to do that." I knew that Karzai would vehemently object. The idea that we (the U.S.) would push for a more definitive demarcation was out of the question as far as I was concerned.

Our conventional and special forces (SOF) did their best to avoid the estimated border. But we still had the question of how to deal with the insurgents and their vicious assaults. A convenient marriage of multi-source intelligence and emerging technology offered another option: armed unmanned aerial vehicles (UAVs). More commonly known as "Predator" drones, these quiet, high-flying aircraft equipped with precision weapons could attack and destroy pinpoint targets. These machines flew in and around Afghanistan, but it was a different legal basis than the Title 10 U.S. Code authority under which the U.S. military operated. As these attack operations, usually aimed against identified individual insurgent leaders, would occur in my CENTCOM "battle space," I would be apprised of the proposed operations and asked to assent before mission execution.

In a briefing in late December 2007, CIA Director Mike Hayden advised me that his agency had received worrisome intelligence about a joint Al Qaeda-Taliban campaign to destabilize Pakistan in the wake of

DECISIONS, DISCORD & DIPLOMACY

Musharraf's declaration of emergency rule.[329] Mike said he would send a team to brief me on the details and request my consent for a proposed U.S. attack on specific "high-priority" individuals.

When the team arrived, they shared with me a list of known insurgent and terrorist leaders working both sides of the border, on which they had good intelligence and position data. I was okay with the concept as it would preclude exposing our troops to obvious dangers in attempting to assault these heavily guarded hideouts, as well as eliminating the need to cross the frontier on foot or by helicopter. I did have some issues with individual targeting.

While not seeking the intelligence details on what the Agency was basing its targeting on, I was aware that structures in this part of the world were walled compounds containing several buildings of various uses. While we might identify the compound (the address) as a shelter for insurgents and militants, it was sometimes more difficult to pinpoint the actual individual or building. There were incidents in which innocent civilians were killed on both sides of the Durand Line. I was sensitive to these unfortunate events and made every effort to ensure we had the best information before authorizing an operation to proceed. Using the best information available, I felt obliged to decide whether the potential cost might outweigh the benefit. In any event, I did not want to put these decisions into an "automatic" mode based on a predetermined set of criteria. Rather, take the time to review the circumstances of each case as it arose. For example, risk factors being comparable, I would be much more inclined to authorize a hierarchical approach, striking one of the top five "most wanted" terrorist or insurgent leaders rather than the next five. Implementation of this tactic proceeded at a slow pace during my time at CENTCOM but increased substantially in following years during the Obama Administration, which viewed these strikes as preferable to ground attacks by our forces.[330] The contribution of this approach to a rising civilian death toll was a key factor in the failure of the overall effort in Afghanistan.

CHAPTER 30

ENGAGING WITH THE MEDIA: ACCURACY A CHALLENGE

My approach to the media was shaped by experience over many years.

The first personal training I received was a crash course in media relations and messaging for deploying commanders initiated by the U.S. Navy just before the start of the Gulf War in 1991. It was a good, albeit last-minute, effort as I was already on board the aircraft carrier, completing pre-deployment preparations. Recalling the discussion with a senior Navy public affairs officer in a catwalk adjacent to the flight deck, a rare, isolated spot away from other people on a blustery, late December day in Hampton Roads, the message was simple: "Think about what you want to say in a few phrases and then speak up and distinctly while looking into the camera." With his videographer filming, we did a few practice "takes." I was shivering and too cold to care much then, but I remembered the advice. It was a blur and seemed a distraction at the time, given the many items of combat preparation on my mind. I do not recall engaging in any personal media events during that deployment, as most of my time was at sea conducting flight operations. Still, that early guidance was correct and useful for future engagements.

My immersion and trial-by-fire experience occurred during that 1995 deployment to the Mediterranean involving the Bosnian conflict. Recall that we were hosting a couple of dozen well-known media people for an overnight stay on the aircraft carrier and were surprised by the start of combat operations in the middle of the night. The big takeaway from that two-week extended exposure was the complementary trust established between the embarked media members and me during high-tempo operations, although I regularly received conflicting "guidance" from my seniors in and out of the chain of command. Everyone in that large media group was true to their word; they could report good stories, and I felt comfortable that the public received and understood my messages.

Another great learning experience occurred during exposure to journalists and reporters from whom I learned beneficial details about foreign countries' history, policies, and cultures. In the forefront was the late Richard Halloran, a longtime reporter and writer about East Asian affairs for the *New York Times, Washington Post, BusinessWeek*, and other news outlets. He was truly a mentor and invaluable confidant from whom I learned much more than he ever learned from me. Richard inspired me to reach out to well-informed and competent journalists from whom I could gain insight into new and evolving issues worldwide.

Of course, I crossed paths with a few unprofessional journalists over the years and survived several "ambush" interviews. But by and large, my media encounters were good, often instructive, and mutually beneficial to the interlocutors.

The CENTCOM experience drew much media attention, prompting me to follow the same course of action I had established years earlier. Rather than trying to convince reporters and journalists of the merits of actions we might be taking, I thought it better to invite experienced correspondents to accompany me to the extent they were willing to expose themselves to potential danger in the combat zones so they could see, hear, and communicate firsthand observations to their audiences.

Predominantly professional, skilled, and thoughtful, most journalists I traveled with were easy to work with and straightforward in their reporting. Some interesting highlights:

One of my first interviews on arrival in Iraq in March 2007 was getting reacquainted with CNN correspondent Kyra Phillips (aka "Baghdad Babe"), whom I had known for years. In 2003, she interviewed my son Bill on the aircraft carrier *ABRAHAM LINCOLN* after he returned from the first bombing mission over Baghdad at the start of the intervention in Iraq.

Later, in 2007, Kyra and her CNN colleagues were holed up in a mini fortress at the bottom of a dead-end alley adjacent to the "Green Zone" in central Baghdad. She conducted the interview at a table in an outdoor setting on a top-floor "lanai" with a view of the Green Zone and palm trees in the background. The subject matter was serious, but the setting was quite entertaining as the camera crew recorded the interview through the trees with gunfire and explosions nearby.

Many journalists joined me on trips to Iraq, Afghanistan, and other countries in the region. Several were particularly thoughtful and persuasive in their reporting. From them, I learned insight and nuances

Engaging With The Media: Accuracy A Challenge

that helped me understand and communicate events in my area of responsibility.

New York Times correspondent and former Marine Corps infantryman C.J. Chivers provided the unique perspective of a combat-experienced military officer reporting on events in Iraq and Central Asia. Having previously worked in Moscow as the *New York Times* bureau chief further enhanced his understanding of the complex relationship among people and events in the region, mainly Central Asia. His insight, particularly in military-related matters, was peerless.

Skilled, professional, and perceptive, ABC's Martha Raddatz had extensive experience in conflict zones and a particularly sensitive understanding of the human dimension of war.

Longtime veteran reporter Bob Burns of the Associated Press reported the facts accurately and in detail without editorializing.

Gregg Jaffe of the *Wall Street Journal* had wide-ranging interests, covered stories in detail, and was usually thinking ahead of the immediate issues and challenges with good insight.

David Ignatius of the *Washington Post,* with his deep understanding of complex issues, cut to the heart of situations in a very understandable way.

The journalist and author Tom Friedman was remarkably agile and accurate in understanding issues. However, he once introduced me to some unease as he accompanied me to Iraq and Qatar. Upon arrival in Doha, he asked, "Have you ever done an interview with Al Jazeera?" I replied, "No," but as I thought about it, knowing that much of the Al Jazeera reporting at that time, particularly on Iraq, was extremely negative, I asked, "Why?" He said he was going to their studio that evening for an interview and asked, "Why don't you come with me and check it out?" Although skeptical, I went to the downtown Doha Al Jazeera headquarters with Tom, who had called ahead to let them know that I would accompany him.

On arrival, I was met by the Al Jazeera Director-General, Wadah Khanfar, who took me on a tour of the facilities and then led me to his office to chat while Tom finished his recording session.[331] Wadah invited me to come back anytime for an in-person live interview. As I considered his offer, I thought about a point Tom had made in the car on the way to the studio, "This might be a good opportunity to present the U.S. perspective on issues, particularly Iraq," which, at that time, despite increased security, was still widely denounced in the region, propounded by the largely negative Al Jazeera reporting. I told Wadah that I would consider it and get back to him. Knowing that Washington would not be in favor, I did not even bother to ask.

About a month later, I was in Doha again and decided to give it a shot. They offered me a live 30-minute evening prime-time interview in the Gulf region. I asked for simultaneous translation of my English into Arabic and vice versa using my interpreter. They insisted on using their interpreter but were okay with mine in the studio beside me. I found the correspondent's questions expectedly negative but easy to answer and refute, particularly insinuations I disagreed with.

It was a terrific opportunity to explain our current activities in Iraq and the positive difference they made to the lives of citizens. Immediately following the interview, I turned to "Betty," my interpreter, and asked if she had heard anything in the translation that was not accurate. She identified one point that we explained to the producer, who fixed the transcript on the spot. The interview with the appropriate correction was aired on the same TV, "Prime Time," the following evening. The network estimated that 30 million Arabic-speaking people watched and listened to the interview. Washington was not happy, but I received positive feedback from many people in the Middle East who acknowledged a better understanding of events.

In February 2008, CNN lead Pentagon correspondent Barbara Starr, with whom I had been acquainted for years, accompanied me on a trip to Iraq. We had one hectic day that began in Baghdad, during which I was flying in a USMC V-22 Osprey tilt-rotor aircraft for the first time in Iraq. The plan was to take advantage of the speed of the Osprey to cover the long distances across Anbar province in western Iraq, stopping at several widely dispersed sites to visit with the troops and to see the security improvements firsthand.

Fallujah, Ramadi, Haditha, and finally, al Qaim were on the itinerary in far western Iraq near the Syrian border. Heading back to Baghdad in the afternoon, the pilot advised that we could not land at Baghdad because a sandstorm had reduced visibility to near zero, and conditions at Fallujah were deteriorating. We were also running low on fuel, and he recommended diverting to the Marine camp at Fallujah, about 40 miles west of Baghdad International Airport.

Upon arrival, I was met by newly arrived in Iraq, Major General (later General, Commander US Southern Command and White House Chief of Staff) John Kelly, who offered to put me up for the night at Fallujah as weather conditions in Baghdad were not forecast to improve. I replied, "I have a meeting scheduled with General Petraeus that I need to attend this evening in Baghdad. Could you put together a ground convoy of some kind to get me there?" He said, "I'll get to work on it," and about 30 minutes later, introduced me to a young officer who would lead my escort group of Marines and vehicles. Directing me to one of the new MRAP (Mine-Resistant Ambush-Protected) trucks, the remainder of the heavily armed escort group piled into a half-dozen up-armored Humvees.

By this point, Iraqi forces had taken responsibility for security on the four-lane highway between Fallujah and Baghdad, about an hour's driving time away. However, my escorting Marines had just arrived in the country. As I soon discovered, they were not familiar with the territory. Nonetheless, as I entered the MRAP vehicle with Captain Craig Faller, my executive assistant, Barbara Starr, and several other escorts, the Marine Corporal riding shotgun for the driver was proud to show me his newly installed "Blue Force" GPS tracking device. "Sir, we always know where we are with this thing." Reassured, I sat in the back and, before long, was fast asleep as we rumbled down the highway toward Baghdad.

Sometime later, I awakened, realized we had stopped moving, looked out the window, and noted palm trees, a few structures, and what appeared to be a small village. Everyone else in the back of the vehicle was still asleep. I asked the driver and his battle-buddy, "Where are we?" "Dunno, sir," was the reply, "we just stopped, but I will ask the Gunny up front in the convoy." Rousting my EA, I told him to get on the radio and contact his relief, my new EA, Army Colonel (later General and Commander U.S. AFRICOM) Steve Townsend, to find out what was going on and, more importantly, to get us the heck out of there.

The rest of the story was about how Iraqi army security had directed our convoy off the highway because of some issue ahead on the roadway.

Our convoy commander decided to pull into this village while he sorted things out. They had no idea where we were, other than somewhere between Fallujah and Baghdad.

This was, at that time, still an insurgent-frequented area. The two Marines in my vehicle kept staring and tapping at their vaunted GPS device, but they had no idea how to operate it beyond the "on/off" switch. I later discovered it was set on the largest scale map display, with a view of only a couple of hundred yards.

About this time, Barbara and the others awoke and, from the conversation in the vehicle and on the radios, deduced that the team was indeed "lost." I directed a pointed verbal message to Steve Townsend in the front vehicle to "... get this #%!! convoy turned around and back on the highway," as this could be an ambush.

Barbara piped up, "Oh my! This will be a great story... CENTCOM Commander and convoy lost in hostile territory in Iraq...," or words to that effect. About this time, I unloaded on Barbara, "... Don't even think about it. If a word of this leaks out, I will toss you out on the highway, and you can walk back!" (or something nastier).

In short order, the Marines had us turned around and back, moving again on the road, advising the Iraqis that we needed to stay on the highway and to let them pass. We made it into Baghdad without further incident and in time for my meeting. I later apologized to Barbara for my rude behavior. Those on that trip laughed while recounting the incident several times. Barbara was kind and kept the story to herself, I think.

BETRAYAL AND CONSEQUENCES

In keeping with the idea that, eventually, all good things end in this life, an incident with a media member brought my time as CENTCOM Commander to an abrupt halt. During the autumn of 2007, the CENTCOM public affairs officer sent a note advising me that a journalist and part-time instructor at the Naval War College named Thomas Barnett wanted to come on a trip and interview me for a story he was writing for *Esquire* magazine.

I did not know and had never heard of him. I told the PAO to put the request in the pending action pile that we would look at it when reviewing names to potentially accompany us on a future trip. Later, I received a call from another four-star Admiral and longtime friend endorsing this journalist and encouraging me to have him tag along on a trip. I replied, "We will take a look at it," but I was hesitant because I did not know the writer.

My public affairs officer received several more requests from the same individual as I did from my old friend. I told the staff that, before I would consider approving this request, to have him come down to Tampa and check him out. Sometime later, Barnett visited Tampa for a meeting with the staff, who noted his strong academic background, extensive speaking experience on strategic and international matters, and high regard at the War College. I had him in the office for a short chat and found him articulate, well-informed on current affairs, and eager to accompany me on a trip to the AOR.

When I asked why the keenness, he advised that he had been engaged to draft an article for *Esquire* magazine about me and events in the region and wanted to see things firsthand. Although something about him put me a bit off, I thought this might be a good opportunity to have someone describe in detail what we were trying to achieve in the region. Expressing an incomplete sense of prescience, I advised him that we would need to review any draft manuscript. He agreed without reservation but later reneged.

In November 2007, Barnett and several other journalists accompanied us for part of a wide-ranging trip to many countries, interviewing me on several occasions. Barnett later requested a photographer come to Tampa to take some still photos, to which I agreed. A couple of months later, I asked my EA, Captain Craig Faller, if he had received a draft of the article and, if not, to remind Barnett that we needed to see it before they went to print. Craig reported that he had received assurances from Barnett.

In early March, I received a telephone call from my daughter, Susan, inquiring if I was aware of a profile piece that had just appeared in the online version of the April 2007 *Esquire*, which she said would be certain to "cause trouble."[332] Chagrined to review the article my daughter forwarded, I found the author had used the accurately recorded details of his trip with us and my comments as background for a highly politicized personal attack on President George W. Bush.

DECISIONS, DISCORD & DIPLOMACY

The gist of the article described me as opposed to and "brazenly challenging" the President's policies on Iran. The story was demeaning of the Bush Administration and challenged the President to fire me for insubordination. I immediately called Secretary Gates to advise him of the publication.

Over the next few days, several news articles, blog posts, and opinion pieces added fuel to the fire with often inaccurate but negative articles alleging disagreements with the President on policy matters. I sent a handwritten note to the President through Secretary Gates, apologizing for my actions that may have contributed to an uncomfortable political position.

In a surprising and ironic twist, I participated in a classified video teleconference from Tampa with the President and his national security team in the White House situation room the following day. I observed an aide hand a piece of paper, which I assumed was my letter, to Secretary Gates, who read it and then passed it to the President. His only visible reaction was a glance over toward Gates. The next day, I received a phone call from General Jim "Hoss" Cartwright, a longtime colleague and Vice Chairman of the Joint Chiefs of Staff. He stated, "Fox, your note was received, but that wasn't the letter they were looking for."

I had a trip to Iraq scheduled for the next day and decided to continue, as there was no further communication from Washington. The silence conveyed a clear vote of "no confidence" from the President. It was obvious that continuing as CENTCOM Commander would be counterproductive to our efforts in the region. As we flew through the night enroute to Iraq, I sat alone in the back of the C-17 aircraft, concluding that the best way to minimize the distraction this episode was causing on the forces under my command and in Washington was to offer to resign.

Reaching the Pentagon by phone from the aircraft, I asked then-Lieutenant-General Pete Chiarelli, Military Assistant to Secretary Gates, to tell him that I intended to submit a letter of resignation and request for retirement that I was drafting. Discussing the matter with Gates, I advised him that I wanted time to personally tell members of my family, senior subordinate commanders, and immediate staff before any public announcement, to which he agreed. Before forwarding the letter to Washington and landing at Basra, Iraq, I had contacted all the people I

Engaging With The Media: Accuracy A Challenge

intended to notify except for my son, who was deployed on an aircraft carrier.

From Basra, I proceeded to the detention facility at Camp Bucca, responding to an invitation from Major General Doug Stone to view the progress that he had made in rehabilitation efforts with detainees. The circumstances there were heartwarming and a complete turnaround from the chaotic situation of a year earlier. General Stone had most of the detainees under instruction in basic education, life skills, and even art classes. Muslim clerics were conducting sessions refuting the radical Islamic messaging of extremist agitators. Detainees engaged in construction projects to improve the camp itself. The gratifying situation there left me with a feeling of satisfaction and pride at the accomplishments of Doug and his team. This was a notable example of leadership with focused application of resources, achieving desired results, and a positive legacy for the people of Iraq. Inconceivable a year earlier!

Continuing to Baghdad that evening, I received several messages from Washington pressing me to complete my desired notifications. I finally accomplished this by connecting with my son. During a private meeting with General Petraeus, advising him of my decision, we received notification that Gates had publicly announced my resignation at a Pentagon press conference. Shortly thereafter, I began the journey back to Tampa, as there was much to do in quickly winding up affairs at CENTCOM.

In hindsight, I would not alter my general approach to the media: inviting them to come with me and see situations firsthand, offering my commentary or explanations only if needed. But I should have used more discretion on a couple of occasions, for example, allowing Michael Gordon of the *New York Times* to accompany me to an early meeting with Prime Minister Maliki in Baghdad, which he reported almost verbatim in a column, infuriating some of the political leadership in Washington.

Tom Barnett was, unfortunately, an untrustworthy individual. He lied to us. And never passed a hint of apology. Contrary to my interpretation of his previous work, he used his access to fashion a blatant political attack on the President. Another case of deceitfully rationalizing by whatever means to a desired political end. I can only blame myself for inviting him without observing his behavior or investigating his journalistic work beforehand.

But the *Esquire* article alone was just the last in a series of circumstances eroding the satisfaction and confidence of President Bush in my service at CENTCOM. Iran policy was the focal point of the Barnett article and media commentary. Still, it was a bit of a red herring. Although steadily pushing back on media conjecture and hype about potential conflict with Iran, I think it would be accurate to say that my public comments on the subject were in line with utterances by my superiors in Washington. Further, the U.S. National Intelligence Estimate (NIE) issued in December 2007 regarding the Iranian nuclear programs concluded that the country had halted its nuclear weapons program in 2003. There was little public discussion about Iran at the time the article appeared.

A more significant cause of discontent in the White House was likely my consistent push to think beyond the near-term "win" of the successful surge in Iraq and frame U.S. actions toward the long-term security arrangement, an objective not realized. The idea that I would exercise my responsibilities as CENTCOM Commander, involving military decisions in Iraq, was irritating to Petraeus and, by extension, to Bush, who was "all in" with his ground commander in Iraq and dismissive of any advice or input not endorsed by Petraeus.

The intense focus on Iraq as a "must-win" by the Bush Administration overrode virtually all other policy considerations. I understood the primacy of that issue but had a responsibility to offer my recommendations and point out other matters that, in my opinion, were subordinated to "near-term" Iraq, particularly Afghanistan, and the strategic importance of our relationship with China.

President Bush prioritized loyalty to his policies and did not like dissenting opinions. Acutely aware of the rising tension in Washington resulting from my actions, I offered to resign in the autumn of 2007, simply stating, "I must continue to do what I think is right, but if it becomes uncomfortable for you, I will step down." At the time, Secretary Gates waved me off.

My resignation in March 2008 caused a stir but was soon forgotten in everyday activities and the run-up to the 2008 presidential election.

ENGAGING WITH THE MEDIA: ACCURACY A CHALLENGE

The media continued to play a significant role in reporting and influencing regional events following my retirement. Many of the issues remain unresolved or have become even more complex today, and a few of the key leaders and actors are still involved.

It is important to learn from these and prior events to baseline good strategic decisions in the future.

As will be apparent in the Epilogue, decision-making in the years following my departure from active military duty continued down a path shaped by events described earlier in this book.

Today, in 2025, the U.S. remains heavily engaged in the still deadly, turbulent, resource-consuming conflicts of the region. Again, short-term, tactical decisions predominate in the current Trump Administration's actions. It begs the question: Why do we not seem to learn from historical and more recent events? This responsibility is ours to assume.

EPILOGUE

"This episode ... reminds one of the desperate ignorance that underlies many critical decisions," concluded Charles Duelfer in reference to the vacuum in which the Iraqi weapons of mass destruction discussion unfolded.[333] But this assertion could be extended to describe much of my experience observing decision-making in the international arena during these years. The lack of awareness of available basic facts, history, cultures, or even interest in the foregoing on the part of high-level decision-makers has been highlighted in several instances. Ignorance or satisfaction in holding to previously held opinions are common factors in essential decisions going awry. Assumptions are either right or wrong. If the latter, trouble looms. Knowledge and understanding always trump assumptions. More of both could have placed us in better circumstances in Iraq and Afghanistan.

Unsurprisingly, disregarding my resignation, the world moved on. Events played out because of decisions made before and during my tenure commanding USCENTCOM. Following my departure, new decisions, compounding earlier choices, steered the course of history.

The 2008 U.S. presidential election campaign dominated the country's political focus for the remainder of that year, with the Iraq War a hot-button topic of debate among key contenders, particularly senators Biden, Obama, and McCain. For its part, the outgoing Bush Administration continued its primary focus on Iraq, desirous of leveraging the security successes of the surge to salvage its overall Iraq policy. President George W. Bush wanted his successor to inherit the positive consequences of decisions made in his final months of office and to leave in place the best chance to optimize the administration's policy aspirations for its incursion into Iraq, albeit scaled back, given the challenges of the previous five years.

The dominant issue in U.S.-Iraq discussions for the remainder of the Bush Administration in 2008 was negotiating the specific details of the Strategic Framework Agreement and the SOFA, but within a climate of continued vacillation on governance improvements by Iraqi PM Maliki. As previously discussed, negotiations dragged on until the 11th hour, culminating with the signing of the, in my opinion, flawed agreements by Bush and Maliki in Baghdad in December 2008. Security in Iraq

EPILOGUE

generally improved over the next few years. Still, the fractious squabbling among Iraqi political entities continued as the slow drawdown of American forces was implemented.

Meanwhile, in Afghanistan, security conditions slowly deteriorated. With Secretary Gates's approval, the stopgap infusion of several thousand Marines I had negotiated with General Mattis arrived in Afghanistan in 2008.[334] But several years of the Bush Administration's focus on Iraq had dimmed the glowing 2002-03 expectations for a secure and stable Afghanistan. Of course, many factors influenced the course of events: the combination of a resurgent Taliban, ineffective NATO troop employment, regime corruption, the increasingly difficult relationship with Karzai, and the challenge of civilian casualties in a population disdainful of any foreign troop presence.

Already retired, and just before the 2008 presidential election, I accepted a request to meet with the Honorable Susan Rice, then an advisor to candidate Barack Obama, to share my views on current foreign policy issues. Then Senator Obama had previously called me while I was still in uniform to discuss events in Pakistan, but this was the first outreach by the presidential candidate or his team.

Ms. Rice and I met for lunch at the Mayflower Hotel in Washington. After a lengthy discussion, I expressed my concern about the implications for two very clearly enunciated potential policy imperatives for the prospective new Obama Administration. Concisely, Ms. Rice suggested that regarding U.S. troop commitments in an Obama Administration, they intended to be "Out of Iraq" and "Into Afghanistan." My response was to opine that these would be two big mistakes.

In the case of Iraq, the surge had succeeded in improving security, major combat operations were concluded, and a timetable for the U.S. troop drawdown was implemented. Negotiations on long-term security arrangements between our two countries were ongoing. I considered it essential that the U.S. retain a residual troop force, albeit much smaller than current troop levels. Our purpose would be to advise and assist the Iraqi military and provide eyes and ears on the ground in this volatile country. Additionally, almost every Iraqi political leader, except those aligned with Iran, joined the Iraqi military leaders and desired that we retain a residual force in the country. Our troops would not continue combat operations, but those remaining would constitute a small, in-extremis response force to help the Iraqis as required in the immediate future. Furthermore, U.S. troops would be needed to train and assist with the U.S. equipment the Iraqis purchased from us and provide nascent capabilities in the Iraqi Armed Forces, such as air defense and intelligence. Furthermore, I suggested we needed to learn from our historical experience in abandoning countries where we had provided significant military assistance, such as Afghanistan, during the 1980s.

Regarding Afghanistan, I agreed that the current security situation had deteriorated, primarily due to inattention across the full spectrum of national capabilities resulting from the focus on Iraq. But recent historical examples demonstrated conclusively that this country did not take kindly to large occupying armies. Focused military assistance was sorely needed, particularly in training and equipping the undermanned Afghan National Army. I was certain that it would fall upon the U.S. to make up for the unfulfilled military training shortfalls of the other NATO nations. Furthermore, I explained that Afghanistan was quite different from Iraq in many ways, highlighting the lack of a recent history of a strong central government in Afghanistan and the vast disparity in literacy between the two countries, which is much lower in Afghanistan. Although current overall Coalition troop numbers were high, many were not effectively contributing to security. Furthermore, I had personally experienced the extreme sensitivity to civilian casualties that was turning the population away from supporting us.

The response that I received was not reassuring, reflecting the Obama campaign rhetoric to "end the war in Iraq, as troops are needed in Afghanistan." As we soon found out, both initiatives, compounded by a focus on the developing financial crisis of 2008, as well as the fundamental prioritization of domestic affairs over international, ensured that my foreign policy concerns were warranted.

Hindsight improves perception and judgment. The passing of time enables a better understanding of past decisions and appreciation for resulting actions and consequences. The experience of making and observing decisions at many levels has led me to restudy and appreciate the history of human endeavor.

In 1849, the French writer Jean-Baptiste Alphonse Karr wrote, "*plus ca change, plus c'est la même chose*" — the more things change, the

Epilogue

more they stay the same ...[335] Circumstances change, but precedents remain. Technological advances continually transform our environment, but human behaviors recur and persist with ceaseless regularity. What seems unrecognizable at the time often becomes evident after the fact. Thus, we frequently find ourselves in situations that seem unique but are fundamentally not vastly different from prior events. "What's past is prologue," says Antonio in William Shakespeare's *The Tempest*. Words of wisdom. History is instructive, but only if we take the time to research, study, and try to understand it. Examples abound in my experience.

I believe that national power, morally and wisely employed, can and should be a force for good. Military capabilities and readiness are key components of that capacity to improve circumstances for ourselves and other human beings. But in recent years, our nation has been too quick to employ a military option as the primary resource for solving international issues. We have been slow to recognize the inherent limits of military power, as evidenced by lessons learned from Iraq and Afghanistan. Prior experience with conflicts in Vietnam, Lebanon, the Balkans, and earlier in Iraq should have been instructive to me and senior political and military leaders.

What emerges throughout this book are recurring choices at many levels. Situations involving human strife beg for solutions. We are all blessed with individual talents and capabilities. We are responsible for using them, not just for our own benefit, but to improve circumstances for others. Decisions, large and small, influence the course of history at individual and global levels. Shaped by a range of factors from personal experience, the influence of others, competing agendas, knowledge (or the absence of), random events, and good or bad individual traits, our decisions are an ever-present reality. Outcomes are unpredictable, but it suffices to say that every decision will have consequences.

AFGHANISTAN SLOWLY SLIDES INTO DISASTER

The United States' abrupt withdrawal from Afghanistan in 2021, following two decades of effort, more than 2,400 U.S. military personnel, almost 70,000 Coalition and Afghan troops, and an estimated 48,000 Afghan civilians killed, and over two trillion dollars expended, offers ample opportunities for reflection.[336]

Looking back at that October 2001 attack on Afghanistan following 9/11, the initial U.S. goals seemed reasonable and attainable: retaliate for 9/11, disrupt the terrorist sanctuary, and destroy the Al Qaeda and Taliban military bases in Afghanistan.[337] These were all short-term objectives and tactical responses to the 9/11 terror attacks. In hindsight, despite 20 years of engagement in Afghanistan through four U.S. administrations, a comprehensive strategic plan with structured, achievable goals failed to emerge.

Shortly after initial success in 2001, President Bush delivered an address at the Virginia Military Institute in April 2002. His speech acknowledged one of the Institute's most distinguished graduates, alluding to a new Marshall Plan. "By helping to build an Afghanistan that is free from evil and a better place in which to live, we are working in the best traditions of George Marshall... the path that we, too, must follow." Alas, a follow-up plan for Afghanistan did not emerge, and the focus of international engagement soon shifted to Iraq. During that same speech at VMI, President Bush unwittingly provided a prophetic assessment of what was to come, stating, "We know this... from the history of military conflict in Afghanistan. It's been one of initial success, followed by long years of floundering and ultimate failure." But said President Bush boldly and inaccurately, "We're not going to repeat that mistake."[338]

Despite the intense focus on Iraq by the Bush Administration, the President offered sound practical advice to President Karzai during bi-weekly video teleconferences; I participated in these throughout my tenure at CENTCOM. But following my departure in 2008, angst about Afghanistan was rising in the waning days of the Bush Administration, with a planned 20,000 increase in U.S. troop strength. However, we still lacked an agreed-upon strategic objective. By this time, even Secretary of Defense Gates was concerned about the negative impacts of the increasing troop footprint.[339]

After taking office in 2009, President Obama followed through on his campaign promise to send more forces to Afghanistan to remedy what he decried as under-resourcing due to President Bush's focus on Iraq. He increased U.S. troop strength there by close to 20,000,[340] which, in fairness, was planned by President Bush. Again, the increase lacked strategic objectives.

Epilogue

In an address on March 27, 2009, formally acknowledging the cross-border Al Qaeda and Taliban links to Pakistan, President Obama announced "A New Strategy for Afghanistan and Pakistan." The new strategy was primarily a U.S. troop increase, an appeal to allies to increase civilian support to Afghanistan, and "shifting the emphasis of our mission to training and increasing the size of Afghan Security Forces." In reply to his rhetorical question, "What is our purpose in Afghanistan?" He focused on Al Qaeda, alleging that their presence in Afghanistan and Pakistan was a continuing threat to the American people, and restated the Bush goal "to disrupt, dismantle, and defeat Al Qaeda in Pakistan and Afghanistan."[341]

In another principal policy address at West Point on December 1, 2009, following a drawn-out, acrimonious policy review that featured bitter disagreement between Biden and the Obama political advisors opposed to the senior military leadership, Obama announced an increase of 30,000 additional troops to deploy in 2010. Then, in his next sentence, President Obama stated, "After 18 months, our troops will begin to come home." Further, "Our overarching goal remains the same: to disrupt, dismantle, and defeat Al Qaeda in Afghanistan and Pakistan, and to prevent its capacity to threaten America and our allies in the future." And "...we will work with our partners, the United Nations, and the Afghan people to pursue a more effective civilian strategy..."[342] Nothing was new; the policy statements remained broad without specific execution details or a structure for assessment.

This West Point speech reflected the contentious debate over troop numbers within his administration. By announcing the planned withdrawal in 18 months, this timeline dramatically undercut any potential long-term effectiveness, sending a clear signal to the Taliban that they could wait out the American presence.

In hindsight, Obama seemed reluctant to back away from his campaign promises to increase troop levels despite dissent from Vice President Biden and other members of his political inner circle. I sensed his lack of conviction on this matter. By setting a date for the withdrawal, Obama signaled his weak support for the Afghan effort and acknowledged opposition to further troop deployments expressed by other administration members.[343]

DECISIONS, DISCORD & DIPLOMACY

Washington focused on recovering from the severe recession in 2009 and debating U.S. troop levels, but turmoil in Afghanistan escalated on three fronts: (1) the intensifying insurgency by the Taliban, (2) the friction and erosion of confidence between President Karzai and U.S. ambassadors and more recently, with Obama's Special Representative for Afghanistan and Pakistan, Ambassador Richard Holbrooke,[344] (3) and churn in the top U.S. military leadership.

From 2005, Taliban forces had been regrouping in southern and eastern Afghanistan and, by 2009, had expanded their presence in the north.[345] Taliban tactics focused on intimidation of the population and military action against the Coalition, primarily attacks on isolated U.S. outposts and extensive use of IEDs.[346] Despite the surge in U.S. forces, the Taliban continued successful operations, particularly against Afghan Security Forces, relying on their advantageous intelligence network, highly motivated fighters, and flexible adaptation of tactics.

Ambassador Eikenberry's relations with Karzai soured following the alleged leak of cables he sent to Washington that were critical of the latter. Friction between the two continued, exacerbated by Ambassador Holbrooke's none-too-subtle advocacy for other candidates to oppose Karzai in the upcoming Afghan elections.

Beginning in 2008, there were five different American generals in charge of the conflict in Afghanistan in four years: from Army General Dan McNeil to General David McKiernan to General Stanley McChrystal to General David Petraeus to Marine Corps General John Allen at approximately one-year intervals. Interestingly, Generals McKiernan and McChrystal were relieved of command by the political leadership in Washington.

The Obama "surge" of U.S. forces into Afghanistan topped out at about 100,000 during 2010-11. Then it declined for the remainder of the second Obama Administration. The contentious political debates regarding troop numbers in Afghanistan had more to do with domestic political considerations than battlefield strategy. The military leaders advocated a robust counterinsurgency plan requiring additional troops. Yet, planners seemed oblivious to the necessary complements: the unlikelihood of resourcing an adequate and essential parallel civilian reconstruction effort and reliable Afghan leadership to effect follow-on good governance, assuming the counterinsurgency was successful. The

Epilogue

U.S. government spent billions of dollars on a wide range of military and development tasks in Afghanistan, but did not get the desired results.[347]

The Obama troop drawdown was announced shortly after the death of Osama bin Laden in May 2011. The drawdown continued through his second term, declining to about 9000 troops by turnover to the Trump Administration in early 2017.

Before his election, candidate Trump often railed against continuing the U.S. military presence, famously tweeting, "Afghanistan is a complete waste. Time to come home!"[348] Once in office as President, he was persuaded by his national security advisers to reverse course, initially authorizing an additional 4000 U.S. troops. Even so, Trump seemed skeptical about continuing the U.S. presence in Afghanistan as the security situation continued to be stalemated on the ground.

In an address to the nation on August 21, 2017, Trump unveiled his strategy for the war, which did not mention any changes to U.S. troop levels. However, he invited allies and partners to support the new plan with additional troop increases. Acknowledging that his "original instinct was to pull out," he revealed his "three fundamental conclusions about America's core interest in Afghanistan:" (1) The nation must seek an honorable and enduring outcome, (2) a hasty withdrawal would create a vacuum that terrorists would fill, and (3) the security threats we face in Afghanistan...are immense. His "new" strategy would be based on core pillars of (1) a conditions-on-the-ground based approach, (2) integration of all instruments of American power, (3) a new relationship with Pakistan to encourage their commitment to partnership with us, and (4) further develop our strategic partnership with India.

President Trump also clearly enunciated his position on nation-building, stating, "We will no longer use American military might to construct democracies in faraway lands or try to rebuild other countries in our own image."[349] He did not address how this new strategy would be executed, but did authorize an increase in U.S. troop levels, which rose to about 15,500 in 2018.[350] Continued stalemate of the security situation in Afghanistan following the troop increases of 2017-18, coupled with his long-standing aversion to U.S. engagement overseas, resulted in President Trump again reversing course in his policy stance. His December 2018 announcement of the unilateral withdrawal of U.S. troops from Syria and a reduction in the number by half from

Afghanistan prompted the resignation of Defense Secretary Jim Mattis. Soon thereafter, Trump directed negotiations begin with the Taliban and appointed Afghan native and longtime Ambassador Zal Khalilzad as chief U.S. negotiator.

The eventual U.S.-Taliban agreement, after almost a year of negotiation to end the Afghanistan conflict, resulted in the so-called Doha Accords, signed on February 29, 2020. The deal, fatally flawed in my opinion, included clauses that dramatically reduced essential U.S. air support to the Afghan military, agreed to a prisoner swap heavily skewed toward the Taliban, and the complete withdrawal of U.S. forces within 14 months if the Taliban kept their commitments. Important background issues that facilitated this agreement, despite continued Taliban violence, were the worldwide COVID-19 epidemic, the ongoing 2020 U.S. presidential election campaign that diverted attention from Afghanistan, plus President Trump's overarching desire to end the war.

Notably, the Doha deliberations did not include the Afghan government but did propose intra-Afghan negotiations with the Taliban. In hindsight, the Taliban, mindful of President Trump's off-stated desire to get out of Afghanistan, had every reason to be delighted with this agreement, which secured the complete withdrawal of all U.S. troops, much to the chagrin of the Afghan government, which had no say in the discussions, in exchange for a promise by the Taliban to prevent Al Qaeda from operating in areas under their jurisdiction. The subsequent intra-Afghan talks were rancorous and inconclusive. Despite the U.S.-Taliban agreement, insurgent attacks, primarily against the Afghan Security Forces, now operating with scant U.S. air support, intensified dramatically. Nonetheless, the U.S. drawdown proceeded rapidly, with less than 2500 troops remaining in the country by the end of the Trump Administration in January 2021.

Then-candidate Joe Biden campaigned for the presidency in 2019, planning to bring American combat troops home during his first(and only) term. He also stated, "We must end the war responsibly in a manner that ensures we both guard against threats to our homeland and never have to go back."[351]

Once in office, President Biden chose to continue the Trump troop drawdown and, on April 14, 2021, announced the complete pullout of all U.S. troops to be concluded by September 11, 2021, stating, "It's time

Epilogue

for American troops to come home... It's time to end the forever war."[352] Left unsaid was the fate of the almost 25,000 U.S.-funded contractor personnel in Afghanistan in 2021, most of whom were sustaining the Afghan Security Forces and maintaining the U.S.-provided military equipment that the Afghans could not support on their own.[353]

Joe Biden had advocated for the withdrawal of U.S. forces for many years before his decision. Seeing himself as the principal foreign policy advisor during the Obama Administration, then Vice President-elect Biden made the first of many trips to Kabul before the inauguration in 2009 and consistently voiced opposition to the Obama troop "surge." In hindsight, there was not enough thinking and planning about how to effect the withdrawal of the final forces. As is often the case in Washington, once a policy decision is made, it is assumed that it is done. In this case, there were many loose ends resulting in the chaotic final days at Kabul airport, needless loss of life, and national embarrassment.

The big question is, could it have ended differently? Given the two decades of American involvement, resource expenditure, and lives lost or battered, could—or should—the outcome have been more positive?

Addressing this issue in hindsight, I believe most readers would agree that the initial assault ordered by President George W. Bush in October 2001 to disrupt the terrorist sanctuary in Afghanistan and destroy the Al Qaeda and Taliban bases in the wake of the 9/11 attacks on the U.S was a reasonable and appropriate use of military force. However, the original rationale for our presence in Afghanistan never evolved once those tasks were accomplished. It never became a cohesive strategy to provide a basis for the subsequent expansion of the mission, particularly the extensive effort at nation-building.

Additionally, many internal and external factors in Afghanistan were in flux, changing the environment over the years, suggesting a comprehensive policy review. Keep in mind that the U.S. military engagement was never invited, even though it was reasonable and warranted by the events of 9/11. Our extended, however well-intentioned, continued presence eventually morphed into a situation akin to that of the interminable uninvited guest.

The most cited causal factor for the failure of the effort in Afghanistan was the decision to shift focus to Iraq by the Bush Administration from 2002 through 2008. I concur with that opinion based on my extensive involvement with Afghanistan, particularly in 2007-08. Despite personal attention to the issue by President Bush and actions by subordinates down the chain of command, the resources (military and otherwise), attention, and focus were only a tiny fraction of the effort devoted to Iraq. The objectives remained the same as in 2001, and there was never a top-to-bottom strategy review. In addition to 2400 U.S. military deaths, the SIGAR estimate of the total amount of U.S. funding devoted to Afghanistan over the 20 years of our engagement was more than $2 trillion. Ultimately, we had little to show for the loss of those lives and money.

It has been well-documented that security and stability in the country declined, certainly from 2005 onward, as the Taliban reemerged, corruption increased, and governance faltered. Nonetheless, the U.S. pressed on, convincing ourselves that we were making progress, thinking that if we could only improve security, the Afghan government that we created in our own Western image and likeness would be able to take over and thrive on its own.

The primary U.S. actions were military and included several changes in tactical and operational level battlefield strategies based on "lessons learned" from the counterinsurgency experience in Iraq. All these efforts required enduring political will, which by 2008 was rapidly evaporating. By then, the underlying message signaled in ways that, in hindsight, seemingly no one could misinterpret was that the U.S. military would leave sooner rather than later. But we remained engaged for 13 more years despite consistent contrary signals from top American political leadership. Resulting in confusion, misinterpretation by key Afghan leaders, and a general loss of interest by the American population. But the Taliban had figured it out, correctly concluding that time was on their side.

Given the hallmark American penchant for quick results and lack of strategic patience, it is remarkable that the duration of the conflict in Afghanistan exceeded all prior U.S. military engagements in history. During those two decades, many individuals and governments from around the world, particularly hundreds of thousands of American military and civilian personnel, labored mightily to bequeath basic security, functioning governance, fundamental human rights, and a sustainable economy for the Afghan people. Notwithstanding often

Epilogue

Herculean efforts and to the chagrin of those pursuing this desired outcome, the country succumbed to Taliban rule.

In the aftermath of this failed effort, voluminous commentary, finger-pointing, and opinions by pundits, politicians, scholars, and "experts" of every stripe present a complex and often contradictory picture of alleged causality. The events that led to the outcome resulted from years of decisions, large and small, some well-intended and wise, others made in ignorance, haste, ill-advised, or plain stupid. These decisions were made in the context of a little-understood culture in a distant land, with immediate neighbors Pakistan and Iran pursuing different strategic objectives counter to the U.S.

Often influenced or driven by factors that had little to do with the immediate events in Afghanistan, for example, parallel decisions related to Iraq, the global economic situation, domestic politics, or other priorities, choices were nonetheless made over time that dictated the eventual outcome. Retrospectively, as someone with significant decision-making responsibilities, albeit for a brief period, I ponder what I might have missed or done differently.

My initial impressions, back in early 2007, were that the overall situation in Afghanistan was reasonably secure, certainly not as unstable as Iraq at that time. It seemed that we were improving overall stability positively and, most importantly, that most citizens still welcomed us. But based on my understanding of history, a heavy military footprint would not be tolerated for long, and we had a limited amount of time to achieve the desired results.

In hindsight, I now believe I made several misjudgments. First, I understood less about the culture and history than I thought, particularly the complexities of tribal and ethnic relationships and their influence on the population, which I underestimated. The second point was an underappreciation for the extent of the Taliban reemergence and population control at the time of my arrival.

In this regard, the significance of the Taliban Offensive of 2006 and the role of brutal Taliban leader Mullah Dadullah Lang in organizing and leading insurgent operations until his death in 2007 was obscured in reports that I received. We saw the tactical battles and events unfolding but failed to perceive the strategic implications, as recently documented by historian Carter Malkasian.[354] It simply escaped my understanding. The picture that I had was a gradual decrease in security, partially caused by the Taliban resurgence, but not the well-orchestrated, wide-ranging campaign to take control of the country that was already underway.

In hindsight, I appreciated the tactical changes but failed to perceive the strategic. In other words, I saw the trees but not the forest. Furthermore, I do not recall anyone on-scene who grasped the significance of this picture at the time.

The third point was another underappreciation, in this instance, the magnitude of the socio-economic development challenge in Afghanistan. Again, I had the data in hand, courtesy of an assessment that I requested from Ambassador Dawn Liberi regarding the economic and counterinsurgency situation in the country in April 2007. In her report, the ambassador offered a snapshot highlighting the low levels of socio-economic development in the 2006 population of 31 million people. Some numbers included an estimated 53% living in poverty with a 40% unemployment rate, a 43-year life expectancy, literacy rates of 51% male/21% female, primitive infrastructure (only 6% access to electricity, 16% of roads paved, rudimentary water distribution), and 80% of the labor force engaged in subsistence agriculture. Plus, an illicit economy supported by narcotics trafficking was estimated to be growing faster than the licit economy.[355] Given the major security challenges, I never fully grasped the effort that would be required, in time and resources, to change this situation.

In hindsight, these factors merited a big-picture strategic review of what we were doing and how long it might take to achieve the desired results. Whether a policy and strategy course adjustment would have made a difference in the outcome is conjecture. We still had time then to achieve a different result if Afghanistan were a foreign policy priority, but Washington continued to muddle along, consuming countless hours in discussion and debate in an atmosphere of waning interest. The Taliban was the single entity that maintained an unrelenting march to their objective of regaining control of the country. Their singularity of purpose was a hallmark of success.

Considering the outcome of our engagement in Afghanistan, I am haunted by the question that then-President Hamid Karzai asked privately at the end of our first meeting in Kabul. "Admiral, we know that

EPILOGUE

you Americans walked away from us twice in the past. Will it happen a third time?" I knew that he was referring to events in the wake of the assassination of our U.S. ambassador in 1979 and then again in 1989 following the Soviet withdrawal, civil war, and eventual takeover by the Taliban. My reply came without hesitation, "Absolutely not, Mr. President," based on the firm conviction that the U.S. was dedicated to a long-term partnership with Afghanistan. Whether President Karzai was prescient or simply seeking affirmation of my commitment is moot. I wonder if he still remembers that conversation. I cannot forget it.

IRAQ DESCENDS INTO CHAOS

Having achieved its long-sought SFA/SOFA agreements with Iraqi Prime Minister Maliki in the waning days of 2008, the Bush Administration transitioned to the incoming Obama Administration, presuming that it had secured the success of the surge by negotiating an extended drawdown schedule of U.S. forces from Iraq. But even before the inauguration, Vice President-elect Biden made a trip to Baghdad in early January to meet with senior Iraqi and U.S. leaders, leaving no doubt that policy changes were coming. He was quoted as saying, "Iraq was Bush's war, Afghanistan is Obama's war," also inferring that if there were no progress on a political agreement, the U.S. might as well leave.[356]

President Obama had campaigned on a pledge to remove U.S. combat troops within 16 months, leaving a small residual force. On February 27, 2009, in remarks "Responsibly Ending the War in Iraq," delivered at Camp Lejeune, North Carolina, the President announced that the U.S. combat mission would end and those forces withdrawn by August 31, 2010, leaving a transitional force of 35,000 to 50,000 troops with limited responsibilities until the complete withdrawal of all U.S. forces by the end of 2011, which was in accord with the Bush Administration negotiated SOFA.[357]

The new accelerated withdrawal timeline was a compromise between political and military officials in Baghdad and Washington. Meanwhile, General Ray Odierno replaced General Petraeus as Commander of U.S. forces in Iraq, and Christopher Hill succeeded Ryan Crocker as ambassador in April 2009. The Bush Administration's placement of General Petraeus at CENTCOM and General Odierno in Baghdad provided continuity of military leadership. Still, Chris Hill, an

Obama appointee with extensive previous experience in Europe and Asia, was a new face in the Middle East. Ambassador Hill and I had an excellent working relationship at USPACOM. He was then in his prior assignment as Assistant Secretary of State for East Asian and Pacific Affairs. Still, Obama's decision to select him for the position in Baghdad had decidedly negative consequences.

Unfortunately, Hill, Odierno, and their staffs did not mesh well in Iraq. Although typical for Iraq in that many factors were in play, a fundamental difference in philosophical approaches underpinned the relationship. General Odierno had been operating closely with the Iraqis at every level and felt that continuous U.S. engagement was essential. Ambassador Hill believed the military was too involved in the day-to-day business of Iraqi governance and that the U.S. should have more of a hands-off approach. The asymmetry in resources and visibility, with the large military footprint overshadowing the number of diplomatic personnel, plus the fact that Odierno had his own foreign policy advisor, the British Emma Sky, grated on Hill. For her part, Sky held views that Hill was miscast in his role in Baghdad and "...disliked Iraq and Iraqis."[358] The strained relationship between Hill and Odierno was visible to others; as one observer reported, "Not since the days of Jerry Bremer and Rick Sanchez had the civil-military relationship in Baghdad been fraught with so much tension."[359]

Against this background and in accordance with the SOFA schedule, U.S. combat forces withdrew from Iraqi cities and major towns by the end of June 2009, with Iraqi forces assuming responsibility for security in population centers.

Iraqi National Parliamentary Elections for seats in the Council of Representatives (COR), which would then elect the prime minister, took place on March 7, 2010, in a much more benign security environment than previous Iraqi elections, no doubt influenced by the still strong U.S. military presence in the country. The outcome of the hotly contested election was a narrow majority for the secular Iraqiya Party, headed by Ayad Allawi, over Maliki's State of Law Party, with the National Iraqi Alliance Party, led by Ibrahim al-Jaafari, not far behind.

Ostensibly a demonstration of evolving improvement in governance, the elections were marred by low voter turnout (62%) compared to the previous election, late changes in the electoral laws that banned

EPILOGUE

hundreds of candidates for alleged Ba'ath Party connections, and allegations of fraud. It soon became clear that PM Maliki had no intention of giving up power despite the narrow Iraqiya electoral victory. Internal Iraqi political squabbling over the formulation of a new government continued unabated.

By this time, it was also clear that Vice President Biden was the Obama Administration's point person for Iraq.[360] He supported the increasingly authoritarian PM Maliki, who remained in office, as did Ambassador Hill. Both thought Iraq needed a "strongman" in charge, and Maliki was their man.[361] Eventually, near the end of 2010, a new Iraqi government was formed. Maliki continued as prime minister with the support of sectarian and Iranian-aligned Muqtada al-Sadr.

Meanwhile, in August 2010, Chris Hill was succeeded by Ambassador Jim Jeffries, who brought extensive Iraqi experience to the job, and on the military side, Ray Odierno by General Lloyd Austin, likewise an old Iraqi hand. But the countdown to the Bush-Maliki agreement on complete withdrawal of U.S. troops drew closer without a serious political push from either side to renegotiate an extension of some U.S. military presence remaining in Iraq.

In my view, the SFA (Strategic Framework Agreement) was an opportunity for a broad U.S. government engagement with Iraq. The terms of the shortsighted SOFA begged for amendments to extend the U.S. military presence. Still, there was little interest in doing so either by the Obama Administration, nor was any vision or future strategy articulated for Iraq. As Emma Sky observed regarding President Obama, "The administration did not seem to care about Iraq and just wanted to get out... his only interest in Iraq was in ending the war."[362]

The Obama Administration's decision to let the "complete withdrawal" time clock wind down to zero would be a fatefully bad choice and squandered opportunity to strengthen internal Iraqi stability and the long-term U.S.-Iraqi relationship. Without the stabilizing influence of a U.S. military presence and counsel, Prime Minister Maliki reverted to his worst days of sectarian rule, quickly orchestrating an arrest warrant for Vice President and Sunni leader Tariq al-Hashimi, the latter then prosecuted on trumped-up charges and sentenced to death in absentia, having wisely fled Iraq.

The next several years saw increasingly sectarian, biased decision-making by Maliki, including widespread placement of Shia cronies in key positions throughout the government, particularly the military. Typically justifying his choices as countering Ba'athist individuals or influence, Maliki's selections marginalized Sunnis and led to increasing secular tension. During this period, I was contacted by several serving and former Iraqi government leaders seeking assistance to increase U.S. engagement to counter the rising authoritarianism of Maliki. Retired and with little influence on a domestically focused Obama Administration, I viewed with concern the growing countrywide insecurity and return of Sunni extremists, especially in western Iraq, but was not able to help.

The ominous rise to prominence of the former Camp Bucca detainee Abu Bakr al-Baghdadi as leader of Al Qaeda in Iraq (AQI), later renamed ISIS, then Islamic State in Iraq and the Levant (ISIL), also called Daesh in Arabic, portended a return to chaos in Iraq. Reemerging from the remnants of Al Qaeda, fueled by the marginalization of Sunnis by the Maliki government, and capitalizing on the disorder in neighboring Syria, ISIL seized upon the lack of security and deficient governance to "carry out attacks and bolster its ranks" in both countries.[363]

With no U.S. military presence in Iraq, the Maliki government's ostracization of Sunni communities and security failures expedited AQI's return to notoriety. Maliki's heavy-handed and sectarian governance in Anbar province resulted in Sunni protests, a crackdown by security forces, which was followed by a local uprising that drove security forces out of the province, paving the way for AQI resurgence.[364]

In 2011, ISIL began a murderous worldwide rampage, primarily in Iraq and Syria, killing thousands of mostly civilian people and eventually overrunning western Iraq, including all the major towns and cities of Anbar province. The poorly led and demoralized Iraqi army put up minimal resistance and fled before the onslaught. Seizing Mosul, the second largest city in Iraq, and then Tikrit and Samarra in the summer of 2014, ISIL closed in on Baghdad with only the Kurdish Peshmerga putting up determined resistance.

Rising insecurity in Iraq had been overshadowed by other events that captured the attention of the Obama Administration: the "Arab Spring" antigovernment protests around the Arab world, particularly

Epilogue

the revolution and civil war in Libya, the ousting of Egyptian President Mubarak, a tsunami and nuclear disaster in Japan, and the U.S. presidential election in 2012, among others.

In response to an Iraqi request for help, the U.S. began providing military supplies to the Peshmerga in June 2014. President Obama reintroduced U.S. forces into Iraq in August with the new intervention named OPERATION INHERENT RESOLVE (OIR). The American-led coalition then began airstrikes against ISIL in Iraq and later Syria. With his country in chaos and world leaders and others in Iraq calling for his ouster, Iraqi PM Maliki finally but reluctantly resigned and turned over governance to Haidar al-Abadi in August 2014. Meanwhile, the hastily organized OIR, consisting primarily of land and aircraft carrier aviation assets and special forces (SOF) units, predominantly American and British, operated in both Iraq and Syria until 2018, when President Trump announced the withdrawal of all American troops from the latter.

With its army in disarray, the Iraqi government, desperately seeking to avoid the entire country being overrun by ISIL, turned to the numerous, mostly Shia, armed militias to save the day. Beginning in 2014, the now Iraqi state-supported militias, collectively known as the Popular Mobilization Forces (PMF), numbering several hundred thousand fighters, joined with the remnants of the Iraqi army, Kurdish Peshmerga, and U.S. support units and advisors in a long, slow, and costly multi-year campaign to recover the large part of the country occupied by ISIL.

The number of U.S. troops in Iraq was incrementally increased to roughly 5,000 by mid-2018.[365] Although most U.S. troops were training, advising, and assisting Iraqi forces, some were providing artillery fire support and engaged in direct combat with ISIL insurgents. These missions by U.S. troops continued for seven years, when the Biden Administration officially ended the second U.S. combat mission in Iraq in December 2021. As of 2025, about 2,500 U.S. troops remain in Iraq as trainers and advisors to Iraqi security forces.[366]

In hindsight, it seems reasonable to question whether this second 2014-2021 intervention in Iraq, at a cost of over 100 more U.S. military deaths and more than $4 billion expended by mid-2017, would have been necessary had the first intervention ended without the complete withdrawal of U.S. troops. A modest extended military presence, such as recommended in my August 2007 *Long-Term Security Posture in Iraq* report in response to JCS request, could have extended U.S. intelligence and technical support and continued training and advice to the Iraqi military. But those suggestions were ignored as the goal in Washington in late 2007 was short-term, focused on extending the U.S. combat mission to ensure the security gains of the surge.

In reviewing what turned out to be almost two decades of our interventions in Iraq, the original Bush Administration goal of removing Saddam was achieved. Still, the cost was horrendously high and morally dubious, especially in human lives.

The strategic situation today is no better than in 2003. Iraq, at present, is unstable, neighboring Syria is worse, and the primary cause of instability in the entire Middle East, Iran, is emboldened, aggressive, and unquestionably more influential in Iraq. The decisions that set us on this course and subsequent choices resulted in unexpected and unconsidered outcomes. Aside from the few people who encouraged and still support the original decision by George W. Bush to invade Iraq, most consider it an error in judgment and a colossal strategic mistake.

REFLECTIONS

Regrettably and unsurprisingly, evil in the world has not disappeared. An array of challenging ideologies, despots, and competitors bent on the demise of the U.S. and the principles upon which it was founded abounds. Deterrence and dissuasion require a competent and effective military capability to complement other instruments of national power. Establishing and maintaining a robust and ready force, resourced and trained to be a credible deterrent, relying on a firm foundation of moral, political, diplomatic, informational, and economic capability, is essential to our future.

The challenge for leadership is the appropriate balance of these capabilities to be persuasive in deterrence but particularly judicious in military force, given the consequences and unpredictability of that course of action. War may be seen as a necessary response to aggression. Still, such action ought to be undertaken only with full consideration of the human consequences, with knowledge and understanding of the lessons of history. Strategy is built upon fact.

EPILOGUE

War is a human endeavor that touches participants in ways that span the spectrum of impact and emotion. As the individual responsible for all the U.S. military personnel in Iraq and Afghanistan during my time in command of USCENTCOM, I am immensely proud of their dedicated hard work, devotion to duty, accomplishments, and sacrifices. A recent experience reinforced our profound responsibility as leaders in making decisions that impact those whose lives are entrusted to us.

Memorial Day weekend, 2023, I visited Arlington National Cemetery. I walked among the graves in Section 60, where many of the dead from Iraq and Afghanistan are interred. Observing a middle-aged couple sitting on lawn chairs in front of one of the gravestones, I approached and asked if the deceased was a family member. The woman replied, "Yes, this is our son, a soldier killed in Iraq."

When I inquired where they had come from, the man said they now live in Florida, but their son grew up with them in New Jersey, my home state. I introduced myself and said that I had also been in Iraq. I asked when their son had served, wondering if it was during my command. The father said, "He died in 2016, not long after he arrived there."

Thus, he was among the cohort of American troops that were reinserted into Iraq following the 2011 withdrawal to combat ISIL. When I asked them about their son, they described an active young man growing up with a strong desire to serve. Mom said, "He was a good boy and eager to serve in the Army." We chatted for some time, and they talked about his childhood growing up in a small town not far from where I was raised, and his conversations with them while he was stationed in Iraq. They spoke with him by phone shortly before he was killed. They then asked me about Iraq, the land, and the people. The couple displayed no bitterness at their overwhelming loss, only immense pride in their son's service. They said they were grateful to be able to spend the day by his grave at the cemetery and thanked me for stopping to visit with them. This special American couple's stoicism and gracious acceptance of sacrifice were extraordinarily moving and inspirational.

Deeply affected by the conversation with the parents of this American soldier, I left them to their vigil, but the impact and memory of their words remain with me. History is antiseptic and static, but human memories are not. Past decisions will not be undone, but future decisions are up to us. Using wisdom gained from historical decisions could make our increasingly interconnected and interdependent world a better place.

Today, memories prompt me to question, ask, and ponder what other decisions could have been made, a constant conversation in my mind, asking: "What if…"

BIBILIOGRAPHY

Al Saud, Prince Turki Al Faisal. *The Afghanistan File.* Cowes, Isle of Wight. Arabian Publishing, 2021

Barfield, Thomas. *Afghanistan: A Cultural and Political History.* Princeton, New Jersey. Princeton University Press, 2010

Bergen, Peter. *Manhunt. The Ten-Year Search for Bin Laden from 9/11 to Abbottabad.* New York. Broadway Paperbacks. Random House, 2012

Bergen, Peter. *The Rise and Fall of Osama Bin Laden.* New York. Simon and Schuster, 2021

Coll, Steve. *The Bin Ladens. An Arabian Family in the American Century.* New York. Penguin Press, 2008

Draper, Robert. *To Start A War. How the Bush Administration took America into Iraq.* New York. Penguin Press, 2020

Duelfer, Charles. *Hide And Seek. The Search for Truth in Iraq.* New York. Public Affairs, 2009

Ekeus, Rolf. *Iraq Disarmed. The Story Behind the Fall of Saddam.* Boulder, Colorado. Lynne Rienner Publishers, 2023

Feith, Douglas J. *War and Decision. Inside the Pentagon at the Dawn of the War on Terrorism.* New York. HarperCollins Publishers, 2008

Final Report of the National Commission on Terrorist Attacks Upon the United States *(The 9/11 Commission Report).* New York, W.W. Norton, July 22, 2004

Franks, Tommy. *American Soldier.* New York. Regan Books. HarperCollins Publishers, 2004

Gates, Robert M. *Duty. Memoirs of a Secretary at War.* New York, Alfred A. Knopf, 2014

Gordon, Michael, and Trainer, Bernard E. *The Endgame. The Inside Story of the Struggle for Iraq, from George W. Bush to Barack Obama.* New York. Vintage Books, 2012

Gordon, Michael, and Trainer, Bernard E. *Cobra II. The Inside Story of the Invasion and Occupation of Iraq.* New York. Vintage Books, 2007

Hayden, Michael V. *Playing to the Edge. American Intelligence in the Age of Terror.* New York. Penguin Random House, 2016

Hooker, Richard D. and Collins, Joseph J., Editors. *Lessons Encountered. Learning from the Long War.* Washington. National Defense University Press. 2015

Lewis, Bernard. *What Went Wrong? Western Impact and Middle Eastern Response.* London. Oxford University Press, 2002

Mansoor, Peter R. *Surge. My Journey with General David Petraeus and the Remaking of the Iraq War.* New Haven. Yale University Press, 2013

Malkasian, Carter. *The American War in Afghanistan. A History.* New York. Oxford University Press, 2021

Neumann, Ronald E. *The Other War. Winning and Losing in Afghanistan.* Washington. Potomac Books, 2009

Rashid, Ahmed. *Taliban: Militant Islam, Oil and Fundamentalism in Central Asia* Second Edition. New Haven. Yale University Press, 2010

Rumsfeld, Donald. *Known and Unknown: A Memoir.* New York. Sentinel, 2011

Sky, Emma. *The Unravelling. High Hopes and Missed Opportunities in Iraq.* New York. Public Affairs, 2015

Smith, Hedrick, Editor. *The Media and the Gulf War.* Foreign Policy Institute of the School of Advanced International Studies, Johns Hopkins University. Washington. Seven Locks Press, 1992

Whitlock, Craig. *The Afghanistan Papers. A Secret History of the War.* New York. Simon and Schuster, 2021

Winnefeld, Admiral Sandy. *Sailing Upwind. Leadership and Risk from TopGun to the Situation Room.* Annapolis. Naval Institute Press, 2023

Woodward, Bob. *State of Denial. Bush at War, Part III.* New York. Simon and Schuster, 2006

Woodward, Bob. *The War Within. A Secret White House History 2006-2008.* New York. Simon and Schuster, 2008

GLOSSARY

A-10 THUNDERBOLT—USAF ground attack aircraft

A-6 INTRUDER—Navy all-weather attack aircraft

A-7 CORSAIR II—Navy attack aircraft

AEI—American Enterprise Institute (Washington, D.C. think-tank)

AFWTF—Atlantic Fleet Weapons Training Facility (western Atlantic near Puerto Rico)

AIR BOSS—Naval Officer in charge of aircraft carrier flight operations

AJFC—Allied Joint Force Command—NATO command HQ in Brunssum, Netherlands

AL-FAW PENINSULA—extreme SE Iraq, where Shatt Al-Arab (River) empties into the Gulf

Al Qaeda—literally, "the base" in Arabic—a Sunni militant terrorist organization

AL-ANFAL CAMPAIGN—Saddam's genocide against Kurds using WMD (poison gas)

AN-26–Antonov designed Soviet built twin engine transport aircraft

ANA—Afghan National Army

ANBAR—Province in western Iraq

ANP—Afghan National Police

AOR—Area of Responsibility

Decisions, Discord & Diplomacy

AQI—Al Qaeda in Iraq. Also known as ISIS, ISIL, and Daesh in Arabic

AUMF—Authorization for Use of Military Force—Congressional grant of powers to the President in response to the 9/11 attacks

AV-8 HARRIER—USMC vertical takeoff/ landing aircraft

B1, B-2, B-52—USAF heavy bomber aircraft

BBC—British Broadcasting Company

BCT—Brigade Combat Team

BIA—Beirut International Airport or Baghdad International Airport

BIG BEN—Iconic bell tower chiming clock in London

BIO—Biological (as in weapons)

BLACK SEPTEMBER—Military conflict in which Jordan expelled the PLO in 1970-71, also the name adopted by a Middle East terrorist group in memory of that event

BND—German Foreign Intelligence Agency

C-17—USAF Transport aircraft

C-5 Galaxy—USAF heavy lift transport aircraft

CAG—Commander, Navy carrier-based Air Group

CAOC—Combined Air Operations Center

CARTER DOCTRINE—1980 declaration that the U.S. would use military force if necessary to defend its interests in the Persian (Arabian) Gulf region

CAS—Close Air Support

Glossary

CBRNE—Chemical, Biological, Radiological, Nuclear, and enhanced high explosive—inclusive acronym for military threats

CHECKMATE— USAF Pentagon-based Strategic Studies and Planning Group

CIA—Central Intelligence Agency—U.S. Foreign Intelligence Service

CINC—Commander-In-Chief

CJCS— CHAIRMAN, U.S. JOINT CHIEFS OF STAFF

CNN—Cable News Network

CNO—Chief of Naval Operations- head of the U.S. Navy

COCOM—Combatant Commander (e.g., PACOM)

CO—Commanding Officer

COD—Carrier Onboard Delivery Aircraft (Navy)

COLD WAR—Geopolitical conflict between the U.S. and its allies opposing the USSR and its allies

COP—Combat Outpost

COR—Council of Representatives—Iraqi legislative entity

CPA—Coalition Provisional Authority—U.S.-established governing entity headed by Paul Bremer in Iraq, 2003

CSAR—Combat Search and Rescue

CSH—Combat Support Hospital

CSIS—Center for Strategic and International Studies

CSTC-A—Combined Security Transition Command-Afghanistan—U.S. military training and assistance force in Afghanistan

CTF-60 Commander Task Force-60 (U.S. Navy Operational Commander in the Mediterranean Sea)

CVW-8—Carrier Air Wing 8 (Navy carrier-based air wing)

DASD—Deputy Assistant Secretary of Defense

DEPSECDEF—Deputy Secretary of Defense

DIA—Defense Intelligence Agency

DNI—Director of National Intelligence—head of the U.S. intelligence community

Durand Line—demarcation between Afghanistan and Pakistan (established by Great Britain in 1893)

EFP—Explosively Formed Penetrator—lethal anti-armor projectile

EU—European Union

F-111 AARDVARK—USAF Strike-fighter aircraft

F-14 TOMCAT—Navy fighter aircraft

F-8 CRUSADER—U.S. and French Navy fighter aircraft

FAC—Forward Air Controller

FATA Federally Administered Tribal Areas—Geographical and political areas of western Pakistan adjacent to Afghanistan

FBI—Federal Bureau of Investigation—domestic U.S. intelligence and security agency

FEBA—Forward Edge of the Battle Area

Glossary

FIF—Free Iraqi Forces—militia of Iraqi expatriates, 2003

FISC—FOREIGN INTELLIGENCE SURVEILLANCE COURT—established by FISA (Foreign Intelligence Surveillance Act) to govern the collection of foreign intelligence while protecting the rights of U.S. citizens

FLIR—Forward-Looking Infrared

FOB—Forward Operating Base

FRONTIER CORPS—Pakistani military force along the Pakistan-Afghan border

FRS—FLEET REPLACEMENT SQUADRON (Navy squadron that trains aircrew in aircraft they will fly in the fleet)

FSO—Foreign Service Officer

GREAT SATAN—Iranian name for the USA

GTMO—Guantánamo Bay Naval Base (pronounced "Gitmo") in eastern Cuba

GULF WAR COALITION—Allied Forces Opposing IRAQ during the Gulf War

GULF WAR—1991 conflict led by the U.S. coalition to expel Iraqi forces from Kuwait

GWOT—Global War on Terror/Terrorism

HEZBOLLAH—Lebanese Shia Islamist political and military entity sponsored by Iran

HMMWV pronounced "Humvee"— armored military vehicle

HOLLOWAY COMMISSION—Investigative body that reported findings on EAGLE CLAW

ICRC—International Committee of the Red Cross

IED—Improvised Explosive Device

IISS—International Institute of Strategic Studies—London-based think-tank

ILA—Iraq Liberation Act—1998 U.S. Congressional legislation

INC—Iraqi National Congress—Iraqi political party opposed to Saddam Hussein

INTIFADA—rebellion by militant Palestinians against Israel (1980s-2000s)

IRAN-CONTRA—Reagan Administration political scandal

IRGC—Islamic Revolutionary Guard Corps (Iran)

ISAF—International Security Assistance Force—NATO military force in Afghanistan

ISCI—Islamic Supreme Council of Iraq—political party in Iraq

ISI—Inter-Services Intelligence: a highly influential Pakistani Intelligence agency

ISIS—Islamic State of Iraq and Syria, later "Islamic State"—terrorist organization

JOINT CHIEFS of STAFF—U.S. military service chiefs

JROC—Joint Requirements Oversight Council—Vice Chiefs of Staff of the Services

JTF—Joint Task Force

JTF-SWA—Joint Task Force Southwest Asia

KC-135/ KC-10–USAF Aerial Refueling Aircraft

KGB—an intelligence agency of the former USSR

Glossary

KSA—Kingdom of Saudi Arabia

KURD—Indo-Iranian ethnic people, mostly Sunni Muslim, living in the self-proclaimed "Kurdistan" area of Iran, Iraq, Turkey, and Syria

LAF—Lebanese Armed Forces

LEAGUE OF NATIONS—an international body to resolve disputes following the Versailles agreement. Precursor to the U.N.

LEVANT—French word applied to the eastern Mediterranean shoreline

LOAC —Laws of Armed Conflict—international laws, treaties, and customs that regulate conflicts

MAGTF—Marine Corps Air-Ground Task Force

MARSOC—Marine Corps Special Operations Company

MESOPOTAMIA—also known as The Fertile Crescent, in the area of the Tigris and Euphrates Rivers in west Asia

MEU—Marine Corps Expeditionary Unit

MI-17—Soviet-designed helicopter, still in production after 50 years

MI6—United Kingdom Secret Intelligence Service

MNC-I—Multinational Corps Iraq (U.S. forces in Iraq)

MNF—(MULTINATIONAL FORCE-U.N. PEACEKEEPING FORCE IN LEBANON-1980s)

MNF-I—MULTINATIONAL FORCE IRAQ

MNF-I—Multinational Force Iraq (Combined U.S. and allied forces in Iraq)

MNSTC—Multinational Security Transition Command (U.S. military training and assistance entity in Iraq)

MO—Modus Operandi

MRAP—Mine-Resistant Ambush Protected—heavily armored military vehicles

MS—U.S. NAVY COLD WAR MARITIME STRATEGY

NAC—North Atlantic Council (NATO Governing Body)

NATO—North Atlantic Treaty Organization

NBC—National Broadcasting Company

NCA—National Command Authority

NGO—Nongovernmental Organization

NIMBY—Not in my backyard

NSA—National Security Agency

NSC—National Security Council

NSS—National Security Strategy

NSWC—Naval Strike Warfare Center (NAS Fallon, NV)

OCO—Overseas Contingency Operations. (GWOT funding renamed by the Obama Administration)

ODRP—Office of the Defense Representative-Pakistan -U.S. security assistance office in Pakistan

OEF—OPERATION ENDURING FREEDOM—U.S. name for the AFGHANISTAN War

OIF—OPERATION IRAQI FREEDOM—U.S. name for the Iraq War

Glossary

OPERATION DELIBERATE FORCE—NATO Air Campaign to degrade Serbian (and allied militias) military capabilities in response to attacks against civilians in U.N. "safe areas" (August-September 1995)

OPERATION DESERT FOX—December 1998 bombing campaign vs. Iraq

OPERATION DESERT STORM—Operational Name for the 1991 Gulf War

OPERATION EAGLE CLAW—Failed 1979 U.S. Tehran hostage rescue attempt

OPERATION INHERENT RESOLVE—American-led coalition to defeat ISIL in Iraq and Syria

OPERATION MOUNTAIN SHADOW Afghanistan operation in 2007 at Tora Bora

OPERATION NORTHERN WATCH—no-fly and no-ground zone in northern Iraq

OPERATION PHANTOM THUNDER—military operation led by U.S. General Odierno and Iraqi General Qanbar in areas around Baghdad in 2007

OPERATION PROVIDE COMFORT—U.S.-led coalition to protect Kurds in northern Iraq

OPERATION SOUTHERN WATCH—no-fly zone over southern Iraq

OPLAN—Operations Plan

ORE—OPERATIONAL READINESS EXERCISE

OSD—Office of the Secretary of Defense

OSDP—Office of the Secretary of Defense for Policy

Decisions, Discord & Diplomacy

OSIRAQ NUCLEAR REACTOR—A French constructed installation in Iraq, destroyed by an Israeli air strike in 1981

OSP—Office of Special Plans—entity created within OSDP during the Geo. W. Bush Administration

OTTOMAN EMPIRE—Vast Political and military domain spanning three continents, centered in present-day Turkey, ruled for more than 600 years from about 1300 until the end of World War I

PFP—Partnership for Peace (post-Cold War NATO program to foster trust between former Warsaw Pact and NATO nations)

PGM—Precision-Guided Munitions

PLO—Palestine Liberation Organization. A political and military entity representing some Palestinians

PR—Public Relations

PRT—Provincial Reconstruction Team

QDR—Quadrennial Defense Review—U.S. Congressionally mandated review beginning in 1997.

QUDS Force—IRGC entity focused on external (to Iran) military and intelligence operations

RAF—Royal Air Force

REPUBLICAN GUARD—Elite troops of Saddam Hussein's Iraqi army

RH-53D Sea Stallion—heavy lift helicopter

RMA—Revolution in Military Affairs—term describing an initiative undertaken in the late 1990s- early 2000s

ROE—Rules of Engagement

Glossary

RSAF—Royal Saudi Air Force

RSP—Radar Scope Photography

S-3 VIKING—Navy anti-submarine and patrol aircraft

SACLANT—Supreme Allied Commander Atlantic—Cold War NATO Command

SAM—Surface-to-Air Missile

SCO—Shanghai Cooperation Organization—Central Asian group of countries dominated by Russia and China to counter U.S. interests

SEALS—U.S. NAVY Sea-Air-Land Special Operations Forces

SENIOR CAG—Air Wing Commander dubbed "Super CAG" (Navy innovative command structure instituted by Secretary John Lehman)

SFA—Strategic Framework Agreement—U.S.- Iraq accord of 2008

SHATT AL-ARAB—combined Tigris and Euphrates Rivers at the head of the Gulf

SHIA—a branch of Islam and its adherents

SIGAR—Special Inspector General for Afghan Reconstruction—Mr. John Sopko

SOFA—Status of Forces Agreement—an accord specifying the legal status of military personnel in foreign countries

SOF—Special Operations Forces

SR-71 BLACKBIRD—USAF high altitude reconnaissance aircraft

SUNNI—the main branch of Islam, differing from Shia regarding succession to the Prophet Muhammad

SUPER ETENDARD—French aircraft carrier-based strike-fighter aircraft

SUV—Sport Utility Vehicle

SYKES-PICOT ACCORD—British-French plan to divide the Middle East into spheres of influence following WW I

TALIBAN—an Afghan military and political group

TANK—Pentagon conference room where meetings of the Joint Chiefs are held

TLAM—Tomahawk Land Attack Cruise Missile

TORA BORA—a mountainous area in eastern Afghanistan

TREATY OF VERSAILLES—an agreement that ended WW I

TUWAITHA NUCLEAR RESEARCH CENTER – A Facility in Iraq that housed a nuclear reactor

UAE—United Arab Emirates

UNIFIL—(U.N. INTERIM FORCE IN LEBANON-1970s)

UNMOVIC—U.N. Monitoring, Verification, and Inspection Commission (Successor organization to UNSCOM, intended to verify Iraq's WMD disarmament)

UNSCOM—UN Special Commission to monitor Iraq's compliance with WMD-related disarmament following the Gulf War

UNSCR—UN SECURITY COUNCIL RESOLUTION

USACOM—U.S. ATLANTIC COMMAND

USAID—U.S. Agency for International Development

USCENTAF—U.S. Air Forces Central Command

Glossary

USCENTCOM/CENTCOM—U.S. Central Command (Middle East, Central Asia, and Horn of Africa at the time)

USEUCOM/EUCOM—U.S. European Command (Europe, Russia, Israel, and most of Africa at the time)

USIA—U.S. Information Agency—former U.S. government entity for public diplomacy, dissolved in 1999 with functions absorbed into the Department of State

USMTM—U.S. Military Training Mission in Saudi Arabia

USNAVCENT—U.S. Naval Forces Central Command

USPACOM/ PACOM—U.S. Pacific Command (Pacific and Indian Oceans, China, India, and Antarctic area of responsibility)

USSOCCENT—U.S. Special Operations Central Command

USSR—Union of Soviet Socialist Republics- Cold War Russia

VCNO—Vice Chief of Naval Operations- deputy head of the U.S. Navy

VID—Visual Identification

WARSAW PACT —Cold War alliance of communist states in eastern Europe

WMD—Weapons of Mass Destruction (typically Nuclear, Biological, or Chemical)

ENDNOTES

1. Edgar Allan Poe, *The Raven*, *New York Evening Mirror*, January 29, 1845, link to The Edgar Allan Poe Society of Baltimore, (https://www.eapoe.org/works/poems/ravenb.htm).

2. NSA Bahrain History, Commander, Navy Region Europe, Africa, Central Website, Stuttgart, Germany, July 20, 2022, (https://cnreuafcent.cnic.navy.mil/installations/NSA-Bahrain/).

3. Iran Hostage Rescue Mission; Operation Eagle Claw, Special Operations Review Group, *Holloway Commission Report,* August 23, 1980, 33, (courtesy The George Washington University https://nsarchive2.gwu.edu/NSAEBB/NSABB63/doc8.pdf).

4. George W. Bush, Address to the Nation, January 10, 2007, (https://georgewbush-whitehouse.archives.gov/news/releases/2007/01/20070110-7.html).

5. Bernard Lewis, discussion notes from Pentagon meeting, Washington, DC, November 10, 2001

6. Peter Bergen, *The Rise and Fall of Osama Bin Laden,* (New York, Simon and Schuster, 2021, 16

7. James A. Paul, *Great Power Conflict over Iraqi Oil: The World War I Era,* Global Policy Forum Archive, New York, October, 2002, (https://archive.globalpolicy.org/component/content/article/185-general/40479-great-power-conflict-over-iraqi-oil-world-war-1-era)

8. National Army Museum, *History of the First World War, Mesopotamia Campaign,* British Army National Museum Archives, (https://www.nam.ac.uk/explore/mesopotamia-campaign).

9. David E. Omissi, *British Air Power and Colonial Control in Iraq:1920-1925,* Global Policy Forum Archive, New York, 1990, (https://archive.globalpolicy.org/component/content/article/169-history/36386-british-air-power-and-colonial-control-in iraq-1920-1925).

10. Katie Fox and Matt Norman Blog, *Lawrence and Bell,* UK National Archives Records and Research, London, May 10, 2019 (https://blog.nationalarchives.gov.uk/on-the-record-lawrence-and-bell/).

11. See Britannica, *British Occupation and the Mandatory Regime,* London, 2023, (https://www.britannica.com/place/iraq/british-occupation-and-the-mandatory-regime).

12. Ibid Britannica, *History of Kuwait,* (https://www.britannica.com/topic/history-of-kuwait).

13. Ibid Britannica, *The Revolution of 1968,* (https://www.britannica.com/place/iraq/the-revolution-of-1968).

14. Ibid

15. Ibid, Britannica, *Iraq under Saddam Hussein* (https://www.britannica.com/place/iraq/iraq-under-saddam-hussein). and *Iraq: A Population Silenced,* U.S. Department of State Archive, December 2002 (https://2001-2009.state.gov/g/drl/rls/15596.htm).

16. Kate Cooch, *Operation Babylon: Israel's Strike on al-Tuwaitha,* Warfare History Network article, April 2006, (https://warfarehistorynetwork.com/article/operation-babylon-israels-strike-on-al-tuwaitha/).

17. Office of the Historian, U.S. Department of State, *The Reagan Administration and Lebanon, 1981-1984,* Washington, 1984 (https://history.state.gov/milestones/1981-1988/lebanon).

18. Email discussion with French Navy pilot, Capitaine de Vaisseau Xavier Houdaille FN (Retired), January 10, 2022.

19. Discussion with then Lieutenant Preston Swift, U.S. Navy, onboard USS Dwight D. Eisenhower (CV-69), September 1983.

20. Op. Cit., Office of the Historian U.S. Department of State, *The Reagan Administration and Lebanon, 1981-1984.*

21. Author telephone conversation with Rear Admiral Arthur "Bud" Langston, U.S. Navy (Retired) former Commander of Naval Strike Warfare Center, NAS Fallon, Nevada, July 5, 2023.

22. Discussions with Commander Thomas C. Stewart, USNR, 1984 and 2022

23. For background, Phillip D. Voss, *Is the Senior CAG a Good Idea?,* U.S. Naval Institute Proceedings, Annapolis, Maryland, Vol 115, July 1989, (https://www.usni.org/magazines/proceedings/1989/july/senior-cag-good-idea).

24. See Deborah Kidwell, *1991-Operation Desert Shield/Desert Storm,* Air Force Historical Support Division, Washington, DC, 1991, (https://www.afhistory.af.mil/FAQs/fact-sheets/article/458965/1991-operation-desert-shielddesert-storm/).

25. For example, see Steve Coll and William Branigin, *U.S. Scrambled to Shape View of 'Highway of Death',* Washington Post, March 11, 1991, (https://www.washingtonpost.com/archive/politics/1991/03/11/us-scrambled-to-shape-view-of-highway-of-death/05899d).

26. Michael Duffy, *George H.W. Bush Accomplished Much More as President Than He Ever Got Credit For,* Time Magazine, December 6, 2018 (https://time.com/4754901/president-george-hw-bush-accomplishments).

27. Kevin Hymel, *Battle on The Basra Road,* Army Historical Foundation, November 2023, (https://armyhistory.org/battle-on-the-basra-road/).

28. Micah Zenko, Blogpost, *Remembering the Iraqi Uprising Twenty-Five Years Ago, Council on Foreign Relations, New York, March 5, 2016,.* (https://www.cfr.org/blog/remembering-iraqi-uprising-twenty-five-years-ago).

29. Report, *Endless Torment: The 1991 Uprising in Iraq and Its Aftermath,* Human Rights Watch, New York, June 1, 1992, 1 (https://www.hrw.org/report/1992/06/01/endless-torment/1991-uprising-iraq-and-its-aftermath).

30. George Kramlinger, *Operation Provide Comfort,* JSTOR, Air University Press, Montgomery, AL, 2001 (https://www.jstor.org/stable/pdf/resrep13948.9.pdf).

31. Ibid, 17

32. Ibid, 23-24

33. Also referred to as the Military Industrial Commission but I use the language referenced in a letter from General Amer Rashid who headed that organization at the time of Kamel al Majid's defection from Iraq.

34. Charles Duelfer, *Hide And Seek: The Search For Truth In Iraq,* (New York: Public Affairs, 2009), 107

35. UPI Archives, *U.S.-Jordanian Forces Drill in Desert,* August 23, 1995, (https://www.upi.com/archives/1995/08/23/us-jordanian-forces-drill-in-desert/1765809150400/).

36. Op, Cit. Duelfer, 115

37. Rolf Ekeus, *Iraq Disarmed: The Story Behind the Fall of Saddam,* (Boulder, CO. Lynne Rienner Publishers, 2023), 147

38. Op. Cit. Duelfer, 113 (and author discussion with MI6 representative in Jordan on May 31, 2023

39. Ibid, 140

40. Ibid, 145

41. Conversations with Charles Duelfer, June 2023

42. Charles Duelfer, *Comprehensive Report of the Special Advisor to the DCI on Iraq's WMD* (a.k.a. The Iraq Survey Report or the Duelfer Report) Washington, DC, October 6, 2004 (https://www.cia.gov/librtary/reports/general-reports-1/Iraq_wmd_2004/inde3x.html) Only small, non-militarily significant amounts of chemicals were found.

43. North Atlantic Treaty Organization (NATO) Archives, *Peace Support Operations in Bosnia and Herzegovina (1995-2004),* Brussels, April 11, 2023 (https://www.nato.int/cps/en/natohq/topics_52122).

44. Dayton Peace Agreement summary, *General Framework Agreement for Peace in Bosnia and Herzegovina,* Organization for Security and Co-operation in Europe (OSCE), Vienna, December 14, 1995, https://www.osce.org/bih/126173).

45. Darrel Whitcomb, *Searching for EBRO 33,* Air Power History Journal, Vol. 49, No 3, pp 34-39, Air Force Historical Foundation, Dayton,

Mechanicsville, MD, Fall 2002, (https://www.jstor.org/stable/26274341).

46. Ibid, 38

47. North Atlantic Treaty Organization (NATO) Archives, *Finland and Sweden Submit Applications to Join NATO,* Brussels, May 18, 2022, (https://www.nato.int/cps/en/natohq/news_195468.htm).

48. Naval History and Heritage Command report, *USS Cole (DDG-67) Determined Warrior,* NHHC, Washington, March 4, 2022, (https://www.history.navy.mil/browse-by-topic/ships/modern-ships/uss-cole.html).

49. Howard W. French, *No. 2 Admiral Meets with Families of Sub Victims,* (New York Times, February 28, 2001), (https://www.nytimes.com/2001/02/28/world/no-2-admiral-meets-with-families-of-sub-victims.html).

50. Alfred Goldberg et al., *Pentagon 9/11,* Official History of the Terrorist Attack on the Pentagon, Defense Studies Series, Office of the Secretary of Defense, Washington, 2007, 30-34, (https://history.defense.gov/portals/70/documents/pentagon/pentagon9-11.pdf).

51. Naval History and Heritage Command Archives, *The 9/11 Terrorist Attacks: Attack on the Pentagon Oral Histories of each of the three officers,* Naval History and Heritage Command, Washington, September 7, 2023. (https://www.history.navy.mil/research/archives/Collections/ncdu-det-206/2001/9-11-pentagon-attack.html)

52. See Veterans Legacy Memorial ICO Marsha D. Stallworth Ratchford, (https://www.vlm.cem.va.gov/marshadstallworthratchford/28D93C1).

53. Op. Cit. Naval History and Heritage Command Archives, Oral history Kevin Schaefer.

54. Martin Weil, Prominent Physician, Burn Center Leader Dies in Maryland Car Crash, Washington Post, October 1, 2018.

55. James "Sandy" Winnefeld, *Sailing Upwind: Leadership and Risk from Top Gun to the Situation Room,* (Annapolis, Naval Institute Press, 2023), 146.

56. Benjamin S. Lambeth, *Operation Enduring Freedom: An Assessment,* Research Brief, Rand Corporation, Santa Monica, November 29, 2005, 1.

57. Peter Bergen, *The Rise and Fall of Osama Bin Laden,* (New York, Simon and Schuster, 2021), 177.

58. Mark Fields and Ramsha Ahmed, *A Review of the 2001 Bonn Conference and Application to the Road Ahead in Afghanistan,* Institute for National Strategic Studies, (National Defense University, Washington, November 2011), 5.

59. Joseph Biden, *Remarks on the Way Forward in Afghanistan,* (White House transcript, Washington, April 14, 2021), (https://www.whitehouse.gov/briefing-room/speeches-remarks/2021/04/14/remarks-by-president-biden-on-the-way-forward-in-Afghanistan).

60. Jason Sherman, *Abizaid Key in Persuading Senior Leaders to Adopt "Long War" Label,* (Inside Defense, Washington, February,1, 2006), https://www.insidedefense.com/daily-news/abizaid-key-persuading-senior-leaders-adopt-long-war-label).

61. Richard Lardner, *Message-Minded Admiral Ditches "Long War" Phrase,* (Tampa Tribune, April 14, 2007), 1.

62. George W. Bush, *Address to a Joint Session of Congress and the American People*, (White House Archives, Washington, DC, September 20, 2001, (https://georgewbush-whitehouse.archives.gov/2001/09/20).

63. Alex Wagner, *Bush Labels North Korea, Iran, Iraq an 'Axis of Evil"*, (Arms Control Association Archives, Washington, February 2002), (https://www.armscontrol.org/act/2002-03/press-releases/bush-labels-north-korea-iran-iraq-axis-evil).

64. Seamus P. Daniels, Essay, *Bad Idea: Eliminating, Rather than Reforming, Overseas Contingency Operations Funding*, (Center for Strategic and International Studies, Washington, December 18, 2020).

65. Public Law 107-40- Authorization for use of Military Force, September 18, 2001, (See Congressional Record, Vol 147 (2001).

66. Public Law 107-56- Uniting and Strengthening America by Providing Appropriate Tools Required to Intercept and Obstruct Terrorism (USA Patriot Act) Act of 2001, October 26, 2001, (See Congressional Record, Vol 147 (2001).

67. George W. Bush, Presidential Military Order, *Detention, Treatment and Trial of Certain Non-Citizens in the War Against Terrorism*, Washington, November 13, 2001, (https://georgewbush-whitehouse.archives.gov/news/releases/2001/11/20011113-27.html).

68. For background see Jana Lipman, *The United States Has Long Sought to Exploit Guantanamo's Legal Contradictions*, (Washington Post, January 5, 2022).

69. Jennifer K. Elsea, Report: *Naval Station Guantanamo Bay: History and Legal Issues Regarding Its Lease Agreements*, (Congressional Research Service, Washington, August 1, 2022).

70. Author personal notes January 24, 2002.

71. Steve Coll, *the Bin Ladens: An Arabian Family in the American Century,* (New York, Penguin Press, 2008), 137 and 142-145.

72. Ibid., 203.

73. Ibid., 141 and Op. Cit., Bergen, 13.

74. Op. Cit. Coll, 203-212.

75. Op. Cit. Bergen, 23

76. Op. Cit., Coll 152

77. Ibid., Coll, 248.

78. Turki Al Faisal Al Saud, *The Afghanistan File,* (Isle of Wight, Arabian Publishing, 20-21), 77.

79. Op. Cit. Coll, 250. and Op. Cit., Bergen, 46.

80. Op. Cit. Coll, 251 and 295.

81. Ibid., 251.

82. Ibid., 335.

83. Ibid., 282.

84. Op. Cit. Al Faisal, 80.

85. Ibid., 79.

86. Op. Cit. Coll, 336-337 and Op. Cit. Bergen, 46-47.

87. Op. Cit. Bergen, 46

88. Op. Cit., Al Faisal, 104

89. Op. Cit. Coll, 341

90. Op. Cit. Bergen, 59 and author discussion with Ambassador Freeman July 2022.

91. Op. Cit., Coll, 376.

92. Ibid., 406.

93. Op. Cit., Bergen, 73.

94. Ibid., 73.

95. Ibid., 73.

96. Ibid., 87.

97. Liza Mundy, Essay, *The Women Who Saw 9/11 Coming,* (The Atlantic, November 18, 2023). (https://www.theatlantic.com/ideas/archive/2023/11/cia-women-counterterrorism-9-11-al-qaeda-warnings/676041/). Also, Op. Cit., Bergen, 100.

98. Combatting Terrorism Center, *Declaration of Jihad Against the Americans Occupying the Land of the Two Holiest Sites,* (U. S. Military Academy, West Point, NY, 2002), (https://ctc.westpoint.edu/Harmony-program/declaration-of-jihad-against-the-americans-occupying-the-land-of-thetwo-holiest-sites).

99. Lawrence Wright, Essay, *The Agent,* (New Yorker, July 3, 2006), (https://www.newyorker.com/magazine/2006/07/10/the-agent).

100. Op. Cit., Al Faisal, 79.

101. Barton Gelman and Dana Priest, *U.S. Strikes Terrorist-Linked Sites in Afghanistan, Factory in Sudan,* Washington Post, August 21, 1998, 1 (https://www.washingtonpost.com/wpsrv/inatl/longterm/eafricabombing/stories/strikes082198.htm).

102. Archive, The 9/11 Commission Report, aka: *Final Report of the National Commission on Terrorist Attacks Upon the United States,* (New York, W.W. Norton, July 22, 2004), 355. (https://9-11commission.gov/report/), 355-56.

103. Op. Cit., Wright.

104. See Atlantic Fleet Weapons Training Facility (AFWTF) (https://www.globalsecurity.org/military/facility/afwtf.htm), May 7, 2011 for a short overview and maps of the facilities. See also, *Vieques Dispute Continues,* (Puerto Rico Herald, San Juan, September 10, 1999), (https://puertoricoherald.com/issues/vol3n38/viequesdisputearticles-en.html). See also, Minutes from U.S. House of Representatives Armed Services Committee Hearing {H.A.S.C. No. 106-19} *Readiness Implications Concerning the Atlantic Fleet Training Center, Vieques, Puerto Rico,* Washington, September 22, 1999. (https://commdocs.house.gov/committees/security/has265030.000/has26503_0.HTM).

105. *The National Security Need for Vieques:* A study prepared for the Secretary of the Navy by Commander U.S. Second Fleet and Commander U.S. Marine Corps Forces Atlantic, (Pace-Fallon Report), July 15, 1999.

106. Author notes from Pentagon meeting with Secretary of Defense Rumsfeld March 13, 2001.

107. For background see: Jacek Bartosiak, *The Revolution in Military Affairs,* Geopolitical Futures Website, November 25, 2019 (https://geopoliticalfutures.com/the-revolution-in-military-affairs/).

108. Michael R. Gordon and Bernard E. Trainor, *Cobra II: The Inside Story of the Invasion and Occupation of Iraq* (New York, Vintage Books, 2007), 573.

109. For a succinct explanation, see: *Quadrennial Defense Review,* Office of the Secretary of Defense Historical Office, (https://history.defense.gov/historical-sources/qadrennial-defense-review/).

110. Ibid., *QDR Report*, September 30, 2001, (https://history.defense.gov/portals/70/documents/quadrennial/QDR2001.pdf?ver=AFts7axkH2zWUHncRd8yUg%3D).

111. Dow Jones Newswires article, *New York's Pataki Pledges to Help Stop the U.S. Navy's Bombing on Vieques,* Wall Street Journal, April 10, 2001, (https://www.wsj.com/articles/SB986854228748379393).

112. Esther Schrader and Paul Richter, *Political Pressure Helped Vieques Avert Cross Hairs,* Los Angeles Times, June 15, 2001, (https://www.latimes.com/archives/la-xpm-2001-jun-15-mn-10730-story.html).

113. Ibid., and author telephone discussions with Senator Inhofe confirming his advocacy in support of Navy retaining Vieques training facilities, and Mr. John Bonsell, former Legislative Assistant to Senator Inhofe confirming the June 2001 telephone call to the White House, January 18, 2024.

114. David E. Sanger and Christopher Marquis, *U.S. Said to Plan Halt to Exercises on Vieques Island,* New York Times, June 14, 2001, (https://www.nytimes.com/2001/06/14/us-said-to-plan-halt-to-exercises-on-vieques-island.html).

115. Jamie McIntyre, *U.S. to end Vieques bombing in 2003,* CNN, Gothenburg, Sweden, June 14, 2001, (http://www.cnn.com/2001/US/06/14/mcintyre.otsc/).

116. Pamela Hess, *Vieques Decision Stuns Pentagon,* UPI Archives June 14, 2001, (https://www.upi.com/archives/2001/06/14/Vieques-decision-stuns-pentagon/6677992491200/).

117. See report: *Vieques, Puerto Rico Population 2023,* World Population Review 2023, (https://worldpopulationreview.com/us-cities/vieques-pr-population).

118. Op. Cit., Pace-Fallon Report.

119. For insight, see: Stewart Brand, *John Rendon: Long Term Policy to Make the War on Terror Short,* Seminars about Long Term Thinking, The Long Now Foundation, July 14, 2006,

120. Mie Augier and Major Sean F.X. Barrett, Interview: *General Anthony Zinni (Ret.) On Staying Honest with the Troops and Translating Experience,* Center for International Maritime Security, March 15, 2022, (https://cimsec.org/general-anthony-zinni-ret-on-staying-honest-with-the-troops-and-translating-experience/).

121. Donald Rumsfeld, *Known and Unknown: A Memoir,* (New York, Sentinel, 2011), 425.

122. Tommy Franks, *American Soldier,* (New York, Regan Books, Harper Collins Publishers, 2004) 355-356.

123. Author notes from JROC meeting with Secretary Rumsfeld, June 21, 2001.

124. Archive, The 9/11 Commission Report, aka: *Final Report of the National Commission on Terrorist Attacks Upon the United States,* (New York, W.W. Norton, July 22, 2004), 399. (https://9-11commission.gov/report).

125. Discussion between author and General Powell at my office in Alexandria, Virginia, August 2020.

126. Robert Draper, *To Start a War: How the Bush Administration Took America Into Iraq,* (New York, Penguin Press, 2020).

127. Bob Woodward, *The War Within; A Secret White House History 2006-2008,* (New York, Simon and Schuster, 2008), 432.

128. Op. Cit., Draper, 89.

129. Ibid., Draper, 10, 14.

130. Douglas J. Feith, *War and Decision: Inside the Pentagon at the Dawn of the War on Terrorism,* (New York, Harper Collins, 2008), 293. See also: Department of Defense Office of Inspector General (Report No. 07-INTEL-04, February 9, 2007), *Review of Pre-Iraq War Activities of the Office of the Under Secretary of Defense for Policy.* (https://www.dodig.mil/reports.html/article/1142221/review-of-pre-iraq-war-activities-of-the-office-of-the-undersecretary-of-defense-for-policy). See also: Op. Cit., Draper, 15, 16. See also: Max Follmer, *Karen Kwiatkowski: The Soldier Who Spoke Out,* (Huffington Post, March 28, 2008). See also: Seymore M. Hersch, *Selective Intelligence,* (The New Yorker, May 4, 2003).

131. Op. Cit., Draper, 125-130. See also: Richard Bonin, *Arrows of the Night: Ahmad Chalabi and the Selling of the Iraq War* (New York, Penguin Random House, 2012).

132. Op. Cit., Draper, 127. Also confirmed in discussion with General Mike Hayden, former CIA Director, May 5, 2023.

133. Public Law 105-338- Iraq Liberation Act of 1998, October 31, 1998, (See Congressional Record Vol. 144 (1998), (https://www.congress.gov/bill/105th-congress/house-bill/4655). Original legislation, H.R. 4655 drafted by Stephen Rademaker, Staff Director, House Foreign Affairs Committee, See also: Op.Cit., Draper, 127.

134. Charles Duelfer, Opinion article, *In Iraq: Done in by the Lewinsky Affair,* Washington Post, February 24, 2012.

135. Discussion with author and Hon. Mary Beth Long in my office, Alexandria, Virginia, March 24, 2022.

136. Op. Cit., Gordon and Trainor, 546.

137. Rolf Ekeus, *Iraq Disarmed; The Story Behind the Story of the Fall of Saddam* (Boulder Colorado, Lynne Riener Publishers, 2023), 229, 256, and 272. See also: Charles Duelfer, *Hide and Seek: The Search for Truth in Iraq,* (New York, Public Affairs, 2009), 250-258.

138. Op. Cit., Franks, 376.

139. Author notes from Pentagon JCS meeting with General Franks and Secretary of Defense Rumsfeld, June 3, 2002.

140. James Steinberg, Michael O'Hanlon, and Susan Rice, *The New National Security Strategy and Preemption,* Article about use of force and legitimacy, (Brookings, December 21, 2002), (https://www.brookings.edu/articles/the-new-national-security-strategy-and-preemption/).

141. Author notes from Pentagon JCS meeting, August 7, 2002.

142. Op.Cit., Woodward, 328-29.

143. Op.Cit., Gordon and Trainor, 164.

144. Matthew Engel, *Scorned General's Tactics Proved Right,* The Guardian, Washington, March 28, 2003, (https://www.theguardian.com/world/2003/mar/29/Iraq.usa).

145. Op. Cit., Draper, 211-12, 370-72, 388. See also: Op. Cit., Duelfer, 470-71.

146. Author notes from Pentagon meeting August 12, 2002

147. Op. Cit., Draper, 371-72.

148. Author notes from Pentagon JCS meeting with Secretary Rumsfeld. September 28, 2002.

149. Author briefing to Secretary of Defense William J. Perry, Pentagon, October 2005.

150. Op. Cit., Franks, 409.

151. Author notes from Pentagon JCS "Tank" meeting, December 13, 2002.

152. Michael R. Gordon and Bernard E. Trainor, *The Endgame: The Inside Story of The Struggle for Iraq, from George W. Bush to Barack Obama*, (New York, Vintage Books, 2013), 8.

153. Author notes from office call with Secretary Rumsfeld, Pentagon, February 2005.

154. Charles Duelfer, *Comprehensive Report of the Special Advisor to the DCI on Iraq's WMD* (The Iraq Survey Report or the Duelfer Report) Washington, DC, October 6, 2004 (https://www.govinfo.gov/app/details/GPO-DUELFERREPORT).

155. Op.Cit., Ekeus, 265.

156. Ibid., 265.

157. Ibid., 265-66.

158. Samir Sumaidaie, *Reflecting on the Iraq War 20th Anniversary*, Discussion at George Mason University, April 21, 2023.

159. Michael R. Gordon and Bernard E. Trainor, *The Endgame: The Inside Story Of The Struggle For IRAQ, From George W. Bush To Barack Obama*, (New York, Vintage Books, 2013), 321.

160. Susan Cornwell, *Pelosi's Judgement Questioned Over Armenia Issue*, (Reuters article, October 21, 2007), (https://www.reuters.com/article/idUSN19325846/).

161. John J. Sheehan, USMC (Retired), opinion piece, *Why I Declined To Serve*, (Washington Post, April 16, 2007) (https://www.washingtonpost.com/archive/opinions/2007/04/16). See also Chris Suellentrop, *Czar Search*, (New York Times, April 16, 2007), (https://opinionator.blogs.nytimes.com/2007/04/16/czar-search/).

162. Sheryl Gay Stolberg, *Bush Picks General to Coordinate War Policy*, (New York Times, May 16, 2007) https://www.nytimes.com/2007/05/16/washington/16warczar.html.

163. U.S. Army/ U.S. Marine Corps Field Manual FM 3-24/MCWP 3-33.5 *Insurgencies and Countering Insurgencies*, (Washington, DC, 15 December 2006).

164. Op.Cit., Gordon and Trainor, 301.

165. Peter R. Mansoor, *Surge: My Journey with General David Petraeus and the Remaking of Iraq*, (New Haven, Yale University Press, 2013), see for example p.178-79. See also Op. Cit., Gordon and Trainor, 411-12 these authors draw conclusions based on opinion and are factually incorrect.

166. Dr. Anthony Cordesman, testimony before Committee on Foreign Relations, United States Senate, *Iraq's Transition—The Way Ahead (Part II)*, Washington, DC, May 19, 2004, (https://www.govinfo.gov/content/pkg/CHRG-108shrg96372/pdf/CHRG-108shrg96372.pdf).

167. For example see blog post, *Ray McGovern: Iran-Nuke NIE Stopped Bush on War,* November 24, 2010, (https://truthout.org/articles/ray-mcgovern-iran-nuke-nie-stopped-bush-on-war/).

168. George W. Bush Address to the Nation, *The New Way Forward in Iraq,* (Washington, DC, January 10, 2007), (https://georgewbush-whitehouse.archives.gov/news/releases/2007/01/20070110-7.html).

169. Iraq Study Group Report, *The Way Forward- A New Approach,* (New York, Vintage Books, 2006), (https://www.govinfo.gov/content/pkg/GPO-IRAQSTUDYGROUP/pdf/GPO-IRAQSTUDYGROUP.pdf).

170. Frederick W. Kagan, Working Paper, *Choosing Victory: A Plan for Success in Iraq,* (American Enterprise Institute, Washington, DC, January 5, 2007), (https://www.aei.org/research-products/wprking-paper/choosing-victory-a-plan-for-success-in-iraq/).

171. Op.Cit., Gordon and Trainor, 309, 313, made the same observation.

172. Rich Lamance, *Center for the Intrepid opens its Doors,* (Air Force Print News, San Antonio, TX, January 30, 2007), (https://www.af.mil/news/article-display/article/128212/center-for-the-intrepid-opens-its-doors/).

173. James R. Hagerty, *Arnold Fisher Provided Better Care for Wounded Warriors,* (Wall Street Journal, September 23, 2022, A-11, (https://www.wsj.com/articles/arnold-fisher-provided-better-care-for-wounded-warriors-11663945708).

174. See United States Senate Committee on Armed Services, U.S. Central Command Nomination Hearing, To consider the nomination of Admiral William J. Fallon, USN, for reappointment to the grade of admiral and to be Commander, United States Central Command, (Washington, DC, January 30, 2007), (https://www.c-

span.org/video/?196462-1/us-central-command-nomination-hearing).

175. Op. Cit. Mansoor, xi (Foreword by David Petraeus). See also, David Petraeus article, *How We Won in Iraq,* (Foreign Policy, October 29, 2013), (https://foreignpolicy.com/20-13/10/29/how-we-won-in-iraq/).

176. Mahmoud Mourad and Mohammed Wali, *Egypt's Former Military Ruler Tantawi, Key Figure in 2011, Dies at 85,* (Reuters, September 21, 2021), (https://www.reuters.com/world/africa/egypts-former-military-ruler-tantawi-dies-aged-85-2021-09-21/).

177. Agence France Presse report, *Maliki to Woo Regional Leaders for Egypt Talks,* (Arab News, Baghdad, April 22, 2007), (https://www.arabnews.com/node/297484).

178. Ibid., 109-112.

179. Op. Cit., Gordon and Trainor, 328.

180. Operation Iraqi Freedom- Iraq Significant Activities (SIGACTS) database; charts, December 2007 SIGACTS, (Global security.org, Washington, May 7, 2011), (https://www.globalsecurity.org/military/ops/iraq_sigacts.html).

181. Ibid., See also, Hannah Fischer, *Iraqi Civilian Death Estimates,* (Congressional Research Service Report for Congress, August 27, 2008), CRS-2 from Federation of American Scientists Report, (https://sgp.fas.org/crs/Mideast/RS22537.pdf).

182. Op. Cit., Mansoor, 77-78.

183. Richard Cobbold, *Analysis: Iranian Seizure of Royal Navy Sailors,* (Royal United Services Institute, March 26, 2007), (https://rusi.org/explore-our-

research/publications/commentary/analysis-iranian-seizure-royal-navy-sailors).

184. Op. Cit., Mansoor, 149, 167 and Op. Cit., Gordon and Trainor, 317.

185. Emma Sky, *The Unravelling: High Hopes and Missed Opportunities in Iraq*, (New York, Public Affairs, 2015), 157. See also Op. Cit., Mansoor, 65-67.

186. Douglas R. Satterfield, *The Most Dangerous Road in the World*, (The Leadership Maker blog, February 1, 2022). (https://www.theleadermaker.com/the-most-dangerous-road-in-the-world/).

187. For background see; Matthew W. Lewis et.al., Article: *New Equipping Strategies for Combat Support Hospitals*, (Rand Corporation, Summer 2012), (https://www.rand.org/pubs/periodicals/health-quarterly/issues/v2/n2/02.html).

188. For background on *"The Awakening"*: Op. Cit., Sky, 177. See also Op. Cit., Mansoor, 120-147.

189. James P. Pfiffner, U*S Blunders in Iraq: De-Baathification and Disbanding the Army*, (Intelligence and National Security Vol. 25, No. 1, 76-85, February 2010), https://pfiffner.gmu.edu/files/pdfs/articles/CPA%20Orders,%20Iraq%20PDF.pdf

190. Carter Malkasian, *The American War in Afghanistan. A History*, (New York, Oxford University Press< 2021), 136.

191. Craig Abram, *Combined Security Transition Command Afghanistan (CSTC-A)*, *(*The NCO Leadership Center of Excellence First Person Account, Combined Arms Research Library, August 1, 2009), (https://cgsc.contentdm.oclc.org/digital/collection/p15040coll2/id/7233/).

192. Author notes from meeting with President Karzai, Kabul, April 2007.

193. Author discussion with Mary Beth Long former DoD DASD for Narcoterrorism November 29, 2023.

194. ABC TV story, *Leaks Fallout: Former Top Diplomat Says Eikenberry Must Go,* (ABC News December 5, 2010), Comments by Zalmay Khalilzad on "This Week" December 5, 2010, (https://abcnews.go.com/thisweek/leaks-fallout-top-diplomat-eikenberry/story?id=12317442).

195. Karen DeYoung, *U.S. Trucking Funds Reach Taliban, Military-Led Investigation Concludes,* (Washington Post, July 24, 2011), (https://washingtonpost.com/world/national-security/us-trucking-funds-reach-taliban-military-ledinvestigation-concludes/2011/07/22).

196. See *ISAF's Mission in Afghanistan (2001-2014),* (NATO Mission Summary, updated May 30, 2022), (https://www.nato.int/cps/en/natohq/topics_69366.htm).

197. For another description and the eventual solution to the problem see Robert M. Gates, *Duty. Memoirs of a Secretary at War,* (New York, Alfred A. Knopf, 2014), 478.

198. Confirmed by author in personal meeting with Commander, Allied Joint Force Command HQ, May 2007.

199. Op. Cit., Malkasian, 178.

200. Dwight Jon Zimmerman and John D. Gresham, June 28, 2005: *One of the Worst Days in U.S. Special Operations History*, The History Reader blog, excerpted from Uncommon Valor: The Medal of Honor and the Six Warriors Who Earned It in Afghanistan and Iraq, (New York, St. Martin's Press, 2010), (https://www.thehistoryreader.com/military-

history/june-28-2005-one-worst-days-u-s-special-operations-history-2/).

201. For an accurate and insightful description of the situation in Eastern Afghanistan in 2007 see, Elizabeth Rubin, *Battle Company is Out There,* (New York Times Magazine, February 24, 2008), (https://www.nytimes.com/2008/02/24/magazine/24afghanistan-t-html).

202. Author phone call with General George Casey, U.S Army Chief of Staff, January 3/4, 2008.

203. For a detailed explanation of the factors behind this complex issue see, Op.Cit., Malkasian,178-215

204. See Inspector General, United States Department of Defense Report, *Alleged Misconduct: Lieutenant General Francis H. Kearney III, U.S. Army, Deputy Commander, U.S. Special Operations Command,* (DoD IG Report No. HO7L105376221, July 10, 2008), Did not substantiate the charges and stated that "LTGEN Kearney acted reasonably and within his authority.".

205. Wire story, *Death of an Afghan Icon: 20 Years Since the Assassination of Ahmad Shah Massoud,* (France 24 News, September 9, 2021), (https://www.france24.com/en/asia-pacific//20210909-death-of-an-afghan-icon-20-years-since-the-assasination-of-ahmad-shah-massoud).

206. Op. Cit., Malkasian,

207. For a short history and updated background, see: *Conflict Between India and Pakistan,* (Center for Preventive Action, June 28, 2023 from Council on Foreign Relations Global Conflict Tracker), (https://www.cfr.org/global-conflict-tracker/conflict/conflict-between-india-and-pakistan).

208. The specific amount is extremely difficult to pinpoint due to a multitude of funding categories and officially recognizable time spans. For example, one declassified but heavily redacted report, *Inspector General United States Department of Defense Assessment of DoD-Managed Programs in Support of the Government of Pakistan, Report No. SPO-2009-004, May 20, 2009,* indicates about $1.5B in Coalition Support Funds (CSF) (https://media.defense.gov/2017/oct/31/2001836209/-1/-1/1/SPO-2009-004.PDF), but another report, a transcript of a congressional hearing, *Oversight of U.S. Coalition Support Funds to Pakistan,* by the House Committee on Oversight and Government Reform, June 24, 2008, recorded an amount of $5.56B, (https://www.govinfo.gov/content/pkg/CHRG-110hhrg50348/html/CHRG-110hhrg50348.htm). Whatever the exact amount, it was large.

209. Joseph R. Biden and Leslie H. Gelb op-ed, *Unity Through Autonomy in Iraq,* (New York Times, May 1, 2006), (https://www.nytimes.com/2006/05/01/opinion/o1biden.html). See also, Max Fisher essay, *Why DC Loves Biden's Terrible Plan to Divide Iraq,* (VoxMedia blog, August 5, 2015), (https://www.vox.com/2015/8/5/9097133/iraq-biden).

210. Peter R. Mansoor, *Surge. My Journey with General David Petraeus and the Remaking of the Iraq War,* (New Haven, Yale University Press, 2013), 104.

211. Michael R. Gordon and Bernard E. Trainor, *The Endgame. The Inside Story of the Struggle for Iraq, from George W. Bush to Barack Obama,* (New York, Vintage Books, 2012), 389.

212. CNN News Report, *2007 Now Deadliest Year for U.S. Troops in Iraq,* (CNN, Baghdad, November 6, 2007), https://www.cnn.com/2007/World/meast/11/06/iraq.main/index.html.

213. Op. Cit., Gordon and Trainor, 339.

214. Author notes from discussion with Sgt. Major Jeff Morin, USMC, May 23, 2007.

215. Op. Cit., Mansoor, 72, 112.

216. Ibid., 77.

217. Author discussion with Dr. Bassima Al-Jadri in Baghdad, May 2007.

218. Emma Sky, *The Unravelling. High Hopes and Missed Opportunities in Iraq,* (New York, Public Affairs, 2015) 187-195.

219. Robert M. Gates, *Duty. Memoirs of a Secretary at War,* (New York, Alfred A. Knopf, 2014), 120.

220. Ibid., 124.

221. White House archives, *President Bush Meets with His Eminence Abdul-Aziz al-Hakim, Leader of the Supreme Council for the Islamic Revolution in Iraq,* (George W. Bush White House Archives, December 4, 2006), (https://georgewbush-whitehouse.archives.gov/news/releases/2006/12/images/20061204-7_d-0721-515h.html).

222. Author notes from meeting with Abdul Aziz al-Hakim, Baghdad, May 12, 2007.

223. Reuters News Report, *Iraqi Shi'ite Leader in U.S. for Cancer Treatment,* (Reuters, Washington, May 19, 2007), (https://.www.reuters.com/uk-iraq-hakim-cancer/iraq-shiite-leader-in-u-s-for-cancer-treatment-idUKN1922220532).

224. Author notes from meeting with Ammar al-Hakim, Baghdad, November 20, 2007.

225. See webinar, *A Conversation with Sayyid Ammar al-Hakim: Shi'ism, Pluralism, and the Future of Iraq,* (Harvard Divinity School, Project on Shi'ism and Global Affairs, May 6, 2021), (https://shiism.hds.harvard.edu/event/shiism-religion-pluralism-and-future-iraq-sayyid-ammar-al-hakim).

226. George W. Bush, *President Bush Addresses CENTCOM Coalition Conference,* Remarks at MacDill Air Force Base, Tampa, Florida, May 1, 2007, (https://georgewbushwhitehouse.archives.gov/news/releases/2007/05/images/20070501-4_d-0312-3-515h.html).

227. Edward Wong and Wissam A. Habeeb, *Baghdad Car Bomb Kills 20 on Bookseller's Row,* New York Times, March 6, 2007, (https://www.nytimes.com/2007/03/06/world/middleeast/06iraq.html).

228. Author notes from walkabout in Baghdad book market, June 11, 2007.

229. Author observations from second visit to Mutanabbi Street and Shabandar Café, Baghdad, November 11, 2007.

230. Author notes from visit to Bayji Oil Refinery, Iraq, June 11, 2007.

231. Paul Brinkley, *A Cause For Hope: Economic Revitalization in Iraq,* Military Review July-August 2007, archive, Army University Press, Ft. Leavenworth, Kansas, (https://armypress.army.mil/portals/7/military-review/Archives/english/militaryreview_20070831_art004.pdf).

232. Radio Free Europe report, *Georgia Sends More Troops to Iraq,* Transcript Radio Free Europe/ Radio Liberty, July 20, 2007, (https://www.rferl.org/a/1077730).

233. Reuters News Report, *U.S. General Wants Big Reduction in Iraqi Detainees,* (Reuters, Camp Bucca, Iraq, November 28, 2007), (https://www.reuters.com/article/idUSL2820026).

234. Article, *Timeline: The Life and Death of Abu Bakr al Baghdadi,* Wilson Center, Washington, October 28, 2019, (https://www.wilsoncenter.org/article/timeline-the-life-and-death-abu-bakr-al-baghdadi).

235. Article, *Looking Back: Munday Dubs 13th MEU Troop Surge COIN Ops 'Undeniable' Success,* (13th Marine Expeditionary Unit website archives, November 9, 2007), (https://www.13thmeu.marines.mil/news/article/532527/looking-back-munday-dubs-13th-meu-troop-surge-coin-ops-undeniable-success.html).

236. Op. Cit., Mansoor, 178.

237. Bob Woodward, *The War Within; A Secret White House History 2006-2008,* (New York, Simon and Schuster, 2008) 139, 145-46, 331.

238. Ibid., 399 and 401.

239. Tom Bowditch, *Notes on Iraq and CENTCOM; 15 July-25 July 2007,* (Notes from meeting between General Petraeus, Admiral Winnefeld and Doctor Bowditch, Baghdad, July 17, 2007), 5. See also, Op. Cit., Mansoor, 178-79. See also, Joel D. Rayburn and Frank K. Sobchak, Editors, *The U.S. Army in the Iraq War: Volume 2, Surge and Withdrawal; 2007-2011, (*Carlisle, Pennsylvania, U.S. Army War College Press, January 2019), 232-234.

240. Sandy Winnefeld, *Sailing Upwind: Leadership and Risk from TopGun to the Situation Room,* (Annapolis, Naval Institute Press, 2023), 253.

241. Op. Cit., Bowditch,1-2.

242. For a concise discussion see; Amy Belasco et al., *Congressional Restrictions on U.S. Military Operations in Vietnam, Cambodia, Laos, etc.,* (CRS Report to Congress, found at Defense Technical Information Center, January 16, 2007), (https://apps.dtic.mil/sti/citations/ADA462084). Note the date of report preparation at the request to Congress.

243. Tom Bowditch, *Notes on Iraq and CENTCOM; 27 June-15 July 2007,* (Notes from discussion between author, Admiral Winnefeld, Dr. Bowditch, and Colonel Johnson, CENTCOM HQ, Tampa, FL. June 27,2007), 1-2,

244. Ibid., 2.

245. Ibid., 6.

246. Joel D Rayburn and Frank K. Sobchak, Editors, *The U.S. Army in the Iraq War: Volume 2, Surge and Withdrawal; 2007-2011,* (Carlisle, Pennsylvania, U.S. Army War College Press, January 2019), 232-234.

247. Tom Bowditch, *Notes on Iraq and CENTCOM; 15 July-25 July 2007,* (Meeting between General Petraeus, Admiral Winnefeld and Doctor Bowditch, Baghdad, July 17, 2007), 5.

248. Ibid., 6.

249. Ibid., 5.

250. Peter R. Mansoor, *Surge. My Journey with General David Petraeus and the Remaking of the Iraq War,* (New Haven, Yale University Press, 2013), 178-179.

251. Interestingly, this opinion was also conveyed to me independently in an email exchange on August 30, 2007, with Wall Street Journal correspondent Greg Jaffe, then on assignment in Iraq,

252. Michael R. Gordon, *U.S. Is Seen in Iraq Until at Least '09,* (New York Times, July 24, 2007), (https://www.nytimes.com/2007/07/24/world/middleeast/24military.html).

253. Ibid., 3.

254. Tom Bowditch, *Notes on Iraq and CENTCOM; 18 July-25 July 2007,* (Includes Tank Session on 25 July), Washington, July 25, 2007, 4-7.

255. Author notes from White House meeting with President Bush, Washington, August 31, 2007.

256. Peter Baker et al, *Among Top Officials, 'Surge' Has Sparked Dissent, Infighting*, (Washington Post, September 9, 2007).

257. The Sunni realignment, led by tribal Sheikhs, from support of Al Qaeda to siding with the American forces.

258. Author notes from meeting with President Bush, Al Asad Airbase, Iraq September 3, 2007.

259. Ibid.,

260. Ibid.,

261. Renee Montagne and Jamie Tarabay, *U.S. Ally Sheik Abu Risha Killed in Anbar Province,* (Transcript NPR Morning Edition, Washington, September 13, 2007). (https://www.npr.org/2007/09/13/14383382/u-s-ally-sheik-abu-risha-killed-in-anbar-province).

262. Michael Barone, *The Petraeus and Crocker Testimony: General and Ambassador Make a Strong Case for a Continued American Presence in Iraq,* (U.S. News and World Report, Washington, September 12, 2007),

(https://www.usnews.com/opinion/blogs/barone/2007/09/12/the-petraeus-and-crocker-testimony).

263. Carol J. Williams, *Sadr Orders His Militia to Stand Down,* (Los Angeles Times, August 30, 2007, (https://www.latimes.com/archives/la-xpm-2007-aug-30-fg-sadr30-story.html).

264. CNN News Report, *NYT Editor Slams Paper Over 'General Betray Us' Ad,* (CNN, New York, September 23, 2007) (https://edition.cnn.com/2007/us/09/23/nyt.moveon/index.html).

265. David H. Petraeus, *Report to Congress on the Situation in Iraq,* (Congressional testimony, September 11, 2007, found at Defense Technical Information Center, (https://apps.dtic.mil/sti/citations/ADA473579).

266. For a detailed explanation of this issue that continued past the second Crocker-Petraeus Congressional testimony in April, 2008, see, Anthony H. Cordesman, *The Failed Crocker-Petraeus Testimony and a "Conditions-Based" Strategy for Staying in Iraq,* (Center for Strategic and International Studies, Washington, April 10, 20080 (https://www.csis.org/analysis/failed-crocker-petraeus-testimony-and-conditions-based-strategy-staying-in-iraq).

267. United Nations press release, *Security Council, Acting on Iraq's Request, Extends 'For Last Time' Mandate of Multinational Force,* (UN Press, New York, December 18, 2007), (https://press.un.org/en/2007/sc920-7.doc.html).

268. Author notes from visit to Fallujah, Iraq February 18, 2008.

269. Author notes from Video Conference with White House, October 29, 2007.

270. White House archives, Declaration of Principles for a Long-Term Relationship of Cooperation and Friendship Between the Republic of

Iraq and the United States of America, (George W. Bush White House archives, November 26, 2007), (https://georgewbush-whitehouse.archives.gov/news/releases/2007/11/20071126-11.html).

271. For a fascinating view of Ambassador Loftis and the SOFA negotiations that supports my original objection offered to Secretary Gates, see a Dissertation done at the Georgetown University Walsh School of Foreign Service by Jaffar Al-Rikabi, an Iraqi citizen, now Senior Economist with the World Bank, Jaffar Al-Rikabi, *Iraq and the Theory of Base Politics: Cooley, Institutionalism and Culture,* (Georgetown University, Washington, April 16, 2010), (https://repository.library.georgetown.edu/bitstream/handle/10822/553437/alrikabijaffar.pdf?sequence=1).

272. For details see, Matthew C. Weed, *U.S.-Iraq Strategic Framework and Status of Forces Agreement: Congressional Response,* (CRS Report for Congress, July 11, 2008, found at University of North Texas digital library), (https://digital.library.unt.edu/ark:/67531/metadc462024/).

273. Author discussion with Dr. Mowaffak al-Rubaie in margins of CENTCOM Coalition Conference, Manama, Bahrain, October 30, 2007.

274. Robert M. Gates, *Duty; Memoirs of a Secretary at War,* (New York, Alfred A. Knopf, 2014), 237.

275. Author discussion with Defense Minister Al-Obeidi, Tampa, Florida, January 8, 2008.

276. For background see, Ambassador Richard J. Griffin, *Private Security Contracting in Iraq and Afghanistan,* Assistant Secretary of State for Diplomatic Security Testimony before the House Committee on Oversight and Government Reform (as prepared for delivery),

October 2, 2007, (https://2001-2009.state.gov/m/ds/rls/rm/93191.html).

277. For a basic summary of the event see, U.S. Department of Justice, Office of Public Affairs Press Release, *Four Former Blackwater Employees Found Guilty of Charges in Fatal Nisur Square Shooting in Iraq*, (U. S. DOJ, Washington, October 22, 2014), (https://www.justice.gov/opa/pr/four-former-blackwater-employees-found-guilty-charges-fatal-nisur-square-shooting-iraq). The four men were later granted pardons by President Trump. See Karen DeYoung, *Trump Pardons Blackwater Contractors Convicted in Deaths of 14 Iraqi Civilians,* (Washington Post, December 22, 2020), (https://www.washingtonpost.com/national-security/trump-pardon-blackwater-contractors-iraq/2020/12/22/603da1f4-44).

278. Alissa J. Rubin, *U.S. Military Reforms Its Prisons in Iraq,* (New York Times, June 1, 2008), (https://www.nytimes.com/2008/06/01/world/africa/01iht-detain.4.13375130.html).

279. At the request of the late Congressman John Murtha, then Chair of House Appropriations Committee, MGEN Stone drafted a detailed and persuasive presentation to support his detainee initiatives (October 18, 2007) that was effective in securing funding.

280. Emma Sky, *The Unravelling; High Hopes and Missed Opportunities in Iraq*, (New York, Public Affairs, 2015), 262.

281. U.S. Department of State archives, Strategic Framework Agreement for a Relationship of Friendly Cooperation between the United States of America and the Republic of Iraq, (Washington, November 17, 2008), (https://2009-2017.state.gov/documents/organization/122076.pdf).

282. U. S. Department of State, Agreement Between the United States of America and the Republic of Iraq on the Withdrawal of United States

Forces from Iraq and the Organization of Their Activities during Their Temporary Presence in Iraq, from Office of Undersecretary of Defense (Acquisition and Sustainment) archives, (Washington, November 17, 2008), (https://www.acq.osd.mil/LOG_CSD/.policies.html/SE_SOFA.pdf).

283. Ed Pilkington, *Shoes and Insults Hurled at Bush on Iraq Visit,* The Guardian, Baghdad, December 15, 2008, https://www.theguardian.com/world/2008/dec/15/george-bush-shoes-iraq).

284. Author telephone discussion with Ambassador Ryan Crocker July 13, 2023.

285. For background and detail see; Richard Phillips, *A Captain's Duty: Somali Pirates, Navy SEALs, and Dangerous Days at Sea,* (New York, Hyperion Books, 2010).

286. For background see; Julie Moffett, *Central Asia: Joint Military Exercise Deemed a Success,* Archived transcript, Radio Free Europe/Radio Liberty, Washington, September 09, 1997, (https://www.rferl.org/a/1086503.html).

287. See USA.gov, U.S. Agency for Global Media for background, (https://www.usagm.gov/).

288. Discussion between the author and Captain Michael Nordeen, U.S. Navy, December 11, 2023.

289. Reuters News Report, *U.S. Soldier Shoots Kyrgyz Truck Driver at Airbase,* (Reuters, Bishkek, August 09, 2007), (https://www.rueters.com/article/us-kyrgyzstan-us-idUSL0684769520061206).

290. See Jason Wahlang, *Turkmenistan's Neutrality-Based Foreign Policy: Issues and Challenges,* Issue brief, (Manchar Parrikar Institute for

Defence Studies and Analyses, New Delhi, July 20, 2022, (https://www.idsa.in/issuebrief/turkmenistan-neutrality-based-foreign-policy-jwahlang-200722).

291. HT Correspondent, *Turkmenistan, Afghanistan to Build New Rail Link,* Hindustan Times, New Delhi, March 13, 2011, (https://www.hindustantimes.com/world/turkmenistan-afghanistan-to-build-new-rail-link/story-uolrCE5pQR9981OBVsqv.html).

292. Barry Bearak, *A Nation Challenged: Yesterday's Hero; Kabul's New Rulers Lament a Leader Who Died Too Soon,* New York Times, November 25, 2001, (https://www.nytimes.com/2001/11/25/world/nation-challenged-yesterday-s-hero-kabul-s-new-rulers-lament-leader-who-died-too-soon.html).

293. Radio Free Europe report, *Tajikistan/ Afghanistan: Road Bridge Opens With Aim Of Strengthening Trade,* Transcript Radio Free Europe/Radio Liberty, August 26, 2007, (https://www.rferl.org/a/1078359.html).

294. For background see; Bruce Pannier, *'We made Mistakes': In Uzbekistan, A Rare Admission Over Andijan Killings,* Archived transcript, Radio Free Europe/Radio Liberty, February 18, 2020, (https://www.rferl.org/a/uzbekistan-andijon-assacre-officials-willingness-talk-analysis/30442215.html).

295. Jim Hoagl, *Ousted from Uzbekistan,* Washington Post, August 7, 2005, (https://www.washingtonpost.com/archive/opinions/2005/08/07).

296. For background and additional information see, C.J. Chivers, *Seeking a Path in Democracy's Dead End,* New York Times, February 3, 2008. (https://www.nytimes.com/2008/02/03/weekinreview/03chivers.html).

297. For confirmation see U.S. Department of State archives, *Resumption of Detention Visits by the International Committee of the Red Cross in Uzbekistan,* (Washington, March 19, 2008), (https://2001-2009.state.gov/r/prs/ps/2008/mar/102399.htm).

298. Tom Gjelten, *U.S. Now Relies On Alternate Afghan Supply Routes,* (Transcript NPR Morning Edition, Washington, September 16, 2011), (https://www.npr.org/2011/09/16/140510790/u-s-now-relies-on-alternate-afghan-supply-routes).

299. U. S. Department of State, *Roadmap for Peace in the Middle East: Israeli/Palestinian Reciprocal Action, Quartet Support,* (Archives, Bureau of Public Affairs Release, Department of State, Washington, July 16, 2003), (https://2001-2009.state.gov/r/pa/ei/ris/22520.html).

300. Adam Entous, *Palestinian Forces Enter Jordan Under U.S. Program,* (Reuters, Allenby Bridge, West Bank, Israel, January 24, 2008), (https://www.reuters.com/article/idUSL24362531).

301. For background about Syrian nuclear reactor discussion in the U.S. see; Michael V. Hayden, *Playing to the Edge, American Intelligence in the Age of Terror,* New York, Penguin Random House, 2016), 255-270.

302. Ehud Barak, *When Israel Struck Syria's Nuclear Reactor; What Really Happened,* (Middle East Quarterly, Fall 2022, Volume 29, Number 4, Middle East Forum, Philadelphia).

303. For background see; Eric Schmitt and Thom Shanker, *In Long Pursuit of bin Laden, the '07 Raid, and Frustration,* (New York Times, May 5, 2011). (https://www.nytimes.com/2011/05/06/world/asia/06binladen.html?hpgrp=k-abar&smid=em-share).

304. Anthony Cordesman, *Afghan Public Opinion and the Afghan War: Shifts by Region and Province, A Breakout of the Data in the ABC*

News Poll, (Center for Strategic & International Studies, Washington, April 10, 2009, 5, https://www.csis.org/analysis/afghan-public-opinion-and-afghan-war.

305. Discussion between author and Major General Eikenberry, Kabul, November 23, 2006.

306. Shashank Bengali, *U.S. Hands Troubled Dam To Afghans,* Los Angeles Times, May 5, 2013, https://www.latimes.com/archives/la-xpm-2013-may-04-la-fg-afghan-dam-201130505-story.html.

307. SIGAR (*Special Inspector General for Afghanistan Reconstruction*), For Master List of all Reports 2008-2023, see https://www.sigar.mil.

308. Amy Belasco, *The Cost of Iraq, Afghanistan, and other Global War on Terror Operations since 9/11*, (Congressional Research Service Report, December 8, 2014, Table 9, page 58, DoD's Flexible Funds for War: Training Afghan Security Forces), https://www.everycrsreport.com/reports/RL33110.html.

309. See Institute for the Study of War Report, *Afghanistan National Army (ANA),* (Institute for the Study of War, Washington, December 13, 2023), data referenced to "Official Website of the Afghan National Army Kabul 2007," (https://www.understandingwar.org/afghanistan-national-army-ana).

310. MG Bob Cone, who succeeded MG Bob Durbin in Kabul, advised me via email of MI-17 and AN-26/32 aircraft deliveries in November and December 2007 and January 2008, much to the delight of the Afghan Air Force.

311. For a good summary of the foolishness, see; Mark Thompson, *Whirlybird-Brained: U.S. Making Wrong Chopper Choice for Afghanistan,* (Analysis from Project on Government Oversight, Washington, June 25, 2018),

(https://www.pogo.org/analysis/whirlybird-brained-us-making-wrong-chopper-for-afghanistan).

312. Op. Cit., Gates, 214.

313. Author notes from briefings with 203 Kandak, Khost, Afghanistan and discussions with Father (Captain, U.S. Navy Retired) Jim Danner, Honolulu, August-September 2021.

314. American Forces Press Story, *CENTCOM Commander Attends Khost Leadership Conference,* (Defense Visual Information Distribution Service, Washington, November 5, 2007), (https://www.dvids.net/news/13668/centcom-commander-attends-khost-leadership-conference).

315. Luke Harding, *Taliban Blow Apart 2,000 Years of Buddhist History,* (The Guardian, March 3, 2001), https://www.theguardian.com/world/2001/mar/03/afghanistan.lukeharding

316. Author notes from meeting with Governor Atta Mohamad Nur, Mazur-i-Sharif, Afghanistan, November 26, 2007,

317. Stephen M. Saideman and David P. Auerswald, *Comparing Caveats: Understanding the Sources of National Restrictions upon NATO's Mission in Afghanistan,* International Studies Quarterly, (2012) Vol. 56, Number 1, pp67-84, (National War College, Washington, March, 2012), https://nwc.ndu.edu/portals/71/images/publications/comparing%20caveats.pdf?ver=VIpJr7MoUq8hERfzoji3uQ%3D.

318. Author notes from conversation with BG Josef Blotz, Balkh, Afghanistan, November 2007.

319. U.S. Department of Defense archives, Central Command Chiefs of Defense Conference in St. Petersburg, Florida, January 15, 2008,

https://www.defense.gov/multimedia/photos/igphoto/2001146934/
.

320. Author discussion with Australian Ambassador to Tehran Greg Moriarity, October 29, 2007, at Manama, Bahrain.

321. Alexandra Zavis, *Meeting Gets Testy Between U.S., Iran,* (Los Angeles Times, Baghdad, July, 25, 2007 cited in The Spokesman Review, Spokane, Washington, July 25, 2007), https://www.spokesman.com/stories/2007/jul/25/meeting-gets-testy-between-us-iran/.

322. International Institute for Strategic Studies, *Managing Global Security and Risk: 2007 Global Strategic Review,* Fifth Annual Global Strategic Review Conference, third plenary session, Geneva, September 7, 2007, from *IISS News Autumn 2007*, 2.

323. For background see, Carlotta Gal, *Pakistanis Tied to 2007 Border Attack on Americans,* New York Times, September 26, 2011, https://www.nytimes.com/2011/09/27/world/asia/pakistanis-tied-to-2007-attack-on-americans.html.

324. Author meeting with President Musharraf, Rawalpindi, Pakistan, March 30, 2007.

325. Author notes from meeting with President Musharraf, Islamabad, Pakistan, November 2, 2007.

326. Scott Neuman and Corey Flintoff, *Musharraf Resignation Ends Nine-Year Reign,* (Transcript NPR, Washington, August 18, 2008, (https://www.npr.org/2008/08/18/14052677/musharraf-resignation-ends-nine-year-reign).

327. Author visit at Torkham Gate security station on Afghanistan-Pakistan border with U.S. Army 173rd Airborne Brigade troops, January 23, 2008.

328. See Vinay Kaura, *The Durand Line: A British Legacy Plaguing Afghan-Pakistani Relations,* Middle East Institute, Washington, June 27, 2017, (https://www.mei.edu/publications/durand-line-british-legacy-plaguing-afghan-pakistani-relations).

329. Discussion with CIA Director General Michael Hayden on December 28, 2007.

330. For background on unmanned aerial vehicle (drone) attacks in Afghanistan and Pakistan see, Michael V. Hayden, *Playing to the Edge; American Intelligence in the Age of Terror,* (New York, Penguin Random House, 2016), 336-44 and 425-26.

331. Author notes from visit to Al Jazeera, Doha, Qatar with journalist Tom Friedman, August 24, 2007.

332. Thomas P.M. Barnett, *The Man Between War and Peace,* (Classic Esquire magazine, April 1, 2008), https://classic.esquire.com/article/2008/4/1/the-man-between-war-and-peace).

333. Charles Duelfer, Opinion article, *In Iraq: Done in by the Lewinsky Affair*, Washington Post, February 24, 2012, (https://www.washingtonpost.com/opinions/in-iraq-done-in-by-the-lewinsky-affair/2012-02/21/gIQA7dKfYR_story.html).

334. Robert Gates, *Duty: Memoirs of a Secretary at War (*New York: Alfred A Knopf, 2014), 214.

335. Jean-Baptiste Alphonse Karr, aphorism in the journal *Les Guepes*, January 1849.

336. Special Inspector General for Afghan Reconstruction (SIGAR) Report, *What We Need To Learn: Lessons from Twenty Years of Afghanistan Reconstruction,* (Washington, August 2021),

(https://www.sigar.mil/pdf/lessonslearned/SIGAR-21-46-LL-Executive-Summary.pdf).

337. George W. Bush, Address to the Nation, October 7, 2001, (https://georgewbush-whitehouse.archives.gov/news/releases/2001/10/20011007-8.html).

338. George W. Bush, Remarks at VMI, Lexington, VA, April 17, 2002, (http://www.cnn.com/transcripts/0204/17/se.02.html).

339. Op. Cit. Gates, 216-219.

340. Amy Belasco, *Troop Levels in the Afghan and Iraq Wars, FY2001-FY2012: Cost and Other Potential Issues,* Table 1, Congressional Research Service, Washington, July 2, 2009, 9, (Defense Technical Information Center), (https://apps.dtic.mil/sti/citations/ADA503796).

341. Barack Obama, *Remarks by the President on a New Strategy for Afghanistan and Pakistan,* Washington, DC, March 27, 2009, (https://obamawhitehouse.archives.gov/the-press-office/remarks-president-a-new-strategy-afghanistan-and-pakistan).

342. Barack Obama, *Remarks by the President in Address to the Nation on The Way Forward in Afghanistan and Pakistan,* USMA, West Point, NY, December 1, 2009, (https://obamawhitehouse.archives.gov/the-press-office/remarks-president-address-nation-way-forward-afghanistan-and-pakistan).

343. Op. Cit. Gates, 371.

344. Ibid, 354.

345. Carlotta Gall, *Taliban Open Northern Front in Afghanistan*, New York Times, November 26, 2009, https://www.nytimes.com/2009/11/27/world/asia/27/kunduz.html.

346. Rob Evans, *Afghanistan War Logs: How the IED became Taliban's weapon of choice*, The Guardian, July 25, 2010, https://www.theguardian.com/world/2010/jul/ieds-improvised-explosive-device-deaths.

347. John F. Sopko, Special Inspector General for Afghanistan Reconstruction, Hearing Before the Committee on Oversight and Accountability, U.S. House of Representatives, April 19, 2023, (https://oversight.house.gov/wp-content/uploads/2023/04/SIGAR-testimony-23-22-TY.pdf).

348. Donald Trump, Twitter comments of March 2013, as reported on CNBC, August 21, 2017, (https://www.cnbc.com/2017/08/21/what-trump-said-about-afghanistan-before-he-became-president.html).

349. Donald Trump, Remarks on the Strategy in Afghanistan and South Asia, Fort Myer, Virginia, August 21, 2017, (https://trumpwhitehouse.archives.gov/briefings-statements/remarks-president-trump-strategy-afghanistan-south-asia/).

350. National Security Archive, *Afghanistan 20/20: The 20 year war in 20 Documents*, Table: U.S. Troop Levels in Afghanistan, 2002-2021, (Washinton, DC, August 19, 2021) 1. (https://nsarchive.gwu.edu/briefing-book/Afghanistan/2021-08-19/afghanistan-2020-20-year-war-20-documents).

351. Council on Foreign Relations, New York, NY, July 30, 2019, Candidate Joe Biden reply to questions on the war in Afghanistan, (https://www.cfr.org/news-releases/2020-democratic-presidential-candidates-answer-cfrs-foreign-policy-questions).

352. Remarks by President Biden on the Way Forward in Afghanistan, Washington, DC, April 14, 2021, (https://www.whitehouse.gov/briefing-room/speeches-

remarks/2021/04/14/remarks-by-president-biden-on-the-way-forward-in-afghanistan)

353. Congressional Research Service Report, *Department of Defense Contractor and Troop Levels in Afghanistan and Iraq: 2007-2020*, Table 1, page 8, from Federation of American Scientists, (https://sgp.fas.org/crs/natsec/R44116.pdf).

354. Carter Malkasian, *The American War in Afghanistan: A History*, (Oxford University Press, New York, 2021).

355. Dawn Liberi, USAID, Memorandum to Commander USCENTCOM, *USAID Economic/COIN Activities in Afghanistan*, April 23, 2007.

356. Emma Sky, *The Unravelling: High Hopes and Missed Opportunities in Iraq*, (New York, Public Affairs, 2015), 272.

357. Remarks by President Barack Obama, *Responsibly Ending the war in Iraq*, Camp Lejeune, North Carolina, February 27, 2009, (https://obamawhitehouse.archives.gov/blog/2009/02/27/responsibly-ending-war-iraq).

358. Sky, Op. Cit, 312-13.

359. Michael Gordon and Bernard E. Trainor, *Endgame*, (Vintage Books, New York, 2012), 585.

360. Ibid, 610.

361. Sky, Op. Cit, 322, 335.

362. Ibid, 321, 338.

363. Article, *Timeline: the Rise, Spread, and Fall of the Islamic State*, Wilson Center, Washington, DC, October 28, 2019, (https://www.wilsoncenter.org/article/timeline-the-rise-spread-and-fall-of-the-islamic-state).

364. Report, *The Islamic State,* Center for International Security and Coperation, Stanford University, Palo Alto, CA, updated April 2021, (https://cisac.fsi.stanford.edu/mappingmilitants/profiles/islamic-state)

365. Jane Arraf Report, *Along the Iraq-Syria Border, U.S. Troops Focus on Defeating ISIS,* NPR *News,* July 2, 2018, (https://www.npr.org/2018/07/02/625406747/along-the-iraq-syria-border-u-s-troops-focus-on-defeating-isis).

366. Report, *U.S.-led troops end Iraq combat mission, as planned-military officials,* Reuters, Baghdad, Iraq, December 9, 2021, (https://www.reuters.com/world/middle-east/iraq-security-advisor-says-international-coalition-ends-combat-mission).

INDEX

al-Abadi, Haidar, 341
Abbot, Charles Stevenson "Steve," 47–48, 56, 74
Abbot, Lloyd "Doc," 47, 98
ABC, 315
Abdullah II, 181
Abizaid, John, 104, 155, 173, 190, 238
ABRAHAM LINCOLN, USS, 148–149, 314
Abrams, Elliott, 139
Abu Ghraib, 198
Abu Hafs, 115
Abu Ubaida, 115
Adams, Dave, 300
Afghan Air Force, 296–297
Afghan National Army (ANA), 204, 207, 211–213, 295–300, 326
Afghan National Police (ANP), 204, 207, 295
Afghanistan
  Al Qaeda, 9, 101–104, 106, 115–116, 208, 329
  Biden's withdrawal plan, 332–333
  CENTCOM visit, 202–214
  civilian casualties, 210–211, 303–304, 310, 312
  Coalition forces, 103–104, 203
  command responsibility and decision making, 334–337
  Doha Accords, 332
  favorable opinion of the U.S., 293
  geography, 203, 288–289
  government, 284
  infrastructure, 204
  insurgency, 203, 292, 310–311
  Iranian opposition to U.S. operations in, 7
  Korengal River valley, 209–210
  Lion's Den, 114
  nation-building, 293–294, 331–333
  NATO regional commands, 208–209
  Northern Alliance militias, 103
  Obama's troop surge, 206, 328–330, 333
  Obama's troop drawdown, 331
  OPERATION ENDURING FREEDOM, 103–104, 208, 288
  OPERATION MOUNTAIN SHADOW, 251, 290–291
  Pakistan and, 212–213, 214–216, 274, 292–293, 307–312

Pech River valley, 209–210
  poppy eradication, 205–206
  Provincial Reconstruction Teams, 208–209, 300–304
  security forces, 211–213
  security in, 202
  socio-economic challenges, 336
  Soviet invasion of, 4, 5, 111–112
  Taliban, 102, 103–104, 114, 117, 208, 212, 292, 301, 332
  Taliban resurgence, 202–203, 324, 329–330, 334–336
  Tora Bora, 103, 114, 117, 119, 287–291
  transitional government, 103
  Trump's withdrawal plan, 331–333
  U.S. casualties, 209, 334, 343
  weather, 203–204
  withdrawal plans, 104, 115, 325–326
  withdrawal outcomes, 327–337
Afghan-Soviet War, 113, 115, 117, 212, 215, 274, 297
Agency for Global Media, 276
AJFC. *See* Allied Joint Force Command
Al Jazeera, 178–179, 252, 315–316
Al Qaeda, 9, 101–104, 106, 107, 115–116, 120–121, 137, 200, 208, 212, 329
Al Udeid airbase, 178
Al-Anfal campaign, 21
Alexander, Ron, 28, 38
Allawi, Ayad, 338
Allen, John, 330
Allied Joint Force Command (AJFC), 208
Al-Thager Model School, 110, 113
American Enterprise Institute (AEI), 2–3, 167
al-Amir, Fahad Ahmad, 179–180
al-Amiri, Hadi, 225
Amiri Diwan, 180
Amos, Jim, 160
Amphibious Ready Group, 74
Andijan incident, 282–284
Andrews Air Force Base, 9
Arab Bureau, 18
Arab Spring protests, 185, 341
Arabian Peninsula, 6, 7, 18
Arafat, Yasser, 23
ARKANSAS, USS, 75
Arlington National Cemetery, 343

Armenian genocide resolution, 156–157
Armitage, Richard, 158
Army War College, 246
Arthur, Stan, 51–52
Asia-Pacific region, 1, 8
Associated Press, 315
al Attiyah, Hamad, 179
Authorization for Use of Military Force (AUMF), 106, 107
al-Awani. Maamoon Sami Rasheed, 254, 256
axis of evil, 105
Aziz, Tariq, 78
Azzam, Abdulla, 112–116

Ba'ath Party, 19, 140, 339
Badeeb, Ahmed, 113
Badr Brigade, 224–225
Baghdad International Airport (BIA), 193
Baghdad Operations Command, 194
al-Baghdadi, Abu Bakr, 233
Bahrain
   CENTCOM visit, 178
   Manama airfield, 51
   Port of Manama, 4
   security responsibilities, 262–263
Bakiyev, Kurmanbek, 277–278
al-Bakr, Ahmed Hassan, 19
Balad Airbase, 196, 197, 289
Baltic states, 89
Banister, Jeff, 227
Barnett, Thomas, 318–322
Barzani, Massoud, 198, 254, 255, 260
Barzani, Nechirvan, 198
Batiste, John, 131, 132
Battle Update Assessment (BUA), 195–196
Bayji oil refinery, 229–230
Begin, Menachem, 185
Beirut International Airport (BIA), 24, 28, 29
Bell, Gertrude, 17, 221
Bennett, Gina, 118
Berdimuhamedov, Gurbanguly, 279
Berndt, Marty, 75
"Betty" (translator), 222, 227–228, 316
Bhutto, Benazir, 308–309

Biden, Joe, 217, 324, 329, 332–333, 337, 339
Biden Administration, 104, 341
Bien, Lyle, 57
bin Laden, Mohammed, 110, 111
bin Laden, Osama
  Af-Pak border presence and influence, 111–114, 119
  Al Qaeda, 115–116
  Al-Thager Model School, 113
  Azzam and, 112–116
  death, 331
  declares war on United States, 118, 120
  education, 110, 111
  family background, 110
  grievance over Ottoman Empire collapse, 15
  Lion's Den, 114
  marriage and family, 111, 114
  Muslim Brotherhood, 110, 111, 112
  self-exile from KSA, 116, 119
  September 11 attacks, 101–104, 106, 109, 120–121, 137
  in Sudan, 116–117, 119
  in Tora Bora, 103, 114, 117, 119, 288–291
  U.S. intelligence on, 118
bin Laden, Salem, 110, 111, 114
bin Salman, Mohamed, 110
biological weapons, 21, 146
Birdwell, Brian, 100
Black September, 23
Blackwater contractors, 264–266
Blix, Hans, 143
Blotz, Josef, 303
Bodde, Peter, 215
Bonn Conference on Afghanistan, 295
Bosnian War, 75, 81–87, 147
Bowditch, Thomas "Tom," 237–238, 241–242-243, 245–248, 250
Bremer, Paul, 143, 201, 224, 264
Brigade Combat Team (BCT) concept, 145
Brinkley, Paul, 230–231
Brook Army Medical Center, 168
Brown, Doug, 226
al-Bulani, Jawad, 196
Bureau of Intelligence and Research, 118
Bureau of Naval Personnel, 94
Burns, Bob, 315

Bush, George H.W., 58, 59, 152–153
Bush, George W.
  2000 presidential election, 92, 122
  CENTCOM Coalition partners meeting, 226
  Detention, Treatment, and Trial of Certain Non-Citizens in the War against Terrorism, Presidential Military Order, 107
  Esquire magazine article, 319–322
  freedom agenda, 151, 152
  GWOT, 104–109
  invasion of Iraq (2003), 152–153, 342
  Iraq invasion contingency planning, 136–140
  military response to Al Qaeda, 102, 333
  national security priority, 121
  "New Way Forward" in Iraq, 14, 166–168, 170–172
  shoe-throwing incident, 268
  trip to Al-Asad, Iraq, 254–256
  Vieques, 131, 132, 133
  Virginia Military Institute speech, 328
Bush, Jeb, 131, 152
Bush Administration, 122, 123–124, 128, 129–130, 324
BusinessWeek, 314

CAG. *See* Carrier Air Group (CAG) commander
Camp Bucca, 198–199, 232–233, 266–267, 321
Camp Cropper, 198
Camp Eggers, 204
Camp Taji, 220
Camp Victory, 194, 195, 241
Capalbo, Joe "Condo," 85
Carrier Air Group (CAG) commander, 46
Carrier Air Wing Eight (CVW-8), 40, 46, 60, 74
Carter Administration, 113
Carter Doctrine, 4
Cartwright, Jim "Hoss," 320
Casey, George, 3–4, 161, 209, 220
CBRNE. *See* weapons of mass destruction
CENTCOM. *See* U.S. Central Command
Center for Strategic and International Studies (CSIS), 158, 163
Center for the Intrepid, 168–169
Central Asian Battalion (CENTRAZBAT), 275
Central Command Forward Headquarters, 178
Chalabi, Ahmed, 140–142, 151
chemical weapons, 6, 21, 150

Cheney, Dick, 2, 96, 139-140, 238
Chiarelli, Pete, 320
Chief of Staff of the Army, 2
China, 1, 7, 8
Chivers, C.J., 315
CIA, 38, 121, 138, 311–312
Clark, Vern, 88, 92, 93, 126, 127, 130–131, 147, 148
Clary, Lt., 26
Clemenceau, FS, 25
Clexton, Ed, 31
Clinton, Bill, 133, 141–142
Clinton, Hillary, 168
Clinton Administration, 120, 122, 124, 129–130, 150
close air support (CAS), 28
CNN, 82, 314, 316
Coalition Provisional Authority (CPA), 143, 201, 224, 264
COCOM. *See* Combatant Commander
Code Pink, 169
Cohen, Bill, 162, 163
Cold War, 5, 7, 9, 20, 25, 40–41, 43, 88, 89, 127
COLE, USS, 92, 120, 122
combat outposts (COP), 168
combat search and rescue missions (CSARs), 84–86
Combatant Commander (COCOM), 136
Combined Security Transition Command-Afghanistan (CSTC-A), 204
confirmation hearings, 165–172
Conner, Patrick, 53
Connor, Gene, 41
Cook, Frances, 156
Cooke, Barry, 53
Cordesman, Tony, 158, 163
Cornwall, HMS, 192
Cosgriff, Kevin, 178, 272–273, 307
Cothron, Tony, 50
counterterrorism, 104–109
Crocker, Ryan, 217–218, 224–225, 233, 242, 243, 245, 253–255, 256–258, 266-268, 307, 338
CSIS. *See* Center for Strategic and International Studies

Danner, Jim, 299–300
Dayton, Keith, 285–286
Dayton Peace Accords, 84
DeLeon, Rudy, 122–123, 124, 129, 135

Deley, Drew, 84
Dempsey, Marty, 196
Department of Homeland Security, 105
Detention, Treatment, and Trial of Certain Non-Citizens in the War against Terrorism, Presidential Military Order, 107
Doha Accords, 332
Dowd, Ken, 274
Draper, Robert, 138
Duelfer, Charles, 79, 141–143, 151, 324
Dunleavy, Dick, 43
Dunn, Patrick, 97
Durand Line, 311, 312
Durbin, Bob, 204, 208, 295
DWIGHT D. EISENHOWER, USS, 4–5, 6
Dwyer, Robert, 53

East of Suez, 6, 8, 16
EFPs, 170, 192, 197, 200, 231
Egypt, 184–187
Ehime Maru, 92
Eikenberry, Karl, 206, 293, 330
EISENHOWER (IKE), *USS*, 22, 24, 29, 34
Ekeus, Rolf, 77-78, 143, 152–153
Ellis, Bob, 34, 39
England, Gordon, 131–133
enhanced interrogation techniques, 108–109
ENTERPRISE, USS, 102
Erskine, Bob, 93
Esquire magazine, 318–322
Euphrates River, 15, 17, 59

Fahd, King, 116
Faisal, Prince, 181
Faisal I, 17–18, 19
Faisal II, 19
Faisal of Saudi Arabia, 110
Faller, Craig, 171, 224, 283, 317, 319
FBI, 120, 121
Federally Administered Tribal Areas (FATA), 112, 214, 216, 292–293, 307, 311
Feith, Doug, 139, 143
Fertile Crescent, 15
Findlay, Rusty, 173

Fisher, Arnold, 168–169
Fisher, Elizabeth, 168
Fisher, Ken, 168
Fisher, Zachary, 168
Flagg, Dee, 98
Flagg, Wilson "Bud," 98
Flanagan, "Bud," 88
Flatley, Jim, 34–37
FOBs. *See* forward operating bases
Foch, FS, 25–26, 31
Foley, Tom, 92
Foreign Intelligence Surveillance Court (FISC), 106
foreign service officers (FSO), 204
forward air controllers (FAC), 27–29
Forward Edge of the Battle Area (FEBA), 53
Forward Operating Bases (FOBs), 3, 168
France
   downed aircraft rescue mission, 84–86
   mandates, 22
   MNF activity in Lebanon, 24–26
   supplies to Iraq for Osiraq, 21
   Sykes-Picot Accord, 16
Franks, Tommy, 136, 138, 143–144, 149, 152
Free Iraqi Forces (FIF), 142
Freeman, Chas, 116
Friedman, Tom, 315–316
Frost, David "Frosty," 47–51, 56, 57, 62

Galvin, John, 62
Gates, Robert, 1–2, 9–13, 160, 162, 173, 180, 199, 217–218, 223–224, 236, 238—240, 242–243, 247, 253, 254, 261, 262, 273, 285, 289, 298, 308–309, 320, 321, 325, 328
Gemayel, Bachir, 24
Geneva Conventions, 108
Geographic Combatant Commands, 2
Georgia (country), 231–232
Gfoeller, Mike, 182
Ghanem, Alia, 110
Gheit, Ahmed Ali Aboul, 186
Giambastiani, Ed, 249
Gingrich, Newt, 140
Global Strategic Review conference, 307
Global War on Terror (GWOT), 104–105, 136, 137, 208, 226

Goldwater-Nichols Act, 88
Gordon, Michael, 249, 321
Graham, Lindsey, 171
Great Britain
    invitation to Navy to share facilities in Bahrain, 4
    mandates, 17, 18, 22
    Mesopotamian campaign, 17
    Royal Air Force, 17
    Sykes-Picot Accord, 16
    withdrawal from East of Suez, 6, 8
GREENEVILLE, USS, 92
GUAM, USS, 140
Guantánamo Bay Naval Base (GTMO), 108–109
Gulf Cooperation Council (GCC), 182, 247
Gulf of Oman, 5
Gulf States, 8–9
Gulf War (1991). *See also* Iraq War
    aftermath, 59
    cease-fire, 57–58, 59
    CENTCOM, 9–14, 57–58, 60–62
    Coalition forces, 51–52, 53–54, 57–58, 61–62, 70–71, 127
    command responsibility and decision making, 46–55, 57–59, 61–64, 65, 69–71
    FEBA, 53
    German allies, 51
    Highway of Death, 58
    intelligence sharing, 49–50, 52
    media coverage, 56, 58
    no-fly zone, 63–64, 71
    Republican Guard, 54, 57–58
    USEUCOM, 62
GWOT. *See* Global War on Terror

Hadley, Steve, 131, 158–160, 253, 273
al-Hakim, Abdul Aziz, 224–225
al-Hakim, Saeed Ammar, 225–226
Hale, David, 181
Halloran, Richard, 314
Hamad al-Khalifa, 178
Hamilton, Lee, 130
Handy, Peggy, 12
Hannah, John, 139
al-Hashemi, Tariq, 196, 254–255, 339–340

Hayden, Mike, 287, 311–312
Helmly, Ron, 215
Henson, Jerry, 96
Hernandez, Rhett, 182
Hezbollah, 24, 35
Hill, Chris, 156, 338, 339
Holbrooke, Richard, 330
Holloway, Jim, 125–127
Holloway Commission, 7
Hornburg, Hal, 82
Horner, General, 68, 69
Human Rights Watch, 59
Hussein, King (Jordan), 23, 75, 76, 181
Hussein, Saddam
   blamed for 9/11 attacks, 151
   blamed for September 11 attacks, 128, 137–139
   Bush Sr. assassination attempt, 152
   conflict with Kuwait, 18
   Gulf War (1991), 56, 58–59
   insurrection against, 63
   regime of, 19–21, 53, 150
   seizure of power, 16, 140
   Shia and Kurd oppression, 60, 70
   as target for regime change, 137, 139, 141, 144, 150, 153
   WMD stocks destruction, 152
Hussein, Safa al-Sheikh, 221
Hussein, Uday, 75

IEDs, 170, 197, 200, 218, 223, 330
Ignatius, David, 307, 315
Implementation and Follow-up Committee for National Reconciliation (IFCNR), 221
INDEPENDENCE, USS, 33
India
   British withdrawal from, 213
   Line of Control, 214
   Pakistan and, 115, 213–214, 216
Indian Ocean, 6
Indyk, Martin, 76
infrastructure, 293–294
Inhofe, Jim, 131–132
International Institute of Strategic Studies (IISS), 307
intelligence sharing

Al Qaeda, 121
Gulf War (1991), 49–50, 52
International Security Assistance Force (ISAF), 207, 208, 302–304
intifadas, 23
Intrepid Fallen Heroes Fund, 169
Iran
    America declared "Great Satan," 5
    axis of evil designation, 105
    CENTCOM contingency planning for, 155
    "Contain, Protect, Deter" (CDP actions), 155
    encouragement of Shia-Sunni violence in Iraq, 157
    Iraqi invasion of, 6, 20–21
    nuclear programs, 322
    oil supplies in, 16, 20
    revolution, 5
    Revolutionary regime, 8
    Saudi concerns about, 183–184
    Shia-Sunni religious conflict, 8–9
    Tehran embassy hostages, 4–7
    U.S. relations with, 7, 306–307
    weapons provided to Shia insurgents, 231–232
Iran-Contra scandal, 6, 43
Iranian Revolutionary Guard Corps (IRGC), 192, 307
Iran-Iraq war, 6, 20–21, 43, 47, 59, 60
Iraq. *See also* Gulf War (1991); Iraq War (Second Gulf War)
    axis of evil designation, 105
    Ba'ath Party, 19, 140. 339
    British mandate, 17, 18
    CENTCOM visit, 189–201
    chemical weapons use, 21
    climate and weather, 193
    defense systems, 47
    elections, 338–339
    factories, 230–231
    French weapon systems, 51
    geography, 64, 65, 192–193
    Great Britain's presence in, 16
    Haditha, 3, 316
    Highway of Death, 58
    historic background, 15–21
    Hussein family defections to Jordan, 75–80
    infrastructure, 201
    invasion of Iran, 6, 20–21

invasion of Kuwait, 4, 8, 21, 46
Iranian opposition to U.S. operations in, 7
Kingdom of Iraq, 18
Kurdish opposition, 59, 60
Military Industrialization Corporation (MIC), 75
Mukhabarat secret police, 20
no-fly zones, 63–64, 71, 92, 121, 122, 137, 151
nuclear reactor, 21
oil for food program, 79–80
oil supplies in, 15, 16
Popular Mobilization Forces (PMF), 341
post-Saddam Hussein, 8
public opinion on, 3
Republic of Iraq, 15, 19
Republican Guard, 54, 57–58
Revolt (1920), 17
sanctions on, 78–79, 141, 151
sectarian conflict, 8
Shia opposition, 60, 70–71
Shia-Sunni religious conflict, 8–9, 18, 20, 157, 194
sovereignty concerns, 248–249, 262
stalemate, 9, 14
suspected WMD, 137, 142, 324
troop surge, 14, 162
USAID Mission, 163
weapons inspections, 143, 151
Western Anbar province, 3
WMD programs, 71, 75, 77–80, 145–146
Iraq Interim Governing Council, 142–143
Iraq Liberation Act (ILA) (1998), 141–142, 150
Iraq Study Group Report, 167
Iraq Survey Group (ISG), 151
Iraq War (Second Gulf War). *See also* Gulf War
2003 invasion, 150–153
Anbar Awakening, 243, 254, 260
Baghdad Security Plan, 218
benchmarks, 170
Blackwater contractors, 264–266
Bush's "New Way Forward," 166–168, 170–172
Bush's trip to Al-Asad, 254–256
Camp Bucca, 198–199
Camp Victory, 194, 195, 241
civilian casualties, 191, 234, 264–265

"Clear, Hold, and Build" tactics, 170
Coalition forces, 196–197, 198, 200
command responsibility and decision making, 238–239, 245–249
contingency planning for, 136–140, 143–149, 152
controversy over way ahead, 245–254
counterinsurgency plans, 160–161, 168, 170, 218
detention facilities, 198–199, 232–233, 266–267, 321
diplomatic efforts toward a long-term agreement, 259–264
Fallujah incident, 264
insurgent activities, 194–195
intelligence assessments, 154–155
lack of progress in, 1, 2
logistic support, 193–194
long-term U.S. security posture, 258–259
media coverage, 314, 316–322
Al-Mutanabbi Street bombing, 227–228
Nissour Square incident, 264–265
Obama's withdrawal plan, 337–339
operational and tactical strategy changes, 190–191
Office of Special Plans (OSP) justifications for, 139–140
partisan political divide, 154, 166, 236
Planning Order, 250–252
Provincial Reconstruction Teams, 158
Saudi complaints about, 183–184
security responsibilities, 240–241, 243, 261–263, 267
SOFA negotiations, 267–269, 324–325, 337–338
troop drawdown plans, 240, 242–243, 250–254, 258–259, 267
troop surge, 158, 160, 167, 223, 236, 241, 269
U.S. casualties, 191, 193, 197, 218, 223, 234, 236, 247, 343
withdrawal plans, 248–249, 325–326
Iraqi Highway One, 193
Iraqi National Congress (INC), 141
ISAF. *See* International Security Assistance Force
Isakov, General, 278
ISIS, 157, 233
Islamic Revolutionary Guard Corps (IRGC), 31
Islamic State of Iraq and the Levant (ISIL), 269, 340, 343
Islamic Supreme Council of Iraq (ISCI), 224
Israel
    invasion of Lebanon, 23–24, 114
    Muslim grievances against, 111
    PLO terrorist attacks, 23
    statehood, 22

wars with Egypt, 184–185
Italy, 16

al-Jaafari, Ibrahim, 338
Jack, Gary "GarJack," 85
Jacobson, Tracy, 280, 281
al-Jadiri, Basima, 220–221
Jaffe, Gregg, 315
Jamal, Arsala, 300
Jamerson, Jim, 62
Japan, 92
JCS. *See* Joint Chiefs of Staff
JOHN C. STENNIS, USS, 272
JOHN F. KENNEDY, USS, 33, 67
Johnson, Jay, 42
Johnson, Ron, 243
Joint Campaign Plan (JCP), 218
Joint Chiefs of Staff (JCS), 1, 249–252
Joint Improvised Explosive Device Defeat Organization (JIEDDO), 223
Joint Requirements Oversight Council (JROC), 137
Joint Strategic Assessment Team (JSAT), 218
Jones, Jim, 62
Jordan
   Air Force, 76
   CENTCOM visit, 181–182
   Iraqi defections to, 75–80
   Palestinian presence in, 22, 181–182
Jordan, Marion, 100
JROC. *See* Joint Requirements Oversight Council
JTF. *See* Joint Task Force

Kagan, Frederick, 2, 167
Kamel al-Majid, Hussein, 75, 77–80, 145–146
Kamel al-Majid, Saddam, 75
Karimov, Islam, 282–285
Karr, Jean-Baptiste Alphonse, 327
Karzai, Hamid, 103, 202, 204–207, 210, 211, 216, 291, 294, 295, 297–298, 304, 309–311, 325, 328, 337
Kashmir, 214
Kayani, Ashfaq Parvez, 115, 215, 307
Kazak Battalion (KAZBAT), 275
Kazakhstan, 275–277

Keane, Jack, 2–3, 10, 162, 167, 238, 239, 246–247
Kearney, Frank, 211
Keating, Tim "Timbo," 71, 93–94, 162
Kelly, John, 148, 317
Kelly. Barney, 41
Kenney, Kristie, 156
Khalilzad, Zalmay, 191, 196, 332
Khaliq, Abdul, 299
Khanfar, Wadah, 315–316
Khashoggi, Jamal, 110
Khuzestan, 20
Kimmitt, Bob, 158
Kingdom of Saudi Arabia (KSA)
   bin Laden family in, 110–111
   CENTCOM visit, 182–184
   foreign intelligence, 113
   land disputes, 18
   September 11 perpetrators, 109
   support for Afghanistan, 111
   women in, 71–72
KITTY HAWK, USS, 102
KSA. *See* Kingdom of Saudi Arabia
Kuhn, Muriel, 98
Kurdish people
   Barzani clan, 65
   chemical attacks against, 21, 63
   desire for statehood, 64–65
   federalism proposal, 217
   hostile cross-border activities, 156
   insurgency, 156
   opposition to Saddam, 59, 60
   Peshmerga militia, 63, 64–65
   political alliances, 65
   refugees, 60–65
   Sunni opposition, 18
   Talabani clan, 65
Kuwait
   CENTCOM visit, 179–180
   Gulf War (1991), 14, 46–55, 56–59
   Highway of Death, 58
   Iraqi invasion of, 4, 8, 21, 46
   looting in, 56
   oil supplies in, 21, 53

statehood, 18
U.S. bases in, 180
Kyrgyzstan, 277–278

Lamb, Graeme, 197
Lang, Dadullah, 335
Lang, W. Patrick "Pat," 163–164
Lawrence, T.E., 17–18
Laws of Armed Conflict (LOAC), 108–109
Lawson, Richard, 36
League of Nations, 17, 18
Lebanon
   1983 deployment, 22–34
   1984–85 deployment, 34–40
   1986–87 deployment, 40–43
   Armed Forces (LAF), 24, 27–28
   barracks bombing, 31, 43
   Civil War, 22, 29, 48
   French mandate, 22
   Israeli invasion of, 23–24, 114
   Israeli withdrawal, 25
   MNF activity, 24–26
   topography, 27
   U.S. Embassy bombing, 24
Lehman, John, 34, 40, 48
Levin, Carl, 166
Lewinsky, Monica, 141–142
Lewis, Fred, "Bad Fred," 40, 42, 48
Lewis, Bernard, 15, 18
Libby, Scooter, 139
Liberi, Dawn, 163, 280, 293, 336
Libya, 41, 341
Loftis, Robert, 261
Long, Mary Beth, 142
Long War, 104
Lute, Doug, 160
Luti, Bob, 140
Luti William, 139–140
Lyons, James "Ace," 31, 43

MacDill Air Force Base, 173, 226
Macke, Dick, 34
Mahdi, Adil, 196, 254, 255–256

al-Maliki, Nouri, 187, 196, 200, 201, 217, 220–221, 254–255, 260, 268, 321, 324–325, 337–341
Malkasian, Carter, 336
mandates, 17, 18
Manila terrorist bombing, 122
Marine Corps Special Air Ground Task Force (MAGTF), 74
Marine Special Operations Company Foxtrot (MARSOC-F), 210–211
Marshall, Andy, 128
Marshall, George, 328
al-Mashhadani, Mahmoud, 191–192
Massoud, Ahmed Shah, 211, 280
Mattis, Jim, 160–161, 298, 325, 332
McCain, Carol, 171–172
McCain, Doug, 172
McCain, John, 166, 168, 169, 171–172, 324
McCain, Roberta, 172
McChrystal, Stanley, 196, 200–201, 208, 212, 219, 233, 243, 285, 287, 289, 291, 330
McFarlane, Bud, 25
McGee, Bob, 85
McGovern, Ray, 164
McGurk, Brett, 267
McKiernan, David, 330
McNeil, Dan, 207, 208–209, 288, 302, 330
media coverage
   access to news, 6–7
   Bosnian War, 85–86, 313
   Esquire magazine article, 318–322
   guidance on media relations, 313
   Gulf War (1991), 56, 58
   Iraq War (Second Gulf War), 314, 316–322
   journalists as sources of information, 313–314, 315
   Petraeus-Crocker Joint Campaign Plan, 249–250
   Petraeus's congressional testimony, 254, 257
   September 11 attacks, 106
Mesopotamia, 15
Mesopotamian campaign, 17
Middendorf, J. William, 126
Middle East
   Chinese influence in, 7, 8
   partitioning of, 16
   Russian influence in, 7, 8
   Shia-Sunni religious conflict, 8–9

U.S. engagement in, 4–9
U.S. presence in, 73
Miller, Paul David, 90
Mine-Resistant, Ambush-Protected vehicles (MRAPs), 223, 317
Mixon, Riley, 66–67
MNF. *See* multinational forces
MNF-1. *See* Multinational Forces-Iraq
Mohamed bin Laden Company, 110, 116
Mohammadi, Bismillah Kahn "BK," 211–212, 280
Monroe, William, 178
Moranville, Ken, 41–42
Mori, Yoshiro, 92
Moriarty, Greg, 306
Morin, Jeff, 219–220
Morris, Dave "Snake," 66
Moss, Brian, 97
MOUNT WHITNEY, USS, 90–91
MOUNTAIN SHADOW operation, 251, 290–291
MSR (Main Supply Route) Tampa, 193
Mubarak, Hosni, 187, 341
Mueller, Raffaello, 284–285
al-Mufraji, Abdul Qadar Obeidi, 191, 196, 263-264
al-Muhaya, Saleh, 183
Mukhabarat secret police, 20
Mullen, Michael, "Mike," 239, 306
Multinational Corps Iraq, 190
multinational forces (MNF), 24
Multinational Forces-Iraq (MNF-1), 3–4
Murtha, John, 266
Musharraf, Pervez, 213, 215–216, 283, 290, 294, 307–312
Muslim Brotherhood, 110, 111, 112

National Commission on Terrorist Attacks Upon the United States, 138
National Intelligence Director (DNI), 138
National Intelligence Estimate (NIE), 322
National Intrepid Center of Excellence, 168
National Security Strategy (NSS), 144
NATO
   Combined Air Operations Center (CAOC), 82
   eastern expansion, 88–89
   headquarters, 74
   International Security Assistance Force (ISAF), 207, 208, 302–304
   Partnership for Peace (PFP), 89, 275

    regional commands in Afghanistan, 208–209
    SACLANT, 88
    Striking Fleet Commander, 90–91
Natter, Bob, 93–95
Naval Air Station Fallon, 47
Naval Aviation Plans and Requirements, 66
Naval Strike Warfare Center, 34
Nazarbayev, Nursultan, 275
NBC, 82
Nelson, Michael "Mike," 69–71
Neumann, Ron, 204–205
NEW JERSEY, USS, 29
NEW ORLEANS, USS, 76
New York Times, 314, 315, 321
news, access to, 6–7. *See also* media coverage
Nichols, Dave, 173
NIMITZ, USS, 6–7, 22, 40–43, 48, 272
9/11 attacks. *See* September 11 attacks
9/11 Commission, 138
Niyazov, Sapamurat (Turkmenbashi), 278–279
Noeth, Michael, 97–98
non-government organizations (NGOs), 59, 90
Nordeen, Mike, 276–277
Norland, Richard, 283–285
North, Gary, 310
North Arabian Sea, 5, 6
North Atlantic Council (NAC), 81
North Korea, 1
    axis of evil designation, 105
Northern Distribution Network (NDN), 285
nuclear weapons, 21, 213, 275, 287, 322
Nur, Atta Mohammad, 302

al-Obaidi, Ali M., 229–230
Obama, Barack, 325, 328–331, 337–339
Obama administration, 105, 268–269, 312
OCO. *See* Overseas Contingency Operations
O'Connor, Sandra Day, 152
Odierno, Ray, 162, 168, 190–191, 194-196, 200, 218, 221, 233, 254, 256, 337–339
Office of the Commander-in-Chief (OCINC), 220–221
O'Grady, Scott, 75
oil

in Iran, 16
in Iraq, 15, 16
in Kuwait, 21
security of Persian Gulf supplies, 4, 20
Oman, 306
Omar, Mullah, 103, 117
O'Neill, John, 118
OPERATION DELIBERATE FORCE, 81–87
OPERATION DESERT FOX, 141–142
OPERATION DESERT STORM, 4, 14, 51–55, 61–64, 66, 68–70, 73, 147
OPERATION EAGLE CLAW, 7
OPERATION ENDURING FREEDOM, 103–104, 208, 288
OPERATION INHERENT RESOLVE, 341
OPERATION MOUNTAIN SHADOW, 251, 290–291
OPERATION PHANTOM THUNDER, 218–219, 236, 243–244
OPERATION PROVIDE COMFORT (PC), 60–65, 70, 90
OPERATION SOUTHERN WATCH, 71
operational readiness evaluation (ORE), 44
operations plan (OPLAN), 144
Oruzbayev, General, 278
Osiraq, 21
OSP. *See* Office of Special Plans
Othman, Sadi, 222
Ottoman Empire, 15–17, 22, 111, 156
Overseas Contingency Operations (OCO), 105

Pace, Peter, 1–3, 9, 11, 12, 124, 130, 168, 217, 239, 249-251, 253, 254, 285
Pace-Fallon Report, 123–124, 130, 133
PACOM. *See* U.S. Pacific Command
Pakistan
  Afghanistan and, 111, 212–213, 214–216, 274, 292–293, 307–312
  Al Qaeda in, 212
  CENTCOM visit, 214–216
  Durand Line, 311, 312
  Federally Administered Tribal Areas (FATA), 112, 214, 216, 292–293, 307, 311
  India and, 115, 213–214, 216
  Inter-Services Intelligence (ISI), 112, 114–115
  Line of Control, 214
  post-9/11 operations in, 115
  Taliban in, 212

U.S.-funded Coalition Support Funds, 215
Palestine
    Black September, 22
    British mandate, 17, 22
    intifadas, 23
    presence in Jordan, 22, 181–182
Palestinian Authority, 285–286
Palestinian Liberation Organization (PLO), 23–24
Partnership for Peace (PFP), 89, 275
Pataki, George, 131
Patterson, Anne, 215, 290, 308
Pelosi, Nancy, 156–157
Pentagon, September 11 attacks, 93–100
Perle, Richard, 139
Persian Gulf, 4, 20, 53
Peshmerga militia, 63, 64–65
Petraeus, David
    Afghanistan command, 330
    at CENTCOM, 338
    congressional testimony, 245, 254, 256–258
    counterinsurgency work, 160–162, 168
    Iraq ground command, 10–11, 12, 170, 172, 173, 190–191, 194–197, 200, 212, 217–218, 220-222, 224, 226, 231, 233, 236–239, 240–241, 245–254, 259, 263-266, 285, 290, 305, 310, 317, 321, 322, 337
    Senate confirmation hearing, 165
Petraeus-Crocker Joint Campaign Plan (JCP), 249
Phillips, Kyra, 314
Phillips, Richard, 273
Pilling, Don, 81
piracy, 272–273
Pletka, Danielle, 139, 141
Popular Mobilization Forces (PMF), 341
Powell, Colin, 11, 65, 88, 90, 138, 145, 149, 155
Powell, Craig, 96
precision-guided weapons, 147–148
"Predator" drones, 311
preemption, 144
presidential elections
    2000, 121, 122–125
    2008, 324–325
    2012, 341
    2020, 332

preventive war, 144
Prince, Erik, 264–265
Provincial Reconstruction Teams (PRT), 158, 208–209, 300–304
Prueher, Joe, 26, 31
Public Law 107-40, 106
Public Law 107-56, 106–107
Puerto Rico, 123–124, 129–135
Putin, Vladimir, 89, 282

Qaboos, Sultan, 306
Qaddafi, Muammar, 41–42
Qatar, 178–179
Quadrennial Defense Review (QDR), 128
Quds Force, 192

radar scope photography (RSP), 37–38
Raddatz, Martha, 315
Rademaker, Stephen, 141
Radio Baghdad, 56
RAF. *See* Royal Air Force
Rahmon, Emomali, 280–283
Ralston, Joe, 156
Rashid, Amir, 78
Ratchford, Marsha Stallworth, 98–99
Reagan Administration, 25, 41
Rendon, John, 135
Revolution in Military Affairs (RMA), 127–128
Ricciardone, Frank, 156, 184, 187
Rice, Condoleezza, 125, 128, 156, 180, 192, 253, 254, 261, 276, 282, 308–309, 325
Richards, Thomas, 43
al-Rishawi, Abd al-Sattar, 254
Riyadh International Airport, 72
Rodriguez, David "Rod," 203, 207, 212, 288
Rogers, Bernard, 35, 36, 43
Rogers, Dave, 67, 69–70
Roosevelt Roads Naval Station, 133
Rossello, Pedro, 124
Rove, Karl, 131
Royal Air Force (RAF), 17
al-Rubaie, Mowaffak, 262–263
Rumsfeld, Donald, 3, 92, 108, 125–129, 132, 136, 137, 143–146, 151, 160, 223

Rumsfeld, Joyce, 126
Russia
    invasion of Ukraine, 89, 163
    invasion paranoia, 89
    Middle East influence, 7, 8
    Sykes-Picot Accord, 16
Ryan, Mike, 82

Sabah, Nasser, 180
al-Sabah, Sabah al Jaber, 180
SACLANT. *See* Supreme Allied Commander Allied Forces Atlantic
Sadat, Anwar, 184–185
Sadler, Brent, 82
al-Sadr, Muqtada, 256–257, 339
Safavi, Seyed G., 307
Safavi, Yahya Rahim, 307
Salafist Jihadists, 104, 109
Saleh, Amrullah, 280
Salih, Barham, 196
Salman, Prince, 71, 178
Sarabi, Habiba, 300–301
al-Sarayeh, Khalid, 181
Sattar, Sheikh, 256
al Saud, Abdullah bin Abdulaziz, 183–184
Saudi Arabia. *See* Kingdom of Saudia Arabia
Saudi Bin Laden Group (SBG), 116
Scaparrotti, Mike, 173
Schaefer, Kevin, 99–100
Schoomaker, Pete, 2
Schultz, George, 24
Schwarzkopf, Norman, 59, 61
Schweitzer, Marty, 299, 300
Scowcroft, Brent, 153
Senate Armed Services Committee Confirmation, 165–172
Senate Committee on Foreign Relations, 217, 257
September 11 attacks
    aftermath, 94–100
    American Airlines Flight 77, 94, 98
    command responsibility and decision making, 94–96
    intelligence failures, 138
    Iraq blamed for, 137
    motivations for, 7, 15
    Pentagon, 93–94

    recovery process, 106
    response to, 104–109, 150–151
    responsibility for, 101–104
    World Trade Center, 93
Shakespeare, William, 327
Shalikashvili, John, 62, 65, 90
Shanghai Cooperation Organization (SCO), 278
Sharif, Nawaz, 308
Shaw, Jonathan, 198
Sheehan, Jack, 11, 12, 88, 90, 159–160
Shia dissidents, 59, 60, 70–71. *See also* Shia-Sunni religious conflict
Shia-Sunni religious conflict, 8–9, 17–18, 157, 194, 260
Shinseki, Eric (Ric), 145
Shulsky, Abram "Abe," 139
Sky, Emma, 221, 338, 339
Small, William (Bill), 35
Smith, Leighton "Snuffy," 81–83, 84–85
SOFA. *See* Status of Forces Agreement
Somalia
    as a failed state, 9
    pirates, 272–273
Soufan, Ali, 118, 120
Soviet Union
    Cold War, 5, 25, 40–41
    collapse of, 88
    invasion of Afghanistan, 4, 5, 111–112
    support for Iraq, 20
Spane, Robert "Rocky," 62
Special Operations Forces (SOF), 102, 200–201, 208, 287, 289
STARK, USS, 20
Starr, Barbara, 316–318
Status of Forces Agreement (SOFA), 254, 261–262, 267–269, 270–271, 324–325
Stewart, Tom, 38
Stone, Doug, 199, 232–233, 266–267, 321
Strategic Framework Agreement (SFA), 262, 267, 339
Stump, Bob, 125, 128, 132
Sudan, 116–117, 119
Sumaidaie, Samir, 153
Super CAG program, 48
surface-to-air (SAM) missiles, 82
Sutherland, Dave, 244
Swift, Preston, 27

Sykes-Picot Accord, 16, 22
Syria
   Armed Forces, 23–24
   Ba'ath Party, 19
   encouragement of Shia-Sunni violence in Iraq, 157
   French mandate, 22
   frustration with America, 163–164
   nuclear reactors, 251, 286–287

Tajikistan, 280–282
Talabani, Jalal, 196, 254
Taliban, 101, 103–104, 114, 117, 208, 212, 292, 301, 324, 329, 332, 334
Tamim, ben Hamad, Emir, 179
Tantawi, Mohamed Hussein, 185
Tarantino, Dave, 96
Taylor, "RAK," 67
Tenet, George, 138
al Thani, Hamad bin Khalifa, 178–179
al Thani, Hamid bin Jassim, 178
THEODORE ROOSEVELT (TR), *USS*, 46, 47, 49, 50–53, 60, 82–83, 97
Thomas, Dave, 96
Tigris River, 15, 17, 59
Tito, Josip Broz, 74
Tomahawk land attack cruise missiles (TLAM), 83, 120, 146
Townsend, Steve, 244, 317–318
translators, 221–222
Treaty of Versailles, 17
Trump, Donald, 331–333
Trump Administration, 323
Tueller, Matthew, 179
Turkey, 61–63, 156–157
Turki al Faisal, Prince, 113, 116
Turkmenistan, 278–280
Tuttle, Jerry, 25–27, 29, 31–34
Tuwaitha nuclear research center, 21

"ugly American" image, 106
Ukraine, Russian invasion of, 89, 163
United Nations
   International Security Assistance Force (ISAF), 207
   Iran-Iraq cease-fire, 21

Iraq sanctions, 78–79, 141, 151
   Monitoring, Verification, and Inspection Commission (UNMOVIC), 78, 80, 143
   oil for food program, 79–80
   Security Council Resolution 688, 63, 71
   Security Council Resolution 1723, 259
   Special Commission (UNSCOM), 77–79, 142, 143
   Weapons Inspection teams, 143, 151
unmanned aerial vehicles (UAVs), 311
Untermeyer, Chase, 178
U.S. Agency for International Development (USAID), 163, 293–294
U.S. Army/U.S. Marine Corps Counterinsurgency Field Manual, 160, 168
U.S. Atlantic Command (USACOM), 88, 89–90
U.S. Atlantic Fleet, 88
U.S. Central Command (CENTCOM)
   areas of responsibility, 2, 76, 102, 169–170, 173, 177–188, 202–216, 272–285
   chiefs of defense (CHOD) Conference, 305–306
   Coalition Conference, 305
   Coalition Village, 226
   Gulf War (1991), 9–14, 57–58, 60–62
   Iran contingency planning, 155
   Iraq contingency planning, 136–140, 143–149
   key activities briefings, 155
   March 2007 Iraq trip, 189–201
   preparation for, 154–164
   resignation from, 320–323
   Senate Armed Services Committee Confirmation, 165–172
   Special Operations (SOCCENT), 211
   staff size, 173
   Strategic Guidance, 174, 175–176
U.S. European Command (USEUCOM), 35–36, 62, 70, 75, 286
U.S. Information Agency (USIA), 276
U.S. Joint Forces Command, 89
U.S. Middle East Force, 178
U.S. Military Training Mission (USMTM), 68–69, 71, 182
U.S. Naval Aviation, 84
U.S. Naval Forces Central Command (USNAVCENT), 69
U.S. Naval War College, 4
U.S. Navy
   Atlantic Fleet Weapons Training Facility (AFWTF), 123–125, 132–133

    combat readiness, 147–149
    decision-making, 88
    Middle East presence, 4–5
    Vice Chief of Naval Operations (VCNO), 92
U.S. Navy SEALs, 84, 85, 102, 209, 272–273
U.S. Pacific Command (PACOM), 1, 2, 11, 173
U.S. Security Coordinator for Israel and the Palestinian Authority, 285–286
U.S. Special Operations Command, 226
USA Patriot Act (2001), 106–107
USACOM. *See* U.S. Atlantic Command
USAID. *See* U.S. Agency for International Development
USEUCOM. *See* U.S. European Command
USNAVCENT. *See* U.S. Naval Forces Central Command
Uzbekistan, 282–285

Vester, Linda, 82
Vice Chief of Staff of the Army, 2
Vieques, 123–125, 127, 129–135
Virginia Military Institute, 328
Visual Identification (VID), 69

Wahabi, Mohammed Abdul, 119
Wald, Chuck, 70
Wall Street Journal, 315
Walter Reed National Military Medical Center, 168, 197
War on Terrorism. *See* Global War on Terror
Wardak, Abdul Rahim, 207, 211, 296, 297, 309
Warden, John, 49–50, 69
Warsaw Pact, 88–89
Washington Post, 314, 315
weapons of mass destruction (WMD), 75, 77–80, 128, 136, 145–146
West Bank, 23, 286
Winnefeld, James "Sandy," 102, 237–238, 241–243, 245–246, 248, 250
WMD. *See* weapons of mass destruction
Wolfowitz, Paul, 124, 125, 127, 129–133, 139, 141, 144–145
Wood, William B., 205–206
Woodward, Bob, 138–139
World Trade Center garage bombing, 117, 120
World War I, 17, 18
World War II, 4, 19, 22, 89
Wright, Lawrence, 121

Wurmser, David, 139

Yemen, 9, 92, 116
Yovanovitch, Marie "Masha," 277–278
Yugoslavia, 74, 81–87, 86

Al-Zawahiri, Ayman, 114, 115
Zebari, Babaker, 183, 263, 267, 306
Zinni, Tony, 62, 136

About William J. Fallon

On September 11, 2001, Admiral Fallon was meeting with Chief of Naval Operations Admiral Vern Clark in the Pentagon when American Airlines Flight 77 struck the building. As Vice Chief of Naval Operations, he immediately directed the evacuation and recovery of Navy personnel from the burning building, then pivoted to orchestrating the Navy's role in retaliatory strikes against Al Qaeda and Taliban forces. This defining moment exemplified the decisive leadership that would characterize his commands during America's most challenging military period in a generation.

Over his 40-year naval career, Fallon commanded at many levels of warfare, flying combat missions off aircraft carriers during Vietnam, later directing all U.S. military operations across three continents. As Commander of U.S. Central Command (2007-2008), he oversaw 230,000 troops engaged in two simultaneous wars during the Iraq surge and Taliban resurgence in Afghanistan.

Before CENTCOM, he led U.S. Pacific Command, managing military relationships with 43 Asia-Pacific nations while containing North Korean nuclear ambitions and navigating China's military modernization. His diplomatic acumen was demonstrated as Presidential Envoy to Japan, following the collision of *USS Greeneville* with fisheries training ship *Ehime Maru*.

A graduate of Villanova, the U.S. Naval War College, and the National War College, he has an M.A. from ODU and was a Wilhelm Fellow at MIT.

About John F. Lehman Jr.

Widely regarded by naval historians and defense analysts the most influential and effective Navy Secretary since Theodore Roosevelt, Dr. John F. Lehman Jr. served as the 65th Secretary of the Navy from 1981 to 1987 under President Ronald Reagan.

A longtime Naval Reserve aviation officer who flew tactical aircraft for more than two decades before retiring as a Captain, Lehman was a principal advocate of the 600-ship Navy and leading champion of the U.S. Maritime Strategy of the 1980s—initiatives credited with strengthening American sea power in the final phase of the Cold War.

Before becoming Secretary, Lehman served on Henry Kissinger's National Security Council staff and as Deputy Director of the Arms Control and Disarmament Agency.

He holds degrees from Saint Joseph's University, Cambridge University, and a Ph.D. from the University of Pennsylvania.

Following September 11, he served on the National Commission on Terrorist Attacks upon the United States (the 9/11 Commission). He currently serves as Chairman of J.F. Lehman & Company.

REQUIRED STATEMENT BY THE DEPARTMENT OF DEFENSE FOR ALL AUTHORS SUBJECT TO THE PREPUBLICATION REVIEW PROCESS

The views expressed in this publication are those of the author and do not necessarily reflect the official policy or position of the Department of Defense or the U.S. government. The public release clearance of this publication by the Department of Defense does not imply Department of Defense endorsement or factual accuracy of the material.

www.ingramcontent.com/pod-product-compliance
Lightning Source LLC
Chambersburg PA
CBHW050059170426
43198CB00014B/2393